D1601104

BEYOND PSYCHOLOGY

An Introduction to Metapsychology

BEYOND PSYCHOLOGY

An Introduction to Metapsychology

Third Edition

For Maýolaine,

with love.

Frank A. Gerbode, M.D.

IRM Press, Menlo Park

First edition 1988
Second edition 1989
Third edition 1995

IRM Press
431 Burgess Dr.
Menlo Park, CA 94025
USA

Library of Congress Catalog Card Number 95-80494

ISBN 1-887927-00-X

ACKNOWLEDGMENTS

Many people have contributed valuable ideas, experiences, and suggestions and have helped to transform what was a mere collection of ideas into a completed work. Lynn and Neil Fetter, Peter Rowell, Martin Rattner, William Hendrick, and Don Palmer were regular attendees during months of weekly lectures and discussions I held on the subject of metapsychology during the writing of this book. They contributed many helpful ideas and suggestions. I am also indebted to Dr. Lewis Gann, Dr. Robert Moore, Michael Hanau, Amos Jessup, Dr. Elaine Parent, Paulette Mahurin, Barry Fairburn, Dr. O.W. Markley, Charlotte French, and Lewis Randall, all of whom waded patiently through the initial draft of my manuscript and offered myriad helpful suggestions and comments, most of which were incorporated into the final draft, and to Gail Gerbode, who contributed several important ideas to the book. I would like to thank David and Julia Mayo for their willingness to spend hours discussing technical and philosophical points and for their frank criticism of my work, which has always proved quite fruitful. Dr. Edward F. Becker, a classmate at Stanford University and still a close friend, was also part of my reason for studying philosophy. I cannot think of a person equally skilled at the art of philosophic dialogue. Our debates and discussions, continuing up to the present, have saved me from many philosophical blunders (though, no doubt, not from all). I learned from him that to disagree with someone is a wonderful opportunity to learn.

I would like to thank Patrick O'Connor, Ph.D. for his valuable work done in editing the final English manuscript, to Chuck McDougal for his detailed commentary on the work, to Larry Voytilla for his help with the illustrations, printing, and production of this book, and to Michele Rae Vierra, who did a superb job of editing and proofreading the entire manuscript.

I feel I must also give a special acknowledgment to Gerald French, friend of my youth, whose intelligence, loyalty, and support have been the source of much of my strength, through sometimes trying times. He always had faith in me when I did not have faith in myself.

CONTENTS

Illustrations

Exercises

FOREWORD

This book lays the foundation for a way of helping another person to improve rapidly and profoundly the quality of her[1] life. This approach is unique in that it is both directive and non-judgmental. It provides guidance, yet allows the person being helped to reach her own understandings and make her own judgments without receiving interpretations, approval, or disapproval. Since anyone can stand to improve the quality of her life in some way, anyone can benefit from the techniques discussed in this book. Nevertheless, at present, these methods are directed toward people who are of average or above-average mental stability and who are not severely disturbed or psychotic. They are not psychotherapy and are no substitute for therapeutic intervention in severe cases. I hope that one day ways will be found of applying the principles of metapsychology to the task of helping these very needy people. Meanwhile, the techniques discussed herein can help the vast majority.

Like any other general subject of study, metapsychology is not committed to a specific method, although methods exist as applications of metapsychology, nor to a fixed belief system, although theories exist within the subject of metapsychology. It

---

1. Throughout this book, I will use either the male or the female pronominal form to indicate, male, female, or unspecified gender.

picks up where psychology, as the science of behavior, leaves off. Hence the name "meta-psychology" has the correct connotation of being a study that goes "beyond" psychology — beyond the study of behavior to the study of that which behaves — the person himself — and the person's perceptual, conceptual, and creative activity, as distinguished from the actions of his body. In this sense, "metapsychology" restores the original meaning of "psychology" as "the study of the psyche, or spirit", and the applications of metapsychology reflect the perennial common goal of therapies, religions, and traditional philosophies, whether one calls this goal the attainment of sanity, of enlightenment, of happiness, of wisdom, or of salvation.

Throughout this book, I will be constantly consulting experiences that I believe we all have in common, as the basis for the points I am going to make. By consulting his own experience, the reader can verify or falsify for himself each of these points. I have assisted this process by including occasional brief exercises. These exercises will greatly enhance the reader's understanding and will allow each reader to verify for himself the points made in the book. My only claim for acceptance of the ideas I am presenting is the assumption that different people have a great deal in common in what they experience and the way in which they experience it. This interpersonal commonality of experience *is* the fundamental truth that the metapsychological approach provides.

It took me many years of thinking and exploring a variety of different fields to arrive, eventually, at the conviction that this approach was best. Along the way, many different people and schools of thought have influenced my thinking.

It was John Goheen, then Chairman of the Stanford University Philosophy Department, who first kindled my interest in philosophy. In a seminar, Dr. Goheen, every bit the quintessential philosopher (complete with flowing white hair and abstracted manner) speculated: "Perhaps it is love that gives meaning to life." For some reason (possibly because it was true), this statement made a deep impression on me. Dr. Goheen remained my mentor throughout my undergraduate years. It was under his tutelage that I studied Aristotle's *Nichomachean Ethics* (on which

I did my Senior Honors Thesis) and R.M. Hare's *The Language of Morals*. Both of these works greatly facilitated my thinking about ethics and communication.

After studying philosophy for a year at Cambridge University, however, I decided that my studies lacked purpose and applicability. I had always felt that philosophy ought to eventuate in a form of wisdom that would enable a person to lead the Good Life and to help others to do so. Modern philosophy, as I experienced it, seemed to lack wisdom.

I turned to psychiatry in the belief that psychiatrists must have a practical knowledge of life. After all, were they not daily involved in helping people solve their problems? For some reason, perhaps because my father was a physician, it never occurred to me to become a psychologist. During my five years at Yale Medical School, I was fortunate to receive a Freudian analysis from Dr. James Kleeman, a man whose personal characteristics, warmth, and ability to create a safe and therapeutic environment set a standard that has stayed with me ever since. I am sure I have incorporated many elements of his manner into my own style of helping. At least I hope I have.

During my residency training at Stanford University Medical Center, I had the valuable experience of working with Paul Watzlawick and others at the Mental Research Institute in Palo Alto. They showed me that a very unorthodox[2] way of helping people could be quite effective.

During this time, I was profoundly disturbed by the work of Truex, Carkhuff, and others, who showed that the effectiveness of many current psychological approaches was by no means established.[3] I had also observed a lack of agreement amongst my teachers and colleagues with respect to diagnosis, prognosis, and recommended modes of therapy. In fact, there *was* no widely

---

2. Unorthodox, that is, at that time.
3. Truax, C.B. and Carkhuff, R.R. *Towards Effective Counseling and Psychotherapy* (Aldine Publishing Company, Chicago, 1967).

agreed-upon science or method in psychology. Each practitioner ultimately had to make up her own mind about what to do with each individual case. I was disheartened to find that the practical, predictable method for helping people I had hoped to find in psychiatry was not there. Also, having read several of Thomas Szasz's brilliant books, I became profoundly uneasy with the idea that helping someone to become happier had to be a medical or quasi-medical ("therapeutic") action.

Therefore, while completing the last two years of my residency, I began to look outside of the more traditional schools of psychology and psychiatry. I looked into Gestalt therapy and encounter groups; I attended Esalen functions; I tried Psychocybernetics and Yoga.

Then came a thirteen-year interlude about which I have mixed feelings. These years were spent intensively studying and practicing the techniques of dianetics and scientology. Many people have advised me not to mention this episode in my life because the idea of scientology sometimes conjures up disreputable images in the public mind. And thus, I was told, people would be predisposed to discredit *my* ideas. But these thirteen years, for all their negative aspects, proved to be a valuable learning experience. Eventually it became necessary for me to make a clear distinction in my own mind between:

1.   The organization (and its founder, L. Ron Hubbard), both of which have been perennially embroiled in controversy, and
2.   The theories and techniques themselves, many of which are quite humanitarian and have very positive effects.

Once I had made this distinction, I made a point, in early 1984, of severing all connections to the scientology organization. What I am doing today has nothing to do with that organization, a fact about which both the organization and I are happy.

Despite our parting of the ways (which was not without drama) and despite the advice of some of my friends, I feel it would be wrong not to acknowledge the wealth of information I found in the scientology materials. I have been able to put these materials to good use in my attempts to understand and align the data from all the various disciplines I have studied and to see the truths that all these disciplines contain. There was one year in which scientology and psychiatry overlapped. During the day, I practiced "conventional" psychotherapy, and in the evenings I functioned as a scientology practitioner. I found my work in the evening to be much more effective than the work I did during the day. This fact *forced* me to take the scientology materials seriously.

These materials were produced by many different people, not just by Hubbard. In fact, the scientology materials are of particular interest in part *because* of these many contributions. The materials were accumulated over a period of more than thirty years by a group of tens of thousands of practitioners who had a very high degree of uniformity in their practice and who were linked very closely within a single organization. These practitioners could therefore compare notes and refine their ideas and techniques in a way that no group of psychologists or psychiatrists (with their disparate ideas and techniques and lack of organizational connections) could possibly do. It may be that there has never been such a large, organized, and homogeneous group of practitioners in any other helping profession. Certainly the number of practicing scientologists in the U.S. was, at least at one time, of comparable magnitude to the number of psychiatrists!

The wealth of practical and theoretical data accumulated thorough the actions and interactions of this group is extraordinary. There are probably hundreds of thousands of detailed case histories in scientology archives. There are hundreds of books and thousands of tapes containing detailed descriptions of theories and methods. Much of this material is confusing, repetitive, wordy, and contradictory; some of it is secret; some of it is intensely interesting. I do not think anyone could read or listen to *all* of this material in any finite amount of time. I spent many years studying it, however, and I feel I have learned the most important parts.

Hubbard and the many others who have contributed to this collection of data, including important but less well-known individuals like David Mayo, Jan and Dick Halpern, and Jack Horner, have surely made a significant (if generally unrecognized) contribution to the helping professions. Techniques and theories developed by these individuals have found their way into many different commonly-used methods, including Co-Counseling, Life Spring, The Forum, and even Gestalt Therapy.[4]

Many of the ideas presented in this book are inspired by this wealth of scientology material. Those who are familiar with the material will therefore recognize certain similarities between ideas and techniques mentioned there and those presented in this book. They will also see many differences. What I am presenting, in fact, is definitely *not* scientology but something entirely different.

Other writers who have impressed me deeply include Sigmund Freud, Carl Rogers, Abraham Maslow, Michael Polanyi, Thomas Kuhn, Eugene Gendlin, and Charles Tart. All these thinkers have helped me to crystallize my thoughts concerning the subject of metapsychology.

* *

This book is organized in three parts. Part One deals with the basic philosophical underpinnings and theory of metapsychology, Part Two provides a useful categorization of the the various disabilities or undesired conditions that may arise in a person's life, and Part Three presents a theory of personal enhancement and some examples of the very effective techniques currently used by practitioners of applied metapsychology.

---

4. For a further discussion of this influence, please see:

    Bartley, William Warren III. *Werner Erhardt* (Clarkson N. Potter, New York, 1978) pp. 149ff.
    Grof, Stanislav. *Beyond the Brain* (State University of New York Press, New York, 1985) pp. 187, 196f, 379.
    Perls, F. *The Gestalt Approach* (Science and Behavior Books, Ben Lomond, CA, 1973) p. 95f.
    Winters, J.A. *A Doctor's Report on Dianetics* (Julian Press, New York, 1951) — Introduction by Fritz Perls.

Appendices 1 and 2 contain some helpful procedures that a person can use by himself or with others to enhance the quality of life. I hope that these will provide a good illustration of some of the basic techniques used in applied metapsychology, and if the reader can derive some personal benefit from them, so much the better. Appendix 3 is a partial list of centers that use metapsychological techniques, in case the reader wants to investigate this subject in more depth.

The viewpoint I am consistently trying to take in this book is that of the world as seen by an individual person at a particular time. While I may sound as though I am making startling and counter-intuitive statements about "objective reality" (because it will be tedious always to prefix my statements by "from the viewpoint of a particular person at a particular time"), please realize that the only absolute assertions I intend to make are about the ways people construct and perceive their own worlds. If you find yourself outraged by something I am saying, before throwing the book down in disgust, try checking to see if, in the situation being described, *you* would experience the world that way and, if so, realize that *that's* what I am talking about.

I encourage the reader to check each of my points against her own personal experience. The goal of metapsychology is to describe universal characteristics of experience, so what I have to say should either ring true when compared to carefully observed personal experience or stand disproved by that experience. I would be interested in hearing from any reader who, on thoughtful consideration of one of my points, finds that her own experience contradicts what I have said. Such feedback will be quite helpful in refining the subject of metapsychology.

There is an extensive glossary, containing some technical terms I have had to introduce, as well as a great many English terms to which I have had to give a restricted or specialized meaning. It is hoped that the reader will make very free use of this glossary, especially if he encounters a term that is puzzling or that has a seemingly odd usage.

Foreword to the Third Edition

The First Edition of this book, published in 1988, sold out very rapidly. The necessity of putting out a second printing gave me the opportunity to correct some errors, make some minor modifications of terminology, and add some new material, especially an expanded section on *having* in Chapter Two (pp. 60-72), a new section on intention and time in Chapter Three (pp. 107-119), and some technical modifications in Part Three. The improvements contained in the Second Edition were based on the advantages of hindsight and on the very helpful feedback I received from readers of the First Edition.

In the six years since the second edition came out, metapsychological thinking has progressed considerably, as has the methodology of viewing and facilitating. These changes have been incorporated into articles in the Journal of Metapsychology and into various revisions of our course manuals, but had not yet found their way into *Beyond Psychology* itself. During this time, we have had further insights into the nature of personal power (formerly called "vitality" — see especially pp. 191-201) and other theoretical points, and we have modified, expanded, and improved the General Curriculum (see pp. 458-470). Other improvements are reflected in changes in the text, which has been lightly re-edited throughout. This third edition incorporates all these changes and so constitutes the latest available data on metapsychology, a subject that continues to change and evolve.

Frank A. Gerbode, M.D.
Menlo Park, California
January, 1995

Introduction

In any discussion concerning help, it is necessary to clarify who or what is being helped and who is to decide what constitutes "help". A policeman, a judge, a politician, a philanthropist — all clearly have a mandate to help a group, a nation, or mankind as a whole. The results of their interventions must therefore be judged by their overall effects on the target group, not by their effects on any one person. People who are in the business of personal enhancement — teachers, counselors, therapists, priests, ministers, and personal consultants — are aiming to help a client (a person who has come to them for help) and their responsibility is to the *client*, not to anyone else. In personal enhancement, a successful outcome exists when the client is satisfied, not when, for instance, a group of people surrounding the client are satisfied with his behavior or personal characteristics. When a client is not satisfied with the "help" he has received, personal enhancement has not occurred, even if the *counselor* is content with the effects of his intervention.

Let us look at a situation a school counselor might be confronted with. Suppose a bright student, being bored, is always annoying his teachers by figiting, talking, or asking challenging or irritating questions. If the counselor, through behavior modification or medication, succeeds in creating a docile child out of this bored intellectual rebel, the counselor and the teachers may be happy, but has a good result really been achieved if the child feels dulled or intimidated? If a client comes to a counselor in order to achieve happiness and completes the counseling miserable but externally functioning or behaving well in life, that is not a successful outcome for this kind of help. In other words, help, *to the client*, results in a more satisfactory life as experienced by *him*, independent of anyone else's evaluations. It is therefore necessary *at least* to consult the client to determine what constitutes help for *him* and, subsequently, whether the proffered help is really effective. That is one reason why individual help is of necessity client-centered, or "person-centered", to use Carl Rogers' more recent term.

There is another sense in which personal enhancement is necessarily person-centered. Personal enhancement occurs when the client becomes more able, when he has greater potential for success — a clearer idea of his goals and improved means to achieve them. Anything, then, that would tend to *lower* awareness or ability is detrimental, rather than helpful. But how does one go about improving ability?

Consider what goes into teaching a person to play better tennis. It does not help to give the student a course in the physiology of muscle movement and a vector analysis of the forces and movements involved in a tennis stroke, nor to teach him aerodynamics and the Bernoulli principle as applied to spinning balls, even though these *are* amongst the physical determinants of a tennis game. Such descriptions are useless toward improving a person's tennis game. In order to improve someone's tennis game, or any ability, one must address:

1.   Things that a person can experience directly.
2.   Things that a person can do knowingly.

If you tell a person to exert a tension force of 10 pounds on his right latissimus dorsi, he will not be able to do so because his latissimus dorsi (though it exists physically) is not part of his experience as a tennis player. Nor can a person successfully calculate the torque he would have to exert on the handle of the racket in order to create an appropriate angular velocity on the tennis ball. Or, more technically, how to get the Bernoulli forces to operate in such a way as to cause the ball to curve downward at a rate of speed calculated to cause it to land inside the court, given its initial velocity and direction of flight. Rather, you must tell the student what sort of movement he *can be aware of making* that would eventuate in a successful stroke. He can and must learn how it *feels* to hit a ball properly. Unless the action of playing tennis can be brought down to an *experiential* level, a person cannot improve his tennis game. Similarly, a person cannot learn mathematics by learning about the chemical or electrical changes that might be occurring in his brain in order for a certain piece of mathematical knowledge to be there.[5] Rather, the student must learn how it *feels* to solve a problem; he must learn how to *think* mathematically. He must learn how to *experience* mathematics. The brain may or may not act as a complex electronic calculator, but it is impossible to get a person to "punch his neurons" in order to get a result. A person cannot experience the act of calculating that way, even if what is happening *does* involve the firing of certain neurons.

Freud started out as a neurologist, but he eventually recognized that talking about neurological structures or mechanisms was not going to help people handle their difficulties with life. He concluded that one had to talk with the client and consult the client's experience. Thus the idea of the "therapeutic alliance" was conceived. It seemed also that experience itself followed certain laws. Freud coined the term "metapsychology" to describe the study of these rules, or the study of "that which leads behind consciousness".[6] Others, such as Jung, Adler, and Horney, followed, each with his or her own theoretical schema to explain the organization and laws of experience.

After a time, however, it became apparent that a peculiar phenomenon was occurring. Freudians began having Freudian

---

5. Assuming that anybody *knew* what those neurological changes should be. It may or may not be the case that mental events are caused by neurological events. The causation might be in the other direction; in fact, it might go both ways. Fortunately, since we are dealing with *experiential* matters, and people don't *experience* their brains, we don't need to decide this question.

6. "Metapsychology" first appeared in a letter to his friend, Wilhelm Fliess, on the 13th of February, 1896. Two years later, he explained its meaning, "I may use the name of metapsychology for any psychology that leads behind consciousness." [*The Complete Psychological Works of Sigmund Freud*, v. I, p. 274]

dreams; Jungians began having Jungian dreams: clients always seemed to "find" those structures or entities postulated by their therapists. Concomitantly, it seemed that clients tended to resent the interpretations and interventions of their therapists. They sometimes felt dehumanized and manipulated. Also, these interventions often failed to achieve a satisfactory result in a short period of time. It seemed that the imposition of a theoretical framework was creating an artificial view of the world and in certain ways preventing the client from arriving at his own insights.

Enter the founder of person-centered therapy, Carl Rogers. Rogers realized that the client somehow had to discover his own truths, that it was not helpful to spoon-feed insights to the client concerning supposed mental entities that the client could not perceive. He saw the debilitating effect of expressing therapeutic interpretations or evaluations. Such evaluations tend to blunt the client's ability to perceive the truth for himself, since a person has to arrive at his own truth. If the client merely accepts a therapeutic evaluation (even a correct one) without perceiving its truth directly, it has only intellectual validity for him and not the experiential validity needed for a truly therapeutic result.

Further, it was found that when a therapist *invalidates* the client or his observations by expressing disapproval for the client directly or through facial expression or manner, or by using belittling evaluations, the client seems to become fearful and less open. In this state, the client is less communicative and less perceptive. Rogers therefore introduced the concepts of nondirective therapy and of "unconditional positive regard" for the client as a therapeutic necessity. In the Rogerian scheme, the role of the facilitator or therapist is merely to make it very safe for the client to think and say *anything* and to let the client know his communication was understood by repeating or paraphrasing it back to him. The Rogerian counselor acts as a companion on the client's quest toward self-understanding and self-realization.

When this approach is properly done, clients have found it very helpful and congenial, and they have achieved a certain degree of improvement with it. For many, receiving Rogerian counseling must surely be a unique opportunity to think and feel freely and to express freely these thoughts and feelings. This approach, however, also seems to be fairly slow and limited in what it can achieve. Clients may feel good about having companionship, but frustrated at not receiving much in the way of help or guidance. A similar difficulty exists in the Freudian free-associative approach. Although the analysand has to view and relay the material to the analyst, for most, analysis appears to be rather aimless and inefficient in the absence of a clear-cut theory of how experience is formed and in the absence of direction from the analyst. It appears that in helping another person one is caught between the Scylla of interpretation (or evaluation) and the Charybdis of aimlessness.

Is it possible, then, to have a non-evaluative, non-invalidative method, one that matches the experience of the client every step of the way and yet one that can use a directive approach to achieve rapid and profound results? The answer lies in the fact that being directive is not necessarily the same as being evaluative or invalidative. It is possible to direct a person's attention without telling the person what he is to perceive. One can show a person a painting without telling him anything about the painting, or ask a client to examine his relationship with his father without telling him anything about that relationship. But in order to be directive without being evaluative, it is necessary to know what the client's world looks like from the viewpoint of the *client*, and to know what the client (or any person) does to build up a particular world of experience. If all the rules governing experience can be expressed in a way that corresponds to a person's own perceptions, and if he can see how he is doing certain things to handle his world or to construct it, then a client can be directed — in a way that is non-evaluative — to alter his experience (his life) to a more satisfactory one. If one can describe the actions a person must consciously take to relieve depression, directing a client to take these steps constitutes an effective, directive, but non-evaluative method. It can be done without referring to anything (such as the Id, Ego, Anima or Animus) of which the person cannot directly be aware.

An effective directive helping procedure, then, consists of giving the client tools that he can consciously use to change the quality of his experience. It need not involve any manipulation on the part of the person helping (the facilitator), nor any act of perceiving or acting *for* the client. The client consciously does all the needed actions and perceiving for himself, under the *direction* of the facilitator.

The facilitator, then, acts like an expert car mechanic talking to the owner of a car over the phone and helping him repair it. The mechanic, like the facilitator, must get the car owner to describe to her what the car looks like, perhaps what it sounds and feels like, what the various instruments show, and how the car behaves when the owner does certain things. Perhaps she gets the owner to rev the engine or turn on the headlights and describe what happens. The mechanic can suggest various actions, like "Open the hood and take the lid off the big, black round thing sitting on top of the engine," to help the owner get a better view. Finally, from the owner's description of what he sees, the mechanic can decide what is wrong and can then describe the various tools needed and where they can be found. She can then walk the owner through the steps necessary to repair the car, all the while having the owner report on what's happening.

Similarly, an effective facilitator gets the client to do various things to assess the situation and find the problem areas. She then walks the client through various procedures to correct the problem. The *client* does the procedures, not the facilitator, though the client does report frequently on how things are going.

My purpose in writing this book is to propose what I believe to be a clear description of what a client — a person — *is*, and the nature of his experience as perceived by *him* (not by anyone else), a clear description of the nature of his intentions, his actions, and his judgments, as experienced by him, and a clear description of the rules that *he can be aware of* that affect his identity, intention, action, judgment, and perception.

The individual person and her experience, as seen from *her* point of view, make up the proper subject matter of metapsychology. Metapsychology is the study of the person and her abilities, the origin, structure, and function of the mind, and the relationship between person, mind, and physical universe. It is the discipline that unifies mental and physical experience; it seeks to discover the rules that apply to both. Central to metapsychology is a study of how the person, her mind, and her world are seen from a "person-centered" viewpoint in the absence of any external viewpoint or judgments.

Thomas Kuhn made the point that, before a science comes into existence, there is a critical stage in the development of a discipline when a diverse group of thinkers and experimenters find themselves groping towards an understanding of the subject. Then, often abruptly, a paradigm or model appears that is so appealing and useful that it becomes almost universally accepted as the "truth" that defines the current state of the subject. At this point, a science is born, where before there was only a "proto-science" — a mere collection of conflicting ideas and unaligned data.[7]

I feel that we are on the brink of such a revolution in the study of personal experience. Dr. Arnold Lazarus[8] makes the excellent point that the field of psychotherapy is in a "pre-paradigmatic phase". He says that without an agreed-upon theory to work from, we must simply observe what works and use that, without worrying, for the time being, about *why* it works. I feel, however, that the study of human interaction and helping has remained "pre-paradigmatic" for long enough. The basic data and observations needed to understand the subject have always been available to us — as our own experiences. No special instrumentation is required to observe these data. What I would like to propose in this book is a long-overdue paradigm — one that is sufficiently based on intersubjectively agreed-upon observations to be a crystallization point for the formation of a new science: metapsychology.

---

7. Kuhn, T. *The Structure of Scientific Revolutions* (University of Chicago Press, 1970).

8. In a keynote address entitled "On the Need for Technical Eclecticism — Science, Breadth, Depth, and Specificity", given to the Phoenix Conference on the Evolution of Psychotherapy, in December, 1985.

PART I

THE THEORY OF

METAPSYCHOLOGY

Chapter One

The Person and His World

In understanding the relationship between a person and the world he lives in, it is important to remember that people have different viewpoints. It is well known that when an accident occurs it is rare to find one hundred percent agreement amongst witnesses to that accident. One person thinks car A hit car B; another thinks car B hit car A. One person estimates A's speed at 35 MPH, another at 50 MPH. It is a difficult task for an insurance investigator, a judge, or a jury to decide which viewpoint is the correct one. The business of compiling and comparing different reports to reconstruct what an "omniscient observer" would have seen at the time is a good and useful activity — in such contexts as that of determining fault in automobile accidents.

In other contexts, however — especially *helping* contexts, such as teaching or personal enhancement — it is useful to know how a person comes to see the world as she sees it, to understand what conscious and non-conscious actions she takes to arrive at a particular view of her world. It is also useful in such contexts to understand what a person does to make changes in her world, how she consciously acts to create a new environment for herself. In order to help a person sharpen her perception of the world, for instance, the helper (let's call him a "facilitator") must know what to tell his client to *do* so as to perceive better. A facilitator therefore needs to know what the client is *currently* doing in order to perceive, and what the client can *consciously* do in order to move from her current mode of perception to improved perception. It is of no help to a facilitator to concern himself with bodily mechanisms (such as neurological changes) of which the client cannot be directly aware. Rather, he must focus on actions of which the client *can* be directly conscious. When learning how to help someone, it is useful to study the rules that determine how a person experiences herself and the world around her. These rules themselves cannot be merely invisible physiological mechanisms; they must *themselves* be evident in the experience of the individual.

Moreover, a person's view of the world and the objects it contains will very likely change as time goes by. She plays different roles; she acquires more knowledge and data; the context changes. A person arriving at Disneyland may see a pine tree. On closer examination, that "pine tree" is found to be an elaborately-shaped piece of plastic. So at one point, the person sees a pine tree; at a later time, she looks at the "same object" and sees a piece of plastic.

The following questions must be addressed by anyone who truly intends to help someone:

1. What are the elements that make up a person's world of experience?
2. By what kinds of actions can a person become aware of existing conditions in her world?
3. What criteria does a person use to decide which of many possible world-views is valid?
4. What criteria does a person use to decide which new conditions to create?

For certain purposes, it is important to judge which view is "objectively" correct. If one were looking for firewood, one would want to know whether a "tree" is made out of plastic or wood. But for the purpose of learning how to help people who are seeking to improve the quality of their lives, judging the correctness or incorrectness of a particular idea is not the crucial issue. What is crucial is to help a person examine the *process* by which she has arrived at such a view and to give her tools for changing that view, if she wishes to do so. Likewise, what is important is not judging the correctness or appropriateness of a particular person's action but helping her look at how she decided to act in that way and, if she wishes, helping her find for herself alternative ways of fulfilling her intentions. If a person thinks there are green snakes on the wall, if she thinks that she is causing plane crashes by having "bad thoughts", or if she believes she can never recover from the loss of a spouse, the truth or falsity of these beliefs is not as important for helping her as the question of how she arrived at these views of the world.

The Person-Centered Viewpoint

This person-centered orientation is crucial to the context of personal enhancement and, in fact, to any form of interpersonal communication. The only way of helping another person — or even communicating to him — is to change something about his world-view. In order to do so effectively, one must first be at least somewhat aware of what the person's current world-view looks like and one must have some idea of how that world-view came about — from the point of view of the person. To change a person's world-view, one must take one of two mutually exclusive actions:

1. Apply force, duress, deception, or manipulation (physical, emotional, or financial) to get the person to accept the world-view you are proposing.
2. Understand why the person has the world-view he has and what the *person* can do to change his world-view if he chooses.

Under (2) is included:

1. Demonstrating facts to him that he can perceive.
2. Helping him to remove duress and force that is impeding or distorting his view of the world.
3. Helping him to acquire skills that he can use to change his world.

Each of these actions requires that the facilitator (or communicator) be able to see what the world currently looks like to the other person and to help him adjust his own world in a way that makes sense to him. One cannot change a person's world-view just by pointing out that his world-view is false and exhorting him to correct it. Such invalidation of the other person's views is counter-productive. One cannot get another person to change his mind just by telling him that he is wrong. To him, his view *is not* false. One might be able to succeed with a combination of invalidation, force, intimidation, and trickery, but this is hardly a desirable method. Absent the use of force and deception, one must start with what is true for the other person and understand *why* it is true for him, then show him an acceptable way of making the transition from his current world-view to a new world-view. In other words, one must go about one's work from a person-centered viewpoint — from an understanding of the present-time viewpoint of the other person and how the person can change it.

Personal Identity

There have been innumerable philosophical arguments concerning the nature of the "self". The "self" has fallen into disfavor with modern analytical philosophers, who complain that this concept is based on grammatical and categorical misunderstandings.[1] Likewise, behaviorists do not speak of the "self" but only of physical behavior. Yet everyone, even a dyed-in-the-wool behaviorist, *acts* as though her own existence were a basic fact of life. Therefore, I am going to accept pragmatically (with the majority) the concept that I exist, you exist, and others exist. For the rest of this book I am going to refer to myself, you, and other people as "persons". I do this deliberately because I wish to distinguish us definitively from *things* that exist but are not sentient, such as chairs, mountains, and typewriters.

Assuming we exist, it is fair to ask: "What is our nature?" In attempting to answer this question, the best initial approach is to describe at least part of what a person can clearly see she is *not*. We will not, necessarily, then have a clear idea of what a person conceives herself to *be*. When I enumerate what a person is not, I do not mean to imply that a person is everything else! But we will be *closer* to understanding what a person is. I have already, by definition, distinguished people from non-aware objects such as tables, chairs, planets, stars, etc. But the question inevitably arises: "What about the body?" and "What about the brain?"

To begin to clarify the issue of personal identity, I give the reader two exercises:

Exercise 1. Change of Focus — I

A. Read the above two paragraphs with a view to seeing how they align with your experience.
B. Now go through them again, but this time notice how each character is formed. Notice the spacing and the typestyle.
C. Note the change in focus from the first reading to the second.

---

1. For instance, see Dennett, D.C. *Content and Consciousness* (Humanities Press, Atlantic Highlands, NJ, 1969).

Exercise 2. Change of Focus — II

A. Throw a small object into the air and catch it.
B. Do the same thing again, but this time try to notice the exact speed and direction of the motions you are making with your shoulder, upper arm, forearm, wrist, hand, and fingers in executing the motion, and the exact trajectory of the object.
C. Were you able to do it?
D. Note the change in focus from the first time through to the second.

Focal and Subsidiary Awareness

In any act of awareness, a person has attention *focused* upon certain things while being aware of other things but not attending to them. When reading a book, I generally attend to the thoughts and concepts and, sometimes, to the words of the writer, but I am not, generally, attending to the letters or to the typographical details, such as the exact shape of the lower-case "a". Yet I must, in some sense, be *aware* of the letters and their shapes in order to read the words, and I must be aware of the words in order to understand the concepts. When throwing something into the air, a person generally focuses on the object thrown and the position of one's hand. Yet one must somehow "take into account" all of the bodily movements used in executing the motion successfully. Awareness that is focused on something is called "focal awareness". Awareness of something on which a person is *not* focused, where that awareness contributes to a focal awareness, is called "subsidiary awareness".

In Exercise 1, Step A, you were focally aware of the concepts conveyed by the paragraph and only subsidiarily aware of the letters and their shapes. In Step B, the focus was shifted to the letters and you became focally aware of them. In Exercise 2, Step A, you were focally aware of the object, your hand, and their paths through space. In Step B, the focus was on various parts of your body and their motions. You probably had a hard time catching the object while maintaining this "closer-in" focus in Step B.

The principle of focal and subsidiary awareness is also well illustrated by the concept of a figure and a ground. Whenever one perceives something, one perceives it against a backdrop of something else. If something else were not there for contrast, the object would be invisible.[2] In looking at a picture on the wall, I focus on the picture, but I am also subsidiarily aware of the wall as its ground. The subsidiary awareness of the wall makes it possible for me to see the picture. In some cases, it is easy to shift one's focus back and forth, the ground becoming the new figure and the figure becoming the new ground. Try the following exercise:

Exercise 3. Figure and Ground — I

a. Look at Figure 1. What do you see?
b. Shift the figure and the ground.
c. Now what do you see?

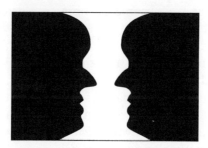

Figure 1. Example of a figure and ground.

This sort of selection of figure and ground occurs all the time in life, as we shift from one context to another. The figure is what

---

2. Camouflaged, in fact. A chameleon uses this principle quite effectively.

we are focusing on, and the ground is what we are aware of but not focusing on at the moment. In other words, there are two kinds of awareness:

> **Definition**:   Focal awareness is awareness of that to which a person is currently attending.

> **Definition**:   Subsidiary awareness is awareness of that to which a person is not currently attending, but knowledge of which contributes to an act of focal awareness.

How does this distinction help us to understand what a person conceives himself to be at a certain time or what identity a person has at a certain time? A principle that will aid our understanding is one proposed by Michael Polanyi, a physical chemist turned philosopher:

> "Our subsidiary awareness of tools and probes can be regarded now as the act of making them form a part of our own body. The way we use a hammer or a blind man uses his stick, shows in fact that in both cases we shift outward the points at which we make contact with the things that we observe as objects outside ourselves. We may test the tool for its effectiveness or the probe for its suitability, e.g., in discovering the hidden details of a cavity, but the tool and the probe can never lie in the field of these operations; they remain necessarily on our side of it, forming part of ourselves, the operating persons. We pour ourselves out into them and assimilate them as parts of our own existence. We accept them existentially by dwelling in them."[3]

A person tends to merge with the tools she uses to perceive and create and regards them as part of herself. She regards as *outside* herself that of which she is focally aware, that which she uses her

---

3.   Polanyi, Michael. *Personal Knowledge* (University of Chicago Press, 1962) p. 59.

tools to perceive or act upon. In other words, from the person-centered viewpoint, *a person is never that which she is perceiving or acting upon.* A person is separate from that of which she is focally aware. From one moment to another, a person may extend, contract, or change that of which she is aware. There-fore, at different times, her identity may extend, contract, or shift.

Acts of Perception

People use various means of perception. They use each of the senses, but they also use telescopes, microscopes, radio, telev-ision, glasses, hearing aids, and the like to perceive the world. If you are skilled in the use of an instrument of perception it "becomes part of you", in your experience. Bodily sense organs require no less skill than non-bodily perceptual aids. Acquiring skill in using eyes, ears, nose, tongue, skin, and other physical organs as perceptual channels is a major developmental task for an infant or small child. It takes a much longer time for an infant to learn to use his eyes than for an adult to learn to use a tele-scope. Studies of children who were locked up in institutions or dark closets for much of their early lives or otherwise deprived of the opportunity to exercise bodily abilities show conclusively that a failure to practice the use of sensory or motor apparatus in early years can lead to an inability to use these sensory or motor organs. These studies also show that they experience difficulty in learning how to use these bodily tools, even when they are returned to the normal world. Similarly, a person who has not heard and spoken French as a child will have some difficulty speaking and understanding it for the first time in adulthood.

When a person looks at a house, he experiences the house as separate from himself. Yet the act of looking at the house also *connects* him to the house. When a person cuts down a tree, he experiences himself as separate from the tree, yet the act of cut-ting down the tree also connects him to it. In an act of percep-tion, a person considers himself as separate from what he per-ceives. And in an act of creating or changing something in the world, a person considers himself as separate from that which he creates or changes. In the case of perception, it is the act of perception itself that both separates and connects the person and the perceived phenomenon. In the case of changed or created objects, it is the act of creating or changing that both separates and connects the person and the affected object. Both creation and perception are *actions* of a person. Therefore a person, by his *actions*, is both connected to, and separated from, the objects that make up his world.[4] Try the following exercise:

Exercise 4. Self-Definition

a.   Feel the texture and temperature of your chair.
b.   Raise your right arm six inches. Where is it?

Note that in Step A, you were aware of the chair as separate from you, and your arm was a part of you, whereas in Step B, you were aware of your arm and it was experienced as separate from you.

Instrumental Skills

In addition to perceptual skills, a person also becomes skilled in performing certain non-perceptual actions, such as playing a musical instrument or throwing a football. Polanyi calls these "instrumental" skills. As with perceptual skills, instrumental skills develop with practice. A young child needs to learn to use her body just as much as a teen-ager learns to use a car. After the use of the body is mastered, as one uses the body to act on something else, the body is included as a part of oneself. After

---

4. The notion of a "person", as here outlined, corresponds reasonably well to Edmund Husserl's notion of the "transcendental ego"; "perception and creation" correspond reasonably well to Husserl's notion of "acts of consciousness". See his *Cartesian Meditations* (Martinus Nijhoff, The Hague, 1960).

that, as one gains skill in using tools, the self-concept is extended past the borders of the body to incorporate these tools. A carpenter using a hammer to drive a nail incorporates the hammer as an extension of herself, just as a good motorist includes her car as a part of herself.

Finally, a person is separate from that which he conceptualizes at a particular time. When a person understands a word or symbol, the concept that he gets is "seen by the light of understanding". At that moment, it is experienced as separate from him. New concepts are based on and defined by already understood concepts: the concept "five miles" is based on the concept "five" and the concept "mile". Concepts, in other words, may be used as tools and construction materials for constructing other concepts. While one is using one or more concepts as conceptual tools, one is aware of the *new* concept on which one is focusing at that moment. The subsidiary concepts that are being used to construct the new concept are experientially a part of oneself and are not regarded as separate thoughts.

Learning and Personal Growth

What do we mean when we refer to "personal growth", "increased awareness", or "increased ability"? Simply this: each time a person succeeds in perceiving, creating, or understanding, she tends to extend herself to *incorporate* what she has perceived, created, or understood. The focus of attention or action moves outward. Each successful act involves the incorporation of an element of instrumental, conceptual, or perceptual skill into the person.

Although I have distinguished between perception, creation, and understanding, normally all three activities are present simultaneously in any given act. Driving a nail (a creation of a change) involves a correct perception of the nail in relation to the hammer and a concept of how to drive a nail. Viewing a star through a telescope involves skill in manipulating the telescope and a concept of what a star is and what a telescope is. One's understanding of what air is — that it exists and has weight — can be

considerably enhanced by an experiment in which one weighs a
deflated basketball, then pumps it full of air, re-weighs it, and
perceives that it is heavier. One's ability to have this understanding involves being able to perceive a scale properly and knowing
how to use a pump and a scale. Because of the value of physical
demonstration in developing understanding, most science curricula
include laboratory work. Part of learning a subject is developing
instrumental skill.[5]

Unlearning and Relearning

Sometimes a person reaches a point of diminishing returns in
his attempts to extend his capacity to understand, perceive, or
create. When this happens, he must "step back" from his point
of extension and examine things that previously were a part of
him. He must, in other words, *unlearn* previously incorporated
patterns of conception, perception, or creation that limit his ability. Then, having learned better skills, he can exercise them and
extend himself outward again.

One example of this process is the famous Cartesian Reduction, in which Descartes reduced his scope of knowledge to the
simple proposition, "I think, therefore I am." Having thus "puri-
fied" his thoughts, he proceeded to re-extend and recreate his
ideas using the concept of God as a basis for this re-extension.
Another example, involving instrumental skill, is that of a "hunt-
and-peck" typist who has reached a limit in her typing speed. In
order to make a major gain in speed, she must "step back" and
put her attention on what she is doing when she types the letter
"a", instead of just *typing* the letter "a". She suffers a temporary
"reduction in identity" from being a *typist* to being a *student* of
typing. She "retreats" to a point from which she can examine the

---

5. Unfortunately, the instrumental aspect of learning is often neglected in
   some forms of education, much to the detriment of the students'
   understanding.

motion of typing the letter "a" in terms of finger position and motion. Here is where training and practice come in. If a simple action is practiced enough, a person can then do the action without attending to it. In other words, the person re-extends to incorporate the improved method of typing and can now again focus on typing the letter "a" or on typing sentences, and if the training was properly done it all goes a lot faster. Furthermore, after relearning the skill, the person will be able to extend herself further in the area of typing. Perhaps now she can focus on the *content* of what she is typing, where before she was focusing on typing the letter "a". Typing the letter "a" has now become a part of her.

The price of optimum extension is often a temporary contraction under controlled conditions, followed by a greater re-extension.

The sense of contraction and introversion that follows failure could thus be viewed as a natural adaptive function. When this introversion is *used* and pursued systematically and thoroughly, an improved *modus operandi* is arrived at. But if, having failed, a person does not use his introversion to repair or enhance his skill, then he simply retreats from that area of life. Consequently, his extension into that area may be chronically or permanently blunted.

Identity

In the above discussion, we have made some progress toward understanding what a person conceives himself to *be* at a particular time. A person plays many roles and extends or contracts his self-definition depending on what the context demands. I am going to use the word "identity" to refer to a particular role or self-definition that a person has at a particular time, including the various skills, assumptions, and characteristics that contribute to that self-definition. This usage of the word "identity" is a specialized one. I do not mean to imply that a person is changing his basic nature from time to time nor to make any other metaphysical assertions about "ultimate human nature" or what a person

"really is".[6] Having made these qualifications, I offer the following definition:

> **Definition**: An <u>identity</u> is a package of viewpoints, tools,
> subsidiary awarenesses, and conceptual, perceptual, and
> instrumental abilities that can be incorporated as part of
> the self in order to fulfill an intention. "Identity" can
> also include the way in which a person chooses to appear
> to others.

A person has no fixed identity. In order to fulfill an intention, she *assumes* an identity. In doing so, she incorporates into
herself the conceptual, perceptual, and instrumental tools with
which to carry out the intention. In carrying out an intention, a
person views, understands, or creates things "outside herself", as
she currently defines herself — that is, outside her current identity. A skilled musician "becomes" her instrument, her skills, and
her musical knowledge and acts to create a piece of music that is
separate from herself. Conceivably, she can even "become" the
music if she is trying to do something else with it, such as
impressing her boyfriend. At another time, the same person
might "become" a teacher, incorporating teaching skills as part of
herself in instructing students. At yet other times she is "being"
a car en route to rehearsals, or "being" a lover, or "being" a
mother.

When speaking of personal expansion or extension as a goal,
what we really want is to develop the *ability* to extend or contract
freely at will. To realize his full potential, a person must be able
and willing to assume different identities at different times without
becoming "stuck" in any of them. It was fine for Louis XIV to
say, "*L'état, c'est moi!*"[7] while he was using France to accomplish

---

6. This usage could be confusing, in that "identity" may seem to mean "that
which makes something unique". That is not how I wish to use the term.
As I use "identity", two or more people could have a common identity,
e.g., the identity of a schoolteacher. Or an identity *could* be unique, such
as the identity of "Albert Einstein".

some international purpose, but to the degree that he became chronically *fixed* in this viewpoint, he suffered.

A desire for fame or power is not the only thing that can fix a person in an identity. Commonly, people get fixed in identities that are somehow "safe". They may have observed that someone else with this identity is doing well in life, so they decide they have to "be" that person (who serves as a "role-model"). Or the identity may be *constructed*, rather than adopted. A self-deprecating identity is sometimes constructed because, being already self-attacking, it is regarded as safe from external attack.

The goal of personal extension is not to extend oneself greatly and then remain indefinitely in an overextended state. A person must also be able to *shed* identities at will and become something simpler and less specialized. I have observed many instances of what I call the "Great Person Syndrome". This occurs when a person, having made some genuinely fine contribution in a certain area (and having extended greatly in that area), incorporates the area chronically as a fixed identity. How often have we seen an able politician who cannot stop being one? Or a great actress who is always acting? A person thus fixed in being a certain identity loses the ability to assume other identities, such as that of a marital partner or a friend. Certainly, as a minimum, we all need to have the ability to be a student from time to time if we are going to learn anything new. A person who loses the ability to be a student ossifies and will eventually substitute fixed ideas for actual knowledge, fixed patterns of behavior for real creative activity, and a fixed viewpoint for real perception.

Identities often become fixed when they are assumed, not for the purpose of creating, perceiving, and conceiving, but for the purpose of *being* viewed, perceived, and conceived in a certain way by others. In the latter case, the person is assuming the role of an object for other persons. And an object does not think, perceive, or create.

---

7. "I am the state."

In other words, the person "becomes" an object; she becomes interest*ing* instead of being interest*ed*.

I have not yet really answered the question "What is a person?" I have discused the ability of a person to extend, to contract, or to shift his identity to fit the exigencies of the moment. But is there an identity that stays constant, that underlies the identities that one assumes at different times?

Certainly there appears to be a hierarchy amongst identities.[8] A person in a particular identity can assume subsidiary or "junior" identities while still retaining the "senior" identity. An actor may one day "be" Hamlet, another day "be" Macbeth or Tartuffe. A musician may at one time be a guitarist, at another time a pianist, at another time a singer. As guitarist, she may be sometimes a rhythm guitarist, sometimes a classical guitarist, sometimes a folk guitarist, or a flamenco guitarist. In fact, if she does her job correctly, she should assume a new identity to fit the mood of each piece she is playing.

Presumably, too, a rhythm guitarist can "step back" and just be a guitarist, then step back again to just be a musician, then step back to just be an artist, then again to just be something else that is "senior" to being an artist (whatever that may be for that person). At some point, it seems one would reach a limit to this "stepping back" process. It seems that one would eventually arrive at the "basic identity" of a person — an identity from which the person or individual is unable or unwilling to retreat. A person with a fixed identity, such as that of a "Great Person", reaches this limit early on, through being unwilling or unable to retreat from that identity. A person who feels insecure or uncertain of receiving approval may adopt a fixed identity to handle the situation. Someone who is being "Mr. Cool" or being a "Marlboro Man" may become very queasy at the idea of climbing down off of this identity and "just being himself", i.e., being a higher-

---

8. Though not a *strict* hierarchy, in that a single ability or identity may be subsumed under different identities.

level identity. I, myself, can recall a time when I was somewhat fixed in the identity of "being a psychiatrist" — an identity for which I received social approval and recognition. At cocktail parties, I would find myself acting in a kindly, non-threatening manner and trying to get people to tell me their innermost secrets! I also acted this way with my parents, much to their dismay.

Abilities and identities are very closely related. Both are ruled by an intention. If one has truly assumed the identity of "a guitar player", then one must have the ability to play the guitar. There is no such thing as a guitar player who cannot play the guitar. Nor is there anyone who can play the guitar who is not being a guitar player when she does so. An ability could be regarded as related to a *lower-level* identity that serves the purposes of a higher-level one. Therefore, an ability is often thought of as a *means* to some other end beside the exercise of the ability. In other words, there is a difference in emphasis. "Identity" emphasizes what one *is*, one's location, viewpoint, and boundaries, whereas "ability" emphasizes what one can *do*. An identity, then, is a tool for getting something done, a means to an end, a role one assumes in order to play a certain game or to engage in a certain activity. As one's purpose determines what tools one will use, so a purpose or intention "rules" an identity. When one is finished with a particular job, it is customary and desirable to put away one's tools and pick up the tools appropriate to the next job. Similarly, when one has stopped working on a particular purpose and turns to another purpose, one must be willing and able to lay aside the corresponding identity — with all its conceptual, perceptual, and instrumental tools — and assume a new one that corresponds to the next purpose.

A fully-functioning person is able to extend *or* contract his scope of identity at will, or to shift entirely to a different identity. Indeed, an inability to shift one's identity when necessary is the source of a great deal of unhappiness in life. A person who is fixed into the identity of a "victim", for instance, is chronically miserable.

What is the limit of renunciation of, or "stepping back" from, identities to more senior and less specialized identities? Is there a "basic identity" that a person cannot renounce or shed? Although for the purposes of this book, I do not need to answer this question, it is an intriguing one. Traditionally, in various spiritual practices that advocate this renunciation, the goal is to become one with the "Divine spark" within, that is "smaller than a mustard seed". Many religious practices involve systematic renunciation of identity, sometimes referred to as the seeking of a state of "egolessness".

And what is the theoretical limit of *outward* extension of identity? Conceivably, if a person were able enough, she could incorporate — and thus become — the entire universe. Some forms of meditation involve "becoming one" with an object of perception. If a person did this to all objects, however, there would be nothing left "outside" her to experience. The universe would vanish — for her. Such a universal identity would have to be free of all purposes, for a purpose must be directed toward the creation of an effect *outside* the identity which has that purpose. If nothing were outside an identity, that identity could have no purpose. Coextensiveness with the universe would thus entail a Nirvana-like state of purposelessness.

One could also conceivably achieve a state of purposelessness by refusing to assume an identity at all. If one renounced all "desires" (purposes), one would not have any identity since an identity is assumed for, and ruled by, a purpose. All that would remain, then, is the universe, with no self separate from it. But since no self exists as something separate from the "rest" of the universe, it might appear that the self *is* the universe. Some mystics have held that, at a certain point, the state of complete renunciation and the state of complete extension or coextensiveness with the universe "wrap around" and are identical states. To quote Huston Smith:

> "All the levels of reality are within man, for microcosm mirrors macrocosm; man mirrors the Infinite.... That which man seeks externally in the highest heavens he seeks internally in the depths of his soul. Spiritual space, like physical, is curved. We journey far to reach our origin."[9]

According to this view, one learns one's true "inner" Divine identity in the very act of achieving oneness with the universe and in the act of renouncing identity.

For our current purposes, we do not need to decide on these speculative matters. It is enough to say that a major goal of personal enhancement should be a high degree of ability to assume identities of increasing or decreasing seniority at will, i.e., a high degree of "vertical" mobility of identity. "Horizontal" mobility of identity, i.e., the ability to shift to another point in another hierarchy of identity (e.g., to shift from being a musician to being a lover) ultimately depends on vertical mobility. One can only make such a "horizontal" shift through being able to shift, first "upward" to a common, more senior identity (such as oneself, as a communicator), then "downward" again to another more junior identity. The senior identity provides continuity for such a horizontal shift.

It is thus very important to be flexible in assuming and shedding identities. I refer to this basic ability as "versatility":

Definition: Versatility is the ability to assume or shed identities.

A major task of metapsychology has been to discover techniques for helping a person achieve a high level of versatility. Some effective ones have been found.

Characteristics of a World

A person's own existence is indubitable, but it is equally indubitable to him that he is surrounded by something, and that something is what he generally refers to as "the world".

---

9. Smith, H. *Forgotten Truth* (Harper and Row, New York, 1976) p. 20f.

Definition: A <u>world</u> is the totality of what exists for a particular person at a particular time.[10]

What the world consists of has been a subject for endless debate and disagreement. By looking at the notion of a world from a person-centered viewpoint, however, it is possible to sort out those characteristics that are common to *any* person's world.

Entities

A person's world is composed of parts: events, objects, or states of affairs. Twenty-five hundred years ago, Heracleitus observed that so-called objects are actually just events — manifestations of change. A river, for instance, is just a flowing of water, even though it appears to be an "object". An object can also be looked upon as a *relationship*, a "state of affairs", e.g., a relation of closeness between more elementary particles, such as atoms and molecules. Elementary particles themselves are nowadays thought of as more like events or relationships than like objects. Likewise, an event (like the Russian Revolution) can be regarded as an object, from the point of view of an historian. Another kind of event, such as the procreation and raising of children, can be regarded as a relationship: a "family". Since an object can sometimes be viewed as an event or a state of affairs (and *mutatis mutandi*), I have chosen to use the term "entity" to apply to any of these possible ways of looking at things:

Definition: An <u>entity</u> is an object, event, or relationship (state of affairs) that is part of a person's world, i.e., that exists, for a person, at a certain moment.[11]

---

10. This definition includes the *relationships* between things as well as the things themselves, because a relationship is a "thing" too. See below.
11. The word "entity" has been used, popularly, to refer to spiritual beings, often demonic ones. That is not what is meant, here! It is used to mean "something that exists".

A person's world, then, partly consists of entities (events, objects, and states of affairs) that can be perceived by him at a certain time, partly of entities that cannot be perceived by him at that time — but that are *known* by him at that time — and partly of concepts he has at that time.[12]

Phenomena: Perceivable Entities

Because "phenomenon" is a term that does not prejudice the issue of whether a perceived entity is an event, a state of affairs, or an object, I shall follow Husserl and use the word "phenomena" to designate those parts of a person's world she *perceives*:

Definition: A phenomenon is an entity that a person can perceive.

By "phenomenon", I do not mean, necessarily, a *scientifically* observable or *measurable* entity (event, relationship, object, or state of affairs). I simply mean an entity that is directly perceivable by a person — something a person can look at, smell, taste, feel, hear, or possibly perceive through an extension of the body, such as a telescope, or a radio, or through conceptual tools.

A phenomenon is not *inferred* from what is perceived, nor an *interpretation* of what is perceived, but that which can be perceived *directly*. Entities that cannot be perceived directly are not phenomena, in our definition of the term.

---

12. Note also that the past or future also exist for a person in present time: one can remember the past, or dream of the future, as a present-time activity, in which case the past, or future, becomes an entity.

Facts: Knowable Entities

Phenomena themselves exist, but some of them also seem to suggest the existence of non-phenomenal entities (objects, events, or states of affairs). These entities, though not perceivable, are nevertheless part of a person's world.[13] For instance, the falling of an apple indicates the existence of gravity, though gravity cannot be directly perceived. I will use the word "facts" to describe entities that exist for a person without being perceivable by him.[14] By "fact", I mean simply an entity (object, event, or state of affairs) that exists *for a person* without being perceivable:

> **Definition**: A fact is an entity that exists for a person but that is not perceivable and is not a mere concept.

---

13. A similar viewpoint is taken by the school of Radical Constructivists, who feel that each person's world is constructed by that person. This assertion should be refined somewhat. Some parts of a person's world are *created* by the person and other parts are *received* by the person as interpretations of other data. Interpretation and creation are not quite the same thing and the term "construction", I think, tends to confuse the two. See Watzlawick, P., Ed. *The Invented Reality* (Norton, New York, 1984). I will have more to say on these matters in Chapter Two.

14. The word "fact" seems apropos, because one speaks of *knowing* facts, but not, for instance, of smelling facts, seeing facts (with the eyes), touching facts, hearing facts (with the ears), and so forth. On the other hand, one does not speak of "knowing" phenomena. I don't *know* a painting I am looking at (except in the restricted sense of "being acquainted with") or *know* the smell of perfume I am smelling; I *perceive* these phenomena. In other words, we speak of *perceiving* phenomena but of *knowing* facts.

I realize I have been somewhat presumptuous in appropriating the word "fact" to describe something from an entirely person-centered viewpoint. People usually think of facts as true absolutely, not just true for an individual at a particular time. But no one has been able to come up with a better term. And even from a person-centered viewpoint, when a person regards something as a fact, she regards it as true. That is, it *is* true — for her! So this connotation of the word is not entirely inappropriate.

The objects in the room, my hands, a photograph I have in my hand, my feelings and emotions — any mental images and everything I can receive through my various senses — all these are phenomena. Other entities (such as "motherhood", electrical fields, photosynthesis) are facts. I am not able to perceive these things, but they exist for me. All of the above are entities and all (whether phenomena or facts, perceivable or not perceivable) are part of my world.

To rephrase what was said in the last paragraph, a person's set of entities (in other words, his world) *includes* his set of phenomena, but it also includes his set of facts — other entities (objects, events, conditions, or states of affairs) that the person is not able to perceive but which nevertheless exist for him, and not just as concepts.

Concepts: Conceivable Entities

Concepts are the third category of entities that make up a person's world. As phenomena are entities that are perceivable, concepts are entities that are *con*ceivable. Concepts (as I use the term) are not mental pictures. A concept of something is not the same as a picture of that thing. Pictures may be associated with a concept, and concepts with a picture, but a picture and a concept are two distinct entities. For instance, when I conceive the concept of a horse, I may or may not "get" several pictures of horses. None of these pictures, nor the group of pictures taken as a whole, is a concept. Since they are *perceivable*, all such pictures are classifiable as phenomena.

The Relationship Among Phenomena, Facts, and Concepts

Phenomena (*per*ceivable entities) and concepts (*con*ceivable entities) are known more directly than facts. There is nothing I know more directly or with more certainty than that I am perceiving the phenomena I am perceiving right now and conceiving the concepts I am conceiving right now. Along with a certainty of his own aliveness, a person's immediate perceptions and conceptions — his phenomena and his concepts — are that of which he has the greatest certainty.[15] The question could be asked, "What about illusions, phenomena that we *know* are illusory?" In this case, however, the *entity* that is perceived is an illusion, not the entity that the illusion may appear to be. Consider the optical illusion shown in Figure 2. The boxes appear to be of unequal size, though in fact they are exactly equal. But if I know it is an illusion, I do not say that I am perceiving boxes of unequal size. I say, rather, that I am perceiving an optical *illusion* in which the boxes look unequal. If I said that I was perceiving unequal-sized boxes, I would not be looking at it as an illusion but as a reality.

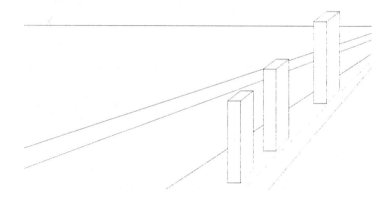

Figure 2. An optical illusion.

To illustrate the relationship between phenomena and facts, let us look at what happens when a person learns to use a microscope. I can recall my first experience trying to use one. Like

---

15. It is interesting to speculate *why* we should be so certain of what we perceive and conceive. I do not know the answer to that question, but answering it might lead to new insights. See also the section on "quasi entities", pp. 37-41.

most beginners, what I first perceived were vague blobs and patches of light. Some of these blobs turned out later to be flecks of dust; I came to see others as air bubbles and still others as different types of cells.

Acquiring skill in the use of a microscope involves learning the *rules* for inferring the existence of these various entities from the phenomena that appear under the microscope. The student learns that certain almost perfectly round and sharp-edged blobs are bubbles, certain rather opaque blobs are dust particles, whereas other blobs that are transparent, granular and have a darker center, are cells. The student is then able to interpret the phenomena she sees. At this stage, the student still sees the blobs and patches of light, but has learned what these blobs "mean". They "mean" bubbles, cells and dust particles.

In time, the student extends her identity as a "microscope user" or "microbiologist" through acquiring perceptual skill in using the microscope. She completely internalizes (makes a part of *herself*) the *rules* of inference that she formerly used to interpret the phenomena under the microscope. She then no longer consciously or focally sees "blobs" and has to *interpret* them as bubbles, cells, or dust. Rather, she simply seems to *perceive* cells, dust particles, and bubbles *directly*. The "blobs" that she formerly saw have become, in a sense, "transparent", in that they are seen with *subsidiary* awareness. What the person now perceives *focally* are simply cells, dust particles, and bubbles. As a mere student, she saw blobs; as a microbiologist, she sees more meaningful entities.

Let us look at this example in terms of facts and phenomena. The student perceived certain phenomena (blobs and whatnot) when she first looked through the microscope. There were no particular facts corresponding to these phenomena. That is, the student did not, at first, know how to interpret these blobs. They "meant nothing" to her. A little while later, the student had learned the rules for relating the blobs she perceived to their meanings: cells, bubbles, and dust. At this stage, the phenomena seen were still blobs, but, based on the rules of inference, the student said, "I perceive a blob that has sharp edges. I must be looking at a bubble." Here, the blob is a phenomenon and the bubble a fact. The student *infers* the existence of a bubble from the blob she sees, using the rule she learned about sharp-edged objects. Now a bubble exists for her, but she does not yet *see* a bubble when she looks through the microscope. What she *sees* is still a blob. She has a phenomenon (the blob) from which she infers a fact (the bubble). At a later stage, the student simply *sees* a bubble. Here, she no longer perceives blobs; her experience, on looking through the microscope, is that of perceiving bubbles. Now the bubble, which was formerly a fact, has become a phenomenon.

What a person *perceives* at a given time depends, as I mentioned above, on the identity the person has assumed at that time. The same entity may be a fact for a person (such as a student) at one time and a phenomenon at another when the person has undergone some personal growth and has incorporated a skill as a subsidiary awareness (such as that of a microbiologist).

Now, even though a person is skilled as a microbiologist and ordinarily does not see "blobs" anymore, she ought to be able to "step back" from this identity. She should be able to disincorporate and de-automatize the inferences and assumptions that are part of that identity, and look through the microscope in such a way that she perceives blobs, instead of bubbles. If she does this, she can then "make" the blobs phenomena (where before they were not perceived at all), and "make" the bubbles mere facts again (where before they were phenomena).[16]

Although I have given a specific perceptual skill as an example, this principle is completely generalizable. Any phenomenon can be regarded as a fact if one "steps back" in this way. As I have just mentioned, facts can also become phenomena, by the

---

16. The ability to "step back" in this way is vital to a teacher, who needs to be able to guide the students from the viewpoint they currently have to a more sophisticated viewpoint (e.g., the viewpoint of a trained microbiologist). People have a varying ability to do this. Those who are stuck in a "knowledgeable" identity may be poor teachers since they are unable to assume the relatively ignorant viewpoint of their students and guide them to a more knowledgeable one.

person "stepping forward" into an identity. Facts are inferred from phenomena using various "rules of inference", such as "Where there's smoke, there's fire," or "If something feels cool and wet, it is probably a liquid." In "extending" his identity, a person includes or incorporates the rules by which the facts are inferred. These rules then become automatically or subliminally known. Then, instead of seeing smoke, he "sees" fire, and instead of feeling something wet and cool, he "feels" a liquid.

A phenomenon is just a phenomenon. It is not doubtable *as such* at the time it is perceived. In order to doubt a phenomenon, it is necessary to "step back" and view it as a conclusion or an interpretation, inferred from other data or phenomena. In "stepping back", however, the person has ceased to view the phenomenon as a phenomenon. At one time an entity may be a phenomenon; at another time it may be a fact. Nevertheless, at any given time, in any given identity, a person has a definite and discrete set of phenomena and facts.

These, together with the person's concepts, make up his world.

Quasi-Entities

By calling concepts, facts, and phenomena the three basic types of entities, I am stating that these things are what definitely exist for the person. But there appear to be other things that have an indefinite or partial existential status. One might say that these "quasi-entities" exist as possible or probable existences — existences of which we are not certain.

When I know a fact, I am certain about it. But I have many "quasi-facts" — things that I am not certain of but that have a certain degree of probability. One could call these "beliefs", "considerations" or "opinions", but these words do not necessarily specify a condition of uncertainty (one can consider, opine, or believe with certainty), and they refer more to the *act* of believing, (considering, opining), than to the *object* of that act. There isn't really a good term, so I will use the suffix "-oid" to indicate the indefinite existential status of the object of such an act. Hence a "factoid" is something that is like a fact but about which one does not have complete conviction.

Let's talk about phenomena next. What is the status of the experience in which I think I might be perceiving something but am not sure? Is that speck on the horizon a boat? It seems as though it might be one, but I am not sure. You could say that what I actually perceive is an indistinct form only — something that might be interpreted as a boat. But you might also say I quasi-perceive a boat. In other words, I have a boat as a quasi-phenomenon or "phenomenoid". Since I am not sure that it is a boat, I don't yet have a boat as an actual phenomenon. It seems that there is a lot of looking that goes on, the object of which is something indefinite. So there is a definite place for the idea of a "phenomenoid". The practice of Focusing, for instance, uses phenomenoids a great deal.[17] In Focusing, a great deal of time is spent trying to determine precisely what phenomenon a phenomenoid is supposed to be.

Finally, about concepts: A concept, to be an actual concept, must be sufficiently clear so that it is meaningful to say "yes" or "no" to it. In other words, it must be a clear possible fact. But there seem to be some cases in which I have a quasi-concept or "conceptoid" — a sort of intimation, but I am not yet sure what possible fact I am trying to conceptualize. I have not yet achieved clarity and distinctness, to use Descarte's phraseology. In other words, the concept, as a concept, has not yet been fully brought into existence. Often it seems to help to try to put a conceptoid into words. Sometimes, when one does this, it "crystallizes" into a actual concept. But it is important to remember that a concept need not be expressed — or even expressible — in words in order to be an actual concept. And, on the other hand,

---

17. See Gendlin, E. *Focusing* (Bantam Books, New York, 1982).

the fact of having said certain words does not mean that a concept has been expressed. For instance, a poem from Dylan Thomas proclaims:

"This world is half the Devil's and my own,
Daft with the drug that's smoking in a girl
And curling round the bud that forks her eye."

You can get a conceptoid out of this, perhaps, but not an actual concept, because you only get some kind of "intimation"; you can't really get enough meaning to have something to which you could say "yes" or "no". Thus linguistic expression is neither a necessary nor a sufficient condition for the formation of a concept. You can have words without a concept and a concept without words. So I would not agree with those who say that it is only by means of language that clear concepts are obtained, and that the clarity of such concepts is obtained only by their rendering into words.

The status of all quasi-entities may vary along a continuum from a very slight degree of certainty to just short of total certainty. A phenomenoid may have varying degrees of clarity. A shape on the horizon may vary from being only slightly suggestive of a boat to being almost certainly a boat, before it becomes certainly a boat and thus a full-fledged phenomenon. A factoid may vary from seeming only slightly more probable than not to seeming almost certain, before it becomes a certainty and thus a full-fledged fact. And a conceptoid may vary from a vague intimation to something that almost makes sense, before it becomes actually meaningful and thus graduates into being a full-fledged concept.

In fact, entities may exist for me without my being totally certain of them. There are some facts of which I am more certain than other facts, some phenomena that I perceive more clearly than others, and some concepts that are clearer than others. In other words, there is some point, in general, at which a quasi-entity graduates to the status of being an actual entity, short of the attainment of *total* certainty. This point seems to correspond to the point at which one is willing to act "as if" one had total certainty, the point at which one can *accept* that entity without necessarily being completely certain of it.

A conceptoid need not be completely clear in order to be accepted as a concept. Even so, when accepted as a concept, it may now be assented to or dissented from. In other words, a conceptoid may pass the threshold into being a concept (i.e., capable of being assented to or dissented from) before it has become fully clarified. I can agree that something exists (or does not exist) without being entirely clear about what it is that I suppose to exist or not exist. I only need to have *enough* of a concept of it to be able to say "yes" or "no".

Thus it is legitimate to say, "I agree that electrons exist. But what is an electron, exactly?" or "I know that Mary loves me. But what is love?" Much of the province of intellectual endeavors like science or philosophy consists, I believe, in making the nature of existence clearer by clarifying the concepts of things already believed to exist.

A person who needs glasses but doesn't have or use them may nevertheless learn to see people's faces and recognize them. The faces he sees are phenomena that are sufficiently clear to be identified, and he will treat them as the faces that he has identified them to be. But he can achieve a greater degree of certainty about what he is perceiving by putting on a pair of glasses.

I know that a particular person is my friend. His friendship is a fact to me — one I can act on. But if he did something especially wonderful for me, I would be even more certain of his friendship.

Certainty is a matter of degree, and rarely, if ever, do we attain total certainty about something. But there is a point at which we attain a degree of certainty that is sufficient for practical purposes, and at that point, a quasi-entity attains the status of being an actual entity. This is the point at which we make the "leap of faith" which enables us to act, where:

> **Definition**: Faith is a degree of certainty that is sufficient for action.

Faith provides the demarcation point between quasi-entities and actual entities. Faith usually falls short of total certainty, but it is the point at which we feel we can cease considering a matter and begin acting. At this point, one might say, we cross the "faith threshold". A person with a very high faith threshold would require a great deal of certainty before acting and so might be quite inactive — as Hamlet described himself to be — whereas a person with a very low faith threshold might be prone to precipitous action with inadequate consideration. The optimum appears to be somewhere in between.

This means that what is an entity in one context may only be a quasi-entity in another. As a beginner, looking through a microscope, I may be pleased merely to be able to distinguish things that are cells from things that are not cells. For me, in this context, a cell is a phenomenon. But if I am trying to determine what kind of cell it is, I may see it as a sort of amoeba, or a sort of paramecium and it is a phenomenoid rather than a phenomenon, because the standard of certainty and clarity is greater. I may have a concept of "verb" that is sufficiently clear for most purposes, but that concept may need to be clarified if I want to be successful at diagraming sentences. I may have the concept of an integral as "the area under a curve", but I will need a more precise concept in order to do integral calculus. And I may feel sure of the fact that I can get along well with a girl named Susan, but if I am going to marry Susan, I will require a higher degree of probability before I will call it a fact that we will be able to get along.

It is characteristic of certain disciplines, such as the sciences and philosophy (and metapsychology), that a very high standard of certainty and clarity is required — more than for most everyday circumstances. And it is also characteristic of these disciplines that an ever-greater standard of certainty and clarity is called for. Such searches for certainty and clarity are amongst the most fruitful of Man's endeavors.

The Person-World Polarity

In talking about the person and her world, I am not talking about two completely separate entities. Rather, I am talking about a bipolar situation: the person and her world are opposite poles, like the north and south poles of a magnet.[18] The person, as the actor, the perceiver, the knower, contacts her world by assuming a certain identity. At one pole is the person; at the other is that which the person perceives, that which she knows or understands, that upon which she acts, and that which she creates by means of that identity — the totality of what exists for that person at that moment — that person's universe or world:

Definition: A world is the totality of what exists for a particular person at a particular moment.

For the purposes of this book, I define a particular person's "world" as the opposite pole to that person. By doing this, I do not mean to negate the possibility of there being an absolute truth or "absolute reality" in some sense.[19] It appears that as people learn more and more from their experience, they discover more

---

18. A person's world could not exist without the person. This is not necessarily to say that *no* world would exist if a certain person did not experience it, but any such world would, *ex hypothesi*, certainly not be *that* person's world, with the special characteristics it has for that person. And if a certain world does not exist for *any* person, then no one can truthfully claim that it *does* exist, so we can safely neglect such a world, from the person-centered viewpoint. It is also difficult (though perhaps not impossible) to conceive of a person who has no world. The north pole does not exist without the south pole; both are part of the same magnet. Yet there is apparently some evidence for the existence of a magnetic monopole, and there are those who argue for the existence of consciousness without an object of consciousness. See Merrell-Wolfe, F. *The Philosophy of Consciousness Without an Object* (Julian Press, New York, 1973).

19. To do so would probably be self-contradictory, because I am putting forward what *I* think is the truth, so I must think there is such a thing as a truth that applies for all people, although I do not know how one could be certain that there is such a thing as absolute truth or absolute reality.

and more commonalities in that experience. And as a person acquires an ever-greater understanding of these commonalities, she approaches a viewpoint that could be regarded as "absolutely true". Whether she can ever *reach* "absolute truth" is questionable, but it seems fairly certain that she can have progressively truer and truer concepts about the world. For instance, Newton's Laws of motion are true, but Einstein's General Relativity equations are truer, and some combination of Quantum Physics and Relativity is probably the "truest" truth currently available to us about the material universe. Likewise, there is truth to be found in behaviorism and in Jungian and Freudian psychology, but I believe that the metapsychological approach provides a "truer truth".

Perhaps paradoxically, the way to arrive at something approximating *absolute* truth is through a study of *relative* truth, i.e., through a study of the person and what is true for him most directly (namely, what he perceives and thinks) and then by a further study of the way in which he builds up a world-view from these perceptions and concepts. As different people become more aware, they tend to *converge* in their world views, instead of diverging. This convergence seems to imply that we are all progressing toward the same truth. "Great minds" are said to think alike. Possibly, as I have suggested, there is a connection amongst persons: some unity of consciousness which, when contacted, serves as a source of intersubjective truth — the equivalent of "objective" truth. The purpose for taking the person-centered viewpoint is to arrive at *inter*subjective truth by a close study of what is true for individuals and how they relate to their worlds.

It is universally observed that phenomena are spatially located and separated from each other in time and space.[20] When a phenomenon is viewed as an object, it can appear to *move*. Such motion can take the form of *translation* (an external change

---

20. And, possibly, in other dimensions. See Chapter Three, pp. 120-137.

in space with respect to time), *transformation* (an internal change in space with respect to time), or both. When a phenomenon is viewed as an event, it is viewed as having *duration*, rather than motion. Thus, as an object, a car is seen to translate and to transform (to move around, get older, get rusty, etc.) over time, while as an enduring event or state of affairs consisting of a cohering of particles in a particular relationship to each other, the car is seen to persist for a certain period of time. Its span of existence starts when the parts are put together into the relationship and ends when the parts fall apart, out of that relationship.

All phenomena "resist" the actions of a person. Phenomena have a degree of immutability or resistance to being changed by a person. For an object, immutability is solidity (resistance to transformation) or mass (resistance to translation); for an event or state of affairs, immutability is a tendency to persist. When we say a wall is solid, we are stating, experientially, that it resists our attempts to deform or transform it. If we say a bowling ball has mass, we are saying it resists our attempts to change its location (or translate it). Both mass and solidity are thus forms of immutability, or resistance to impulsion. For an event, such as the rolling of a ball, immutability is momentum. For a state of affairs or relationship, immutability is persistence or resilience.

Immutability is relative to the ability of a person to apply force. A two-hundred pound weight is relatively immutable to a person of ordinary strength but quite mutable to an Olympic weight-lifter. A toddler cannot lift a forty-pound suitcase. To her, it is an immutable object. To an adult, it can be moved easily.

Any phenomenon has a degree of opacity, or we would not be able to perceive it at all. If we say something is opaque, we are saying that it resists our attempts to perceive *through* it.[21] Paradoxically, the very quality that resists our powers of

---

21. Incandescent objects are experientially opaque because their brightness prevents us from seeing what lies behind them.

perception (and prevents us from having "X-ray vision") is what makes it possible to perceive things! Our definition of opacity has been expanded to cover all senses. In this sense, a speaker grill is opaque to visual perception but transparent to sonic perception; a double thickness of glass is visually transparent but sonically relatively opaque; sensitive skin is transparent to touch; callused or numb skin is opaque to the sense of touch. Opacity is relative to the perception channel being used. It is also relative to the acuity of that perception channel, as well as to the strength of the signal coming through. A wall is less sonically opaque to a blaring horn than to a whisper; it is more transparent to sound for a person with sharp ears than for a relatively deaf person. It may be opaque to light and sound but quite transparent to X-rays or radio waves, if such means are being used as perceptual channels.

Some phenomena may be said to have "meaning". Such phenomena, known as "tokens", are either symbols (such as words or gestures), or indicators — phenomena that can be explained, such as rain clouds or smoke. In some cases, this "meaning" is easier to grasp than in other cases. It is relatively easy to understand the significance of a rain cloud (it means rain) and relatively difficult to understand the significance of a sudden, apparently hostile encounter with an ordinarily amiable person. It is easy for most Americans to understand English but difficult for them to understand Russian. A phenomenon that is understandable is considered to be intelligible, and any phenomenon can be said to have a degree of intelligibility. Nevertheless, any phenomenon also has a degree of *un*intelligibility. That is, phenomena resist understanding to a varying degree. In other words, it is either easy or difficult to grasp the underlying significance of a phenomenon. Understanding a phenomenon is not automatic. It requires an act of interpretation, which may be relatively easy or difficult, depending on the person and on the phenomenon. The resistance of phenomena to understanding is clearly relative to the knowledge and intelligence of the person in question. Russian words are unintelligible to most Americans but quite intelligible to most Russians. An X-ray photograph is intelligible to a radiologist and relatively unintelligible to an untrained person.

Perceptually, the opposite of resistance is something like opportunity, "freedom", or, more simply, "space and time". Perceptually, space is transparency, or non-resistance to perception. One feels surrounded by space if one can see, feel, or hear for a certain distance. If seeing, hearing, or other senses are resisted, then one feels "closed in". Space and time can also be viewed as a lack of resistance to change. Inability to act is characteristically explained (literally or figuratively) as an insufficiency of time or space. A person who finds it impossible to get her work done characteristically complains that she doesn't have enough time. A frustrated person feels as though she is encountering "barriers", as though "doors are closed" to her. One needs time and space in which to act.[22]

Each side of the person-world polarity affects and determines the other side. An ability on the person side corresponds to a certain freedom, opportunity, space and time, granted by the world. In order for me to have the ability to do something, the world must grant me an opportunity to do it. In order for me to be able to play the guitar, the world must give me the opportunity

---

22. Other dimensions may be required as well. See Chapter Three, pp. 120-137. It might be argued that space and time themselves may be forms of resistance or barriers. The distance from here to the moon might be considered a barrier to taking Sunday outings there. The real barrier, however, is not the space intervening between the earth and the moon but gravitational and inertial resistance to motion. If there were no gravity and no inertia, a tiny impetus would send one hurtling to the moon at an indefinitely high speed. Likewise, an interposition of time between now and a certain event is not a barrier. On the contrary, it *allows* that event to take place by making it possible to fit in the actions between now and then that are necessary to make it happen. This is not to discount the fact that the existence of space or time might be counter to one's intentions. Resistance is often necessary in order to act. One of the principle difficulties to getting things done in a weightless condition is that the resistance normally supplied by the force of gravity is not available, so things do not stay put. If one needs a certain kind of resistance in order to get something done, its absence can be very frustrating. It is also possible to defeat an opponent by not resisting, as masters of certain Eastern philosophies and martial arts (e.g., Taoism and Tai Chi) are wont to do.

by containing guitars, music, strings, and the like, and the time and space in which to use them. Conversely, in order for me to have opportunity in my world, I must have the ability to *take* the opportunity. In order for the existence of time, space, guitars, music, and strings in the world to give me the opportunity to play the guitar, I must attain the *ability* to play it (See Figure 3).

THE PERSON   **THE WORLD**

Life,   Opportunity,
Ability,   Freedom,
Vitality   Space and Time

Figure 3. Overall person-world polarity.

Abilities also have their counterparts on the world side of the person-world polarity. On the person side are the various abilities of the person — the ability to know, to perceive, and to create; and on the world side are the various qualities that permit the exercise of these abilities: intelligibility, transparency, and mutability. As I have mentioned, intelligibility is the other side of understanding; transparency relates to perception, and mutability to strength (See Figure 4).

Wisdom,
Knowledge,   Intelligibility
Intelligence

Perceiving   Transparency

Moving   Mutability

Figure 4. Basic abilities and their worldly counterparts.

Also, corresponding to inability on the person side of the person-world polarity is a lack of opportunity, prohibition, barriers, and resistance on the world side (See Figure 5). To an incompetent person, the world appears to be replete with impossibilities and barriers; to an able person, the world is filled with possibilities and opportunities. Conversely, in the face of a large number of barriers, prohibitions, and resistances, a person feels himself to be very unable, whereas in the face of many opportunities, space, and time, a person feels himself to be able. On the negative side, then, we have:

Figure 5. Inability and its worldly counterparts.

And, specifically, corresponding to an inability to understand or comprehend on the person side of the person-world polarity is unintelligibility on the world side. Things seem unintelligible to an uncomprehending person, and a person feels stupid when confronted with something unintelligible. Corresponding to insensitivity or imperception on the person side is opacity on the world side. The world looks relatively opaque to a person with weak eyesight; conversely, if a person is in the middle of a London fog, he finds that his ability to perceive has been impaired. Corresponding to weakness on the person side is immutability on the world side. As I said above (p. 44), the world appears immutable to a weak person, and a person faced with things that he cannot change feels weak (See Figure 6).

Understanding, perception and creation normally work together despite being conceptually separated here. To overcome any one of the three varieties of resistance often requires the assistance of the non-corresponding abilities. One can overcome the opacity of a wall by using one's understanding and one's ability to move objects around. For example, one can set up an X-ray device (to which the wall is transparent) or bore a peep-hole. A one-inch plank is relatively unbreakable (immutable) to an ordinary, bare-handed person, but to a karate expert with special

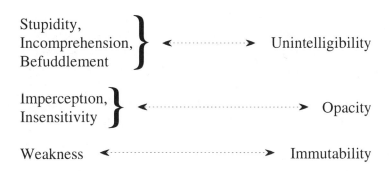

Figure 6. Basic inabilities and their worldly counterparts.

ability to understand and perceive, it is easily broken. Finally, one can use one's ability to perceive and act to understand something. Experimentation and laboratory skills are a good example. Intellectual tasks become much easier if one also makes diagrams or models (bringing perception and action into the task as well).

Personal Reality

To the degree that a phenomenon is thought of as an event or process, we tend to think of it as composed of energy. To the degree that we think of a phenomenon as an object, we think of it as composed of matter. To the degree that we think of it as a relationship or state of affairs, we think of it as a pattern in space and time, a "form". Phenomena seem to partake of all three aspects: form, matter, and energy. A working steam engine may be thought of as partly energy and partly matter, arranged in a certain form in space and time. We have seen that an experience consists of phenomena, separated by various dimensions, e.g., space and time. An experience is made up of matter and energy, separated by various dimensions, and containing various forms.

Now, here is a central point: I have said that in order for a person to exercise an ability, there must be some degree of "space", freedom, or absence of resistance that permits the ability to be exercised. It is equally true, however, that, in order for an ability to be exercised, the ability must meet *some* degree of resistance. For instance, if something is *entirely* transparent to all channels of perception possessed by a particular identity, then it is entirely insensible (invisible, inaudible, etc.) to that identity and thus cannot be perceived. If something is entirely mutable, then we also cannot detect it by being impeded in any way by its presence: it has no solidity, no mass, no momentum, and no persistence. Finally, if something is completely intelligible, then it vanishes as a phenomenon; it becomes a part of the person. If the *words* on this page, for instance, are completely intelligible, you no longer notice them; they are "transparent", and you notice only the *meaning*. You perceive the written words themselves only on a *subsidiary* level, incorporated as part of yourself.[23]

Personal growth occurs through the acquisition of various abilities (including perceptual abilities), as in my example of learning to interpret blobs seen under a microscope. The same is true of learning a foreign language. A new foreign language student looking at a book written in a foreign tongue is at first very aware of the spelling and arrangements of the foreign words. If she looks at the very same book after she has learned the foreign language thoroughly, she is no longer likely to be aware of the words, their spelling, or their syntax. Instead, she is now aware of the concepts the author is expressing, and the words, spelling, and syntax become "transparent". She can, of course, "step back" and deliberately try *not* to understand the meaning of the words, in order to find out something else about them. A proofreader or typesetter must learn to ignore the meaning of the words and attend to the shape or size of the letters. A linguist must learn to pay close attention to the phonetic structure of the words. In these cases, the words and letters (or sounds) are not being understood, so they are perceptible.

---

23. Did you only become aware of the words just now, as I mentioned them?

A puzzle is no longer a puzzle for a person who has figured it out. Until then, the person's attention tends to be fixed on it, so the puzzle remains "there", experientially. For instance, a person could be puzzled about the nature of glass. How can it be that when you melt sand and then recool it under certain conditions, you get the odd substance called "glass", instead of just solid sand, or rock? Sand is made up of tiny fragments of rock. Rock is not terribly fragile and has a high, definite melting point. When you melt sand and allow it to cool, you get glass. Unlike rock, however, glass is quite fragile and does not have a definite melting point. It just gets softer and softer as you heat it up. How, you might wonder, can you have a solid with no definite melting point? Like the proverbial question "Why is grass green?", this conundrum about glass could persist indefinitely as a problem for someone. The answer to the puzzle is that glass is not solid at all. It is liquid, a supercooled liquid, a substance that stays liquid below its melting point without crystallizing. It is similar to a supersaturated solution like honey, which may take a long time to crystallize. Like honey, the cooler glass gets the more viscous it gets. When its viscosity is so great that one cannot get it to flow appreciably at all, then it appears solid, i.e., non-transformable. In reality, it is just a very viscous liquid that flows *very* slowly. Over the centuries, "solid" glass does flow appreciably. That is why old glass windows tend to become quite distorted. Very ancient glass can also eventually start to crystallize. Once a person has these data, he understands why glass is the way it is, and that problem disappears forever.

If a person were not baffled about anything, there would be nothing left to understand. If he had unlimited ability to perceive (total X-ray vision), then *nothing* would be visible, since everything would be transparent. And if he had unlimited power to create motion, nothing would have mass or solidity for him. So, paradoxically, *the existence of a world results from a partial inability to perceive, to create, or to understand* — or from not fully exercising these abilities. An increase in the exercise of a person's ability to perceive, create, or understand *dissolves* part of his world.

The purpose of metapsychology is to increase a person's ability to perceive, to create, and to understand, or, obversely, to decrease the opacity, the unintelligibility, and the immutability of the person's world. That does not mean that a person always *has* to exercise abilities when he has them. In fact, having an ability to *do* something also implies having the ability *not* to do that thing. It is just as important for a person to be able *not* to perceive, create, or understand, if he chooses not to do so, as it is for him to be able to *do* these things.

When I spoke of identity, I stated that in theory, extending oneself to a point of oneness with the universe would obliterate the universe. Alternatively stated, if there were no opacity, no unintelligibility, and no immutability for a person, there would be *nothing* for that person. In other words, if a person were to exercise an infinite ability to perceive, to understand, and to create, the universe would disappear for that person.[24]

I have defined existence as the quality of being a concept, a fact, or a phenomenon. Yet the one "entity" connected to a person that is never a phenomenon for her is the person herself! We thus transcend any phenomenon we can perceive. Any "evidence" a person has for her own existence is always indirect. I never perceive myself as an object. I do not (and cannot) "look inside" to find out things about myself. *Whatever* I see is always "outside" myself in fact and by definition, since "outside oneself", at any particular time, is *defined* as whatever one experiences or acts on at that time. I am therefore not a phenomenon that I can put at a distance and examine.

Other people than myself are also "invisible men", to use R.D. Laing's phrase.[25] I can never perceive another person. I

---

24. I'm not entirely sure that it would be a good thing to make the universe disappear, but in any case, we have far enough to go in the direction of increased ability that we need not worry about this eventuality right now! Also, if we did acquire such a degree of ability, we could choose not to exercise it, or we could put the universe back, or create another one!

25. Laing, R.D. *The Politics of Experience* (Ballantine Books, New York, 1967), p. 18.

can only see the form, perhaps, of some identity assumed by another person, e.g., the body. But that is not the person herself. I have reason to believe or know that other people exist, but they cannot be phenomena for me, any more than I can be a phenomenon for myself.

These thoughts bear on the nature, or definition, of "reality".

The Nature of Reality

In philosophy, the study of what exists is called "ontology" or "metaphysics". In some circles, the latter term has come to mean occult, spiritual, or spiritualistic practices. This is not what I am talking about here. Metaphysics, in the traditional sense, is concerned with the discovery of the ultimate nature of reality, as contrasted with appearances, or as contrasted with anyone's opinion about what might be real. That is also not my interest here. Pursuing "metaphysics" in this sense would be contrary to the person-centered approach. My interest is to explore what reality is from the viewpoint of a particular person or group at a particular time.

From the person-centered viewpoint, what exists experientially for a specific individual — what he feels he *knows* — is what is real *for that person*. In other words, reality, as I am using the term, is *owned*. When I speak of reality from the person-centered viewpoint, I must specify *whose* reality I am speaking of. I undoubtedly think, or feel I *know*, certain entities exist that you think or feel *you* know do not exist, and vice versa. It is a commonplace observation that people have widely differing views concerning the world they live in. For some people, Atlantis existed; for others it did not. There are some people in undeveloped countries who would be certain you were lying if you told them that people had gotten into big metal huts that vomited fire and pushed them all the way to the moon. Likewise, most Westerners would not believe, as a New Guinea aborigine might, that it is possible to stop a neighbor's yams from growing by cursing them. Differences between individual or group realities are often vast. These differences are partly based on differences in the phenomena people experience and partly based on differences in the ways in which they *interpret* these phenomena, i.e., differences in the *conclusions* they draw concerning what they perceive. If I have *seen* an extraterrestrial and you have not, this fact could cause a difference in our realities. If you and I watch the same political speech, and I see it as an example of "knee-jerk liberalism", whereas you see the same speech as a "wonderful, humanitarian discourse", then our differences in reality (in this respect) are based on differences in interpretation.

I have noted that the totality of what a person conceives to exist — the total number of the entities that exist for her — includes all the phenomena she perceives. It also includes many entities (facts) that she does *not* perceive. I have never seen Tasmania, yet I know Tasmania exists because I've seen it in atlases, and I've heard of "Tasmanian devils". Likewise, no one has seen an electron. It is, in fact, impossible to do so in principle, according to Heisenberg. Yet we know or believe that electrons exist. They are real to us. We draw conclusions concerning existence from phenomena of which we *are* directly aware, using various concepts we have concerning these phenomena and their causes and effects, and using various intellectual tools, such as logic and Occam's Razor. Phenomena are epistemologically prior to our notions about what exists (what we regard as facts). We have a direct, indubitable knowledge of phenomena through perception and only an indirect, less certain knowledge of that which we infer from phenomena.

Reality and Concurrence

The complete set of entities that exist for a person comprise that person's world. Because there is more than one person, there is always the possibility of agreement or disagreement amongst persons concerning the existence of entities — objects, events, or states of affairs. What exists for one person does not necessarily exist for another.

But between any two persons, we will find some entities on which they agree or *concur*. Therefore, I will introduce the following definition of "concurrence":

Definition: Concurrence is an agreement between two or more people that one or more entities exist. In other words, it is a shared assent to those entities.

And here I come to a practical, person-centered definition of "reality", a term I have been using somewhat loosely up to this point:

Definition: Reality for an individual person, is that person's world, what he believes to exist. Reality, for two or more people, is a "common world" — a set of entities that are shared as a result of concurrence.

If a single person thinks something exists, then that thing is real to her. If she thinks that something does not exist, then that thing is unreal to her. If she is not sure whether or not something exists, then she is also unsure whether that thing is real or not. If she is unsure about the existence of many things, we would say that her concept of reality is shaky. The world seems *generally* unreal to a person in this condition. If she is generally certain about things, her world seems very real to her. If two or more people share entities, the set of all shared entities for a particular group of people is *their* reality. So we can speak of "Sam's reality", "Jennifer's reality", "Sam and Jennifer's reality", and these three realities will be different. "Sam and Jennifer's reality" will be the intersection of "Sam's reality" and "Jennifer's reality", based on Sam and Jennifer's concurrence.

In using the term "reality" in this person-centered way, I am, again, not trying to make any assertions about an objective, external world or about where an external world came from.[26] From

---

26. For practical purposes, there is little point in talking about such a world, since all a person will ever encounter are the entities that comprise his *own* world, which include a certain number of entities — such as others' reports and their behavior — that constitute evidence of what the *entities* that

the person-centered viewpoint, then, it is best to talk of "realities" (plural), instead of the singular "reality". The danger in talking about "reality" is that a person might be tempted to regard his own reality as the infallible truth about the external universe. To insist that my world is *the* one and only world might be all right (though dogmatic and short-sighted). But to go on and try to force other people to concur with my reality on the ground that it is "the one true reality" is a form of "existential imperialism" or "existential chauvinism" that is far worse than any conceivable *national* imperialism or chauvinism.[27]

Fortunately, it is not necessary to use force to get others to concur on substantial parts of a reality. One can *demonstrate* the existence of something to another person. Demonstrating to someone that something exists consists of getting the other person to concur on that thing by appealing to *his* experience. In fact, demonstrating *is*, by definition, pointing to something in someone else's experience.

A person acquires an entity when he either perceives something for himself (in which case, he acquires a phenomenon) or when he agrees with or assents to a concept. The concept could be expressed by another person or conceived by himself. In

---

comprise others' worlds might be. He can never know "*the* world" in any other sense. If he does somehow (perhaps through intuition, telepathy, or ESP) come to know what is in the "outside world" or in another's world, then that knowledge becomes forthwith part of *his* world, so what he knows is still part of his world. And then the only point of talking about it would be to try to make it real to others.

27. Unfortunately, many people and groups *do* attempt to force their concepts on others, and it is eminently possible to change another's concepts by imposing duress or engaging in deception. Few people are capable of maintaining their point of view in the face of a high degree of physical, emotional or financial threat, or of recognizing deception when they see it. I feel that much, if not all, that is evil in the world is based on the imposition of ideas by duress and by deception. Duress and lies, not money, are the root of all evil.

either case, by assenting to the concept, he acquires a fact. This observation allows us to improve our definition of fact:

Definition: A <u>fact</u> is a concept that is accepted as real.

or

Definition: A <u>fact</u> is a concept to which a person gives assent.

If a "possible fact" is not yet agreed to or accepted, then it is just a *concept*, not a fact. In other words:

Definition: A <u>concept</u> is an entity that may or may not exist, to which a symbol or statement may refer. It is an idea or thought, not a picture or phenomenon. It may be *represented* by a symbol, but it is not a symbol. A person converts a concept into a fact for himself by assenting to it, or into a fiction by dissenting from it. A concept is, in effect, a "candidate fact" or "potential fact". It is something that "offers itself" as a possible fact but which may or may not yet be accepted as such. It is a possibility that may become, or turn into, a reality.

A fact, then, is a concept that, by being believed, is elected from candidacy to full acceptance.[28]

---

28. This position may seem to contradict my assertion that a concept can be an entity as well. Certainly a possibility can exist or not exist, so if a concept is a possibility, certainly a concept can be an entity. But the concept is not the entity that it will become if it is accepted as true. It exists as a possibility; when assented to, it will exist as a fact.

There are (at least) three kinds of possibility:

1. Empirical
2. Logical
3. Conceptual

An empirical possibility is a fact that might be the case in the real world. For instance, there might be a green car parked in front of the local grocery store. On the other hand, a unicorn is not an empirical possibility. There are no unicorns in the real world. A logical possibility is something that

Even within a single person's world, the degree of reality or credibility of a concept may vary along a continuum. Something with which a person agrees firmly, something of which she is very certain, is very real to her. Something of which she is only *fairly* certain is of moderate reality.[29] Something of which she is very unsure has very little reality. There can also be degrees of *unreality*, ranging from things she does not *think* are the case to things she is quite sure do not exist. The reality of a concept can thus range in the following manner: from a high degree of certainty, through high probability, likelihood, mere possibility, unlikelihood, improbability, and a high degree of improbability, to impossibility.

Whereas reality can have different degrees for one individual person, the scope or breadth of concurrence or shared reality amongst two or more people can also vary. An Eskimo and a Hawaiian, for instance, probably do not have much shared reality; next-door neighbors, siblings, or members of a church may share a great deal.

A major purpose of communication is to increase the breadth of concurrence amongst people.

---

does not involve an internal contradiction. "A is red and A is not red" is logically impossible; "Unicorns exist" is logically possible. Note that all logical impossibilities are also empirically impossible, although the reverse is not the case. Finally, conceptual possibility is the quality of being something of which it would make *sense* to say that it exists, that it does *not* exist, or that it *might* exist. What *kind* of possibility is a concept? It certainly need not be an *empirical* possibility. I can conceive of a unicorn even though I do not believe it to be empirically possible that a unicorn exists. Nor need it be a logical possibility. I can conceive of the concept "A is red and A is not red", although this is not a *logical* possibility. "A is red and A is not red" *can*, however, be assigned a truth value, namely "false". So it *is* a conceptual possibility, Naturally, if something is not a conceptual possibility, it can be neither a logical nor an empirical possibility. A person *has* a concept when she creates or receives a conceptual possibility. Our use of language reflects this notion of concepts. The term "conceivable" is often used to mean "possible".

29. A "quasi entity", in effect. See above, pp. 37-41.

Chapter Two

Ability

In Chapter One, I touched on some of the basic abilities that people have, including the ability to assume an identity, to understand, to perceive, and to create. It is now time to spell out these basic abilities in greater detail.

Basic abilities fall into three areas:

1. Being
2. Having
3. Doing

Being

A person has the ability to *be* or assume different identities. A person has the ability to "extend into" or *assume* a more specific or "junior" identity from a more general or "senior" identity in order to act on a more extended but also a more specialized scope. He also has the ability to "step back" from or *shed* junior identities in favor of senior or more general identities. I will use "assumption" and "shedding" to describe these two actions:

Definition: <u>Assumption</u> is specialization and extension of identity through the incorporation of previously external elements (such as skills, tools, or concepts) as part of the self.

and

Definition: <u>Shedding</u> is the relinquishing of an identity in favor of a more general identity through the disincorporation of previously incorporated elements.

And, as we have seen (p. 29), the ability to shift identities is called "versatility":

Definition: <u>Versatility</u> is the ability to assume or shed identities.

When a person assumes a certain identity, he incorporates and is enabled to use various conceptual, perceptual, and instrumental tools so as to become aware of the various entities around him and to create changes in them. The scope and nature of a person's identity largely determines the sort of entities he is surrounded by and the types of actions he can take with these entities. A guitar player is surrounded by music, audiences, notes, phrases, and pitches and can affect his audience, change his pitch, play notes, and so forth. An automobile driver is surrounded by street signs, dividing lines, other cars, pedestrians, and the like. He can perform such actions as putting on the brakes, changing gears, accelerating, turning, and honking his horn.

Having

A person can and does *have* a certain world when she assumes a certain identity. Concepts, phenomena, and facts are the basic constituents of this world, the basic entities the person *has*. So it could be said that a person can *have* each of these types of entity.[1]

Let us review a few definitions:

Definition: A <u>world</u> is the totality of what exists for a particular person at a particular time — all the entities that person *has* at that time.

Definition: An <u>entity</u> is an object, event, or relationship (state of affairs) that is part of a person's world, i.e., that exists, for a person, at a certain moment.

Note that in discussing the ability to *have*, I am not concerned with where the entities that a person *has* come from. They could be created by the person; they could be from the outside world, they could be from God, or from the material universe. In any case, a person clearly has them.

Having as Potential Causation

Having is intimately connected to causation. We have those things over which we can exert some form of intentional causation or action; we do not have those things over which we cannot. This leads me to a useful definition of having:

---

1. The word "have" is used in different ways, and confusion can result from failing to differentiate between its different meanings. We sometimes use "have" to refer to entities (by which I mean to include objects, events, characteristics, and states of affairs) conceived as being *within* a person's current identity (as where one says, "Mary has a bad temper."). At other times, we use "have" to refer to entities *outside* that identity (as when we say, "Mary has a blue Chevrolet."). In the first sense, we are using "have" to mean "includes", and in the second sense, we are using "have" to mean "possesses". In the first sense, what is "had" is conceived of as internal to that which has it; in the second sense, what is "had" is conceived as external. The first usage of "have" really falls under the category of *being*, so it is not relevant to our discussion of having as *distinct* from being. "She has a bad temper," is really only another way of saying, "She is bad-tempered." For the purpose of clarity, I propose to use "have" in the second sense rather than the first.

Definition: Having is the ability to be causative (or to act) with respect to an entity.

Just because I *can* act on something doesn't mean that I have to *be* acting on it at any particular time. I can have a book in my attic and not be handling it, seeing it, reading it, or even thinking of it at any particular time. But the fact that I have the book does mean that I *can* read it or touch it if I wish (or not, if I prefer not to). Obviously, having, as above defined, can admit of different degrees. I have at least one firehouse in my city, and a local football team to root for. But the degree to which I have these entities is less than the degree to which I have my car — or my body — because the degree to which I can act on my car (or my body) is greater than the degree to which I can act on the San Francisco Forty-Niners or the local firehouse.

Prehension

A second concept is contained in having: namely, the concept of being *currently involved* in causation or action with respect to something. As I said above, I can have a book without reading it, but I "have" it in a more immediate sense when I hold it in my hands or scan it with my eyes. It is useful to distinguish between being *able* to act on something and *actually* acting on it. One is an ability or *potential* action; the other is an *actual*, current action, an *exercise* of ability. I have adopted a rarely used (but real) term — "prehension" — to describe this immediate, currently active sense of having:

Definition: Prehension is the condition in which an entity is the direct object of a person's current action.

When you prehend something, you have it in your immediate grasp, physically, perceptually, or cognitively. You are *doing* something with it. You may *have* a cat, but only when you see it, pick it up, or think about it do you *prehend* it. You can *have* knowledge of who the second president of the United States was, but only when you are actually thinking, "Adams was the second president of the United States," are you *prehending* that fact. Thus we can now define having in terms of prehension:

Definition: Having is the ability to prehend.

Getting and Gaining

Between having and prehending, there is an intermediate phase, during which one is "putting attention on" or "taking hold of" something. This phase is called "getting":

Definition: To get an entity is to come to prehend it.

This usage is similar to that used in referring to computers. The action of "getting" on a computer is that of taking a datum from some peripheral storage location and bringing it into the central processing unit for immediate use. The computer already "has" the data — i.e., it is *able* to "get" it — but it must *actually* "get" the data before it can use it or change it. "Get" is also commonly used to mean "coming to have". In the interest of conceptual precision, however, we will not use "get" in this sense but in the sense of coming to prehend something — either something that one already has or something that one is just beginning to have. Sometimes the act of coming to *have* something coincides with that of coming to *prehend* that thing, as when one is suddenly handed a check. In such a case, one prehends something without having it *first*, although one does have it in the instant of prehension. More often, perhaps, the things we get are things we already have.

This usage of "get" gives us yet another valid definition of having:

Definition: Having is the ability to get.

because obviously you can prehend something if and only if you can *come* to prehend it.

We will use the word "gain" to refer to the action of coming to have something (as distinguished from the action of coming to *prehend* something):

Definition: To gain an entity is to come to have it.

The word "gain" might be thought of as synonymous with "receive", but "gain" can also mean "create", as when you "gain control" over something or "gain an advantage". Our usage is the broader one including both creative and receptive modes of coming to have.

Note that whenever you *get* something, you must have *gained* it. In fact, we could redefine "gain" as follows:

Definition: To gain an entity is to acquire the ability to get it.

Releasing and Losing

There is a transition phase between prehending something and no longer prehending it. We will refer to the act of letting go of something, no longer acting on it, as "releasing" it:

Definition: To release an entity is to cease to prehend it.

Whether one still *has* an entity after one releases it depends on where one puts it, when one releases it. If you have a piece of paper in your hand and then throw it into the fire, you not only cease to prehend it, you also cease to have it. On the other hand, if you carefully file the paper, you continue to have it. We will use the term "losing" to refer to the action of ceasing to have something:

Definition: To lose an entity is to cease to have it.

Note that you can lose something by releasing it and putting it somewhere where you can no longer prehend it, but you can also lose something without releasing it at all, as when your house burns down while you are at work.

Summary of Terms

The state:	Prehension	Non-prehension
The definition:	Acting on	Not acting on
Coming into the state:	Getting	Releasing

The state:	Having	Not having
The definition:	Ability to prehend	Inability to prehend
Coming into the state:	Gaining	Losing

As I mentioned in Chapter One (pp. 31-33), the entities that a person has (or prehends) are of three types;

1. Concepts (conceivable entities)
2. Phenomena (perceivable entities)
3. Facts (knowable entities)

These were defined as follows:

> **Definition:** A concept is a possibility that may or may not become an actuality.

> **Definition:** A phenomenon is an entity that a person is able to perceive.

> **Definition:** A fact is an entity that exists for a person but that he is not able to perceive.

The moon is a phenomenon for me; the moon's orbit around the earth is a fact, and the concept of a cow jumping over the moon is a concept (a concept that happens to be false).

The state of having any of these three types of entities and the state of prehending that type of entity are not the same state. You can *have* a concept without thinking of it, but you only *prehend* it when you *are* actively thinking of it. You can *have* a fact (such as the fact that grass contains chlorophyll) without thinking about it all the time. You only *prehend* this fact when you are consciously thinking about it (cognizing it). You can *have* a phenomenon (like a table, or a view of the ocean) without actually *prehending* the phenomenon at any given moment.[2]

Ways of Prehending

I can now proceed to discuss the ways in which a person prehends each of the three types of entities.

I will use the word "conceptualizing" to describe the state of prehending a concept. "Conceptualizing" is a term that does not prejudge the issue of the concept's point of origin, which is important, because in saying that someone prehends something, we do not want to have to specify where it comes from.

There is no such word in English with respect to phenomena. The word "perceive" clearly means the *receipt* of a phenomenon from outside, and words like "imagine" and "picture" clearly involve the *creation* of a phenomenon by a person. The term "visualize" comes as close as the English language allows, but this term clearly connotes *visual* imagining or perception. Because we need a word that can cover all the senses, I have had to coin the analogous term "perceptualizing" to describe the state of simply *prehending* a phenomenon.

---

2. This raises an interesting question: Where and what is an entity, for a person, when he *has* it but is not prehending it? Is a concept still a concept when it is not being thought of? Is a phenomenon still a phenomenon when not being perceived or pictured? And is a fact still a fact for a person when she is not thinking about it? Where do these things "go" when we release them, and from where do we get them when we get them? Berkeley tried to solve this riddle by saying, essentially, that to exist is to be prehended. And then he invoked God as the being who continues to prehend entities when no human is doing so. Physical scientists similarly invoke the existence of an objective physical universe to serve as an agency that can hold entities in physical form, even when no person is aware of them. Since, like Kant, I don't know what form, if any, phenomena, concepts, or facts may have "in themselves", I will sidestep these troublesome issues and simply continue to use the same terms to describe these entities when they are, and are not, being prehended.

So far, we have:

Definition: Conceptualizing is the state of prehending a concept.

and

Definition: Perceptualizing is the state of prehending a phenomenon.

But how does a person prehend *facts*? Conceptualizing only gets a person as far as prehending a concept but falls short of prehending a fact. I will refer to the act of prehending a fact as "cognizing":

Definition: To cognize is to prehend — to be currently aware of — a fact. The fact so prehended is called a "cognition".[3]

Assent and Intention

I have mentioned earlier[4] that an act of *assent* is involved in making a fact out of a concept, an act in which the person determines a concept to be true. The acceptance of a concept as a *fact* requires a decision, a determination. Anyone can get the concept that "Brazil has double-digit inflation" and have no doubt about having that concept, without being sure that Brazil does, in fact, have double-digit inflation. But, given a concept, a further action of assent is required to arrive at a fact. It is when we say "Yes!" to a concept that we acquire a fact. So "Brazil has double-digit inflation" is only a concept, but when I agree with that concept,

---

3. We will see that the concept of a cognition is vital to the subject of facilitation: the appearance of a new cognition or "realization" is one of the indicators that a viewing procedure should be ended. See Chapter Eight, pp. 407,429.
4. See pp. 56-57.

give my assent to it, it becomes a fact, for me. And so it is with all of the facts I have — originally they were concepts, and then, by being assented to — agreed with — they graduated to the status of being facts, for me.

The Meaning of "Yes"

There are actually two and only two different meanings of "Yes!". The first is simple agreement. Someone says, "The cat is on the mat," and I say, "Yes!", which means "I agree!" The second is a form of promising: you say, "Will you please put out the cat?" and I say "Yes!" Here, by saying "Yes!", I have promised to comply with your command. Agreement and promising are interpersonal forms of assent, but more basic are the in*tra*personal forms, the kinds of assent we make by ourselves. When I promise myself to do something, I am making a *commitment*, whereas when I agree with myself about something — assent to the truth of that thing — I am doing something quite different: I am *accepting* something. The former is a creative form of assent — an assent to the creation of a new activity or condition, in effect — whereas the latter is a receptive form of assent, a decision to accept something as true or real. So far as I know, there are no other forms of assent.

Two Kinds of Assent

Understanding has been defined as the act of receiving a fact, whereas postulating is the act of creating one; both involve giving assent to a concept.

In the case of understanding, the assent is receptive: acceptance.

In the case of postulating, the assent is creative: commitment.

We complete an act of understanding by considering a concept and then accepting it as true. We start an act of postulating by considering a concept and then committing ourselves to *making* it be true.[5]

We can therefore say:

> **Definition:** Assenting is the act of saying "yes" to a concept and thereby converting it into a fact. Receptive assent is acceptance; creative assent is commitment.

"Assenting" could also be defined as follows:

> **Definition:** Assenting is the act of gaining a fact.

Considering

Of course a person does not have to decide that a concept is *true*. He can decide it is false or decide it has a certain probability or improbability. The term "considering" denotes the action by which a person makes this decision:

> **Definition:** Considering is the action of coming to decide whether to convert a concept into a fact by giving assent to it, to convert it into an unreality by dissenting from it, or to convert it into a probability by giving it something between full assent and full dissent. In considering, one weighs the pros and cons of accepting a concept and then finally decides that it is factual, probable, improbable, or non-factual.

The outcome of considering a concept is:

1. Assent to it (which converts it into a fact).
2. Dissent from it (which converts it into a falsehood).[6]
3. Something in between (which converts it into a probability).

The ability to consider is a *skill* that people possess in different

---

5. I shall have more to say about assent and intention later (pp. 111-112).
6. Dissent is really only a form of assent — assent to the "obverse concept", the concept that is the negation of the concept in question. To dissent with

degrees. Different people have varying abilities to assent, dissent, or assign something a probability. People who are chronically antagonistic or who are afraid of commitment may have trouble agreeing with what other people say, so they will either be chronic dissenters or chronically indecisive. People who are rash or impatient and who make snap judgments are not good at withholding judgment and thinking in terms of probabilities. Other people seem unable to disagree with others (perhaps out of a desire to appease them). They will appear either as "yes-men" or as being very wishy-washy. A person with a good ability to consider things can readily arrive at facts — i.e., assent, dissent, or assign a probability. Such an ability is vital to success in any undertaking and, indeed, to happiness. What people do when they engage in the act of considering, and the criteria they use to decide what to accept as true or real, are important topics, but ones we will leave for later.[7]

Knowing

As we have seen, the process of coming to accept something is equivalent to coming to *know* that thing.[8] And as long as a

---

the concept "a red car in front of my house" is to assent to the concept "no red car in front of my house".

7. See Chapter Four, pp. 155-166.

8. It might seem that in order for a person to accept a concept, he would first have to know it was true. If he knows it is true, however, then he has *already* accepted it. Knowledge requires the prior exercise of judgment, and the outcome of that judgment is a decision on whether the concept is true, false, probable, or improbable. Only when he has made this judgment and has decided to accept, reject, or assign a probability to a concept can a person say that he *knows* something is true, false, or probable to a certain degree. A possible exception to this rule might be where a person has an intuition that carries its own conviction, not requiring consideration or determination. This kind of "pure intuition" might be regarded as direct knowledge, not requiring a separate act of acceptance.

person knows something, he has it as a fact. Therefore, we could say that:

Definition: Knowing is the state of having a fact.[9]

From a person-centered viewpoint — i.e., from the viewpoint of an individual person — accepting something brings that thing into existence. It permits the person to *have* that thing. As Polanyi points out:[10]

> "*[T]ruth is something that can be thought of only by believing it.* It is then improper to speak of another person's mental operation as leading to a true proposition in any other sense than that it leads him to something the speaker himself believes to be true,"

If I *know* something and you do not agree with it, you call it a "belief" of mine; if you do agree, you call it "knowledge". But subjectively, to me there is no difference between my knowledge and those of my beliefs of which I am certain.[11] I may be quite certain that UFO's exist. I say, therefore, that I *know* they exist. You may be equally certain that they do not exist. So you *know* UFO's do not exist, but you see me as *believing* (not *knowing*) that UFO's exist. On the other hand, if you are also certain that UFO's exist, you will say that you *know* UFO's exist and that I also *know* UFO's exist. In both cases, my belief and certainty are the same. The difference in your description of it depends on whether you agree with me or not on this point. That clearly does not mean that everything I believe or you believe is

---

9. Actually, to be precise, we say we "know" something when we can access it mentally without resorting to physical actions like looking it up in a book.

10. Polanyi, Michael. *Personal Knowledge*, p. 305 (Italics Polanyi's).

11. The word "belief" is, unfortunately, used in different ways. In one sense, it means a relatively weak sense of certainty, as opposed to "knowledge", which connotes a strong sense of certainty. But in another sense, it can mean a strong certainty. As I use the term, I intend it to mean, simply, "certainty". In this sense, from the person-centered viewpoint, it is synonymous with "knowledge".

necessarily true "objectively", or that others will regard it as true. If one departs from the person-centered viewpoint, it is quite possible to say a person can believe things that are quite untrue. But from the person-centered viewpoint (from a person's viewpoint at a certain time) those things he believes with certainty *are* true for him at that time. There is no distinction, from that viewpoint, between belief with certainty and knowledge. This is not to say that people are in any way arbitrary in granting assent or belief. Nor do I mean to say that a person cannot change his mind or reconsider, based on new evidence. He can see, from a new viewpoint, that his old beliefs were false.[12]

Doing

In addition to *having* a world, a person can perform various *actions* with respect to his world:

Definition: An <u>action</u> is an instance of causation by a person. It is the exercise of an ability.

Actions can be classified according to the "direction" in which they occur. Certain actions originate with the person and result in changes in various parts of the person's world. Other actions consist in the receipt of entities (concepts, phenomena, and facts) from the world. I will use the term "creative ability" (or, simply, "creativity") to describe a person's ability to originate actions that make changes in her world. A highly creative person is able to "get a great deal done" in the world; many changes in the world originate from her. Creativity can, of course, take many forms. A creative person can be artistic, creating new visual, auditory, tactile, and kinesthetic experiences (such as sculpture, dance, music, and painting). She can also be intellectual, being involved

---

12. I will have more to say on this subject in Chapter Four, pp. 169-172.

in the creation of new concepts. Or she can simply cause a great many changes in the physical universe, such as by building houses — or nations. Any kind of bodily action, even a small action like lifting a finger, is a creative act, in that a new condition (e.g., a lifted finger) is created in the world. I will be using a very specific definition of "creativity":

> **Definition**: Creativity is the ability to originate actions that cause changes in the world, the ability to bring new entities into existence.

Apart from creativity, however, a person also has a basic ability to *receive* the various elements of her world. This ability might be called "receptivity" or "awareness":

> **Definition**: Awareness is the ability to receive.

A very aware person finds it easy to acquire information from her world. Things are generally not hidden from her. Her perception and understanding are good. It is possible to be very aware without necessarily having to *create* anything. Some forms of meditation stress "pure" awareness that consists of only receiving and not putting anything out. And some forms of creation (such as sending letters or indulging in various practical jokes) do not involve any feedback on the results of the action. These might be regarded as "purely" creative actions.

Awareness and creativity do not usually exist in isolation from each other, however. In creation, awareness is in the service of creativity; in a receptive action, creativity is in the service of awareness. While engaged in the creative action of building a house, one uses one's awareness to see the tools and the materials, to get feedback on what one is doing, and to admire the final product. But the ruling force is the creative intention to build the house. While engaged in the receptive action of trying to understand the General Theory of Relativity, one may perform the creative actions of looking at the book, turning the pages, drawing diagrams, talking to others, and so forth, but the ruling force is the receptive intention to understand. Study is a receptive action, but by introducing various creative elements into the act of studying, the learning process is greatly enhanced.[13] Thus, under normal circumstances, creativity and awareness work together, each enhancing the other.

Creative Actions

Creativity is the ability to bring into being the three basic types of entities in the world: concepts, phenomena, and facts.

Creating Concepts — Conceiving

A person creates concepts by thinking them, or (a term I prefer) "conceiving" them. A more expanded definition of "concept" is:

> **Definition**: A <u>concept</u> is something that may or may not be factual, to which a symbol or statement may refer. It is an idea or thought, not a picture or phenomenon. It may be represented by a symbol, but it is not the symbol. A person converts a concept into a fact for himself by assenting to it, or into a fiction by dissenting from it. It is, in effect, a "candidate fact" or "potential fact". It is something that "offers itself" as a possible fact but which may or may not yet be accepted as such, or *assented to*.

where

> **Definition**: <u>Assent</u> is the action of saying "Yes!" to a concept. It is one possible outcome of considering, the other two being dissent and assignment of a probability.

I can proceed, then, to the following definition:

---

13. For more discussion of this topic, see Chapter Six, pp. 307-312.

Definition: <u>Conceiving</u> is the act of creating a concept.

To illustrate these ideas, try the following exercise:

Exercise 5. Concepts and Pictures

a. Conceive of something.
b. Did you get a specific mental picture along with the concept?
c. See if you can conceive of something without getting a specific picture.
d. Can you do that?
e. Is what you are conceiving of existent, non-existent, or possibly existent?

You may find that a confusion of different mental pictures accompanies the concept. People tend to find, however, that concepts do not correspond one-for-one with pictures. There may, in fact, be no pictures associated with a concept.

Creating Phenomena — Picturing

The second basic kind of entity in a person's world is a phenomenon. There are both physical and mental phenomena. The former are perceived via the physical senses; the latter are viewed via "non-sensory" perception.[14] A person can *create* phenomena for herself by imagining or (a preferable term) "picturing" them:

Definition: <u>Picturing</u> is the direct creation of a phenomenon by a person.

A phenomenon can be perceived through any number of percep-

---

14. More data on non-sensory perception is to be found later in this chapter (p. 83).

tual channels. In picturing, one can create pictures that contain the same kinds of perceptions: tactile, auditory, visual, and so forth, or any combination of these.

By picturing, one can bring a new phenomenon into existence. I am not now speaking of creating physical objects. I am speaking at an experiential level. Whether some chemical process occurs in the brain that actually causes the phenomenon to appear, or whether a person, while picturing, causes changes in the brain, is a matter of conjecture. Moreover, it is irrelevant to the person-centered viewpoint because the essence of the person-centered viewpoint is that it deals with what a person can be aware of, and the person has no direct awareness of neurological events in her brain. It is also irrelevant from the person-centered viewpoint whether there is an actual physical object corresponding to a perception. I might perceive a table in a dream, when no corresponding physical table is there, yet it would still be true to say that I have the *experience* of a table.

So when I say that I, or any person, can create phenomena, it is equivalent to saying that a person can create experience. A person can create an experience of a table that is as much an experience as — although perhaps qualitatively different from — an experience of a table that is physically present. And a person can uncreate certain experiences by simply ceasing to create them.[15]

The following exercise is best done with the eyes closed, so I suggest you get someone else to read off the steps to you, and that you signal to that person when you have done each step so that she can give you the next. If you don't have anyone available to do this for you, you can still do the exercise:

---

15. An uncreation could also be regarded as a creation — of empty space and time.

Exercise 6. Creating a Picture

a. Close your eyes and make a picture of a white horse that you have not seen before.

b. Include in the picture the sound of it whinnying, the feel of its mane in your fingers, the temperature and smell of the horse. If you can, get the feeling of riding it. Get as many senses into the picture as possible.

c. Did you have a *concept* of a horse before you made a *picture* of one?

d. Note who is creating this picture.

e. Note where the picture of the horse is located.

f. Uncreate it — make it disappear.

g. Open your eyes.

Experientially, all of this happens without any intervention from the physical universe, even though an EEG or some other biomonitoring device might indicate that there are physical correlates.

As you may have noticed, the process of picturing seems to include conceiving as a necessary first step. One conceives of what one is going to picture and makes a picture to fit the concept. It is hard to see how a person can make a picture without first having some concept of what he is going to make a picture *of*. For instance, in picturing a horse, the person first gets a concept of a horse and then makes a picture that fits that concept.[16] The total process, then, is as given in Figure 7.

           Conceiving   *Picturing*
Person ·····> Concept ·····> Phenomenon

Figure 7. The creation of concepts and phenomena.

---

16. Did that happen for you?

Creating Facts — Postulating

I have now shown how a person can create concepts and phenomena. But how can a person create a fact? The answer lies in the definition of a "concept". When considering occurs in conjunction with the creative action of conceiving, and the result of the consideration is assent, something new is created: a fact. Let us say a person conceives of the possibility that there is no limit to the number of prime numbers. If he assents to that concept, then, for him, there *is* no limit to the number of prime numbers! In the act of assenting, a person creates for himself a new reality, a new fact. Often these facts are *future* realities. If I conceive of the concept of going to a movie and then assent to that concept, I create a new future event for myself (a fact, since it isn't perceived yet). The creation of such facts often has physical consequences. If I conceive of the concept that my hand is going to rise a few inches into the air and then assent to that concept, my hand will move, where before it was not moving.[17] This combination of conceiving and assenting is the creative action called "postulating":

Definition: Postulating is the combined actions of conceiving and assenting, leading to the creation of a fact.

From a person-centered viewpoint, a person moves his body by postulate. I raise my arm by deciding, considering, or *knowing* that it is going to rise. I call this kind of practical knowledge "postulating", because one is creating a reality with this kind of knowing that did not exist before (the state of affairs of having a raised arm) — one is creating this state of affairs by making a postulate. This exercise should illustrate this point:

---

17. Assuming, of course, that my hand is not paralyzed or restrained.

Exercise 7. Moving the Body by Postulate

a.   Decide to raise your little finger NOW.

b.   Note what happened.

Probably, your little finger rose. If it did not, I submit that you really did not assent to the concept that your finger was going to go up. Or you made a conflicting decision not to raise it.

If a person operates through some physical extension of herself or her body, such as a bicycle, she will still be causing things to happen by postulate, but on a wider scope. How does one turn a corner on a bicycle? One does not experience this act as the act of moving various muscle groups in various combinations. Most people have no idea — and never did have any idea — what muscular actions take place in the act of balancing on a bicycle (any more than they realize what they do to raise arms or legs). They decide to turn, and it happens. They decide to raise their arms, and it happens.[18]

While a person is being a certain identity, her postulates will correspond to that identity. Since postulating is a form of practical or creative knowledge, if one knows — believes with certainty — that one *cannot* do something, one will not be able to do it or even to postulate it, until one changes one's opinion on the matter. An important and demonstrable corollary of this observation is that *a large number of a person's abilities, disabilities, failures, problems, and successes depend largely on her own*

---

18. Actually, Polanyi [*Op cit*, p. 49f] gives a rather nice account of how we actually *do* maintain balance on a bicycle: "When [the cyclist] starts falling to the right he turns the handlebars to the right, so that the course of the bicycle is deflected along a curve to the right. This results in a centrifugal force pushing the cyclist to the left and offsets the gravitational force dragging him down to the right. This maneuver presently throws the cyclist out of balance to the left, which he counteracts by turning the handlebars to the left; and so he continues to keep himself in balance by winding along a series of appropriate curvatures. A simple analysis shows that for a given angle of unbalance the curvature of each winding is inversely proportional to the square of the speed at which the cyclist is proceeding."
Did you know you were doing all that?

decisions and beliefs.[19]

Postulating is creative or practical knowing, a combination of conceiving and assenting.

To each *action* performed by a person there corresponds an *entity* in that person's world. What constitutes the "world", of course, includes the world of physical entities as well as mental pictures and concepts.

As I have said, the basic creative actions are conceiving, picturing, and postulating. The act of conceiving connects the person with the *concept* conceived, which lies on the world side of the person-world polarity. The act of picturing connects the person with the picture itself, which lies on the world side of the person-world polarity. In postulating, the acts of conception and assent (commitment) connect the person to the resulting fact, which lies on the world side on the person-world polarity. One cannot conceive without a corresponding concept being present, picture without a corresponding phenomenon, nor postulate without a corresponding fact.[20]

PERSON		WORLD
Picturing	················>	Phenomenon
Conceiving	················>	Concept
Postulating	················>	Fact

Figure 8. Basic creative actions.

---

19. It is possible, using certain techniques, to help a person to rapidly change his beliefs to new beliefs that are more enabling and less disabling and thus dramatically to improve a person's ability and willingness to try. These techniques form part of applied metapsychology.
20. In the latter case, the fact postulated is often a *future* fact, or a fact about the future.

As mentioned above (p. 64), one can gain entities — concepts, phenomena, or facts — in either a receptive or creative mode. A fact is gained when a person gives his assent to a concept. Making a fact is done receptively when the concept being assented to (accepted) is arrived at by a receptive action (interpretation). It is done creatively when the concept is arrived at by a creative action (conceiving). One can intend to create a certain condition in the world, or one can intend to receive a certain condition from the world. In both cases, what was a mere concept is converted into a fact. In both cases, a reality is brought into being. The difference between creation and reception lies in the *source* of the concept. If the concept is created by the person (conceived), then assented to, the result is the appearance of a new condition in that person's *world*. If the concept is arrived at as a result of interpreting data originating in the world, then assented to, the result is the appearance of new understanding or knowledge in the person's mind.

Creation begins with conceiving, with the creation of a concept. Once one has a concept, one can go in two directions. One can use one's ability to make mental pictures (picturing) and create a mental phenomenon, or one can assent to the concept and thus make a fact. In the first case, having done the creating, it is possible to turn around and perceive the creation. In the second, one can turn around and know the fact. The creation and the subsequent reception are two different actions, although what is received may be useful in providing feedback in order to enhance the act of creation.[21]

It is obvious, then, that a person can create all three types of entities that make up her world: concepts, phenomena, and facts. But there are many entities in her world that she does not create. These are the entities she *receives* from outside herself via her receptive actions.

---

21. I wonder whether it is possible to picture without perceiving what is pictured?

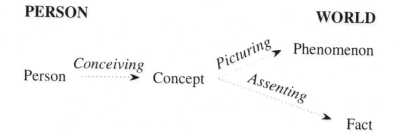

PERSON   **WORLD**

Person   *Conceiving*   Concept   *Picturing*   Phenomenon

Assenting

Fact

Figure 9. Sequence of creative actions.

Receptive Actions

As the creative actions of a person relate to what she *gives out*, so the receptive actions relate to what the person *takes in*. They include perceiving, explaining or interpreting, understanding, and intuiting.

Much of what we receive from the world outside us is called "data". "Datum" can be a useful term, but only if it is accurately defined, because it is used in many different ways in ordinary language:

> **Definition**: A <u>datum</u> is something that is "given" to a person, in other words *accepted* by her. A datum is either a phenomenon or a fact.

A person receives phenomena, or is aware of phenomena, by the action called "perceiving":

> **Definition**: <u>Perceiving</u> is the action of receiving a phenomenon.

When a person sees a table, hears music, feels warm, tastes food, looks at a mental picture, or dreams, she is perceiving, and what she perceives are phenomena: the taste of the food, and sound of the music, the warm feeling, and the like. Although perceiving is receptive, it is not *inactive*. What a person perceives in a given situation is very much affected by the knowledge and viewpoint that she has at a particular time and by the identity she has assumed at that time.[22] This is not to say that perception is *creative* from the person-centered viewpoint. A person perceiving does not experience what she is doing as an act of *creating* something, but as an act of *receiving* information from somewhere.

Some forms of perception are clearly non-sensory. For instance, if a mental picture suddenly appears, it is clearly a phenomenon that I am perceiving, but the instrument of perception is not any of the physical senses:

Definition: Non-sensory perception is perception of a phenomenon that does not occur through any physical senses.[23]

Another way in which it is possible to receive concepts is directly — not via interpretation or explanation of data. I shall call this receptive ability "intuition":

Definition: Intuition is the receipt of concepts by a person directly from his world, not via interpretation or explanation of data.

Frequently, concepts "just occur" to us. Sometimes, it appears that we process data unconsciously and then the answer "just appears" in the form of a concept from no identifiable source.

---

22. A great deal of psychological work has been done to show how a person's "mind set" determines what she will perceive in a certain situation. Perception has been shown to be heavily "theory laden". At one time, it was fashionable to talk about "raw sense data": perceptions that are devoid of any interpretation by the percipient. In recent years, however, the concept of "raw sense data" has fallen into disfavor, both amongst philosophers and amongst psychologists. And rightly so, I believe. Perception always contains an element of interpretation.

23. Note that this is not exactly the same thing as what is called "extrasensory perception". In non-sensory perception, what is perceived need not be events thought to occur in the physical world or in someone else's mind. If I look at a mental picture of my mother, or listen to a song "in my head", I am engaging in non-sensory perception, but probably not engaging in "extrasensory perception", in the normal sense of the term. Whether "extrasensory perception" exists or not has been hotly debated. Non-sensory perception is not debatable.

When I have been puzzling over a difficult problem, the answer to the problem may suddenly appear as a flash of insight, quite unexpected and unrelated to what's going on at the moment. It is perhaps debatable exactly where the concepts received through intuition come *from*. Some are surely the result of "subsidiary" interpretation of data. In this kind of intuition, the data and the interpretation process occur "unconsciously". That is, these actions are incorporated as part of the identity one has assumed at a particular time and are therefore not perceptible. I can look at someone and get the concept that that person is angry without thinking about how I am reaching that concept and without thinking the person *looks* angry. Many people think that apparent episodes of telepathy or clairvoyance are merely this kind of subliminal perception and interpretation of subtle phenomena. Others feel that intuition may somehow constitute a "direct contact with truth", or a conceptual communication from "higher consciousness" or from higher spiritual beings. From the person-centered viewpoint, though, what occurs is the sudden appearance of a concept "from nowhere", without any attempt to *conceive* the concept.[24]

As I have said, corresponding to each *action* performed by the person is an *entity* in the person's world. Corresponding to the receptive action of perceiving is the phenomenon perceived in the person's world. Perception does not occur without something

24. Harman, Willis, and Rheingold, H., in *Liberating the Unconscious for Breakthrough Insights* (Jeremy P. Tarcher, Inc., Los Angeles, 1984) discuss this phenomenon at great length and give various techniques for enhancing intuition.

The work already done by Puthoff and others, e.g., Targ, R. and Puthoff, H.E. *Mind Reach* (Delacorte Press, 1977), supports the idea that "pure", non-computational intuition and true ESP ability are universal. In developing intuition and non-sensory perception, it might be important to learn how to differentiate subjectively between these receptive actions and creative actions like conceiving or picturing — "analytical overlay", to use Puthoff's term. One would think that exercises on becoming purely receptive, on willfully ceasing to engage in creative actions, would be helpful in developing non-sensory perception and intuition.

being perceived. Corresponding to an act of intuition, there is the concept intuited. Corresponding to an act of interpreting, there is a concept, an interpretation of a datum, in the person's world. Intuition and interpretation, in the sense in which I am using these terms, do not occur without the appearance of a corresponding concept.

PERSON		WORLD
Perceiving	◄·············	Phenomenon
Intuiting	◄·············	Concept
Interpreting	◄·············	Concept

Figure 10. Basic receptive actions.

Receptive actions follow a certain sequence (see Figure 11).

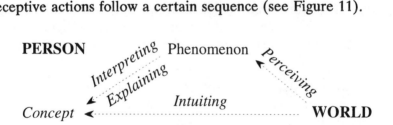

Figure 11. Sequence of receptive actions.

The sequence starts with the world as defined above (p. 61). The world and the person combine forces to give rise to phenomena by the receptive action of perceiving and to facts by understanding. These are the *data* from which other facts can be arrived at:

Definition: A <u>datum</u> is a fact or phenomemon.

Some of these data are interpreted or explained. This act of interpretation gives rise to concepts. If these concepts are accepted as true, then they in turn may constitute data and may generate further interpretations and explanations, leading to further concepts and facts. It is also possible that a person could receive concepts or facts directly by means of intuition.

The reception of concepts, facts, and phenomena can begin either with an act of intuition or with an act of perception. The outcome of an act of perception is the appearance of a phenomenon. The outcome of an act of intuition is the genesis of a concept, or, perhaps, a fact.

Some of the facts and phenomena (data) that are received may be taken as having certain *meanings* or implications. These are assumptions (in the case of facts) and tokens (in the case of phenomena):

> **Definition**: An assumption is a *fact* that refers to, indicates, or implies another concept or fact. An assumption is a fact that has *meaning*, a premise.

> **Definition**: A token is a *phenomenon* that indicates or refers to a concept or fact, a phenomenon that has *meaning*. The word "red" (spoken or written) is a token that refers to the concept of a certain wavelength of light or a certain type of visual phenomenon; dark clouds can be a token of rain.

For instance, if I perceive someone is crying, I may take that phenomenon as a token of grief or unhappiness (although they could be tears of joy). If I find out that the President of the Philippines has been deposed, I may take this fact as an assumption from which I could get the concept that the Communists have infiltrated the government, or that the military has taken over.

Starting from such a datum, I can make one or more interpretations and come out with various concepts about what the meaning of that datum might be (see Figure 12).

         Interpretation
Datum ············➤ Concept 1, Concept 2, Concept 3 ...
         Explanation

Figure 12. Reception of concepts.

At this point, a person has various concepts, some coming "directly" from intuition, others having been derived from interpretation of data. Each of these concepts is something that might or might not exist. And the person has various perceptions.

But I have not yet explained what needs to occur in order for the person to receive *facts*. A person must use his ability to *consider* to arrive at facts, whether creatively or receptively. Having received one or more concepts, and having considered them, he decides which of these concepts are true, which are false, and which have various probabilities. He must, for instance, decide, on observing a person crying, whether the concept that the person is sad is true, false, or probable, and whether the concept that he is happy is true, false, or probable. For each concept, then, what happens is shown in Figure 13.

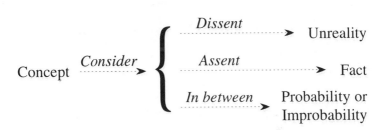

Figure 13. Possible outcomes of considering a concept.

An interpretation of a datum, absent an assent to (acceptance of) that interpretation, is a mere concept — a *potential* fact. What makes it an *actual* fact for a person is his act of acceptance. This combination of interpreting and accepting is called "understanding":

> **Definition**: Understanding is the combination of interpretation and assent (acceptance) that results in the acquisition of a new fact, a conclusion.

Both understanding and postulating, then, involve a combination of a concept and an act of consideration and assent. The only difference is that in postulating the concept is created by the person and the assent is an act of commitment, whereas in

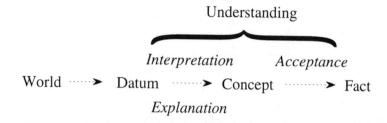

Figure 14. Understanding — a combination of interpretation and acceptance.

understanding, the concept is arrived at by interpretation of data and the assent is an act of acceptance (see Figures 14 and 15).

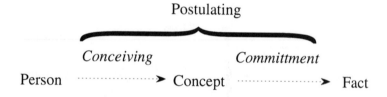

Figure 15. Postulating — a combination of conceiving and commitment.

Facts are a major constituent of a person's world; by understanding he receives them, and by postulating he creates them.

All the actions that a person undertakes are various instances and combinations of these basic actions (see Figure 16).

Intention, Action, and Inaction

It is good to be able to do things, but it is just as important for a person to be able *not* to do things. It is questionable whether we should even describe as an "ability" something a person does compulsively. Wiggling the ears is an ability, but if a person cannot stop herself from wiggling her ears, that is more of a disability than an ability. We would probably say that she has a neurological problem or "tic" that is causing the ears to twitch.

Some people are unable to stop having disagreeable mental pictures. For instance, combat veterans who are victims of Post-
Traumatic Stress Disorder cannot stop picturing scenes of past
combat situations. Some people get stray tunes — auditory pictures — that they cannot exorcise. Others compulsively experience sexual fantasies. When a person has insomnia or is deliri-
ous, she finds herself compulsively trying to conceptualize something or to solve problems. This, too, is not an ability, but an
inability to stop the process of conceptualization. It is often
advantageous to be able to stop oneself from postulating certain
things. Some people show a repeating pattern of failure — such
as a series of failed marriages — because they are continually
creating a future that contains marital disaster. Or people decide
that they are going to fail and then live up to that expectation.
Depression is largely a state of uncontrolled negative decision-
making. Fixed negative postulates can become self-fulfilling prophecies.[25]

Likewise, one should be able to turn a receptive ability on or
off. One should be able to look *away* from something as readily
as one can look *toward* it. Some forms of meditation develop this
ability by practicing a systematic turning away from all sensory
impressions and all mental contents — an "emptying" of the
mind. One should also be able not to compulsively *interpret*
something. Much of Zen Buddhistic work (and that of other
meditative disciplines that do not involve turning away from
experience) involve acquiring the ability not to *interpret* experience but just to be *aware* of phenomena as they arrive.

25. For some reason, it is the negative postulates that tend to become fixed.
Positive postulates (decisions that one is going to do well), however, also
tend to be self-fulfilling. The methods of Dale Carnegie (*Power of Positive
Thinking*), Maxwell Maltz (*Psychocybernetics*), and others are attempts to
capitalize on the self-fulfilling effects of positive postulates.

PERSON   **WORLD**

Basic Forms of Prehending

Perceptualizing ◄·······························► Phenomenon

Conceptualizing ◄·······························► Concept

Cognizing   ◄·······························►   Fact

Basic Creative Actions

Picturing   ·······························► Phenomenon

Conceiving   ·······························► Concept

Postulating   ·······························►   Fact

Basic Receptive Actions

Perceiving ◄······························· Phenomenon

Interpreting ◄······························· Concept

Intuiting   ◄······························· Concept

Understanding ◄·······························   Fact

Figure 16. Summary of basic actions.

Finally, one should have the ability to withhold assent if needed, and not accept as a fact every interpretation or concept that is offered. People that cannot withhold assent become slaves to the opinions of others and often get quite confused when others' opinions differ. One should be able to recognize when something does not make sense. The ability to recognize nonsense as such has a lot to do with having a sense of humor. When we laugh at something, we are recognizing its absurdity.[26]

The receptive abilities are ways in which a person receives his experience. But since they *are* abilities, a person must be at least potentially able to choose *not* to exercise them. The person is therefore not entirely passive when he engages in receptive actions. The person must *decide* to accept a concept as factual in order for agreement to occur; he must *decide* to pay attention in order to perceive, and he must *decide* to think about a phenomenon in order to interpret it.

A characteristic of any action is that there is an underlying *intention* behind it. One intends to conceive of something, so one thinks and creates the concept. One intends to make a phenomenon, so one engages in the creative action of picturing and creates the phenomenon. One intends to do something, so one postulates it and brings it about. On the receptive side, one intends to receive a phenomenon, so one looks and does so; one intends to receive a thought or concept, so one interprets a datum (such as a sentence) or consults his intuition and does so; and one intends to receive or know the truth or the facts, so one sorts out different possible concepts or interpretations and accepts one or more of them, thus creating one or more facts.

People sometimes speak of "unintentional acts". For instance, if someone taps my kneecap in a certain way, my foot jerks forward, whether I intend it to do so or not. In this case, however, it is clearly not an act of *mine*, but an act of my body. If someone pushes or throws me off a cliff, it is not an act of mine

---

26. See also the discussion of humor in Chapter Six, p. 297.

either, but a bodily motion impelled by others. If I am reaching across a table for the salt and I knock over a glass of water, one could say that knocking over the water is an "unintentional act". From my viewpoint, however, it is not an act of mine at all, any more than being thrown off a cliff is. It is an unforeseen *consequence* of an act of mine (the act of reaching for the salt), just as, if I buy a bright red dress for a friend and two months later, while wearing the dress, she is gored by a bull, it could not be said that *I* caused her to be gored. It is not an act of mine precisely because it is not foreseen by me and therefore not intended.

The Resultant Intention

When involved in a given activity, a person may have many different intentions that influence her actions. These intentions often oppose or fail to align with each other. More often than not, in fact, there is more than just a pair of opposing intentions. There are likely to be a variety of intentions pulling in different directions.

We can understand what is going on, here, by using an analogy from physics: that of vectors. If you wish to determine which way an object is going to move, it is possible to add up all the various forces acting on that object, taking into account the magnitude and direction of each force, and determine that the net force is acting on that object and in which direction that force is operating. Each force is described as a "vector" — a quantity that has two components: direction and magnitude. The forces may be combined by a process called "vector addition", and the result is a "resultant vector", which determines what the net effect of all the forces on the object is going to be, and therefore what the object is going to do.

Intentions work in much the same way. Like a force-vector, each intention-vector has two components: magnitude and direction. We call the "magnitude" of an intention its *cardinality*, and we call its "direction" its *objective*. Of course, at this point, the analogy between force- and intention-vectors breaks down somewhat, because the objectives of intentions are not simple directions in space but specific realities that are being sought, and the additive process is therefore much more complex than is vector addition. Nevertheless, the analogy is useful. In making a decision to act, a person takes into account all relevant intention-vectors, with their varying cardinalities and objectives, and adds them together to form a "resultant intention". The resultant intention is what determines the person's action.

The process of considering what to do is nothing more than the process of resolving different intention-vectors into a resultant intention. Often, it is difficult or impossible to arrive at a resultant intention. In this case, there may be no clear balance in one direction or another, and one is irresolute — one cannot and does not act. One can escape from this irresolution only by deciding to cease considering the point at issue and to consider something else instead.

The concept of a "vector addition" of intentions that brings about a resultant intention and thus determines action is closely related to the basic economic concepts of "cost" and "benefit":

Definition: The cost of an action is the sum of all the intention-vectors that would oppose that action.

while:

Definition: The benefit of an action is the sum of all intention-vectors that would favor that action.

The action of considering the cost-benefit ratio of any action, therefore, is equivalent to the action of adding up all the intention-vectors that relate to that action and coming up with a resultant intention with respect to that action. This resultant intention will determine whether — and how — one acts.

Involuntary Actions

Some people claim that they are "forced" to do certain things. People feel they "have" to go to parties they do not "want" to go to. That is, people sometimes feel they knowingly do things that are unintentional. For instance, if I am held up at gunpoint and ordered to hand over my money, one could say that handing over the money is an "unintentional act". But this is an imprecise way of speaking. What the robber succeeded in doing was to give me sufficient *incentive* to hand over my money. The handing over of the wallet was intentional. I could have said, "No," and risked being shot. Just because one choice is *much* more rational than another does not mean the less rational choice does not exist.[27] Therefore, strictly speaking (and our way of thinking on these matters probably needs to be sharpened), no one ever does anything unintentionally. Conversely, if something happens that was not intended by me, it is not an action of mine.

Behind any activity, then, is an intention. In fact, the intention, or intending, is the *proximal* part of the activity, the part that lies closest to the person, and the rest of the activity consists of consequences of the intention.[28] Though it might not seem to be the case, intention is a necessary condition in receptive actions as well. One *intends* to perceive, to interpret data, and to understand. Sometimes, however, it may seem that one does not have

---

27. There is such a thing as an act that is, in itself, unintended, but is performed because the alternative is even more strongly unintended. Such acts might be called "involuntary" acts. For instance, when I am held up and I give the robber my money, that is not something I would do willingly, absent a compelling reason, so we say that this act is done "involuntarily". The line between "voluntary" and "involuntary", however, is a bit vague. I may hate examinations, but if I must take an examination to get my doctorate degree, then I will take it anyway. Is the examination involuntary or voluntary? It seems to be voluntary, even though, in itself, it would not be intended. It could be argued that taking the exam is voluntary because the compelling reason is a *positive* one — getting a valuable degree, rather than a *negative* reason like being threatened with a gun. But if I hate operations and I go to the hospital to get a possibly malignant mole removed, is that an involuntary action or a voluntary one? Most would say that it is voluntary. Or if I hate exercise but exercise daily to prevent arteriosclerosis, is that an involuntary action, or a voluntary, though disagreeable one? It is difficult to distinguish between a positive reason and a negative one. Do I exercise or hand over my wallet to a robber out of fear of death or out of love of life? Would I fear death if I didn't love life? The answer to these questions is difficult but does not affect the fact that all acts are intentional.

28. See Chapter Three, pp. 132-134, for a further discussion of this point.

any choice about perceiving, just as it may seem that one sometimes does not have any choice about creative actions. Nevertheless, it is theoretically possible not to attend to something if one
does not wish to; one can put one's attention in a different direction. For instance, while listening carefully to a sound or trying
to recall a past event, one tends not to attend to what is going on
visually; while concentrating intensely on a visual experience, one
may be inattentive to sounds and other physical sensations. This
phenomenon is seen in an extreme form in hypnosis. Good hypnotic subjects are capable of being inattentive to events that
would be overwhelmingly apparent to an unhypnotized person.
Children are notorious for having a talent for deliberate inattention. The point is that reception is just as causative as creation.
The difference is only one of the *direction* of the action. Creation
consists in pushing things out, while reception consists in pulling
things in. But one can pull just as causatively as one can push!

Automaticities

What about "unconsciously intended acts"? From the
person-centered viewpoint, such acts do not exist. If an action is
done "automatically" as part of a larger action, the person does
not experience himself as doing that action. For instance, if I am
unconsciously tightening my latissimus dorsi when making a tennis
stroke, I do not experience myself as performing the action of
tightening this muscle, so this action does not exist for me. I
could conceivably, "step back" and notice which muscles I am
tightening, at which point I would experience myself as acting in
that way. I could, I suppose, *define* "unconscious intentional
acts" as acts that I would see myself as having done if I stepped
back from my current identity. Once I have stepped back, however, anything I then do is a different act from what was happening before.

Some receptive actions appear to happen automatically, just
as some creative actions appear automatic. These receptive
actions are not actions that we experience ourselves as *doing*, any
more than "unintentional creative actions" are actions we

experience ourselves as doing. They seem to happen without our choice, so we conceive of them as "just happening". But just as it is conceivable that a person could bring automatic creative behavior under control, so it is possible he could bring automatic receptive behavior under control. Some advanced yogis seem to be capable of readily turning their attention away from any experience, even from intense or painful experiences. Much of personal enhancement consists of regaining conscious control over processes that are happening automatically. This applies to both creative and receptive processes.

When a person conceives a concept, pictures a phenomenon, or postulates a fact, the obvious and correct explanation for the existence of the concept, fact, or phenomenon so created is that he created it himself. It is possible, however, to create an entity — a picture, concept, or fact — and then to forget or repress the act of creation. Having done this, a person could then err by trying to explain the existence of the created entity in some other way, such as by the notion that someone *else* created it or that it came from the body or some other physical agency. If he makes this mistake, the entity appears to be "out of his control" and may take on a type of "resistance" (immutability, opacity, or unintelligibility) to his actions.[29] Much of the distress that people undergo is because of this mechanism of repressed creation, followed by a misassignment of source. The classic example is the tale of the housewife who wants to borrow eggs from her neighbor but pictures her neighbor giving her a hard time about it. This picture becomes so real and so solid that the housewife forgets that she created the picture in the first place and mistakes the picture for reality. She finally goes to her neighbor's house and says, "Oh, keep your stupid eggs anyhow!" Many unfortunate interpersonal interactions are based on this sort of confusion

---

29. A solipsist, or a person who believes that in our highest identity we are one with the creator of the universe, would have to say that *all* resistance originates in this way.

between picturing and perceiving, or conceiving and interpreting.[30]

---

30. This mechanism is probably the cause of many forms of paranoid fantasies or hallucinations.

Chapter Three

The Anatomy of Experience

This chapter deals with the elements of experience and the way in which these elements are arranged, classified, and related.

A person can assume any number of identities. From the viewpoint of any particular identity at any given time, a person experiences *herself* as unitary, but experiences the *world* as composed of multiple entities (concepts, phenomena, facts). These entities can be classified as mental or physical.

Some entities appear to require the mediation of the body; others do not. Phenomena perceivable through the bodily senses or their various extensions (such as microscopes) are "physical phenomena". But what shall we call phenomena that are perceivable through non-sensory perception? If you did Exercise 6 (p. 77) you will recall that it is possible to create a picture of a horse and to perceive the picture. Or you can recall some past incident and perceive it or re-experience it. Although it could be argued that we *are* using our physical brains and neural pathways to produce such pictures, I would like to explore this subject at an *experiential*, person-centered level. We do not *experience* ourselves as perceiving these entities through physical means. We do not *see* our brain cells or view neural impulses. Nor do we experience ourselves as interpreting, intuiting, or understanding via the body.

Similarly, some *creative* actions are done through the body or its various extensions and are therefore called "physical actions", whereas other creative actions (such as conceiving thoughts, creating, changing, or destroying mental pictures, and postulating) do not involve bodily mediation, although these actions may be correlated with neurological events and may lead to physical consequences.

The Mind

What we are aware of non-physically is not, under ordinary circumstances, apprehended by others; what is done non-physically is not, ordinarily, done to others or to physical objects. Nor are our non-physical actions perceived by others, although their consequences may be perceived. An artist can create a non-physical picture and then render it as a painting. Others can see the consequence — the painting — but not the non-physical picture. Indeed, the ability to render non-physical phenomena into physical form is surely one of the major abilities an artist has.[1]

Experientially, then, space, time, and phenomena also exist in a non-physical realm. And these phenomena are perceived and

---

1. Mozart is said to have composed his music by "taking dictation". Because of his extraordinary memory and unusual ability to render sounds into musical notation, he could give a very complete rendering of what he heard "in his head". How many others of us might have composed symphonies or other great works of art if we had similar powers to remember and render into physical form our non-physical experiences?

acted upon in much the same way as is done in the physical realm. A convenient and traditional name for this non-physical realm is "the mind":

> **Definition**: The mind is the set of entities that exist for a person but that, under ordinary circumstances, other people cannot be aware of or act upon directly. It is that person's set of "private" entities, or that person's "private" world. Mental actions (creative or receptive) are not *experienced* by the person as being mediated through the body, regardless of neurological correlates that may exist.

For the following exercise, it is best to have someone read off the steps to you, and you should let him know when you have completed each step:

Exercise 8. Mental and Physical Space and Time

a. Note the time.
b. Close your eyes and make a picture of a white horse.
c. Make it tiny; make it large; make it normal-sized.
d. Turn it green, then red, then white again.
e. Move it to the left; move it to the right.
f. Move it up; then move it down.
g. Make it gallop out to a great distance away.
h. Then have it gallop back.
i. Make sure it is quite solid and dense, then try to have an equally solid and dense rabbit be in the same space as the horse and observe what happens.
j. Make the rabbit disappear.
k. Try to make the *same* horse be *simultaneously* to your right and to your left.
l. Could you do it?
m. Make the horse disappear.
n. Open your eyes.
o. Note the elapsed time of the exercise.

If you did this exercise, you will see that mental events do occur in space and time. You will also notice that, even in a mental space, two solid objects cannot occupy the same space at the same time. You can conceive of them as fluid or fragmented and intermix their parts, but you cannot have two solid mental or physical objects in the same place at the same time. Nor can the *same* object be in two different places at the same time. You will note that this mental exercise required a certain amount of physical time — that, in fact, mental time and physical time appear to be the same time-dimension. One dove-tails neatly into the other. It is meaningful to say that you thought of or pictured the horse *before* opening your eyes and looking at your watch. Therefore, there must be a common time-continuum amongst mental and physical events.

Like physical objects, mental objects exist under certain constraints. Even a mental object cannot appear to be in two different places at the same time. Two copies of the mental object may be in different places at the same time, but not a single one. If my imagined horse is seen to be in an imagined stable, it cannot at the same time be out in an imagined pasture. If picture A is on the left side of my mental field of view, it cannot simultaneously be on the right side. A car, imaginary or otherwise, cannot, in one view, both exist and not exist. You will also notice that the "left" and "right", and the "far" and "near" used in describing mental space are the same "left", "right", "far" and "near" used in describing physical space. The two spaces appear to be separate, but not along any of the above-mentioned dimensions.[2]

Although people loosely refer to mental experience as "inner experience", both mental and physical experiences are, in fact, external to the person, or, rather, to the identity the person has assumed and from which she is experiencing. Experience, in other words, is always "external" to the identity experiencing it; a phenomenon is always separate from that which observes it. The observer and the phenomenon observed are opposite poles of the process of observation.

---

2. I will discuss these issues more fully later (pp. 126-133).

I do not plan to address the issue of "mind over matter" in the sense of psychokinesis or telepathy. These are alleged non-physical or mental actions (actions not mediated via the body) that can affect the physical universe or someone else's mental universe directly. I do, however, want to address two other traditionally controversial issues:

1. The "mind-body problem": the problem of how mental events can affect physical events and vice versa.
2. The problem of communication — the problem of how one person, inhabiting one world, can communicate with another person, inhabiting a different world. This problem is exemplified by the age-old question of whether two people really see the same color when they say they are looking at something "red".

Countless volumes of material have been written and are being written about these topics.

The Mind-Body Problem

The "mind-body problem" arises from the notion that mind and body inhabit totally separate universes, each with its own space and time, its own laws, and its own kinds of causation. Events in the mental universe can be regarded as causing each other according to the rules of the mental universe, and events in the physical universe can be regarded as causing each other according to the laws of the physical universe. But there is no common set of laws between the two universes that would permit causation from one universe to the other. Therefore mind-body and body-mind causation seems to be impossible. Yet it appears to occur.[3]

---

3. An additional difficulty with this point of view arises when one asks, "What separates them?" How can two entities be separate if they are not in the same space at all? "Separate" loses its meaning in the absence of a shared dimension along which separateness can occur. I will pursue this point

From the person-centered viewpoint, however, the mind-body problem doesn't exist. According to the viewpoint I have been presenting, mind and body do not inhabit different universes but are part of the same universe, part of the same space-time continuum. A similar point was made by Ernst Mach.[4] The mind and the physical universe are not separated by being in different universes but only by the fact that one is private and the other is public. There is no reason, therefore, why they cannot interact. From the person-centered viewpoint, bodily phenomena are clearly causally connected to mental phenomena and vice versa. If I formulate the intention to raise my arm, the arm rises (under normal circumstances). The intention is non-physical; the action is physical. Subjectively, there is no more doubt of the causal link between the two than of the link between intending to create a mental picture of a horse and having the picture of a horse appear. In both cases, the intention and the outcome are clearly perceived as part of the same process. Similarly, if I feel a pain in my right elbow, there is no doubt about what I feel. Whether there is any physiological or pathological correlate to that pain is irrelevant. The pain is there, and it is clearly perceived as a physical pain, yet it attracts my (non-physical) attention and may well affect my (non-physical) mood or ideation. From the person-centered viewpoint, there is no mind/physical universe split and no mind-body problem.

---

further in this chapter.

4. Mach, Ernst "The Analysis of Sensations", in Beardsley, M.C., Ed. *The European Philosophers from Descartes to Nietsche* (The Modern Library, New York, 1960).

The Problem of Communication

The problem of communication is not so easily dismissed. It is hard, from a person-centered viewpoint, to say how extreme the differences between different people's worlds really are, whether two people really do share the *same* concepts or the *same* experiences when they communicate. In fact, it may seem all too easy to move from a person-centered view to a solipsistic one. Although each person has complete certainty about his own existence, there does not appear to be the same degree of certainty about others' existence. As a solipsist, I could believe that there *are* no other persons or identities, but only a set of phenomena in which I appear to be embedded (some of which appear to be more under my control than others). But it is possible to infer from one's own perceived involvement with a body that other similar bodies — which undergo motions similar to those I induce in my body — are directed or inhabited by beings like myself. This does seem to me to be a simpler assumption than the assumption that while I know I exist, I am surrounded by bodies that contain no such beings as myself. Worse yet is to assume, counter to experience, that I do not exist, but that my body, like all other bodies, is an automaton. The latter assumption is incompatible with living life and can, for practical (or experiential) purposes, be discarded.

Yet since the end of the past century, the prevailing view in behavioristic psychology has been just that: that bodies are just automatons. The whole concept of a mind has come under attack.[5] The "hard-line" behaviorist notion is that people are merely bodies, not experiencing beings. The behaviorist feels that to talk about any mental phenomena is to go beyond the evidence, since one cannot perceive such phenomena directly in others. The behaviorist, then, deals only with various abstractions

---

5. See Gilbert Ryle's *The Concept of Mind* (Barnes and Noble, New York, 1962).

concerning patterns of behavior or physical actions on the part of bodies. With the advent of cybernetics, this viewpoint took a slightly more sophisticated turn. The cybernetic notion is that people, as bodies, are just self-programming computers that are also programmed by their surroundings. By controlling the programming of these computers, one can modify the behavior of the bodies. The notion of how a person experiences life or how he feels (e.g., whether he is happy or not) is either ignored (because there are no experiencing persons) or reduced to observations of behavior (e.g., "happy behavior", like smiling, laughing, or saying "Yum-yum."). Psychology became the study, not of the psyche but of behavior. The paradox is that the behaviorist cannot help thinking, intending, dreaming, and acting, even though to do so is against his ideology!

In recent years, this strict interpretation of behaviorism has softened somewhat. With the introduction of the notion of "mental behavior", the person and experience seem to have worked their way back into psychological thought by the back door. And this is the way it should be, not because it is "humanistic" or "holistic" to look at a person as a person, nor, as Descartes thought, because God would not be so cruel as to deceive us about the nature of things, but because there is a better reason to believe that other people exist. This reason has to do with a rule of scientific reasoning called "Occam's Razor", which states that one "should not multiply entities beyond necessity". In other words, in explaining data, one should not assume the existence of any facts that are not absolutely necessary in order to explain the data. Of two or more possible theories that would account for the same data, one should choose the simplest and most modest. It is simpler to assume that other bodies that look like mine and behave like mine are driven by a similar cause than to assume that other bodies are just machines programmed to *act* as though other beings were running them. So Occam's Razor demands that I adopt the simpler theory. I know my car is powered by hydrocarbon fuel. It is simpler for me to assume that the cars I see, that also go "Vroom, Vroom!" and give out exhaust, are also powered by hydrocarbon fuel than to assume they are really electric or atomic, with cleverly constructed noisemakers that go

"Vroom, Vroom!" at the appropriate times and with little smoke generators and tiny fans blowing the smoke out of the exhaust pipes. The latter explanation is possible, but much too complicated.[6] I am assuming, therefore, that there are other beings like me, that they have minds as I do, and that they have points of view and worlds of their own, which are not the same as my world but which seem just as valid for them as my world seems for me. And I am assuming that the rules by which others' worlds are constructed and operate are much the same as those which govern my world. I assume that the fact that people can communicate to, and understand, each other at all is itself very strong evidence of how much we have in common. I assume that these commonalities can be found, understood, and explored. These assumptions are the essence of the person-centered viewpoint and the key to helping people successfully.

---

6. It is actually making *more* of an assumption — it is *less* skeptical — to assume that every body (other than mine) is a cleverly constructed automaton than to assume that they are inhabited by beings like myself. Without being telepathic, I only have direct evidence about the ownership and control of one body — my own. That evidence tells me that a being (me) is connected to my body and that the body's behavior is at least partially determined by my intentions. Since other bodies behave similarly, I have more reason to think that other bodies have beings connected to them as well than to think that no such other beings exist. Otherwise, I must assume the paranoid viewpoint that other bodies are elaborately programmed to *act* as though they were controlled by beings. Like any paranoid schema, this gets overly complex because then I am faced with the question of who programmed those bodies. If I am the only being around, then according to this view I must have programmed them myself. But I am not *aware* of having done so!

Intention and Time

Recall that I have lumped together events, states of affairs, and objects under the heading of "entities". Any object could be described as an event or state of affairs and *mutatis mutandi*. Even a quintessential "object", such as a desk or a table, must be viewed as four-dimensional, or as a state of affairs persisting in time, in order to exist as an object. A table with no finite time-dimension does not exist as an object. Note that in talking about experiential space and time, I do not want to invoke Einsteinian or relativistic concepts. I am talking about space and time as experienced by people under ordinary circumstances.

Cycles

Any entity — whether a fact or a phenomenon, or whether or not it is conceived as an event, an object, or a state of affairs — has what I will call a "cycle" connected with it. It has:

1. A point of creation (in the case of an object) or starting (in the case of an event or state of affairs).
2. A period during which it is changing (as an object or state of affairs) or persisting or continuing (as an event).
3. A point of destruction (for an object or state of affairs) or stopping (for an event).

A boat is *created* in the boat yard, *maintained* during the time of its use, and eventually *destroyed* — by rot, by fire, by decomposition, by being dismantled, or by breaking up on the rocks. A fire — as an event or state of affairs — starts when it is ignited, *continues* while it burns its fuel, and *stops* when it is extinguished.

The middle of the cycle can be regarded as a period of duration, persistence, or survival, but it is also often a period of growth or decay, and always involves change. Even "unchanged" persistence across time involves at least one change: the change of relationships to other entities. Let us try to think of a counter-example. Suppose we have a bar of platinum-iridium placed in a vacuum or inert gas. It is inside a jar, inside a vault, at a constant temperature (like the Kilogram of the Archives in Paris). Could we say that that object persists without change? Let us discount changes that are invisible to a person under normal circumstances: vibration of molecules, and the like. Nevertheless, that bar of platinum will be acted upon by shifts in the position of objects around it — varying gravitational and electromagnetic fields (from a factual viewpoint). It also moves with the motion of the earth, the solar system, the galaxy, and the local galaxy cluster. From a phenomenal viewpoint, other changes occur. As I walk around, the bar may at one time be close by, at other times distant. It is sometimes visible, sometimes invisible. It may have greater or lesser monetary value at different times. If I learn something more about platinum, I may see the bar in a different light.

The fact is that, both factually and phenomenally, nothing can remain the same unless all people and entities surrounding it also remain unchanged. And this would mean, essentially, that no time elapses. So for any entity, change is an integral part of a cycle.

Issac Watts, in the famous hymn "Oh God, Our Help in Ages Past", describes time as "an ever-rolling stream". And it may be that way, conceptually. But time is not *experienced* in this way. Instead, time is divided up into finite chunks, each of which is defined by a cycle. To identify a piece or "period" of time, we must name the event, object, or state of affairs whose cycle defines that period of time. For instance, the "Elizabethan Period" is the period of time defined by an event known as "the Reign of Queen Elizabeth I". This event started at her coronation, continued through all the vicissitudes of her sovereignty, and ended at her death. Similarly, the period of time defined by "when we were at the movies" started when we walked into the theater, continued while we watched the film, chewed popcorn, whispered to each other, and applauded, and ended when we left the theater.

Even an arbitrary period of time, such as a "minute", is defined by an event. A minute starts when the minute hand leaves one notch on the clock dial, continues while the hand travels to the next notch, and ends when it arrives at the next notch. Or, alternatively, a minute is defined by a 360 degree sweep of the second hand.

A person or entity may inhabit more than one period of time. The "time I did my psychiatric residency" includes "the time I was 30 years old", "the time I lived in New Haven", "the time I vacationed at Provincetown", and many other times.

Activity Cycles

For any given person, different periods of times are defined by the cycles that exist for that person. Among all these cycles, however, certain ones stand out as being the ones that are important to a person at a particular time. These are the cycles that relate to the activities the person is engaged in at that time, where I define "activity" as follows:

> **Definition**: An activity is the action or actions (creative or receptive) that a person takes in order to fulfill an intention.

It is formulating an intention that gives a person something to *do*, i.e., an activity. An activity may be primarily *receptive* or primarily *creative* in nature, depending on the intention that rules the activity. An intention to listen to Beethoven's Fifth Symphony, and the corresponding activity of listening, is primarily receptive; an intention to build a house is primarily creative, and so is the corresponding activity of building.

These intentions bring into being a special kind of cycle, the "activity cycle":

> **Definition**: An activity cycle is a cycle that is brought into being by the formulation of an intention. It lasts as long as the intention lasts, and no longer.

Since activity cycles are the ones that are most important to a person, I will henceforth use the term "cycle" to refer to activity cycles. Also, the word "cycle" is often used more or less interchangeably with "activity".

Some cycles are brought into being by the intentions that rule a person's *creative* activities; others by intentions associated with his various *receptive* activities. Formulating an intention to engage in a creative activity gives the person something to make or create. I will refer to a creative activity as a "task". Formulating a receptive intention gives the person something to receive — an experience. It produces a piece of experience that is "given" to him (or, more accurately, "taken" by him). I will therefore refer to a receptive activity as an "incident". The following definitions summarize these points:

Definition: A <u>task</u> is a creative activity.

Definition: An <u>incident</u> is a receptive activity.

When a person has finished doing a task, the task is ended. When a person has finished having or experiencing an incident, the incident is over. In both cases, the cycle is ended.

It is intention, then, that a person uses to bring about a creative or receptive cycle and thus to create a period of time for that person. What starts a cycle is an intention. If I perform a particular action called "writing a paper", this action starts when I formulate the *intention* to write a paper, continues while I do the research and thinking, physically write the paper, edit and refine it, and ends when I finish typing it up in final form. The *intention* is what holds a cycle together and defines it. A cycle stops when, and only when, the person stops intending the end result of the action, i.e., either when:

1. The end result or goal has been attained (as in the example of writing a paper), or
2. The person discontinues the intention; she stops wanting to achieve the result.

Assent and Intention

This is a good point to clarify the relationship between assent and intention, and in order to do this, it is necessary to take another look at the nature of intention. The reason why intention and activity always go together is that intention is actually *part* of an activity: that part which, in a certain sense, lies closest to the person.[7] Intention is, in fact, the most subjective part of an activity. So in a certain sense, intention is the beginning of an activity, but not its beginning in *time*, since intention and activity are coextensive. Assent, on the other hand, does occupy a particular point in time, namely the point at which an intention is formulated. Unlike an intention, assent does not extend throughout an activity cycle. Actually, in fact, each cycle has *two* acts of assent connected with it, one at each end. Each cycle begins with a *commitment*, which is the formation or beginning of the intention, and ends with an *acceptance*, which fulfills or unmakes the intention and thus completes the cycle. Until you commit yourself — at least to some degree — to doing something, you don't begin doing it. And after you have committed yourself, you continue doing it until a certain act of acceptance occurs. Either you fulfill the intention and finally accept the fact that you have succeeded or you consciously decide to accept the fact of its *non*-fulfillment. Either kind of acceptance ends the intention, the activity, the cycle, and that period of time.

Although an activity is often primarily receptive or creative, at the beginning of each activity there is always a creative act of assent and at the end there is always receptive assent. At the beginning, you are putting out something — a new activity, period of time, identity, and intention, minimally. And at the end, you need to receive data to determine whether or not you have ful-

---

7. We shall have more to say about what type of "closeness" we are talking about, later in this chapter (pp. 126-133).

filled the intention, so that you can accept the outcome and thus terminate the intention, the activity, the identity, and the period of time.

Balancing Acceptance and Commitment

In fact, if you start to accept things on a wholesale basis, you will find that you are completing cycles left and right. If, at the same time, you avoid making any more commitments, the end result, theoretically, is ultimately a complete lack of current activity cycles, intentions, identities, or periods of time. You will find yourself wholly in present time with no desires, nothing to do, and nothing to be. That, I believe, is a pretty good description of the Buddhist notion of Nirvana. And, indeed, we find that many spiritual paths embrace the notion of complete acceptance of everything as a path to enlightenment.

On the other hand, if you keep on making more and more commitments and never accept anything as complete or OK, you will surely become more and more embroiled in a large number of ongoing activities, and life will start to go out of control.

The ideal, I believe, is to retain freedom of choice over acceptance and commitment. That way you can regulate things so that you have just the right amount and kind of activity going on in your life. Whenever too much is going on, you can start accepting things. When life gets boring, you can make more commitments.

Limits on Intention

A person does not intend something that:

1. She knows or believes to be impossible, or
2. Is already completed.

It is, of course, possible to intend to *continue* an activity that is ongoing. For instance, if one is flying a plane, it is possible to intend to *continue* to fly. It is also possible to intend to do something *again* that one has finished doing. While walking from home to the post office, I can intend to go to the post office. After arriving at the post office, I can no longer intend to go to the post office, because I am already *at* the post office. I *can*, however, intend to make the trip to the post office *again* at some future date. Furthermore, I cannot intend to fly to the moon by flapping my arms, because I know that is impossible. I might *wish* I could do so, but I could not *intend* to do so. Often, a person stops intending something that she conceives to be impossible, but if she were to look at the same situation from another viewpoint, she would see that it is really not impossible. People often set unrealistically low limits for themselves and thus fail to achieve what they otherwise could. This is called "having a lack of self-confidence". Some of the more spectacular gains a person can make from applied metapsychology are from revising upwards her estimate of what it is possible for her to do. There are ways of helping a person to do so.

Of course, a person can be in many different periods of time at once. I am currently writing this chapter, so "the time I am writing this chapter" is one period of time. But this cycle is part of a larger cycle, which is the cycle of writing this book, so I am also in "the time I am writing this book". If I intend to visit Scotland some day, and I have that as an ongoing intention, then I am also in "the time I am working on visiting Scotland".

A person does not necessarily have his attention continually on an ongoing cycle. Cycles often lie "dormant" or "inactive" when the circumstances the person finds himself in are not relevant to the cycle in question. For instance, I am trying to get this book finished, but when I am at the beach, playing music, or conversing with friends, I am not usually thinking about the book. However, when I see my desk or my word processing terminal, my book tends to come to mind. In other words, one could say that being in the appropriate environment *reminds* me of the cycle, and the cycle — or the intention — is thereby *activated*.[8]

A person could be said to have a certain amount of awareness and a certain amount of creativity at any particular time.
Awareness and creativity could be considered two aspects of
aliveness or power. Although potentially a person has an indefinite amount of power to "spend" in various ways, it seems that in
practice a person has only a finite amount. There seems to be a
limit to the number of things a person can be aware of at once
and a limit to the number of creative actions a person can engage
in at once. If he is preoccupied, if his awareness and creativity
are directed to something that is in one place, it is, to some
degree, difficult to place his awareness and creativity elsewhere.

I think a computer analogy will help at this point, so long as
we do not take it too seriously or too literally.[9] A computer has a
certain amount of "main" data space available to it, in which it
must perform all of its operations. This readily available data
space is known as "random access memory", or RAM. This
corresponds to the Freudian conception of the "conscious mind"
and contains data of which we are immediately aware, data that
we prehend. A computer also has more remote data space,
which, however, is still "on-line", e.g. on discs or tapes, parts of
which can be read into RAM in order to be used in calculations,
but which are not currently in RAM. This corresponds to the
Freudian conception of the "preconscious mind" — data that can
be readily retrieved but is not currently present. These are data
that we *have*, but aren't currently *prehending*. The Freudian conception of the "unconscious mind" corresponds to archived data
— data that is on tapes, punch cards, or hard copy, filed away
somewhere where we might have to do quite a bit of digging to

---

8. When a cycle is activated, it seems to *impinge* on the person more, to move
"closer" to the person in some way. It is then more easily prehended. We
will have more to say about this mechanism of activation in Chapter 7, with
regard to unpleasant or painful cycles (pp. 345-347,356).

9. In what follows, I urge the reader always to remember that a *person* cannot
be adequately represented by a mechanical model. However, the person's
environment may, to some degree, be understandable in terms of mechanics,
and the person's mind is part of his environment.

find them (i.e., to prehend them).[10]

Pursuing this analogy, I can say that there is a finite amount of working space in which to perform the various necessary operations. In a computer, this working space is used for four purposes:

1. Data input routines (for reading data, when needed, off of discs, keyboard, tapes, etc.)
2. Data storage space (for storing the data that is being worked on)
3. Program space (for storing the instructions that are to be carried out)
4. Output routines (for sending out data or performing actions)

The total amount of RAM is analogous to the total amount of "life" or "personal power" (or, if you prefer, *élan vital*, libido, "psychic energy", or "consciousness") a person has. Thus it can be useful to speak in terms of amount of "power", which would be equivalent, in the analogy, to the number of "bytes" of RAM a computer has.[11] Some part of the RAM, at any given time, will be employed in performing one or more tasks; the rest of the RAM is available for other tasks. Thus, a computer, at any given time, has a certain amount of RAM free in which to perform new

---

10. This computer model is not the only model we could use. Plato, for instance, had an interesting "aviary" model of the mind. ["Theaetetus", in *The Dialogues of Plato* Tr. Jowett, B. (Random House, New York, 1937), v.2; pp. 202ff] He envisaged the mind as like a giant aviary. At any given time, you can have a bird in your hand or in sight, but the rest of the birds have to be sought after or caught. Those in the cage can, however, relatively readily be caught. So the cage corresponds to the Freudian conception of the "preconscious mind". Birds outside of the cage would have to be hunted down and might or might not ever be found, so the space outside the cage corresponds to the Freudian unconscious. The computer analogy, however, is perhaps more apropos for our modern era.

11. The analogy is a bit weak, here, because a computer's ability to get work done also depends on the speed and design of the computer, not just the amount of RAM. But I can chalk up this inaccuracy to "analogical license" and use it as another excuse to assert that people are not computers.

tasks, to store more data for ready access, or to exercise more input or output routines. The more free space there is, the faster the existing tasks will be completed and the more new tasks can be taken up. Analogously, a person has a certain amount of free life, consciousness, or power with which to be aware and to intend, and by awareness and intention, to exercise her creative and receptive abilities. A computer may have wonderful programs, but if it has a very limited amount of free RAM, it will not get much done. Likewise, a person may have a great deal of ability, but in the absence of a sufficient amount of personal power, she also will not get much done. Even a very brilliant person, when in a state of extreme emotional upheaval or depression, will be relatively unproductive. It is simply not true that human misery is conducive to creative activity. The reverse is the case. It *is* true that a person with a great deal of power can confront past unhappiness — even great tragedy — and learn from it, whereas a person of low power must either shy away from her past moments of pain or succumb to them.[12]

If a person has started a creative cycle — if she has started to postulate something, to picture something, or to conceive of something, and if she has not unmade that intention — then:

1. She is still in the middle of that cycle.
2. She is still in the period of time that she delineated by formulating that intention.
3. That cycle remains part of her perceived present time.

A person defines her own present time by her intentions. In this way, present time is expanded to include a part of the future and also expanded backward to include part of the past. For instance, a champion golfer expands her present time to include

---

12. As we shall see in Chapter Four (pp. 193-194), power is a combination of ability + drive (the capacity to have affinity for — to desire — things). Many applications of metapsychology concentrate on restoring a person's power by restoring his drive, his "lust for life". Others concentrate on restoring ability.

the whole action of swinging, hitting the ball, and having it travel to its destination. Throughout the action, she "sees" the entire four-dimensional activity at a single glance. The same is true, to a degree, of all our actions, whether creative or receptive. In the act of intending, we stretch our present time to include a wider segment of time than just one instant. Our intention thus spans time in much the same way as our present-time attention spans space. And the period of expanded present time created by the intention stays with us until the intention is unmade or the action is completed. As noted above, we may be carrying part of the "past" as part of this expanded present time, as well as part of the future. The duration of the intention, from the past through the projected future, is the time-dimension of this expanded "present time". So, to a person, present time consists of all those periods of time governed and created by his intentions.[13]

Some of a person's resources (power, "psychic energy", or consciousness) continue to be tied up in these creative cycles (tasks). In other words, the more there is going on *now*, the fewer resources he has available for new activities. If too many tasks are left incomplete, a person can be greatly debilitated. Certain metapsychological techniques are designed to end these past tasks, either by having the person complete them, by enabling the person to become aware that they are already complete — if they are complete and the person does not realize it — or by making it possible for the person, if he wishes, to simply unmake the intention that created the task or creative cycle. In this way, these techniques "unclutter" a person's present time.

The same holds for receptive cycles (incidents). If a person has been unable to interpret (or perceive, understand, or intuit)

---

13. If one were to suspend one's intentions, one's present time would, theoretically, have no breadth in the time dimension. Thus one would achieve the state touted by Ram Dass of simply "being here now" and of thus being aware without intending. This would be a state similar to that mentioned in Chapter One (pp. 27-29), in which one had "backed up" from all of one's intentions and identities and now had no intentions and no identity, but a sort of "oneness with the universe".

something, he can be left with an incomplete receptive cycle. If the person has intended to become aware of something and has not yet become aware of it, he is held in suspension, waiting for the awareness to come. If he is waiting to perceive something or waiting for something to appear, he can also become fixated. In my youth, I recall sending away for an "atomic ring". For weeks, my awareness or attention was trapped, hovering around the mail box day after day, waiting for the precious package to appear so that the incident of receiving the package could be completed.

A person can also become preoccupied because he wants or intends to agree with something or concur with someone but cannot. A cycle has been started that should end in his concurrence, but he is unwilling or unable to give his agreement. People with marital problems often want desperately to believe that their marriage is a good one. That attempt to believe can lead them to try to ignore all sorts of evidence to the contrary. Often the first task of a marriage counselor is to overcome this desperate desire to believe what they *know* is not true. For such couples, the task of proving to themselves and others that there is "nothing wrong" with their relationship can become a desperate preoccupation.

One can also become preoccupied with trying to find something out (e.g., whether or not UFO's actually exist), or trying to decide which interpretation of a phenomenon is correct. A lover may wonder, "Does the way she acted mean she doesn't love me, or was she just tired?" Unread or unfinished books can also have a deleterious effect on a person's power. Suppose, for example, that I decide to learn Einstein's General Theory of Relativity. I buy a book on the subject but get bogged down in the mathematical formulas after reading ten pages. At that point, say, I put the book down and do something else and "forget about it". I might go on for years with a bit of my awareness fixed on that activity. Someone could do me a big favor by sitting me down and doing whatever is necessary to make me aware that I still have this intention. That awareness gives me the opportunity to pick up the book again and finish it, perhaps with the help of someone who understands General Relativity and who explains things well.

Or I can decide it is all right if I *never* understand General Relativity. *Either* decision results in a noticeable feeling of relief.

Suppose I decide to go to Tahiti, but cannot afford it. I start saving money, but other things always come along that I need the money for. Some part of my intention remains fixed on the completion of that activity until I either unmake the intention — decide it was not so important after all — or go to Tahiti. Again, either decision results in a feeling of relief.

If you want to experience this sense of relief (while improving the quality of your life), I suggest that you try the following exercise:

Exercise 9. Completing Cycles

a. Make a list of all the activities you can think of that you have started but neither completed nor deliberately discontinued.
b. Go through the list, item by item and decide, for each item, whether you still really want to do it or not.
c. If you still intend to fulfill the intention behind that activity, then either:
    i. Do so immediately or
    ii. Schedule a definite time *in writing* when you are going to do so.
d. Otherwise, decide that it is all right if you *never* finish that activity, and definitively abandon it.

Perhaps you once started *War and Peace* and still intend to complete it, some day. When you come to that item on your list, you must decide to do one of the following:

a. Finish it *now*.
b. Make a note on your calendar of when you are going to finish it.
c. Decide that it is all right if you *never* finish *War and Peace*.

If you do this exercise for real, the world will literally seem brighter, because you will have more personal power available to look and act upon it.

Dimensions of Experience

Baba Ram Dass admonishes us, "Be here now." There is a sense, of course, in which we cannot do otherwise. Whatever we are, whatever we do, and whatever we are aware of, *must* be here and now in order for it to be done now, or in order for us to be aware of it now. By definition, everything that *exists*, exists here and now. Entities that only exist*ed* or that *will* exist are not here and now, and are therefore non-existent. This raises the question of how we can *know* the past or the future, since they are not here and now. And it brings up the further question of how statements about the past or future can be true, since the past and future do not exist.

The past and the future nonetheless seem to be a part of a person's world. In other words, they do seem to exist. They cannot be perceived in the same way that present physical objects can be perceived. They may be perceivable as mental pictures through non-sensory perception. And certainly they may exist as *facts* — concepts to which the person has given her assent.

A person's concept of time — and of space — depends on the concept of dimensionality. I define "dimension" as follows:

Definition: A <u>dimension</u> is a quality of a world that permits the separation of its component parts.[14]

A non-dimensional world could contain only one point. Nothing could be separate from anything else in such a world, if, indeed, it

---

14. A conversation with Dr. Harold Puthoff was especially fruitful in arriving at this definition. By "dimension", I do not mean exactly what is often meant in mathematics, where the number of dimensions equals the number of independent variables. Nor do I mean merely qualities that differentiate one entity from another, such as color or smell. By "dimension", I am referring to a "locative" quality — a way in which different objects can be said to be in separate *locations*.

could even be dignified with the title of "world". A one-dimensional world would consist of a line, composed of separate points. Or it could be thought of as stretched out in time, consisting of a succession of points "in the same space", and separated from each other only by time. A two-dimensional world would consist of a plane or surface or possibly of a line that is stretched out sideways over time so as to form a succession of lines (perhaps of varying lengths). A three-dimensional world could consist of planes of various shapes extended in space *or* time. And finally, we have our present world, consisting of at least four dimensions.[15]

The Spatial Dimensions

From the person-centered viewpoint, there appear to be three spatial dimensions and one temporal one. The spatial dimensions separate objects from each other according to *position*.[16]

The person generally defines as *here* the area that she is focusing on at a particular time. She may arbitrarily shrink her *here* to include things closer and closer to the space included in the identity that she is currently "being". I am sitting here, being

15. The existence of twelve or more dimensions is under serious consideration by modern physicists. But since metapsychology is a study of what exists from a person-centered viewpoint, I shall only consider dimensions that are perceptible to a person.

16. From the viewpoint of the person, the spatial dimensions are usually perceived as follows: The person is at the origin (center point) of her world, spatially, and she sees her "normal" direction of view as "forward". In other words, she sees distance in a "forward" direction as positive and distance in a "backward" direction as negative. Apart from distance, the person has two angular coordinates — the angle to the right or left and the angle representing elevation above or below a horizontal plane including the origin. The person sometimes translates these data into an "absolute" reference system, such as longitude and latitude or arbitrary coordinate systems like street intersections, but the basic orientation given above is that which a person has experientially.

a typist, and my word processor is part of my *here*, as is the table, the lamp, the floor under my feet. But by focusing my attention more narrowly, I can "shrink" the extent of what I experience as *here*, so that now the lamp on the table, is not *here* (within my area of focus) but *there* (outside the area of focus). In other words, a person includes, in her sense of what is *here*, a certain area of space surrounding her which contains what she is focusing on. What I regard as *here* depends on the scope of what I am placing my attention on. In typing this chapter, *here* may include my word processor, clothes, my chair, and various papers. But in thinking about space travel, for instance, *here* may be planet Earth, or this solar system. It is hard to conceive of a situation in which *here* could be experienced as a mathematically dimension-less point. In fact, that concept of *here* is an abstraction that lacks experiential validity. This is because a person generally experiences herself as occupying a certain amount of space. How much space a person occupies depends on the identity she has currently assumed, and that amount of space is the smallest quantity of space that she can consider as being *here*. For instance, if the person is currently being a body, the smallest *here* she can have is defined by the limits of her body. Nevertheless, by shedding this identity, she can shrink her *here* even more. If I decide I am not my *whole* body, then I can consider myself to be my brain and regard my right hand as *there*.

The Temporal Dimension

The temporal dimension separates objects from each other according to a factor that I will call "tense":[17]

---

17. Of course, "tense" is meant to apply to *words*, so this is an extension of normal usage to apply to entities that might be expressed in words that have a past or future tense.

Definition: <u>Tense</u> is a directionality in time. There are two tenses: past and future.

Person

Past   *Present*   *Future*

Figure 17. The time dimension.

In time, as in space, the person finds himself in the present at the origin. The past and the future are in opposite directions (see Figure 17). Since (in Western culture, at least) the person normally views himself as facing "forward" in time, future tenses are generally regarded as having a "plus sign", whereas past tenses are regarded as having a "minus sign". In countdowns, time *before* liftoff is "T *minus* 30 minutes", whereas time *after* liftoff is "T *plus* 30 minutes". When the person uses spatial metaphors for time, he generally follows these rules. He "looks forward to" events that have a future tense and he "looks back on" events that have a past tense.

    Now is also never experienced as a dimensionless point. *Now* contains everything that is happening or that a person is focused on doing. *Now* always has a definite duration. If someone asks me "What is happening now?", I could say, "I am typing a sentence," "I am writing Chapter Three," "I am writing a book on metapsychology," or even "I am trying to improve the planetary ecology," depending on where I am focusing my intention. But even the activity of typing a sentence is not something that happens in an instant. It takes a few seconds. A period of time must be described in terms of an activity that is going on in that time. Present time is no exception to this rule. Therefore, with spatial dimensions, what the person includes in his experience of *here* is determined by the scope of that on which he is currently focusing; with the temporal dimension, his experience of *now* is determined by the scope of the activities, both receptive and creative, that he currently considers himself to be engaged in. Some of these activities have long time spans (for instance, the activity of writing a book), some have short time spans (such as the action of typing the letter "r"). But each activity lasts for a certain definite length of time. None is instantaneous. The notion of *now* as a dimensionless point, like the notion of *here* as a dimensionless point, is therefore a mere abstraction. A person "stretches out" his *now* to include entire sections of time defined by the activities on which he is focused.

A person can expand her *now* by extending her area of focus and making very long-range plans, thus acquiring "the long view". The person can also arbitrarily shrink her *now* to positions closer and closer to where she is in time, "living for the moment". Furthermore, the activities a person is currently engaged in are based on the intentions she currently has. As was mentioned earlier, actions are intentional. An act is being performed as long as it is intended and no longer. Conversely, the formulation of an intention is the start of an activity cycle. Therefore, the duration of an activity is equivalent to the duration of the intention. It is equally true to say, therefore, that present time is defined by what a person is currently *intending*, since what constitutes present time is all the *activities* on which a person is currently focused. The act of intending, then, stretches out a person's present *time*, just as the act of expanding one's awareness stretches out a person's present *space*.

Just as a person can only shrink her present space to the outer limits of the identity she is currently "being", so she can only shrink her present time to the outer limits of the *intentions* that are built into her current identity. By shrinking one's concept of *here* until it lies within the outer limits of one's current identity, one can force a change of identity. Shrinking one's *now* until it lies within the limits of the built-in intentions of one's current identity likewise forces a change in identity. As a writer, my current intention is to finish this chapter — it is the "inner" limit of what constitutes *now* for me. But by "stepping back" from that identity to that of a typist, I can shrink my *now*, say, to include only the action of typing this sentence or this word. If I shrink my identity still further, I can consider *now* to be just the time it takes to type the letter "r".

The past contains all those activities that have been completed or ended. These have a "past tense". The future consists of those activities that are not yet started. These have a "future tense". The closer to a person or identity an entity is in time, the less of a past or future tense it has. The farther away it is in time, the more of a future or a past tense it has. So the past and the future do exist — at a greater or lesser distance from the person along the temporal dimension. Naturally, present time tends to be clearer to a person (because it is closer), just as one is more clearly able to perceive phenomena that are closer spatially than those that are further away. The future (for a person at a particular moment in time) consists of entities that the person intends to *have*, whether (as a creative action) by postulate or (as a receptive action) by predicting (i.e., by making a certain interpretation of present data and then accepting that interpretation).[18] In either case the result is the creation of an entity with a future tense. The following exercise will illustrate how a future is created or predicted:

Exercise 10. Creating a Future

a. Decide you are going to touch your chair in five seconds, and then do so.
b. Did you create something in the future?
c. What is the weather going to be like in an hour?
d. Did you predict something?

Some puzzling questions concerning a person's world are not completely resolved using the four-dimensional model. These include:

---

18. A future could also, possibly, be received by being *intuited*. Intuition could reveal a future that exists for a person at a particular moment, but that may turn out not to be what eventually occurs. Nevertheless, from the person-centered viewpoint at that earlier moment, that *is* the future the person then conceives himself to have — and does have.

1. Can a person view or "change" a four-dimensional object? If so, what "time" does he have to effect such a change?
2. What is the relationship of mental space and time to physical space and time?
3. From what "perspective" can a person see an "expanded" present time?
4. In what sense can a person "move" to view a past or future entity?

A special application of the definition of "dimension" given above offers a possible answer to some of these questions. The proposed concept is that there is a fifth dimension in addition to the four spatio-temporal dimensions.

The Fifth Dimension

To approach this concept, let me start by reminding the reader of the definition of "mind":

> **Definition**: The mind is the set of entities that exist for a person but that, under ordinary circumstances, other people cannot be aware of or act upon directly. It is that person's set of "private" entities, or that person's "private" world. Mental creative or receptive actions are not experienced by the person as being mediated through the body.

Clearly, the mind cannot be said to include physical objects that are visibly present in physical space and time. Yet they do appear to occupy a sort of space and time. The question arises, then, what the nature is of mental space and time. In fact, the mind appears to *share* space and time with the physical universe, yet in some sense mental space and time are also "separate". Per our definition of dimension, this "separateness" (if it exists) must be allowed by some dimension — unless we say that the mind is another world the person inhabits, completely separate from the physical universe. If we adhere to the person-centered viewpoint and say that the person has only one "world", then there must be a dimension in this world that separates mental from non-mental entities. I have already offered the reader an exercise[19] which demonstrates that no two different solid and dense mental objects can be in the same space at the same time; the same is certainly true of solid and dense physical objects. What if we try to combine mental and physical objects? Try the following:

Exercise 11. Observing the Fifth Dimension

a. Find some thick, transparent object, such as a glass sphere.
b. Look at the object and at the same time picture a small horse in the middle of it.
c. Have the horse gallop around in the object.
d. Is the horse part of the physical object or separate from it?
e. Is the horse in the same space and time as the object?
f. If so, how are they separate?
g. If not, what is the difference between the space and time the horse occupies and the space and time the object occupies?
h. Now consider the possibility of an actual (though small) solid physical horse running about in that object.
i. Is that a possibility?

If you have the same experience as I, you will find it *is* possible to picture a mental horse in the middle of a physical solid object and that it appears that the mental horse and the physical object are nevertheless separate, or else that there is a separate space and time (somehow "superimposed" on the object) which contains the horse.[20]

---

19. Exercise 8, p. 100.
20. This "superimposition" appears (to me) similar to a "projection" of two three-dimensionally separate objects onto a two-dimensional plane, as in the following diagram:

The ball and the box can be "projected" onto a two-dimensional plane. Similarly, a three-dimensional space can contain a projection of an object remaining in the same space but stretched out in time:

So a different degree of "physicality" or "objectivity" appears to be a quality that is capable of separating objects, experientially, from each other — even if they appear to be in the same spatio-temporal location. In other words, objects can be separated depending on how close they are to each of the two poles of life: the person and his world.

I will refer to this fifth dimension as the *polar* dimension:

> **Definition:** The polar dimension is the dimension that separates entities according to their degree of objectivity or subjectivity.

where

> **Definition:** Objectivity is the quality of an entity being on the world side of the person-world polarity.

and

> **Definition:** Subjectivity is the quality of an entity being on the person side of the person-world polarity.

It appears (pending the discovery of yet *another* dimension) that two phenomena cannot be in the same space, time, and

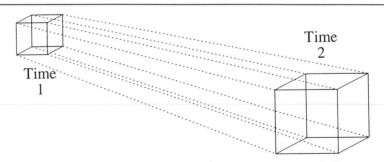

In a similar way, one could regard the combination horse-object as a projection of two four-dimensional objects in the same space and time but separated in another, "5th" dimension. You will find, if you redo Exercise 4, that if you think of the horse as physical, it cannot occupy the same space as the ball; and if you make a mental picture of a solid ball and try to superimpose a solid mental horse in the same mental space, you cannot do that, either. See also Exercise 8, p. 100.

objectivity. They can be in different times and the same objectivity and space, as when successive mental or physical objects occupy the same space. And they can be in different spaces and the same time and objectivity, as when two physical or mental objects are perceived at the same time in different spaces, and, as I just said, we can have two objects of different objectivity in the same time and space.

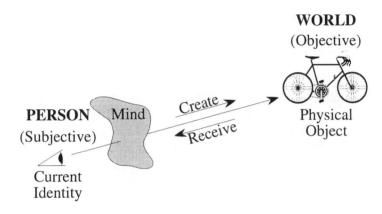

Figure 18. The polar dimension.

In this "polar dimension" (so-called because of the "poles" are seen as occupied by the person on one side and the world on the other), entities are separated according to their "objectivity" (see Figure 18). Entities that are less "objective" and more "subjective" appear closer to the person side of the polarity, while more "objective" phenomena appear more distant and closer to the world side of the polarity. The person, in her current identity, is at the center in this dimension, and it appears that she always looks "outward", i.e., toward the phenomena she perceives. We could say that the polar dimension radiates from the person to each entity in her world.[21]

Movement Along the Polar Dimension

The person can "move" along this dimension by extending or contracting his identity. At any given point, the person may extend "outward", so that he no longer sees what he saw before, but "becomes" it. He can look at positions at or behind the position he is currently occupying only by moving "behind" them or "inside" them (i.e., in a "subjective direction") and looking outward to see them from this new vantage point. As conjectured in Chapter One (pp. 27-29), the limit of "inward" motion — motion in the direction of subjectivity or shedding of identity — might be an arrival at a Supreme Identity. A motion toward objectivity, assumption of identity, specialization, and expansion of scope of action would, perhaps, be limited by arrival at an identity coincident with the physical or "objective" universe — a universe in which all objectivity would disappear, because there would be nothing "outside" to view.[22]

Causation and the Polar Dimension

Using this five-dimensional model, we can talk of causal or polar "priority", which is analogous to temporal priority. When a person creates an effect on his world, he is causally prior to the effect he creates. Personal causation follows the line of polarity. A person causes things along the "polar dimension". A cause is causally prior to its effect, as the person is prior to his world, according to this view. A person is closer, causally, to his mind than to the physical world, in that causation of mental effects

---

21. This is a "radial" dimension, since it goes in all directions from the center.
22. I also pointed out that some philosophies and religions consider the states of "pure subjectivity" and "pure objectivity" the same, in that they appear to "wrap around" into each other.

appears more direct and causation of physical effects more indirect or mediate.[23]

This five-dimensional model is useful because it provides a framework for understanding how a person can have an effect on a four-dimensional world. Suppose a person had only four dimensions in which to operate. Since the universe is a four-dimensional object, the person would find herself imbedded

1. Spatial (Position)
   a. Up — Down
   b. Forward — Backward
   c. Left — Right

2. Temporal (Tense)
   a. Past — Future

3. Polar (Objectivity)
   a. Person — World or
   b. Internal — External or
   c. In — Out or
   d. Subjective — Objective

Figure 19. Summary of Dimensions

in the universe as just another four-dimensional object, like a fly fixed in amber. The present, past, and future would all be pre-ordained or pre-existent; a person would be unable to change the shape of the universal four-dimensional object. But a person — to a greater or lesser degree — experiences herself as able to alter the course of events, not as imbedded in them. Therefore, she considers herself to have an additional degree of freedom that mere events do not have, i.e., another dimension in which to exercise causation.[24] This causal or polar fifth dimension could be

---

23. That is probably why the mind is private — it is closer to the person.
24. See Dunne, J.W. *An Experiment With Time* (The Macmillan Company, New York, 1927) for a detailed analysis of the need for a higher dimension.

regarded as providing the person with an analog of time or a higher sense of "time" (namely, causal priority or posteriority) in which to manipulate four-dimensional entities, thus "changing" these entities and creating (four-dimensional) entities that were not there "before" (in a new sense of "before"). Causation is the analog of "motion" in this fifth dimension, and it is by such "motion" that the person can "change" the future and possibly the past. This dimension also gives the person a "time" in which to "move" to the past or the future, and a "present time" in which four-dimensional segments of the world can be present to her "at once".

Dimensions of an Activity

Where do activity cycles and intentions fit in to this picture of causation and the Polar Dimension? First of all, we can now see in what sense intention is the most proximal part of an activity: it is that part which lies closest to the person in the polar, dimension — the subjective/objective dimension. In other words, intention is the most subjective part of an activity. But intention also extends through the *time* dimension. In fact, as we have seen, formulating an intention starts an activity cycle and creates a period of time that continues so long as the intention persists and only ends when a person unmakes or fulfills the intention. Now that we have *defined* intention as the proximal part of an activity in the polar dimension, it is easy to see why this must be the case: there cannot be an activity without it having an end that lies closest to the person in the polar dimension, just as you cannot have a rod without a tip. Intention is as inseparable from activity as the tip of a rod is from the rod itself.

Now we can also clarify where assent fits into the picture. Assent does not extend throughout the activity cycle. Actually, each completed cycle has *two* acts of assent connected with it, one at each temporal end. Each cycle begins with a *commitment*, which is the formation or beginning of the intention, and ends with an *acceptance*, which fulfills or unmakes the intention and thus completes the cycle. Until you commit yourself — at least to some degree — to doing something, you don't begin doing it. And after you have committed yourself, you continue doing what you have committed yourself to doing until a certain act of acceptance occurs. Either you fulfill the intention and finally accept the fact that you have succeeded or you consciously decide to accept the fact of its *non*-fulfillment. Either kind of acceptance ends the intention, the activity, the cycle, and that period of time.

Although an activity is often primarily receptive or creative, at the beginning of each activity there is always a creative act of assent and at the end there is always receptive assent. At the beginning, you are putting out something — a new activity, period of time, identity, and intention, minimally. And at the end, you need to receive data to determine whether or not you have fulfilled the intention, so that you can accept the outcome and thus terminate the intention, the activity, the identity, and the period of time.

In summary (See Figure 20, p. 134), an activity has two dimensions apart from its spatial ones. At one end in the polar dimension lies the person and her intention; at the other end in this dimension lies the objective of the intention — the desired consequence of the activity. At the subjective end of the activity, at the beginning in time lies an act of creative assent — a commitment; at the end in time lies an act of receptive assent — an acceptance.

Various methods of improving a person's ability to move along the polar dimension have been devised. Certainly, anything that improves a person's causativeness and his ability to be flexible about identities should improve his ability to "move" in this way. Versatility has been defined as:

The ability to assume or shed identities.

It could be redefined as:

The ability to change one's position in the polar dimension.

It is useful, in discussing ways of helping people, to look at the subject of the past and the future from the point of view of what a person can do about them. Clearly, a person influences the future by creative picturing of future events, by conceiving of

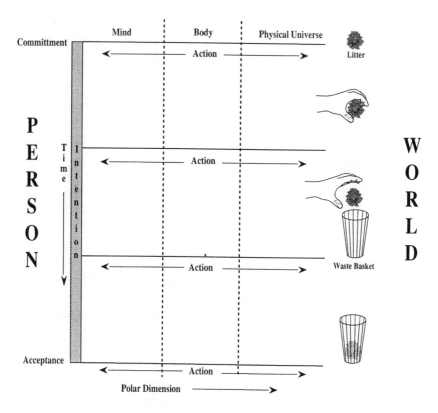

Figure 20. Dimensions of an Activity

possible futures, and by deciding (postulating) that a certain future is to occur.[25] Receptive action with respect to the future is the act of interpreting present events so as to generate a prediction of the future. Receptive actions regarding the past include recalling past entities by picturing them, and interpreting present or past events as implying the existence of other past events (as, for instance, a detective does: interpreting clues to generate knowledge of the past). Intuitions about the past or the future may also be valid receptive actions.

---

25. See Chapter Two, pp. 75-82.

But what about *creative actions* concerning the past? Can we make sense of this concept? Can one create a mental picture with a past tense? Let us see if this is possible.

Exercise 12. Creating a Mental Picture in the Past

a. Recall a time you made a mistake.
b. Picture yourself, in the past, in that same situation, doing what you now perceive would have been the right thing. Make sure the picture is from your viewpoint, as you would have seen things at the time.

This technique is similar to one used by Milton Erickson and his followers.[26] You get the person to create an artificial past for himself that is less traumatic than his actual past. Similar re-creations of the past are used by Gestalt therapists and psychodramatists.[27]

What about *conceiving* something with a past tense? That is not difficult. A concept is a "potential fact" — something that might exist.[28] A concept of the past is something that might *have existed*; a concept of the future is something that might exist *in the future*. Let us see if these can be created.

Exercise 13. Creating Past and Future Concepts

a. Conceive of something that did not, so far as you know, exist in the past.
b. Conceive of something that might exist in the future.

Finally, is it possible to postulate or create a *fact* in the past, something that exists now as a past event but that didn't exist before? Certainly, it is possible to change one's mind about what happened in the past, or to decide something must have happened

---

26. Erickson, M. *Collected Papers* (Irvington, New York, 1980), p. 525ff. Article entitled "The February Man".
27. Perls, F.C. *The Gestalt Approach* (Science and Behavior Books, Ben Lomond CA, 1973) p.93f.
28. See Chapter One, p. 57.

in the past (based on evidence or intuition). But that is a receptive action — an interpretation — or reinterpretation — of data.
For example, if you are in psychoanalysis, you can decide that
you must have had an Oedipal Complex. If you are a Rankian,
you can decide that you must have had birth trauma. You can, in
other words, just as easily know (or believe with certainty, which
from the person-centered viewpoint is the same thing) something
about the past, based on little or no evidence, as you can about
the future. The problem with *postulating* into the past, though, is
that you cannot postulate something that you know to be impossible. Since we seem to know more about the past than about the
future, our options seem more limited. So if you *know* something
did not happen in the past, you cannot decide that it did while
still knowing that it did not. Of course, people do not often make
arbitrary decisions about what the past is; they usually base these
decisions on evidence of some kind, on authority, or on other
considerations having to do with the rules for organizing a
world.[29] But the situation is really not essentially different with
respect to the future. Decisions are not usually made arbitrarily
there either, but that does not mean that they are not made. It is
not, in fact, inconceivable that one *could* make a completely arbitrary decision about the past, if one did not know that what was
decided *did not* happen. Try it:

Exercise 14. Postulating Into the Past

a. Conceive of something that *could* have happened in the past
    (either to you or to someone else) without being inconsistent
    with the rest of experience.
b. Decide that it *did* happen.

You can decide for yourself whether or not this can be done.

If you have talked to friends or relatives from early in your
life, you will probably find that your recollections do not exactly
match theirs. This means that the two of you have probably made

29. See Chapter Four, pp. 156-166.

different decisions about the past, or one or both of you have, at some point, decided to change the past for some reason. If a husband comes home late from the office and the wife sees lipstick stains on his collar, she may decide that she must have made those stains without realizing it. If she later catches her husband in bed with his secretary, she will probably revise her opinion about the past activities of her husband and about the meaning of the lipstick stains. People often make decisions about the past of which they are not aware, whereas they tend to be more aware of the decisions they make about the future. It is possible to help a person considerably by helping her to become more aware of the decisions she has made in and about the past, to revise these decisions, and thereby to build a different, more accurate, and less debilitating picture of the past. Since decisions about the past tend to carry over into the present and future, revising such decisions can have a major effect on a person's life.

If you want to help a person, you must help her become aware of her past, and possibly change it so that she can change her future. As Santayana said, "He who has not studied history is doomed to repeat it." Perhaps this could be rephrased as "He who has not remade his own history is doomed to re-experience it."

Success and Emotion

I defined "activity" as the process of carrying out an intention. The set of all actions a person does by way of carrying out an intention is the activity that corresponds to that intention. Each activity consists in overcoming resistances to understanding, perception, or motion — the overcoming of unintelligibility, opacity, and immutability, or, sometimes, the overcoming of incomprehension, insensitivity, and weakness. Success in the activity occurs when the intention behind the activity is carried out, i.e., when something is created, perceived, understood, etc.

At any given time, from the viewpoint of a certain identity with a particular intention, a person has an impression of how well she is doing in carrying out that intention. This impression is attended by various attitudes and emotions.

How Success Affects Emotion

It is emotionally uplifting (at least to some degree) to be successful at even a small task, and emotionally disturbing to fail. One feels pleased at finding the word that fits into a slot in a crossword puzzle and irritated at not finding it. A lawyer feels happy when she wins a motion or a judgment in court. A doctor is content when she correctly diagnoses or cures a patient. A musician feels glad when he creates music that satisfies his own and others' aesthetic taste and unhappy when he does not. I therefore define "success" as follows:

Definition: Success is the fulfillment of an intention or, equivalently, the completion of a cycle.

A major success, then, is the completion or fulfillment of a major intention, one that is important to the person and high on the hierarchy of intentions. A minor success is the fulfillment of a lesser intention. Often a person who is being unsuccessful in one or more major activities will end up spending a great deal of time on smaller activities in which he *can* be successful. A person who is failing at his job may become obsessed with some hobby or sport or may concentrate on receptive actions (such as watching movies and reading books) where success is almost guaranteed.

By defining success as the carrying out of an intention, it is possible to bypass the various stereotyped social definitions of "success" — such as "making a lot of money" or "being famous or powerful" — and also remain true to the person-centered viewpoint. Success, for any person, *is* the fulfillment of an intention.

An interesting feature of success is that it obliterates intention. It does not seem possible to intend something that one believes to be already a *fait accompli*, since intention is toward creating or receiving a reality that is not already there. If you have already found something, you can no longer *intend* to find it; if you understand something, you can no longer intend to understand it, and if you know something already exists, you cannot intend to bring it into being. You can, of course, intend to find something, to understand something, or to bring about something *again*, but that is a different matter.

Success also obliterates itself. Success exists at the point where an intended entity actually exists. Since success is defined as the fulfillment of intention, once the intention is gone, so is the success. Success, then, is momentary. As has often been observed, success immediately becomes a *past* success. To *continue* to be successful, one must continue to have unfulfilled intentions that are in the process of being fulfilled.

To intend a certain action, one must consider it *possible* to accomplish that action. Hope is defined as knowing that something that the person intends can or might exist. Hope is therefore a prerequisite to intention. If a single or repeated failure causes one to lose hope, then the intention ends. This might be called a "final failure". Final failure, like final success, does theoretically end an intention: in fact, however, a person is more likely to decide that something is very *difficult* than to decide that it is *impossible*. Rather than actually *ending* the activity, he becomes *apathetic* about it.

A continuum exists, therefore, from final success through subsidiary successes to subsidiary failures and, ultimately, to final failure. An intention begins in hope and ends in final failure or final success. It is also possible to re-evaluate an intention or goal and to decide that, although it is possible to carry out that intention, doing so would interfere with carrying out other, more important intentions. I may intend to go to a movie and then, on learning I have some important task to perform, I may re-evaluate that intention and unmake it without having had a final success or failure at it.

In practice, a person often re-evaluates and unmakes an intention at a point far short of final failure. A girl may decide to be a Prima Ballerina. But if she has some failures along the way (for instance, if she is not doing well in her ballet classes), she may look at the amount of effort it would take to bring herself to the Prima Ballerina level and realize that the dedication required would make it impossible for her to lead a normal life, Accordingly, she may unmake this intention. She can unmake it even while being successful if she perceives that it is incompatible with other goals. Of course, to unmake an intention, a person must be aware that she *has* that intention, and she must be able to compare it and relate it to other intentions. In the case of "automatic" or "subsidiary" intentions, re-evaluation might not be possible, so that one could easily travel all the way to final failure on these intentions. Being fixed in a particular identity, for instance, can cause a person to have a fixed intention, and vice versa. It is unlikely, therefore, that a fixed intention will be fulfilled, because the person with that intention is not able to shift identities flexibly to fit different occasions. Ultimately, then, a fixed intention is likely to drive a person to hopelessness and inactivity, or, sometimes, to final failure. A "sex goddess" whose entire identity is based on her physical appearance can feel herself to be quite a failure when she gets too old for the part, unless she manages to shed this identity and assume a different one.[30]

Since an identity is ruled by an intention and engages in an activity, the unmaking of the intention also unmakes the identity and, at the same time, unmakes the activity. If I decide to stop playing my guitar, then I am no longer being a guitar player — until I decide to play it again.

---

30. The intention to survive physically seems to be built into bodies. If a person is fixed in a bodily identity, then death must be viewed as a final failure of major proportions. If one adopts a religious or spiritual outlook and views oneself as a non-physical being rather than as a body, i.e., if one feels one can shed one's physical identity and continue to exist, then this particular final failure appears to be avoidable. Besides, there are extreme situations in which one might have to re-evaluate the importance of bodily survival. If some cause seems important enough, people have been known to make this re-evaluation and to willingly sacrifice their bodies. Death in these circumstances is not necessarily viewed as a failure.

Along with various degrees of success or failure in carrying out a particular intention or being a particular identity, there are corresponding emotions, attitudes, and strategies. These reflect how well a person considers he is doing in the activity. They can be arranged along a continuum or scale, the upper levels of which correspond to an approach toward final success and the lower levels of which correspond to an approach toward final failure. This continuum is called the "Emotional Scale" (See Figure 21).

Definition: The emotional scale is a continuum of emotions, ranked in increasing order of adaptiveness and success, between final failure and final success.

Just above final failure is a level of hopelessness and apathy. At this level, final failure has not yet occurred, but one considers it to be inevitable. "It cannot be done," "I cannot do anything about it," "It would take an infinite amount of effort to be successful", "I don't care anymore" are some of the attitudes at this level. There is no strategy except to do nothing, to disengage from the activity, to stop caring. In other words, the person has not yet unmade the intention behind the activity, but he anticipates and welcomes a final failure that *would* fully unmake the intention and thus relieve his suffering.

A little higher, one feels grief or sorrow at the thought of the impending failure. The intention is still there; one does still care enough to feel grief. One has not yet completely accepted failure or loss. Nevertheless, one is in the *process* of accepting it. The attitudes here are: "Poor me!", "I'm a victim," "I cannot do anything about it," "I'm devastated," "I don't know if I can bear it." The strategy is to elicit sympathy and comfort from others as a substitute for what is lost, and — possibly — to motivate *them* to do something about the situation, based on that sympathy — even if one feels one can do nothing about it oneself. So at this level, there is hope at least that someone else might be able to do something.

A little higher are various degrees and intensities of fear and anxiety. At these levels, one does not yet think that the intention is impossible to carry out, but one sees a high probability that it will prove to be. Naturally, one fears the outcome. Attitudes at

(Final Success — Disengagement)

Elation
Enthusiasm
Cheerfulness
Complacency
Contentment
Ambivalence
Antagonism
Anger
Resentment
Hidden Hostility
Anxiety
Fear
Grief
Apathy

(Final Failure — Disengagement)

Figure 21. The emotional scale.

this level are: "It is a dangerous situation," "I've got to get out of here!." "What am I going to do (or what is going to happen) if I fail?" The strategy is to try to flee from or avoid those circumstances that are leading toward final failure or to flee the failure.

Up to this level, the person has been attempting to withdraw from or avoid the situation that faces her. Above this level, however, the person stops turning away (withdrawing) from her situation and begins to move toward it, to reach for it, though destructively at first. Here are various levels of hate, rage, or anger. At these levels, generally, one is attempting to destroy by force the factors that seem to be leading to failure.

At the lower end of this level, the person still has too much anxiety to engage in *overtly* destructive behavior. Her motion toward her environment is, as yet, quite covert. At this level of hidden hostility, she pretends to be friendly and constructive but secretly acts to suppress, weaken, and destroy others. She is afraid that if others around her are allowed to be powerful, they may destroy her. Therefore, in various subtle and secretive ways, she attempts to undermine their ability. She makes subtly cutting and invalidative remarks. She strongly resents the success of others and will attempt to undermine it. She also attempts to prevent others from having close relationships with others. This is the level of "hidden operations", of intrigue, of malicious gossip; it gives us the stereotypic picture of an "evil" person. Individuals who are chronically at this emotional level tend to be surrounded with unsuccessful, sick, and unhappy people. They prefer weak people because they feel safer in such company, and they will sometimes act covertly to lessen others' power. The attitude at this level is "I've got to stop this viciousness, but God help me if anyone finds out what I am doing." It is therefore somewhat dangerous to associate with such people. They are not, however, fundamentally evil; they are merely manifesting the signs of this emotional level. With help, they can rise to a higher level on the Emotional Scale, though the presence of undisclosed misdeeds may make a covertly hostile person harder to help.[31]

When a person moves up the scale from hidden hostility and becomes more courageous, he becomes *openly* hostile, or angry. The strategy at this level becomes that of overt destructiveness. This strategy, like the other "built-in" strategies I have discussed so far, is not highly adaptive, but it is often better than running away or acting secretly. Attitudes at this level are, "They are evil," "I must destroy them," "I must fight this to the end!"

A little higher, at the level of antagonism, one handles barriers to success by using force to push against them, rather than to destroy them. This push is in reaction to a push from the other side. Attitudes encountered at this level are "I will not let them get away with it," "An eye for an eye," "Give 'em some of their own medicine!". A determination to get revenge is at this level. At this point, one feels that there is just under a 50-50 probability of achieving final success.

---

31. See Chapter Six, the section on misdeeds and withholds, pp. 284-295.

Above antagonism lies the level of ambivalence, where one is unsure of whether one wants to do the task or not. There is a chance of success, but it looks as if it is going to take a lot of work, and the person is not sure whether or not it is worth it. The forces are balanced. The likelihood of succeeding is viewed as about equal to that of failing. The attitude is: "Maybe I'll make it; I'm not sure if I want to do it." One takes half-hearted action at times, but one is easily distracted. This is a level at which one is prone to be rather inactive because one feels neither excited at the idea of a barely probable success nor motivated by a strong possibility of failure.

Next are the levels of contentment and complacency. Here one feels that "Everything is going just fine; it is routine; we are plodding along, making steady progress." There is no great excitement about the prospect of success, but one feels relatively confident about it. The strategy, here, is just to keep on doing what one is doing and not change anything.

Above this are the levels of cheerfulness and enthusiasm, in which one becomes excited and energetic at the prospect of success. Here, one feels one is doing very well indeed, and the activity gets to be fun.

Finally, one can feel elation — usually at the point of some major final success. This is a point of change of identity: either growth and expansion, or the abandonment of an identity whose intention has been fully realized. In helping your child resolve a problem with her homework, you must become a teacher (functionally) until you succeed in helping resolve the problem. Then you resume the identity of a parent. At the same time, you may experience an emotion of elation of greater or lesser intensity. When a musician successfully learns a piece, his ability as a musician is enhanced and he experiences an expansion of that identity. The feeling of elation includes a sense of freedom and expansion.

Emotion and Physiology

We have been discussing the relationship between emotions and success. Yet one's emotional state seems also to be influenced by physical and physiological changes. Hunger, illness, and fatigue (and certain drugs) cause a person to be more prone to feeling lower-level emotions than usual. Certain other drugs, and physical actions that seem to satisfy basic physical needs (such as eating, exercise, and sexual activity), may raise a person's emotional level. These physical effects tend to be temporary and seem mainly to be correlated with the relief of physical discomfort. Swimming in cool water feels good when one is hot; a hot shower feels good when one is cold; food tastes good when one is hungry. Physical needs seem to be "built in" intentions (or "drives") connected with the body.[32] Freud thought these physical intentions (specifically, sexual ones) were the basis for all human motivation. That view, however, has seemed counter-intuitive to many. Indeed, the concept of "drive motivation" is no longer widely accepted. People are not aware of having their activities dictated in this way.

How Emotion Affects Success

Emotions are the person's response to a measure of success or fulfillment of intention. The Emotional Scale, however, itself influences the degree of success one is likely to have because the different strategies present at each level of the scale vary in their adaptiveness. High on the scale, a person uses perception, understanding, and skill to handle a situation; lower down, she uses force, then destructive force, then avoidance, then an appeal for sympathy, and finally no strategy other than inactivity. The

---

32. Certain drugs might be thought of as operating through "fooling" the body into thinking its needs are satisfied (or, in some cases, *not* satisfied).

adaptiveness of each level is directly proportional to the "high-ness" of the emotion. That is, the strategies become more and more maladaptive as you go down the scale.[33]

A significant feature of this scale is that at any level all the strategies at or below that level are "naturally" available to a person, while none of the higher strategies are available. So a person with a high emotional level in an activity has more tools for dealing with this activity than a person who is lower on the Emotional Scale. It may, in certain circumstances, be wise to run away, to fight, or even to elicit sympathy by expressing grief. Ideally, one can also take creative action — the strategy of enthusiasm.

In fact, the effect of emotions on success is so strong that one can make a good prediction of success in a particular activity by observing a person's present position on the Emotional Scale with respect to that activity. Above the level of ambivalence, a person is likely to succeed; below that level, she is likely to fail. This is one way of looking at the saying "Nothing succeeds like success." It is equally true to say, "Nothing fails like failure." This may be the reason why in many languages, the word for "happy" and the word for "fortunate" are the same.[34] Happiness can lead to success, just as success creates happiness. The two concepts are inextricable from each other. In fact, happiness is the condition on the "person" side of the person-world polarity that corresponds to success on the "world" side:

Definition: Happiness is the knowledge that one is being successful at fulfilling one's intentions.

For lack of a better term, I generally refer to the emotions at or below ambivalence as "negative" emotions, because:

---

33. See Chapter Nine (pp. 517-528) for a description of how to replace these built-in strategies with more adaptive ones.
34. Even in English, one of the meanings of "happy" is "fortunate".

1. Their corresponding strategies are more conducive to failure than to success.
2. At these emotional levels, a person has stepped over the line from a general movement toward success to a general movement toward failure.
3. These lower emotional levels are painful or uncomfortable to a person and thus usually unwanted.
4. These emotions tend to persist beyond the situations that trigger them off.

Definition: Negative emotion is emotion connected with failure, i.e., emotional levels at or below ambivalence, such as anger, fear and grief.

I will use the term "positive emotions" to refer to emotions at the upper end of the Emotional Scale:

Definition: Positive emotion is emotion that lies above ambivalence, such as complacency, enthusiasm, and elation.

It is possible to improve a person's success in life by helping her to rise on the Emotional Scale. For various reasons, a person can become chronically locked in a lower-scale (negative) emotion. Unlocking the person from a chronic negative emotion and allowing her to move up the scale has a very salutary effect.[35]

Also, associating with a person who is high on the Emotional Scale tends to raise one's own level on the scale whereas associating with a person low on the scale tends to pull one down the

---

35. Therapeutic techniques (such as those used in certain encounter groups) that are directed toward driving a person into a lower emotional level and causing a display of negative emotion are therefore counter-productive. In general, applying any form of duress, such as group pressure, sleep deprivation, or forcing a person to confront what she does not want to confront, results in a *lowering* on the Emotional Scale rather than an improvement.

scale. Thus, as a matter of survival, it is a good idea to select people high on the scale as one's close personal friends, significant others, or colleagues.

Both work and play are activities. The only difference between them is the emotional level at which they are done. Football, tennis, or chess can be drudgery to a person who has negative emotions toward these games — who is at ambivalence or below on the Emotional Scale with respect to them. Conversely, keeping financial records or pleading a case in court can be a form of play to a person who is enthusiastic about it. Activity is that which needs to be done to carry out an intention. "Work" and "play", a "game" and a "job", are really the same thing: an activity. The difference between them lies only in the emotion one feels toward the activity. Games involve one or more intentions or purposes. In table tennis, the purpose is to get twenty-one points, and, subsidiarily, to hit the ball so that it lands on the other side of the table after clearing the net. The same is true of jobs: there are intentions — things that need to be done — and subsidiary intentions. In both cases, there are also abilities or (equivalently) freedom, space, and time in which to accomplish the purposes, as well as barriers, or "resistances" to overcome on the way. To a person who is happy or emotionally positive, her job is a game; to a person who is unhappy or emotionally negative, life is drudgery or worse. The turning point between a game and a mere job is the point at which "seriousness" enters in. This occurs at "complacency" on the Emotional Scale. The dividing line between a job and drudgery lies at ambivalence.

A person usually feels emotion *toward* something. At any given time, he may have different emotions toward different areas of his life. He may feel antagonistic toward his wife, grief-stricken about the plight of a friend, and enthusiastic about his job. The areas a person feels good about usually do not need any special treatment. The ones in which a person finds himself low on the Emotional Scale are those he needs to work on. Often, however, a person will be found to have a "characteristic" emotional level that pertains to most aspects of his life. One person may handle most situations in an antagonistic way; another person may be quite cheerful about most things. The more successful a person is in life *generally*, the more of his own intentions he is able to fulfill and the higher his characteristic emotional level is likely to be.

By helping a person attain and maintain a characteristically high emotional level, it is possible to help him transform his life into a series of very enjoyable games.

Chapter Four

The Genesis of Personal Reality

How does a person receive and create the reality in which she lives? First, we will take a look at the basic criteria a person uses to choose the sort of reality she wants to have and to discover the truth about the reality she has.

"Truth" and "falsity" apply to statements or declarations, though we shall also speak of "true" or "false" concepts. A true concept is one to which a person assents and a false concept is one with which a person dissents. From the viewpoint of someone who believes in an "objective" or "absolute" universe, truth can be defined as a correspondence between a concept and the state of the universe. From this "objective" viewpoint, the statement "The tree is fifteen feet tall," is true if, and only if, in fact — i.e., in the objective universe — the tree measures fifteen feet from top to bottom.[1]

---

1. To a person who believes that what is true is *absolutely* true, an absolute universe will exist for her, and truth (for her) will consist precisely in this correspondence. But that is from *her viewpoint*. From another's viewpoint, there may be no absolute universe, or there may be a different absolute universe. One person's having an absolute universe doesn't mean everyone

In working from the person-centered viewpoint, we are not concerned with the state of the objective universe but with an individual person's view of his world and with the rules by which this view of the world is constructed.[2] People only experience what *they* experience. From his own experience, each person constructs his own model of the world. It is only possible to help another attain personal enhancement by referring to *his* experience and *his* world.

Moreover, the current model of the universe, given at its most fundamental level in current physics, is itself being made less and less absolute and more and more relative to the one observing it. At a macroscopic level, the General and Special Theories of Relativity come into play. Their basic tenet is that there are no privileged frames of reference. That is, for instance, nothing in the universe can be said to be traveling at any particular speed.[3] Speed is entirely relative, as is direction and even acceleration. The universe differs markedly depending on the viewpoint or frame of reference from which it is viewed. If event A and event B are simultaneous from one viewpoint, A may occur before B in one frame of reference and B may occur before A in another. Object X may be three feet long in one frame of reference and two feet long in another. The absolute model also breaks down at the microscopic level of quantum physics: the fundamental constituents of the universe, namely subatomic particles, have no precise location or momentum until actually observed. The act of observation, in fact, *creates* these particles in their concrete form, where, before being observed, they were only "probability density functions".[4]

---

else has to agree, although *she* may think so. Wars are fought over differing "absolute universes".
2. My reasons for adhering to this viewpoint were given in Chapter One, pp. 11-58.
3. Except photons, which are thought always to travel at the speed of light from any frame of reference.
4. Prior to the act of observation, an electron belonging to a particular atom,

From the person-centered viewpoint, "truth" is defined with reference to concepts:

Definition: The <u>truth</u> of a concept is its condition of being assented to or believed with certainty by a person.

Of course, it is quite commonplace for the same concept to be true for person A and false for person B. For instance the statement, "Some people are mentally ill," is true for most psychiatrists, but it is false for Thomas Szasz.[5] "Men have Oedipus Complexes" is true for Freudians and false for Behaviorists. The statement "Your ancestors will get you if you do not appease them," is true for some tribes in New Guinea but false for most Europeans, while "Men have gone to the moon," is true for most Europeans but false for some isolated African tribes. There may or may not be an "absolute truth", but, for practical (or metapsychological) purposes, we are only concerned with the truth that exists for the individual. When a person declares something to be true (which is the same as simply *declaring* it), she is inviting agreement from others.[6]

From the person-centered viewpoint, reality can have different degrees, ranging from impossibility to certainty.[7] From the

---

for instance, *might* be anywhere. The probability of its being in various positions around a nucleus has a certain value, but no one can say where it is, exactly. It is *almost* certain to be within a fairly narrowly circumscribed area. When it is finally observed, then it is observed in a specific location, and the rest of the places where it "might have been" are no longer places where it "might be". Thus the act of observation brings the particle into being in its observed location. The particle has no definite location absent the act of observation, according to this view.

5. See Szasz, Thomas *The Myth of Mental Illness* (Dell Publishing Co. New York 1961).
6. See Chapter Five, pp. 216-219, for a broader discussion of this point.
7. See Chapter One, p. 58.

same viewpoint, then, truth may also have different degrees, from complete falsehood, through various degrees of probability, to complete truth.

The Learning Cycle

In order to arrive at truth, a process of interpretation must occur by which one deduces, induces, or infers facts from phenomena or from other facts. What is a fact at one time may be a phenomenon at another, depending on the identity or viewpoint a person has assumed.[8] Keeping these ideas in mind, we can look in a little more detail at the process by which we move from existing data to new facts. I call this process the "learning cycle", using "learning" to mean the person's arrival at any new piece of knowledge, not just the arrival at scientific or academic knowledge.[9]

First, however, a general description of the learning process is in order. Learning involves interpretation or explanation. For instance, suppose I see a phenomenon consisting of: small, muddy footprints heading into and out of the kitchen, the cover off the cookie jar, and missing cookies. In addition, I hear my young daughter playing outside. Now, someone else might have taken the cookies, a raccoon (or a neighbor kid) might have come into the house. Or someone could have cleverly placed all these signs there to get me to unjustly accuse my daughter. These are

---

8. See Chapter One, pp. 34-37.
9. A great deal has been written about this subject under the heading of the laws of deduction and induction. The problem with many of these writings is that different people have different ways of deciding on truths, given the evidence, and so discussions of inductive methods may boil down to individual preferences or tastes. One can argue for one method as being better than another, but I doubt that any absolutely correct method will be found for constructing reality from the evidence. Some general rules will be offered later in this chapter, however (pp. 156-166).

all possible explanations or interpretations of the phenomena I observe. The most probable interpretation, however, is that my daughter in fact ate some cookies, and *that* is the interpretation I accept. A detective has to do this kind of thing all of the time. In fact, all of us function as detectives in this respect. Our reasoning, of course, need not always be elaborate. If I hear a bell ringing periodically, I may interpret it as a telephone ringing, based on past experience. This is an interpretation, albeit a simple one.

The general sequence for arriving at any knowledge (or belief with certainty) is given in Figure 22.

Data (phenomena or facts)

> *Inference or*
> *Interpretation or*
> *Explanation*
> ▼

Ideas or concepts
(There might be several interpretations)

> *Consideration*
> ▼

Acceptance (of an interpretation as a new entity)

Figure 22. The sequence of learning.

A person starts, for instance, with perception. He interprets the perceived phenomena as indicating the possible existence of one or more "underlying" entities, (i.e., he gets several different concepts from the phenomena). Finally, he makes a choice, in which one concept is accepted as the correct or most probable interpretation. In the above example, one could arrive at various possibilities (concepts) from observing the muddy footprints and the cover off the cookie jar. One then has to consider these concepts to decide which is true. Once one has accepted one of these concepts, one has a new piece of knowledge. A person could also start with a fact — something he knows other than through perception — and draw conclusions from that. If I know that my daughter stole the cookies, I may conclude that she might have done it because she likes sugar, because she is spoiled, as an act of revenge, etc. I will act in different ways, depending on which of these interpretations I choose to accept.

But how does one go about deciding, amongst the possible different interpretations of existing data, which of these interpretations is true? What are the criteria a person uses to *consider* various concepts? What are the various considerations that determine the *validity* of various interpretations of experience? At this point I must add another step into the learning cycle — *verification* of interpretations. The learning cycle is now seen to be divisible into four steps, not just three:

1. Perception or knowing
2. Interpretation
3. Verification
4. Acceptance

A datum is, as such, unquestioned since it is defined as a fact or a phenomenon and hence has already been judged as real. If it is to be questioned, it must be regarded not as a datum, but as an *interpretation* of some other datum, or as a mere concept. But once we have a concept, we must *consider* it in a certain way (in order to verify it) before we can accept it.

What criteria does a person use to verify (or disprove) various interpretations of experience? Why would a person accept a certain concept as factual or true and reject some other concept as not factual or false? Theoretically, a person could just decide arbitrarily what to accept and what not to accept. Indeed, this is a principal objection that is raised about a subjective viewpoint — its arbitrariness. There does seem to be a need for some restraint on what can be truthfully claimed as real, as Israel Scheffler points out.[10] Otherwise there would be no way for a person to *decide* what to believe and what not to believe. Fortunately, the decisions a person makes about reality are not generally capricious. Phenomena are accepted as existing because they are directly perceived. Facts are accepted as valid interpretations of phenomena when they explain phenomena or relate them to each other in a meaningful way. "Reality" is a "correct" or accepted interpretation of experience. And a person has verification rules that determine the correctness or acceptability of an interpretation. These rules are the means by which the person moves in the learning cycle from having, perhaps, several different concepts as possible interpretations of her experience, to an acceptance of one of them as the correct one. Although different people have differing rules for accepting some interpretations and rejecting others, some principles of verification seem to be universal amongst people. I have already mentioned one of these: Occam's Razor — the principle of keeping explanations as simple as possible. This makes sense, because a person can deal more easily with simplicities than with complexities. It is easier to juggle one ball than to juggle seven.

The Organizing of Experience

The basic principles that people use in organizing their experience are not so different from the criteria one would use in designing a human interface for a computer. A person acts and thinks in such a way as to maximize certain qualities in her experience. These qualities make her experience more *empowering*. One of them is what Freud refers to as "the pleasure principle".[11]

---

10. Scheffler, I. *Science and Subjectivity* (Hackett, Indianapolis, 1982) pp. 1-2, 19.
11. Freud, S. *An Introduction to Psychoanalysis*, Lecture 22 (Permabooks, New York, 1958), p. 365.

The Pleasure Principle

A person tends to interpret, create, and order her experience in as pleasant a way as possible — in a way that provides for as much pleasure as possible.

Relief

Freud viewed pleasure as a process of relief from pain, or "drive reduction". And it is certainly true that a person seeks relief from pain or discomfort, and experiences this as pleasure. It is a pleasure to scratch an itch that is irritating, to drink when one is thirsty. Eating (insofar as it is a relief from hunger), sexual release (insofar as it is a relief from sexual tension), and defecation are all "negative pleasures". Eating and sex can also have an aesthetic component, which is a "positive pleasure" (see below). "Drive reduction" or "negative" pleasure is probably what Maslow had in mind when he used the term "deficiency motivation" (as opposed to "growth motivation"),[12] what Plato had in mind when he spoke of "mixed pleasures" (as opposed to "true pleasures"),[13] and what Aristotle had in mind when he used the term "necessary pleasures".[14] A person will go to some lengths to eliminate pain, even if it means not exercising abilities and awarenesses of which she is capable. A person with a sore leg will not normally run, even though she is capable of doing so.

A person's aversion to the various entities that make up her experience can have very serious consequences for her, as will become obvious in Part II of this book.

---

12. Maslow, Abraham H. *Toward a Psychology of Being* (Van Nostrand Rheinhold, New York, 1968), pp. 21-43.
13. Plato. *Philebus* 46.
14. Aristotle. *Nicomachean Ethics*, VII, iv, 2.

Aesthetics

In addition, a person seeks "positive pleasures", or aesthetic experiences. A person naturally gravitates toward beauty, so she will tend to order her experience in such a way as to maximize beauty and minimize ugliness. Keats wrote:

" 'Beauty is truth, truth beauty!' — that is all
Ye know on earth, and all ye need to know."

That is *not* all ye need to know, but there is wisdom in what he said. Even a scientist, if given two otherwise equally valid explanations of the available data, will tend to choose the one that is the most "elegant" — i.e., the one that appeals to her aesthetic taste.

Order

Secondly, a person naturally wants life, and its various activities, to be relatively orderly, convenient, and manageable. No one is happy when her life is completely out of her control. We like to be masters of our own fates, controllers of our own destinies. Of course, no one pursues order *exclusively*. The pursuit of order is tempered (and often opposed) by the pursuit of pleasure and heuristics. But order in itself is regarded as empowering.

Simplicity

The first major sub-category of order is *simplicity*. As per Occam's Razor, a person will, first of all, opt for simplicity in his data. This means that he will want to have a world with as few separate parts as possible. He will want the elements of his experience to be as *non-complex* as possible. A world which is terribly complex is hard to keep track of. A person will, for instance, prefer a non-complex tax form to a complex one, and a non-complex explanation to a complex one.

A similar criterion to that of non-complexity is that of *continuity*. If a person has a certain task to perform, he would rather be allowed to *continue* it and bring it to completion before he embarks on the next task. A person doesn't like his life to consist of a series of interruptions. Writing that contains a number of interjections — appositions (like this one), clauses, parentheses and irrelevancies — can be quite annoying to the reader, who generally prefers to have a line of reasoning continue to its proper conclusion. "Patchwork" clothing, fragmented art work or music, and "urban sprawl" are displeasing because of their discontinuities.

Part of achieving simplicity is also achieving interpretations of experience that have as wide a *scope* as possible. The more data a particular interpretation of experience can explain, the fewer rules there will have to be, the simpler one's organizational schema will be, and the easier it will be to keep things orderly. It is tiresome to a person to be continually shifting frames of reference. It is far better to try to find one frame of reference, or only a few, that have sufficient scope to cover *all* of experience.

Finally, *ease* also falls under simplicity. A person wants to get things done as easily and as simply as possible. He doesn't want to have to struggle with things; he prefers them to be *easily* controllable. Part of ease is *predictability*. Things can get very difficult if a person has to prepare for a number of different outcomes at any given point. Ideally, the person should have a world view that allows him to predict the future and to predict the effects of his actions.

Stability

The second major sub-category of order is *stability*. A person will seek to have a world that is relatively stable, that is predictable and familiar. A world where the rules are constantly changing and the objects are behaving erratically or randomly going into and out of existence may be fine for a brief "Alice in Wonderland" experience. Many have sought out such experiences (via drugs, or other "kicks") out of boredom or out of a sense that a radical reorganization of experience would be salutary. But, on the whole, a person values stability greatly.

In order to preserve stability, people have a strong conservative tendency. It is much simpler to continue building on an old frame of reference than to go to the trouble of creating a whole new frame of reference and readjusting everything. Every once in a while, it seems that a readjustment must happen, but this is usually a fairly unsettling or even catastrophic experience. For instance, a person who has lived a very quiet, simple existence out in the country may experience a considerable "culture shock" at moving to the city and having to deal with that frame of reference. In the sixties, many people encountered severe stress in trying to switch to the values of "free love" and "open marriage" that were in vogue at that time. Since a major readjustment tends to be a catastrophic experience, people often avoid radical change — even when it may actually be necessary. Precedent and habit have a strong influence in the design of a person's experience. "Social gadflies" and revolutionaries, and people with new ideas, tend to have a hard time in society. They usually have trouble convincing other people of the truth of their views.

It is a well-known observation that the more revolutionary a concept is the more stringent the proof must be in order for it to be accepted. That is why, despite a great deal of scientific evidence in its favor, ESP is still not widely accepted in parts of the scientific community. The evidence, for many scientists, is simply not overwhelming enough to warrant destabilizing their view of the universe. On the other hand, if something fits an old frame of reference well, it requires little or no proof. If I say that I have a headache, and I'm frowning and holding my head, you are likely to accept what I say as true without proof, because headaches are commonplace in your frame of reference. But if I want you to believe that men from Mars are controlling my brain through etheric beams, that might require considerable proof. And that is as it should be. It makes sense for a person not to be wasteful of a useful frame of reference.

Congruity

The third major sub-category of order is *congruity*. Different parts of a person's world should fit together smoothly and not jar with each other. To use a term invented by Leibnitz, the entities that make up a person's world should be "compossible". One type of congruity is *logical consistency*. A person becomes quite confused and unhappy when parts of her world are logically inconsistent with other parts. A person will not allow an entity to be *where* it is not, or to be *what* it is not. She will also not think that an entity exists *and* does not exist, at the same time, from the same viewpoint.[15] But the truth of the matter is that logical consistency is a necessary condition for the ordering of experience. It is not a *sufficient* condition, however, and anyone who maintains that it is sufficient justly deserves criticism.

Apart from *logical* consistency, the different parts of experience must otherwise align or fit in as much as possible with the person's intentions and with each other. Non-illogical inconsistencies include instances of "bad taste" (such as a purple tie worn with an orange shirt), artistic blunders (such as a wrong musical chord), and any other situations where some element of the situation does not "fit". They also include situations and behavior that do not match a person's intention or identity, such as a harsh,

---

15. It has become fashionable, lately, to launch attacks against logical, or "left brain" thinking. Such attacks are reminiscent of the practice of "mortification of the flesh". The body, a natural tool and instrument of perception, has often been attacked as the source of evil and temptation and as a distraction from spiritual improvement. Recently, it seems that the mind or rational faculty of a person is coming under attack. The "right brain" is glorified over the "left brain". "Left-brain thinking" (meaning logical, analytic thought) has come to be a term of opprobrium. I consider this lamentable. The ability to reason and to think logically is just as natural to a person as the ability to feel and to perceive (and, perhaps, to intuit). Attacking this natural ability amounts to a new, especially destructive form of mortification: "mortification of the intellect". All of our abilities and tools should be *used* to construct a better world, not thrown away.

callous manner in a therapist. Incongruities, illogical or otherwise, subvert a person's sense of reality and fragment her experience into non-aligned parts. A person tends either to try to resolve incongruities or, if they cannot be resolved, to eliminate or ignore them.

The validity of any concept is measured against its tendency to promote organization of the person's world, i.e., its tendency to promote all of the above three major principles (and their various sub-categories). A person will tend to accept concepts as true when they are aesthetic, relieve pain, make life simpler, and when they do not conflict with other parts of experience. She will also tend to accept concepts that lead to an expansion of knowledge. She will tend to reject concepts that are overly complex, incongruous, painful, ugly, or boring.

Heuristics

The third major criterion a person uses in creating certain experiences and in choosing amongst different interpretations of experience is "heuristics":

> **Definition;** Heuristics is the quality of a world or part of a world by virtue of which it promotes learning or greater understanding. It is the opposite of "dullness", monotony or tedium.

A person will tend to make *heuristic* assumptions and interpretations — those that permit and encourage further exploration and knowledge. For instance the assumption "Every event has a cause," leads a person to seek for further interpretations of entities, whereas "Cause and effect are illusion" tends to lead a person to abandon the search for further knowledge. If a person thinks that entities do not have causes, he stops trying to explain the world around him. Freud greatly advanced the cause of psychology (and metapsychology) by his assumption that mental events have causes, just as physical events do.[16] Another heuristic assumption is: "There is always more to learn." A person will tend to interpret experience so as to encourage the learning cycle. Aristotle's concept that knowledge is the ultimate good is an excellent heuristic assumption. The notion that life is a learning experience is another.

More specifically, a person will tend to gravitate toward elements of experience that are intelligible. He will read books written in English if he is American or British and in Russian if he is Russian. And he will strive to make intelligible what is currently unintelligible. He will strongly resist others' attempts to restrict his sources of data, and he will naturally gravitate to mysteries, where it appears there is something to be learned. Further, a person has a natural tendency to seek out novelty. He becomes bored if there is too much sameness around him. He cannot learn as much from unvarying experience as he can from new situations. So he desires a certain amount of change. A person wants and needs problems to solve and a certain number of unknowns in his environment in order to continue to learn and expand his knowledge. Otherwise, he is quite unhappy.

Balancing Pleasure, Order, and Heuristics

In organizing experience so as to maximize its empowering characteristics, a person will have to balance each criterion against the others. Excessive emphasis on beauty or pleasure may be a distraction from, and hence inconsistent or incongruous with, an orderly and heuristic life. A person at work could spend her time admiring or taking pleasure in her fellow employees. There

---

16. For instance, in talking about slips of the tongue, Freud attacks the notion that they are mere random events. He asserts, "It is my assumption that the [slip] is not left to psychic arbitrariness, but that it follows lawful and rational paths." [Freud, S. *The Psychopathology of Everyday Life*, Tr. A.A. Brill (Mentor Books, New York, 1958), p. 9].

1. PLEASURE

    a. Relief
    b. Aesthetics

2. ORDER

    a. Simplicity
        i.   Non-complexity
        ii. Continuity
        iii. Scope
        iv. Ease
        v.   Predictability
    b. Stability
        i.   Precedent or habit
        ii. Predictability
        iii. Controllability
    c. Congruity
        i. Logical consistency
        ii. Fitness or alignment

3. HEURISTICS

    a. Intelligibility
    b. Potential for future knowledge
    c. Novelty

Figure 23. The criteria for organizing experience.

is nothing intrinsically wrong with her doing so, but she also needs
to be task-oriented in order to avoid the disorder that would
result from losing her job. A person likes to live an orderly life
but will break her schedule in order to learn something (as when
she goes to a seminar) or to have some pleasure (as when she
takes a vacation). Otherwise, life gets boring or painful. A person who is fixated on learning (a "grind" or a "bookworm") may
need to lighten the intensity of her learning and put some of her
energies into pursuing order and pleasure in order to achieve a
proper balance. A "seeker", whose life is a wonderful learning

experience but excessively disordered, might have to create order by doing what is necessary to acquire a steady job and a home. Ideally, all three criteria — pleasure, order, and heuristics — are maximally satisfied. A person's main striving in life is to achieve that balance.

Note that there are two ways in which a person can act to affect what is "true" for her:

1. A person can engage in *receptive* actions to find truth; she can perceive, understand, intuit, or reframe or reinterpret existing experience to meet the criteria given above.
2. A person can seek (by her *creative* actions) to bring about certain experiences, or to change her world in certain ways, in order to satisfy these criteria.

The first approach might be exemplified by an aesthete who always seems to find a way of looking at existing experience that permits her to see the beauty in it. She can even see beauty in tragedy. It is also exemplified by a scientist, who can spot the hidden order in things, and by a student or teacher, who sees the learning potential in experience. The second approach is exemplified by the action-oriented person, who *makes* things true, by the artist, who *creates* beautiful phenomena, by the physician, who relieves suffering, and by the mathematician, who creates new conceptual realities. All of the person's abilities — both receptive and creative — are thus directed toward modifying or experiencing her world in a more satisfactory manner.

Although I have apparently identified pleasure, order, and heuristics as three separate principles by which a person organizes her experience, these criteria are closely correlated with each other. It is both pleasant and often conducive to learning to have one's world in a reasonable order. Disorder can be both unpleasant and destructive of the concentration needed for efficient learning. Order is also part and parcel of aesthetics: the beauty in aesthetic products consists in the way in which they are ordered. Obversely, pain can be extremely confusing, overwhelming, and disorienting. From the heuristic side, as we learn more, our world becomes more orderly and more pleasant. A great deal of learning has to occur, also, before one can fully appreciate various kinds of art. A child may enjoy music, but she does not have the breadth of enjoyment that a musically trained adult would have. Furthermore, aesthetics are useful in teaching: artfully done visual aids are conducive to learning, and universities go to great expense to maintain a highly aesthetic environment for the students. Theories that have the greatest heuristic value are also generally the most aesthetically appealing and the simplest.

Empowerment, Validity, and Value

The interconnections between pleasure, order, and heuristics are so manifold that it appears as though these three elements are aspects of a single thing, which we could call "empowerment":

> **Definition:** Empowerment is the combination of and balance between pleasure, order, and heuristics that a person seeks to maximize in organizing his experience. It is that, on the world side of the person-world polarity, which corresponds to power on the person side.

The combination of these three elements in the *receptive* action of interpreting and understanding could be called "validity", in that it is a consideration of all these elements that determine what a person will end up accepting as valid:

> **Definition:** Validity is empowerment in experience obtained by receptive actions. A person accepts elements that create the most empowering experience and rejects elements that create a lesser degree of empowerment. A person's view of his world is the most valid one he can piece together, given the available data.

On the other hand, as mentioned above (p. 165), a person also attempts to *create* these elements in his world. One is not, however, normally thought of as *creating* validity. What he does intend to do, by his creative actions, is to change his world so as to make it more *valuable* to him.[17] Thus, the following definition of "value" will serve us well:

Definition: Value is empowerment in experience obtained by creative action. A person strives, by his creative actions, to maximize the value of his world.

The maximizing of validity and value does not involve indiscriminately trying to maximize pleasure, order, or heuristics individually without reference to the other two elements. In his creative actions, a person does not simply try to get as much pleasure as he can, as much order as he can, or as much heuristics (knowledge) as he can. Rather, he tries to get as much pleasure as he can, consistent with also getting a large amount of knowledge and order. He tries to achieve as much order as is consistent with a large amount of knowledge and pleasure. And he tries to learn as much as possible, consistent with also having a high degree of pleasure and order in his life. The Aristotelian "Golden Mean" (the principle of following a middle path between extremes) definitely applies to each of these elements.

The same is true for a person's receptive actions. A person does not arrive at the most valid world-view by:

1. Believing what is most pleasant, without regard to whether that belief increases order and heuristics in his world-view.
2. Accepting a certain view of the world just because it is orderly, regardless of whether it is elegant or permits him further personal growth.
3. Being a perpetual seeker or mystic and remaining oblivious to questions of order and aesthetics.

A person may become overbalanced in one direction or another, but this does not mean he doesn't *seek* to attain a proper balance.[18]

---

17. This fact has implications in the field of economics, as pointed out by Ludwig von Mises in *Human Action* (Contemporary Books, Chicago, 1963).
18. People join mass movements or cults because these promise to put a great deal of order into their worlds. But this order is often bought at the expense of a massive sacrifice of heuristics and pleasure. Individual thinking

People are far from arbitrary in what they accept as empowering (valid or valuable). They follow certain definite criteria, including the three organizational criteria given above. Individuals, of course, have their own specific criteria for what is valid and valuable, in addition to, or as an elaboration of, these major criteria. It does help to know the criteria that a particular person is using to organize his world, especially if one wants to offer him new experiences or new concepts. It is also helpful to know that changing an established viewpoint can be stressful for a person. Knowing that, one can put one's attention on doing what is necessary to eliminate the stress so that the person can afford to look at the new concept.

Certain schemas or systems of thought have proven quite useful to people in organizing their worlds. The physical sciences, for instance, provide a frame of reference that promises a great deal of order — simplicity, congruity, familiarity, continuity, predictability, and ease — and thus they are rightly highly favored. Before the advent of the physical sciences, things were often explained as being "God's Will". This is, indeed, a *simple* explanation in itself, but unless you happen to have a way of knowing what God's will *is* at any particular time, and a way of influencing God, you will have trouble planning for the future. The concept of an objective universe governed by natural laws was a great improvement on the concept that everything happened solely by God's will, in that it meant that a person could predict and control her experience to a much greater degree. Theurgy is a more difficult and less predictable discipline than metallurgy!

Nevertheless, the physical sciences are now increasingly being found to have insufficient *scope* to align or order a major part of experience. They do not do well in predicting or ordering *mental*

---

and intelligence is subordinated to the viewpoint of the leader, and pleasures and aesthetics are frowned upon as distractions from the "all-important" purposes of the group.

entities, for instance, and these are much closer to a person than physical ones and form a major and very important part of a person's life. Nor is the physical science model particularly helpful in improving the aesthetic quality of the world. And, as I mentioned earlier,[19] it is not useful in providing a basis for personal enhancement. It does have heuristic value, but only in the physical areas that lie within its scope. Its physicalistic assumptions preclude its use in learning about non-physical experiences. Hence the relatively recent interest in different psychologies, spirituality, and Eastern religions as possible paradigms for understanding mental experience. And hence the need for metapsychology as a discipline of more general scope.

Falsehood

I have previously asserted that what is true for a person is what she believes with certainty and that what is false for her is what she disbelieves with certainty. I have also stated that even *within* a particular person's world, there are various degrees of truth. Is there any sense, though, in which we can speak of a person believing things that are not true, even for herself? Is there any sense in which a concept can be false for a person, and yet she can believe it? It seems that it would be useful to speak in these terms. Although I do not think that any *particular* belief of mine is false, I acknowledge the possibility — or even the likelihood — that one or more of my current beliefs may be false. It seems impossible that I could be right about *everything*. Yet I do believe what I believe.

The answer to this riddle is to consider the effect of time. From the point of view of a person (the person-centered viewpoint):

---

19. Beginning of Chapter One, pp. 11-13.

A person never *has* a false belief; she only *had* false beliefs.

The concept of unawareness is crucial to this idea. It is through *becoming aware* of new data and relationships amongst data that a person revises, discards, and acquires beliefs. We generally say that another person has a false belief when we think that if that person becomes more aware, she will then change her beliefs, perceiving the falsity of the belief she had when she was *less* aware. In other words, we think, in this case, that if the person looked at various parts of her world, she would revise her *belief* in the "false" concept to a *dis*belief in that concept. And the same is true for me concerning my own beliefs. When I say I probably have some false beliefs, I am actually saying that I am likely to become aware of certain things that will cause me to reject some of the concepts I currently accept.

The notion that a person can have false beliefs is therefore similar to the notion that a person can do something unintentionally. The real meaning of the phrase "unintentional act", is "a consequence of an act the person would have foreseen, and therefore avoided, if she were fully aware of all relevant data".[20] By saying or implying that there are certain "unconscious" truths that a person can discover, we are asserting that there are certain concepts that a person will hold to be true if her awareness increases in a certain way. If a therapist says that you have "unconscious hatred" for your father, she is predicting that if your awareness of your relationship to your father increases, you will then know (or believe) that you hate him.[21] A statement about false belief can be regarded as a prediction concerning a concept a person

---

20. In Chapter Two (pp. 93-95), I pointed out that people don't perform unintentional acts, but that they may perform *involuntary* acts.
21. As I will explain in Chapter Eight, this type of therapeutic assertion is counter-productive. See the sections on interpretation and evaluation in The Rules of Facilitation, pp. 387-388.

currently holds to be true. The prediction is that if a person becomes aware of what is in a particular area, she will then cease to accept that concept as true.

So a person's idea that another person has false beliefs means:

1. She does not agree with the other person's current beliefs.

and possibly:

2. The other person's beliefs are based on an unawareness of certain data.

"False belief" is therefore defined as follows:

> **Definition**: A <u>false belief</u> is a belief based on unaware-ness of entities with which it is incongruent.

For instance, if my daughter thinks a bright purple and orange poster is beautiful, I may consider that a false belief simply because I do not agree. If she says, "I hate you!", I will probably take that as a falsehood because I know she is blotting out many experiences of love and affection in order to make that statement. I know that when she "wakes up" from her tantrum, she will feel differently. If she asserts, "Two plus three equals seven," it is a falsehood in both senses, because I will be able to demonstrate to her that putting two marbles together with three other marbles actually produces *five* marbles.

A negative judgment about another's beliefs can be mitigated by a willingness to reconsider that judgment.[22] Considering is a basic ability. Having considered and reached a conclusion, one ought to be able to make another consideration and possibly come up with another conclusion, i.e., to change one's mind. The abil-ity to change one's mind, to reconsider, is extraordinarily valu-able. An inability or unwillingness to reconsider, or to consider again, is a grave liability since it leads to fixed ideas and stuck

---

22. I am indebted to Peter Rowell for bringing up this point.

identities. A person ought to be able to reconsider his own beliefs when they differ from another's. He should be able to "step back" from the assumption that either his *or* the other's beliefs are true or false. Having done so, he can look — ideally *with* the other person — at the data from which these beliefs were derived. Then he can decide anew on the truth or falsity of the beliefs in question. Improving a person's ability to reconsider is one of the chief concerns of personal enhancement. Many — perhaps most — of the barriers and unsolved problems a person finds himself confronted with in life consist of his own fixed ideas, such as "I'll never be happy", "All men (or women) are untrustworthy", "I'll always be an alcoholic", or "Everyone's in it for the money." Reconsidering a basic fixed idea can cause dramatic and beneficial changes in a person's life.

In seeking to help others, it is particularly fruitful to look at false beliefs as being based on an unawareness of certain things. A facilitator (one who helps another to gain personal enhancement) is supposed to help another person discover the truth about himself and the world and eliminate false concepts. She helps the person establish a view of his world — or a new belief or knowledge about his world — that is based on a greater degree of awareness and conceptual and perceptual ability. The greater "truth" that the facilitator is aiming for, then, is the world the person will have from the viewpoint of a higher degree of ability and awareness. The "falsehood" the facilitator is dispelling is the old world the person lived in because of his relative degree of inability and unawareness.

Nevertheless, an integral part of any effective personal enhancement technique must be that the therapist or facilitator *never* evaluates information for the person; she never tells the person what his new, improved world is to look like. She does not tell the person what it is that he is to discover when he becomes more aware. All of the facilitator's efforts are directed merely toward increasing the degree of awareness. What the person then perceives and comes to believe is for the person himself to discover.

Cardinality

Some parts of experience play a central role in furthering the value and validity of a person's world; other parts have a more peripheral role. Those that are more central are called "important" or "cardinal" parts of experience.

A person may have discovered that in order to avoid social discomfort, embarrassment, or confusion, she has to assume a particular identity — as in my earlier example of my "having" to be a psychiatrist (pp. 26-27). This identity thus becomes "important" to a person, because it is necessary to her sense of well-being. Other things, such as the car she drives or the food she eats, are of secondary importance because she could drive a different car or eat other food without being uncomfortable. An identity that becomes too important to a person can become fixed.

A musician's views on how to perform a trill may be quite central or important to her life, while for others the technique of trilling may be quite peripheral. For an athlete, being in good physical condition is very important. For a society matron, the idea of what constitutes a successful social event may be quite important. A sudden challenge to one of these central entities can be quite upsetting or even catastrophic to a person since the challenge threatens to throw her experience into confusion, pain, or stultification. I shall call these central, important entities "cardinal points":

> **Definition**: A cardinal point is a part of a person's world that, because of its tendency to promote pleasure, order, and heuristics, or because of its relationship to her intentions, has importance for the person.

Something that consistently brings order into a confusion will tend to be a cardinal point. Thus executives and managers tend to be thought of as important. A significant source of pleasure or beauty in the middle of pain or ugliness can be cardinal to a person — for instance, a handsome or pleasant man or a beautiful or enchanting woman. Movie stars, girlfriends, boyfriends, and spouses tend to be important or cardinal for this reason, along with great works of art or other beautiful or pleasurable things.

A great teacher, sage, or guru, or a great scientist may be a cardinal point because of her heuristic value, i.e., her value as a source of knowledge.

So obviously another person can be important (cardinal) to a person. A mother is usually a cardinal point for her young child because without her there would be a great deal of confusion, pain, and ignorance in the child's life. Indeed, any "significant others" have this characteristic of cardinality.

An authority is a cardinal point for a person insofar as he is a source of information, control, pleasure, or relief from pain. A person can be important to me without necessarily being viewed by me as an authority, but an authority is always important to me. What separates authorities from other important people in my life is that I have found that taking their suggestions or obeying their orders is beneficial to me. When they ask me to do something or agree to something (i.e., to accept something as factual), I find that compliance results in more knowledge, order, and pleasure (or at least absence of pain) in my experience. To the degree that obeying an authority seems to result in pleasure or the avoidance of pain, I will tend to continue obeying. So long as I find that accepting the views of an authority brings order into my world-view because of their simplicity and congruity and that it enhances my knowledge to accept these views and to accept the authority as such, then I will continue to do so.

People have a very strong impulse to rely on authorities, and that impulse is well-founded. Indeed, as Nelson Goodman asserts:

> "The many stuffs — matter, energy, waves, phenomena — that worlds are made of are made along with the worlds. But made from what? Not from nothing, after all, but *from other worlds*. Worldmaking as we know it always starts from worlds already on hand; the making is a remaking."[23]

If one is going to construct a world, one has to start from somewhere and, as Polanyi points out:

"The learner, like the discoverer, must believe before he can know. But while the problem-solver's fore-knowledge expresses confidence in himself, the intimations followed by the learner are based predominately on his confidence in others; and this is an acceptance of authority."[24]

In acquiring knowledge, therefore, a person begins by accepting the authority of teachers and parents. In this way, he acquires a stable world to build on.

Ideally at various points in a person's history a miracle occurs: the person gains independence from authorities he formerly accepted without question. His world reaches a point where it has enough order and content to enable the person to find other cardinal points in it beside authorities, and he finds that he can actually achieve greater pleasure, order, and knowledge by making his own construction and synthesis of the world — instead of continuing to rely on an authority to do it for him. This happens not just during childhood and adolescence, but repeatedly in a person's life. Whenever we enter an area of experience that is quite new to us, such as when we are acquiring a new skill, we have, at first, to be willing to accept the authority of our teachers. When we have learned enough, we can be "weaned" and can take over control of the area for ourselves. The process of skillful teaching consists in a gradual turning over of control and determinism from the teacher to the student. When the student has full control, he graduates.

Hypnosis might be said to work in this way. A hypnotist establishes a trance by getting the subject to agree, for the time

---

23. Goodman, N. *Ways of World Making* (Bobbs-Merrill, Indianapolis, 1978) p. 6 [Italics Goodman's].
24. Polanyi, M. *Personal Knowledge* (University of Chicago Press, 1962), p. 208.

being, to accept her, or her statements, as his sole reference point or cardinal point. In other words, by agreement, the hypnotist becomes the sole authority for that person at that time. Once this agreement is made in the context of the hypnotic session, everything the hypnotist asserts will be taken as literally true. The subject will restructure his experience — even to the point of hallucinating some phenomena and becoming oblivious to others — to fit the hypnotist's declarations. The profound sense of peace and relaxation that is often experienced in hypnosis is just the person's response to a great — if temporary — ordering of his experience. This is the same feeling one gets at being "converted" to a new, all-encompassing, religion. Hypnosis is just a mini-conversion experience. Or we could say that conversion is a form of hypnosis.

It is possible for a person to assign cardinality quite arbitrarily to any point in a confusion so as to bring order into the confusion. Generally, a person will prefer *any* point of reference to complete confusion.

Exercise 15. Assigning Cardinal Points

1. Listen to a Bach fugue (or other contrapuntal music with three or more parts) with which you are not very familiar.
2. Listen to the same piece again. This time, single out for your attention one particular part or instrument.
3. Listen to the same piece a third time, singling out a different part or instrument.

You will note that though the piece may have been a bit confusing to you on the first go-round, putting your attention on one part as a cardinal point for the whole piece will greatly enhance your understanding of the piece. Note, too, that you can equally well understand the piece with a different cardinal point. You can use this technique of singling out a part of a confusion as a cardinal point in many different real-life situations. If you are lecturing to a group of people, it is often helpful to single out some one person and talk to her, then single out another person and talk to her. This will tend to place order into the process of public speaking and make it easier. Most cardinal points in a person's experience are not consciously chosen in this way, but it is a useful thing to know how to do.

Needless to say, a person will strongly deny and resist any assertion that tends to undermine one or more of her cardinal points, and she will be strongly motivated to accept as true any assertion that reinforces her existing cardinal points. To attack someone's cardinal points without helping her to find new ones is not a very nice thing to do. If you do have to get a person to change a cardinal point, you are well advised to give the person a new one before you destroy the old, or help make it possible for her to find a new one for herself. If you must take away something that has become important to a child, for instance (a toy, perhaps, that needs to be washed), it is best to get the child interested in something else, so that the old toy is no longer as important to her. Then she will not mind if you take it away. It is unlikely that a child — *or* an adult — will give up a major cardinal point without a struggle. If a person firmly believes in Freudianism and it is an important part of that person's life (if, say, she is a Freudian analyst or is undergoing Freudian analysis), you are not going to accomplish anything by trying to get her to disbelieve in Freudian theory. You will only cause an upset unless you have some other cardinal point of equal aesthetic (or pain-relieving), order-inducing, or heuristic force to substitute for Freudianism in his world.

Revolutions are notorious for attacking cardinal points without providing new ones. Revolutionaries are sure that the "old guard" (who are cardinal points for the society) are wrong and evil. Perhaps such revolutionaries are often right. But they usually have no new cardinal point to substitute for the old guard. So the result is often prolonged confusion, unhappiness, and stupidity which as often as not eventually results in a re-establishment of the old pattern by the erstwhile revolutionaries. Napoleon was a champion of the French Revolution, promising "Liberty, Equality, and Fraternity", yet he ended up imitating — and, in fact, outdoing — the royalty of France (who only had *kings*) by making himself an *Emperor*.

The cardinality of an experience or of a phenomenon determines the *intensity* with which it is experienced. For instance, as I earlier observed (p. 58), the reality of, or the degree of belief in, an entity varies from impossibility through possibility to certainty. But if something is a cardinal point, the question of its reality takes on a greater intensity. My certainty about my driver's license number is high, but this number has no particular intensity in my world because it does not really matter to me what the actual number is. Similarly, I do not think there have been any arachnids with wings, but this uncertainty has little intensity for me. It would have greater intensity if I were an entomologist. On the other hand, my daughter's love for me (or lack of it) does affect me strongly because she is a cardinal point for me (a "*significant* other"). Being uncertain about my daughter's love would be intensely upsetting and disturbing in a way that being uncertain about my driver's license number would not be. We do, in fact, like to be certain about our cardinal points. Some important metapsychological techniques are designed to increase this certainty and to increase the ability to give up false or fixed cardinal points and find better ones.

Closeness and Affinity

Affinity is defined as follows:

Definition: Affinity is the impulse toward closeness.

But what does "closeness" mean, in this context? Closeness can be physical — and we often like to be physically near things and people we like. But the closeness that concerns us here is closeness in *identity*. This could be regarded as closeness in the fifth dimension of experience — the subjective-objective dimension that stretches between the person and his world.[25] As you approach someone or something along this dimension, it comes closer to being a part of you. If you were to reach it, you would have identified yourself with it or *become* it, in a sense that depends on whether you are dealing with an object or a person.

There are two kinds of affinity:

1. Affinity for people.
2. Affinity for entities (such as valued possessions).

Affinity for People

I will refer to affinity for people as "affection". "Affection" describes a relationship between people: a willingness, or even a wish, to approach the viewpoint of another — to see the world that another sees, to share a viewpoint, to commune with another. Affection can include a desire for physical closeness. The closer you are to someone physically, the closer your physical viewpoint approximates his. But the same applies to mental viewpoints. If you could occupy exactly the same viewpoint as another — i.e., if you could occupy the same mental and physical space — you would have to *be* that person (and he would have to be you). So we could say that one has affection for another person to the degree that one wishes to share an identity with that person. Putting these considerations together, we have:

Definition: Affection is the wish to be close to another person, to share a common space, viewpoint, and identity.

---

25. See Chapter Three, the section on the polar dimension, pp. 126-133.

Affection has a negative counterpart — "disaffection":

> **Definition**: Disaffection is the characteristic of being
> unwilling to be close to another person, to share a space,
> viewpoint, or identity with him.

A high degree of affection is referred to as "love", whereas a
high degree of disaffection might be called "hatred".

Affinity for Impersonal Entities

What about affinity toward an impersonal entity, such as an
object or event? We may speak loosely of "loving cappucino" or
"loving to ski", but we are aware that quite a different relationship exists, here. This kind of affinity might be thought of as a
willingness and readiness to be physically close to an object, such
as a painting. If I have affinity for cappucino, I want it around, at
least at times. But that isn't always the case. I have a great deal
of affinity for the Eiffel tower, but I am quite willing to have it be
in Paris and not in my back yard. And I'm rather fond of the sun
and moon, but I don't necessarily want to *live* in either place.
Furthermore, there are three kinds of entity: phenomena, facts,
and concepts. I may have affinity, not only for phenomena, but
also for concepts or facts. I have affinity for the potential fact
that Russia will sort out its internal difficulties. The affinity I
have for internal peace in Russia is not a desire to be close to that
peace. I may have affinity for the idea of a unified field theory
without necessarily wanting to think about it all the time.
Another view of the second sort of affinity is that it is a wish
for or an impulse toward *having* something. If I have affinity for
the sun and moon, or for Van Gogh paintings, I wish to have
them become part of my world and continue to be part of my
world. In other words, I wish to have access to and/or influence
over them, where:

> **Definition**: Access is the ability to engage in receptive
> actions with respect to an entity.

and

> **Definition**: Influence is the ability to engage in creative actions with respect to an entity.

In other words, I want to be causative (or to be able to act) with respect to those entities for which I have affinity.[26]

How does the notion of *having* fit in with the notion of fifth-dimensional closeness mentioned above (pp. 178-179)? When I *have* something very thoroughly, I am (by definition) capable of exercising a great deal of causation over it. And in this case, it can become functionally a part of me — become incorporated in an identity of mine. If my body is well-trained and healthy and I can therefore be very causative over it, it tends to become a part of me, rather than part of my environment. I need not, and do not, put attention on it. My focus of attention moves outward, and the body becomes part of "self", rather than "other". So it is with anything that is thoroughly "had". It becomes so thoroughly permeated with my identity that it becomes a part of me, and I, in turn, enjoy a sense of personal expansion in having something to that degree. I have it to such a degree that I am no longer aware of having it. It disappears from the foreground of consciousness. It is a curious paradox that thoroughly having something causes it to vanish, experientially.

"Having", then, can also be defined as follows:

> **Definition**: Having is (fifth dimensional) closeness to an entity.

---

26. See the section on "having" in Chapter Two, pp. 60-67.

Desire and Abhorrence

Can we now think of another term to stand for the affinity we have toward entities (things)? I believe the term "desire" serves very well:

Definition: Desire is the impulse toward having or continuing to have an entity.

Like affection, desire has a negative counterpart, which we shall call "abhorrence":

Definition: Abhorrence is the impulse toward rejecting or continuing to not have an entity.

A high level of desire could be expressed as "yearning" whereas a high level of abhorrence could be called "loathing". An absence of abhorrence could be called a willingness to have.

Parenthetically, one could say that, to the degree one *desires* another person, one is looking at that person as a thing — an entity — whereas to the degree that one has *affection* for another person, one is viewing that person as a conscious being. There is a definite qualitative difference between love and yearning; affection and desire; disaffection and abhorrence; hatred and loathing. The first of each of these pairs has a personal quality; the second is impersonal.

Affinity and Importance

A second parameter crosses affinity at right angles to it: importance. A person or entity may be more or less important to a person, i.e., it (or he) may be more or less of a cardinal point for that person. It is the importance factor that gives *intensity* to affinity as, earlier in this chapter (p. 178), we saw it gave intensity to reality. Affinity, dislike, or the middle ground between, i.e., ambivalence, can thus be mild or intense depending on the importance factor. Ambivalence, for example, can be extraordinarily intense and uncomfortable in close personal relationships or in important job situations. At the other extreme of intensity, a person can be ambivalent about something like a movie, but it is not an intense experience — just a mild uncertainty about whether one likes it or not. Similarly, love or hate can be mild ("I love Alan Alda," "I hate Victor Mature."). Affinity, one might say, is the "pitch" and importance is the "volume". As importance fades, love tapers off into a mild aesthetic appreciation while hatred becomes a sort of mild dislike, yearning becomes a slight preference, loathing becomes a slight disinclination, and ambivalence fades into indifference.

Closeness and the Emotional Scale

In Chapter Three (pp. 138-145), I defined the Emotional Scale as a scale of success, ranging from final success to final failure. But this scale can also be regarded as a scale of affinity. One's emotional level reflects the degree to which one *has* what one desires. That is just another way of describing success. Although I described the Emotional Scale as a scale of "How well am I doing?", I could equally well have described it as a scale of "To what degree am I getting what I want?" A person is enthusiastic about an activity when he believes he is getting closer to his objective; he has negative emotion (is ambivalent, antagonistic, angry, fearful, or sad) about an activity when he feels he is getting farther away from it. "How well am I doing?" is thus just a special case of closeness, and closeness is primary.

As a person becomes more and more successful in performing an action, he *has* that action to a greater and greater degree. And he comes closer and closer to extending his identity to incorporate that action as part of himself, as outlined earlier (p. 181). If I am successful at learning a certain chord on the guitar, then after I have been completely successful, I can now include that skill as part of my identity as a musician. I have already noted that elation is the point when a success is of sufficient magnitude to allow for an expansion of identity. The highest degree of closeness one could have to something is to *be* it — to incorporate it as part of self.

In order for a part of experience to persist, the degree to which one *has* that part of experience — and one's emotional level with respect to it — must be moderate — not off the top or the bottom of the scale. As I have mentioned, an extremely high emotion (elation) occurs when there is a final success and an incorporation of something as part of oneself. When that happens, the thing seems to disappear. Hence, "too high" an emotion causes an experiential disappearance. On the other hand, "too low" an emotion (too much "distance") likewise causes a vanishment. A person will shy away from things that he dislikes excessively by becoming unconscious of them or otherwise "going away" from them or getting rid of them. The Emotional Scale (in addition to being a scale of power/debilitation, having/not having, and closeness/distance) is therefore also a scale of awareness/unawareness and creativity/non-creativity. At the higher levels, one allows oneself to be more and more aware of something until one is so aware that one "sees through" the thing, and the thing is no longer apparent. Or one gets better and better at doing a task until one incorporates that task as a skill, and is no longer aware of "doing" the task. Instead, one does something else *via* the task. In other words, the task becomes incorporated into oneself as a subsidiary action. At the bottom of the scale, one becomes more and more unwilling and unable to receive something, until one suppresses awareness of the thing altogether. Or one becomes less and less able to create something, until one gives up on it altogether and stops trying to create it. Whether one goes off the top or the bottom of the scale, that aspect of experience disappears.

Affinity, admiration, or pleasure — all these manifestations can lead to a disappearance, through incorporation, of the admired object, identity, or activity. As discussed in Chapter One (pp. 49-52), if a person has a great deal of power, things tend to vanish. An identity never sees *itself*, so if a person is so willing to *be* something that she can *become* it, when she *has* become it, it no longer exists for her. You might say that she *lives* it. An object that is thoroughly admired can become a familiar part of oneself. One may become only "subliminally" aware of it, and it can seem to vanish. An action for which one has a lot of affinity — cooking, for instance — can likewise become incorporated as something one does without noticing that one is doing it. Desire is thus a transition state toward the state of incorporation that occurs when the resultant *having* reaches a certain high level.[27]

Likewise, aversion could be regarded as a transitory state toward getting rid of something (or becoming unaware of it if we cannot get rid of it), which can occur when a certain level of distance is achieved. The tendency to become unaware of entities that are too painful ("repression", to use Freud's term) is the source of the majority of human suffering. Fortunately, there are some very effective techniques for undoing repression and alleviating emotional pain, some of which will be outlined in later chapters.

Paradoxically, it seems that the more aversion one has for receiving, creating, or being something, the more one tends to receive, create, or be it. In Chapter One (pp. 49-51), I pointed out that it is resistance to perception, understanding, or causation that causes entities to be experienced. We now see that the resistance may come from the *person's* side of the polarity in the form of an unwillingness (or aversion). Such resistance can also create immutability, unintelligibility, and opacity. An unwillingness to perceive something actually makes it more opaque, an unwillingness to understand something makes it less intelligible, and an unwillingness to change something makes it less mutable — to the unwilling person. So I can say, "What you resist, you tend to receive," and "What you resist creating, you tend to keep on

---

27. Of course, it is also possible to "step back" from something that we have incorporated and admire it. As a matter of fact it is *necessary* to be at a certain distance from something to admire it — or, indeed, to perceive it at all. There is a difference between the desire we have for something and *having* the thing that is desired. Desire can be very intense and yet remain present and unfulfilled, but when having reaches a certain level, one paradoxically no longer *has* the entity in question but *becomes* that entity.

creating." You have to be willing to perceive something before you can see through it (cause it to vanish, experientially). You have to be willing to change something (make a change) before you are done with it. Otherwise, it is an incomplete receptive or creative cycle. And, it turns out, you have to be willing to *be* something before you can *not* be it.

The psychoanalytical literature is full of instances of "identification with the aggressor". If we translate this phenomenon into metapsychological terms, we have: "Whom you resist being, you tend to become." If you have a low enough affection for someone and if there is a sufficient degree of intensity (importance) in the relationship, you tend to *become* that person (as a fixed identity). We find people who hated their parents becoming like their parents. Children of child abusers, it has been found, tend to be child-abusers themselves. While a person may or may not tend to emulate significant others she loves, she will *perforce* tend to emulate those she hates. People complain of qualities in others that they themselves possess, a fact that accounts for such classic statements as: "People are so cynical! They are just out for the Almighty Dollar," "I hate people who are antagonistic!", or "All men are the same — they have a stereotyped view of women." You do not become the identity that the hated person conceives *herself* to be, but rather the identity that *you* conceive her to be. Since people are usually aware only of the worst qualities of the people they hate, those are the qualities that they then tend to emulate. It is unfortunate but true that people's worst characteristics are often the most contagious.

A person's *resistance* to things is abhorrence; her *striving* for things is desire. One can, without abhorrence, choose for various reasons not to receive, be, or create something, without ill effect. I love steaks, but I can choose not to have one now. I can love being a musician but not choose to be one now, and I can love racing cars and choose not to race just this moment. But when one tries to avoid something out of abhorrence, then the above mechanism is activated, and one finds oneself with a greater or lesser tendency to be stuck with that thing, depending on the intensity or importance factor.

It is a peculiarity, then, that a person's world tends to fill up with objects, identities, and actions to which he has an abhorrence if his abhorrence is great enough so that he does not confront those things and *actually* get rid of them or change them. If a student has such an abhorrence of homework that he does not do it, he has more and more homework to do. If a person cannot confront the disorder in his life, he gets more and more disorder. A person has an impulse to repress things for which he has an abhorrence. In order to get rid of such things, he must, paradoxically, allow himself to become *aware* of them.

On the other hand, one tends not to notice things that do not offer resistance to one's actions by being painful, jarring, or problematical. A bodily feeling of well-being is usually only noticed in contrast to a prior feeling of malaise. When a person has been well for a period of time, he does not notice the wellness of his body. A car that is easy to drive tends to be readily incorporated as a part of oneself. It does not draw itself to one's attention while one is driving it. The desirable things that one has tend not to be noticed unless one steps back to admire them. Undesirable things that one has — things that are not admired — tend to stand out in a situation, as illustrated by the fact that one can draw attention to a word by missspppeling it. Note how the transparency of the words in this paragraph suddenly changes to opacity on the word "missspppeling", while all the correctly spelled words go unnoticed.[28]

---

28. Did you notice the correct spellings of "spell" in earlier chapters (pp. 50, 59)?

Desire and Ability

Just because one desires something does not mean one thinks one is able to attain that thing. As a teen-ager, I was often overwhelmed with a desire for carnal knowledge of the body of Kim Novak, Marilyn Monroe or Brigitte Bardot, without having any illusions about my ability to satisfy this desire by any form of direct action. By excruciating personal experience, I learned that desire and despair may co-exist. Indeed, despair cannot exist without desire.

Understanding

In order to satisfy a desire, one must be *able* to do so. But how does one become able? By acquiring and using creative and receptive abilities — in other words, by attaining understanding and control. The ultimate result of all receptive actions is an act of understanding. We perceive phenomena, interpret these phenomena in various ways so as to arrive at various concepts, and then decide whether to accept one or more of these concepts as factual. At the point where we determine the facts, we can be said to have understood the situation.

There are three basic receptive actions: perception gives us phenomena, interpretation gives us concepts, and considering these concepts and accepting one or more of them gives us a fact or facts. Understanding is the entire transition from existing data (facts or phenomena) to new facts. Thus understanding is the final product of receptive actions.

The act of understanding consists of four parts, the major components of the learning cycle that we discussed earlier in this chapter (pp. 153-156):

1. An interpretation of a datum, resulting in
2. a concept, that is
3. tested or verified, and
4. accepted as factual.

In this sense of "understanding" — because of (4) — the result of understanding is the acceptance of a fact. We *know* (or believe with certainty) what we understand about entities. In another sense of the word "understand", however, one can "understand" a communication without the concept received necessarily being agreed with or thought of as factual. In the latter sense, "understanding" is merely a conceptual sharing. I choose to use the term "comprehension" to carry this meaning, reserving the term "understanding" for our present usage:

> **Definition:** Understanding is the combination of interpretation and acceptance that results in a new fact, a conclusion.

whereas

> **Definition:** Comprehension is the act of correctly identifying the concept or experience that an originator of a communication intends to convey.[29]

---

29. Failing to make this distinction between the two meanings of "understand" has some interesting — and undesirable — consequences. If we conceive that understanding must always mean conceptual sharing with another being, then we must regard all our knowledge as coming from another being out there somewhere. In this interpretation, we must assume that there is a Being who sends us all the phenomena that we do not recognize as clearly coming from other people like ourselves. In other words, this Being, generally thought of as God, sends us the physical universe, or its manifestations, as a message that we must interpret in the way that He intends us to interpret it. This is one way of reintroducing the notion of an "absolute physical universe", albeit a different way from that of the physical sciences. It is based on a Supreme Being with an absolute set of concepts, instead of an absolute physical reality. In this view, a correct interpretation of God's message gives us truth and reality and an incorrect interpretation gives us falsity and illusion. In other words, understanding, in this view, is conceptual sharing with God.

If we always assume that "understanding" (in the sense of comprehending a communication) must result in *acceptance* of what is understood, then we have a difficulty: with this definition of "understanding", whenever one truly understands what another person is communicating, one has to see the truth of it, or agree with it! This can lead to an unfortunate situation if one honestly does not agree with another person about something. In this situation, even if you *comprehend* the concept she is giving you, she can continue to claim you must not be *understanding* her since you do not agree. You then find yourself in an intolerable situation in which you continue indefinitely to feel very stupid and frustrated because you are not able to "understand". Worse yet, in desperation you may decide to agree (against your better judgment) in order to get out of the bind, thus giving yourself an incongruity (because you do not really agree). This situation is most likely to arise with authoritarian communications in which there is a strong insistence on agreement or even a penalty for disagreement. The authority in question may have a vested interest in equating understanding with agreement.

Bishop Berkeley took this approach in his statement that to exist is to perceive or to be perceived. God, according to Berkeley, sends us perceptions and thus in a single act gives us existence and creates a world for us. God also, helpfully, keeps those parts of the world in existence that no one happens to be looking at, at a certain time. Plato's view also fits this model. He saw the visible world as a mere appearance (like shadows on the wall of a cave) which reflects an "absolute" world of Ideals, or Forms, (possibly in God's mind?). Hence our world could be seen as a "communication" from (or of) the Platonic Ideals, and we should correctly interpret our experiences as reflections of these Forms. In fact, any absolutistic view of the universe, such as that of Newtonian physics, contains the idea that there is a reality "out there" that is completely separate from us, but that "communicates" to us via phenomena, and our interpretations are true to the degree that they reflect the "true" physical forms that are "out there". The only difference between this view and Berkeley's or Plato's is that the physical universe plays the role of God: it keeps our worlds in existence and gives us existence. It is thus only a short step from absolute materialism to pantheism.

These rather interesting difficulties can be avoided by using the term "comprehend", rather than "understand", to apply to the act of getting the meaning of a communication.

Control

As understanding is basic to receptive actions, so control is basic to creative actions. In order to create, one must control aspects of the world. To conceive a concept, picture a mental image, or postulate a fact one must be able to control one's mind, and to make things happen in the physical universe one must be able to control physical objects. Any creative act is thus an act of control, and controlling and creating may be regarded as more or less synonymous.

Ability

In acquiring ability, one learns to *control* something. An able officer must be capable of controlling his troops. But this control does him no good unless he also *understands* the tactics and strategy necessary to win battles. He is not an able officer, either, if he has an excellent understanding of strategy and tactics but is unable to control his men. As an armchair politician, I may happen to *understand* perfectly well what it takes to eliminate the federal deficit, but I am not *able* to eliminate it unless I have some degree of *control* over the political process. An ignorant demagogue, on the other hand, may have plenty of political clout, but unless she also *understands* how to eliminate the federal deficit, she is not *able* to eliminate it either. In other words:

Definition: Ability is the potential for action. It is composed of control and understanding.

Note that one may be *able* to do something without either doing it or desiring to do it. I have a good head for figures and good powers of concentration, so I am quite *able* to handle all of my own accounting. But I find it excruciatingly boring, so I prefer to pay someone else to do it instead of me.

Intention — A Combination of Desire and Ability

When you put together desire and ability, however, you then get *intention*. Unlike a desire, an intention requires that one consider oneself potentially able to fulfill it. I cannot intend something that I know I cannot bring about, and I cannot intend something that I do not desire. But I can and *must* intend that which I both desire and feel able to bring about.

I need to make one small point here for the sake of accuracy. One may have an intention which does not eventuate in action if there is some more powerful set of counter-intentions. Such an intention is really only an intention *vector*, not a *resultant* intention that gives rise to action.[30]

As I have said, formulating an intention begins an activity cycle that exists so long as — and only so long as — the intention exists. Thus, intention and action are inextricably bound up with each other. As I have also said, if an action can be regarded as something that stretches from a person to the object of that action — some entity in that person's world — then intention might be regarded as that part of an action that lies nearest to the person (in the fifth dimension), whereas other parts of the action, such as, perhaps, body motions and physical consequences of these motions, lie further away (nearer the world).[31]

These two characteristics of an intention can be combined into a new definition:

---

30. See the section on "The Resultant Intention" in Chapter Two, pp. 92-93.
31. See also pp. 132-133, above.

Definition: Intention is a combination of desire and ability. It is the proximal end of an action being performed by a person.

Drive

In relating to the various entities that make up a person's world, she desires some of them, has aversion to others, creates some, receives others. Ideally, she has a maximum ability to create and receive entities. But ideally, too, she should have a strong and positive regard toward the entities she creates and receives. In Buddhist thought, desire is felt to be an evil.[32] Perhaps in some ultimate sense this is the case, but in ordinary life a person who lacks strong desires is generally listless, weak, and unhappy. She has no "lust for life", does not enjoy life. We say of such a person that she lacks "drive":

Definition: Drive is the ability to desire things or the degree to which one does desire things. It is the level of positive regard toward the world or its parts.

Intention and Power

There are many people who are able to do great things but fail to do so because of lack of drive or ambition. We do not regard such people as powerful. Others have very strong drive

---

32. My friend Dr. Jerry Davis, a student of Buddhist philosophy, tells me that it is not desire but *attachment* — i.e., *fixed* desire — that Buddhists feel must be avoided. If so, their views would accord with mine.

but little ability, and these, too, we do not regard as powerful. Only the *combination* of ability and drive adds up to power, in the common usage of the term.

But note that we have defined *intention* as a combination of desire + ability. It follows, therefore, that intention and power must be closely related concepts. We can, in fact, define "power" (in the sense of "*personal* power") as follows:

Definition: Power is the capacity to intend.

When we think about it, this apparently surprising conclusion makes sense. We conceive of people as having a certain amount of power with which to engage in their daily activities. In Chapter Three (pp. 115-116), I expressed this concept as *elan vitale* or consciousness, but it can also be expressed as being composed of "intention units". At any particular time, a person has only a limited capacity to intend things, a limited number of available "intention units". Much of what we do in viewing is to free up trapped intention units (known as "charge") so that a person becomes more aware and more able to make things happen in the present. But one can also augment the total supply of intention by helping the viewer in other ways such as education. Naturally, as a person becomes more powerful, she becomes more able. But over and above this, she also develops a greater degree of drive, a more expanded lust for life, and this is just as important to her well-being.

Power is a Means, Not an End

I do not mean, here, to glorify power for its own sake. As I shall discuss in the next chapter, the entire purpose for being in a world, with all the entities that it contains, is to use them as a means toward the fulfillment of one's most deeply-seated intention. And that is the intention to attain an ever-increasing degree of communion with one's fellow beings. The universe is meant to be a universe of *discourse*. By becoming more powerful in our dealings with the world, we acquire an enhanced degree of ability to communicate with others and to enhance the well-being of others — which is really the main point of the whole exercise.

The Power Triad — Drive, Control, and Understanding

I have said that power is a combination of ability and drive. But ability is a combination of control and understanding. Power, then, can also be defined as follows:

Definition: Power is the combination of drive, control, and understanding.

Drive, control, and understanding together make up a triad. Increasing one member of this triad increases the other two:

Drive

When one has an increase in drive, one is motivated to engage in a greater number of creative and receptive actions, i.e., to increase one's control and understanding. A person with an intense interest in music will engage in making music and listening to music, where a person who is not interested in music will not.

Control

Control, in turn, augments drive and understanding. Once one has established control over an entity, one has a greater drive towards doing something to or with that entity. We tend to be most enthusiastic about areas of life over which we have the greatest control.

Also, if a person can exercise control with respect to an entity (not necessarily control *of* that entity), he can come to understand it better. What he needs to control in order to achieve greater understanding depends on what he is trying to understand. He may need to control the entity itself, surrounding entities, or his means of perceiving the entity. Being able to control a microscope improves one's ability to see and understand microscopic objects. As I use a guitar more and more, I gain a greater understanding of the instrument and skill in its use. The more control one has in an area, the more understanding will occur in that area.

Understanding With more understanding, one sees more possibilities for control. By understanding the functions of the different parts of an automobile, one is able to control an automobile better. By understanding, one knows which tools to use to achieve which effects.

It is also true that having a greater understanding of a subject enhances one's enthusiasm for that subject (drive). Music appreciation courses enhance one's interest in engaging in musical activities.

Understanding ·········➤ Drive ·········➤ Control

Figure 24. The power triad

The Ascending Power Triad

When one increases one side of the triad, the other two will go up. But when the other two go up, the first side will then also go up, and so you get a positive feedback loop, the result of which (all else being equal) is to cause a greater and greater quantity of all three members of the triad — in other words, a greater quantity of power (see Figure 25). So we can now offer a broader definition of power:

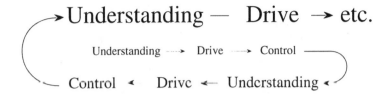

Figure 25. The Ascending Power Triad.

Definition: Power is a combination of drive, understanding, and control that characterizes a person's relationship with the entities that constitute his world. Under normal circumstances, it forms an ascending triad, with an increase in any member of the triad leading to an increase in the other two.

The easiest entry point to this triad is understanding. It is hard to have desire for, or to control, something one does not know anything about and does not understand. But understanding can come from acquiring data in a variety of ways, not just by controlling something. For instance, before I am willing to handle a band saw, I will want to have some data about it. Once I know how it works, how to use it, and what it can do, it will seem both safer and more useful than it did before. In other words, I will now have some desire for it and will be willing and inclined to approach and control it. Then, when I begin to control it successfully, I soon get a *better* understanding of it, and the triad continues to ascend.

Triad of Debilitation

On the other hand, the power triad may go downward. If something happens to make a band saw seem unsafe (e.g., if I cut myself on the saw), then the lowered desire or increased abhorrence that results will lead to a diminished sense of control over the band saw and to a diminished certainty about it (less understanding). If, for some reason, I stop using the band saw (controlling it) then my practical skill and certainty of it (understanding) will diminish and I will not be as willing to deal with it (less drive). Finally, if I forget what I've learned about it (if I have less understanding), or if someone convinces me that I do not know as much about it as I thought I did, then I will have less desire to use the band saw and also less control. This sequence describes a descending triad of *debilitation*.

> **Definition**: Debilitation is a relative absence of drive, control, and understanding with respect to entities. It forms a descending triad, with less drive leading to less control and understanding, less control leading to less understanding and less drive, and less understanding leading to less drive and less control.

Power and Empowerment

An interesting facet of drive, control, and understanding is that they have an intimate relationship with pleasure, order, and heuristics, respectively. The latter are the principles a person uses to decide which interpretation of *experience* to accept or what kind of experience to create.

PERSON		WORLD
Understanding	⬅ ·············· ➤	Heuristics
Drive	⬅ ·············· ➤	Pleasure
Control	⬅ ·············· ➤	Order

Figure 26. Components of power and their worldly counterparts.

From Figure 26, it is obvious that drive is simply that, on the world side of the person-world polarity, which corresponds to pleasure on the person side. Likewise, control corresponds to order and understanding to heuristics. In general, power on the person side corresponds to empowerment on the world side.

The opposite manifestations are shown in Figure 27.

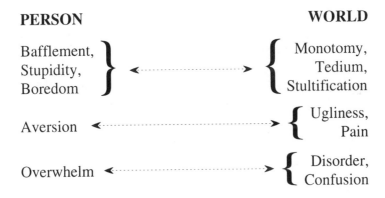

Figure 27. Components of debilitation and their worldly counter-parts.

Entities a person cannot learn from she will see as monotonous, tedious, or stultifying. Those to which the person has an aversion she will see as ugly or painful. Those she is unable to control, by which she is overwhelmed, she will see as disordered or confusing. And, in general, a person feels powerless in areas which contain debilitating elements.

A person will attempt to act so as to bring about a maximum amount of empowerment (pleasure, order, and heuristics, or — equivalently — validity and value) in her life, with respect to her world of entities. Or, to put it differently, a person acts so as to try to enhance her own drive, control, and understanding — that is, her power — as much as possible. Receptive ability or understanding on the person side of the person-world polarity corresponds to validity on the world side; creative ability or control corresponds to value on the world side.

How *successful* a person is in accomplishing these goals, how high a degree of enhancement she will be able to achieve, depends very much on the condition she is in to begin with. Above a certain point (ambivalence on the Emotional Scale), a person will enjoy a gradually or rapidly expanding triad of power and empowerment. Below that point, a person will find the empowerment of her life and her own power decreasing gradually or rapidly. The triad can thus be an ascending power triad or a descending debilitation triad, depending on the person's initial condition. Fortunately, it is possible to help a person who is suffering a descending triad to reverse its direction. In fact the various techniques of applied metapsychology are designed to do just that. But any action that results in a major increase in drive, control, or understanding can help reverse the descending triad.

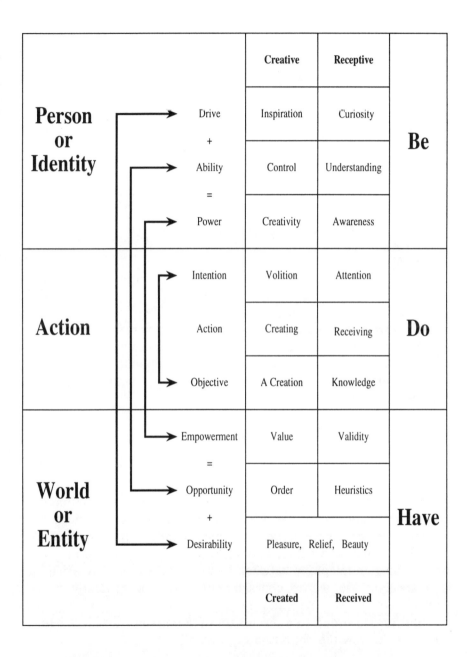

		Creative	Receptive	
Person or Identity	Drive	Inspiration	Curiosity	**Be**
	+			
	Ability	Control	Understanding	
	=			
	Power	Creativity	Awareness	
Action	Intention	Volition	Attention	**Do**
	Action	Creating	Receiving	
	Objective	A Creation	Knowledge	
World or Entity	Empowerment	Value	Validity	**Have**
	=			
	Opportunity	Order	Heuristics	
	+			
	Desirability	Pleasure, Relief, Beauty		
		Created	**Received**	

Figure 28. Summary of person-world correspondences.

Chapter Five

Personal Relationships

I shall now turn from a person's relationship with his world and the various entities comprising it to his relationships with other people. As we shall see, a person's relationship with other people is quite different from the relationship he has with impersonal entities.

Communication

Central to the topic of personal relationships is communication. In dealing with the topic of communication, I wish to include, for the moment, only normal, mundane means of communication such as writing, talking, signaling, etc. There may be such a thing as telepathy between people, but if telepathy exists it is a special case whose characteristics are not generally well-known.

Before I proceed to a discussion of communication, it is helpful first to review the definition of "token":

Definition: A <u>token</u> is a phenomenon that indicates or refers to a concept or (candidate) fact, a phenomenon that has *meaning* to the person perceiving it. The word "red" (spoken or written) is a token that may refer to the concept of a certain wavelength of light or a certain type of visual phenomenon; dark clouds can be a token of rain.

The sentence "The cat is on the mat," presents itself to a person as a phenomenon, such as words written on a blackboard, words printed in a book, or sound waves.[1] This phenomenon exists, and is thus itself an entity, but it also indicates or represents something else: another entity, consisting of a cat on a mat, which may or may not be a phenomenon (or, indeed a fact) for that person at that time. A token, even one used in a communication, need not be symbolic. A TV picture, photograph, or other recording may also be a token, that is, a phenomenon that has a referent or concept connected with it, the referent being that of which it is a picture. Each of the four movements of Vivaldi's "The Seasons" represents or refers to one of the four seasons. Note that the entity whose existence is referred to may or may not really exist, despite its being represented, i.e., it may only be a concept. A picture of Pegasus represents a winged horse, but no such horse exists.

A certain phenomenon may or may not be a token, depending on the context. Suppose a computer malfunctions and puts out reams of paper covered with symbols meaningless to the user. The normal user does not call those symbols "tokens"; he regards them as mere meaningless phenomena, or "garbage". But a systems expert who is debugging the system would very likely regard that printout as containing valuable information. In

---

1. Actually, one could also regard a "sentence" as being something more abstract — a *pattern* that could be expressed as a *variety* of different phenomena, all of which map to the same sequence of phonemes. For our purposes, however, this distinction is not important.

other words, he regards the symbols on that printout as tokens that refer to the state of functioning of the computer, and he will study the printout intensively for what it tells him about the malfunction. Almost *any* phenomenon could be a token. That is, almost any phenomenon could indicate or imply the existence of one or more other entities. Whether it does so in a *specific* context is what determines whether it is a token in that particular context. Whether there is an "explanation" for something at a certain time — and what the nature of that explanation is — depends entirely on the intentions and activities of the person who is aware of that entity, at the specific time in question.

The receiver's way of viewing a phenomenon is really what determines whether a phenomenon is a token or not, and if it is a token, what the token represents. A phenomenon is a token only if it is *viewed* as having a referent, i.e., as signifying a concept. I may say something to you that I intend to be a statement about an entity, but you might not receive it that way, or you might receive it as a statement about a different entity than that to which I intended it to refer. In other words, the referent of the statement for you may be different from what I intended the referent to be. In England, if I say, "I want to go to the bathroom," the natural presumption would be that I want to take a bath or wash up, whereas I might mean that I want to visit the toilet or WC. In this case, the receiver receives an assertion about my desire to bathe, whereas I, being American, meant to give him a statement about wanting to relieve myself. Or I might walk up to someone and say, "*Govoritye po russki?*" and the other person might think I'm talking gibberish, because what I said would not be a token for him. But from my viewpoint, I'm asking him, in Russian, whether he speaks Russian.[2]

---

2. I'm reminded of a rather gruesome story that Thomas Szasz, the great Hungarian-born critic of psychiatry, told about a woman who was kept in a mental hospital for some years because she spoke gibberish. Finally, a Hungarian-speaking visitor discovered she was not crazy at all but was simply speaking Hungarian!

Given this preamble, it is now possible to define communication:

> **Definition:** Communication is the transfer of a token from one person to another, where the concept or phenomenon that the receiver interprets the token as representing is the same as the concept or phenomenon that the originator intended the token to represent.[3]

Note that this is quite a restricted definition. We do not speak, except perhaps by analogy, about "communication" between machines, or between a person and an impersonal entity. The former action is merely a physical interchange of particles, and the latter may be "perception" or "control", but not "communication", as I use the term here.

---

3. This definition, of course, raises certain philosophical problems. From the person-centered viewpoint, for instance, how can one person ever have the *same* token as another? Each is a separate phenomenon appearing to a different person. And the same applies to the apprehension of what the token represents: how can two different people have the same concept or phenomenon? One might take refuge in talking about "equivalent" concepts or phenomena, but I don't think this strategy would really obviate the problem. This problem, to me, is no more nor less mysterious than the difficulty of seeing how different people can communicate at all or share the same world.

Whether one can communicate to animals other than Man depends on whether animals are sapient beings or persons, as we are. If one thinks this a possibility, then one is faced with the task of deciding how far down in the animal kingdom one is going to allow creatures to be considered sapient beings. Is every ant sapient? Every amoeba? Every bacterium or virus? Fortunately, for the purposes of this discussion, we do not have to answer that question.

Components of Communication

Several conditions necessary to the existence of communication are implied in the definition given above. First of all, there must be two persons to participate in each act of communication, not more and not less. This fact is implicit in the idea of a transfer. A transfer is a motion from point **A** to point **B**. It requires a point transferred *from* — an origination point or creation point — and a point transferred *to* — a receipt point. If something stays in the same place (one point), then it has not been *transferred*. So two persons are required, one at each end of the communication channel. On the other hand, the same thing cannot be transferred to more than one other place at the same time. Where one person is talking to more than one other person (as in a lecture situation), multiple acts of communication (or, possibly, *mis*communication) are actually going on, one for each person receiving the communication. What each person in the audience receives as a token — and the concept or phenomenon each gets as an interpretation of that token — may be quite different from what others in the audience are receiving — and different, again, from what the speaker intended. So each transfer must be considered separately on its own merits to determine whether a communication occurred in that case. In other words, a dissemination or distribution of tokens and concepts or phenomena to many people from a single source is accomplished by a number of simultaneous transfers of tokens and sharing of concepts or phenomena. That is, a number of acts of communication are involved.

What else is implied in this definition? The fact that there are two persons, not one, and the fact that a change in space (motion) occurs necessitates a spatial separation between the two viewpoints assumed by the persons, so we say that there must be a *distance* between them.

Third, something travels across the distance from one to the other: the one *sends* a token, while the other *receives* one. This idea is also implicit in the idea of a "transfer of a token".

The token sent must be at least approximately the same as the token received in order for communication to occur. If I run a Christmas tree farm and I say to a customer, "This is the tree," and the customer thinks I said, "This is free," a *mis*communication, rather than a communication, takes place.

Merely receiving the token correctly is not sufficient for a communication to occur. A classic example, from Ripley's *Believe It or Not* is a case of a French general who, after a battle, was complaining about his cold and said, *"Ma sacreé toux!"*, meaning "My damned cough!" His soldiers, however, heard it as *"Massacrez tous"*, meaning "Massacre all of them!", and did so. In this case, the sound received was the same as the sound sent (the two French sentences sound the same), but obviously there was still a miscommunication. Likewise, if I point to a tree and say, "Baum!", you might well be able to hear exactly what I said, but that might not necessarily make it a communication. You might think I mean you are to shoot down the tree or something of the sort. But if you know German, you will know that I am pointing out a tree — stating that a tree is there. This is called *comprehending*[4] the communication, which is equivalent to having the correct interpretation of the phenomenon received as a token, i.e., getting the correct concept or phenomenon — that which the originator intended to communicate. When I hear "Baum" and realize it means the existing entity called a "tree", then, if that was the concept the other person was trying to put across, the communication succeeds. Before I interpret the token, "Baum," it is just a noise.

Note that though I may understand that the other person is asserting the existence of a tree, i.e., that she is stating that a tree is there, that does not necessarily mean I *agree* that a tree is there

---

4. Note that I do not speak of "understanding" the communication. This is in order to avoid ambiguities in the word "understand". When we say we "understand" something, that often is taken to mean that we view an underlying *truth* about it. Here, I am only talking about viewing the underlying *meaning* — the concept the communicator intented to convey. The term "comprehension" is used advisedly: it means "prehension with", i.e., two people prehending the same concept. See above, pp. 62-63, for more on prehension.

or that I concur in the existence of a tree. When a young child points to the moon and says "Lamp!", I comprehend her perfectly, and communication does exist, but that does not mean that *I* think that the moon is a lamp. One can have *phenomenal or conceptual* agreement, therefore, without *factual* agreement or concurrence. We can agree on the *meaning* of an utterance without agreeing on the *truth* of an utterance. In telling me a lamp is there, my child *is* making a statement, but I can comprehend the statement without necessarily agreeing. It is, of course, often the case that I *do* concur. And, short of telepathy, communication is the only way in which concurrence can be arrived at or confirmed. In other words, comprehension, or conceptual sharing, is a necessary but not a sufficient condition for the establishment of concurrence.

When a person receives a communication, the tokens she perceives are sounds (e.g., voice), or light patterns (e.g., facial expressions or gestures or words in books), or sometimes other perceptions, such as touch (e.g., a firm handshake may be perceived as meaning friendship or reliability). She interprets these phenomena as originating in the intentional actions of other people. The intention in this case is to convey certain concepts or phenomena to her. In interpreting these phenomena, she arrives at concepts or phenomena the other person may possibly have wished to convey to her; she may also arrive at the interpretation that it is not a communication at all, but just a noise the other person made, or a communication to someone else. Another possible interpretation is that the real concept the other person is putting across is different from that contained in the surface meaning of the words. All these are possibilities.

From these possibilities, she induces or deduces (i.e., makes a decision and chooses) the interpretation that she judges to be the most probable and accepts that as reality. The reality she arrives at is the reality that a certain concept or phenomenon was what the other person intended to convey to her. At this point, the communication cycle is complete.

The Learning Cycle in Communication

The communication cycle is actually a learning cycle.[5] From the various tokens the person receives, he learns what concept or phenomenon the communicator intended to communicate. When he has arrived at this new knowledge, that learning cycle is complete. If what has been communicated is a *phenomenon*, there is usually no need to do more. But when it is a *concept*, it is usually necessary to go through the learning cycle again in order to decide whether or not to *agree* with the concept communicated. This constitutes a *second* learning cycle. For this step, he takes as a *datum* the fact of having received a certain concept from the communicator. In successfully completing the first learning cycle, he may have expanded his identity a little bit to *include* the prior phenomenon (e.g., the sound of the sender's voice) as a subsidiary awareness, and what he is now *focally* aware of is the fact of having received a certain concept. Or he may simply *assume* (as a fact) the concept that the other person intended to communicate a certain concept. Now he must go through another cycle of interpretation and consideration, eventuating in another view of reality. Starting from the datum that this other person intends him to receive a certain concept, he may reach several different conclusions, among which may be:

1. The other person is lying.
2. He is being truthful but is mistaken.
3. He is lying but (accidentally) correct in his statement.
4. He is being truthful and is correct.

For instance, let us suppose a person says to me "The cat is on the mat." I comprehend her statement, and that completes the communication cycle. Then I must decide whether:

---

5. As described in Chapter Four, pp. 153-156.

1. She knows the cat isn't really on the mat but is trying to trick me.
2. She thinks the cat is on the mat but is *wrong* (the cat is actually outside).
3. She thinks the cat isn't on the mat and is trying to trick me, but it actually *is* on the mat.
4. She thinks the cat is on the mat, and she is right.

I might also have to take into account the past history of this person's utterances in order to decide whether her word should be trusted. When I have completed this learning cycle, I am then in a position to accept or reject the factuality of the concept that the cat is on the mat — or, possibly, to decide I do not yet have enough evidence to make a decision. So a communication cycle often goes through at least two iterations of the learning cycle before the recipient is done with it.

But we do not yet have all the necessary conditions that go together to form a *sufficient* condition for communication.

Communication as an Intentional Act

Communication, from the point of view of the communicator, is an act, and like any other act of a person, it is intentional.[6] If a person does not *intend* to communicate, then he does not see himself as transferring a token to the other person or as intending that it be comprehended, and thus no communication takes place for him. In order for the recipient of the communication to think that the originator is communicating, he has to believe that the originator intends to transfer the token and comprehend the concept or experience that it represents. Otherwise, what we have is not communication but just a form of eavesdropping. For instance, suppose you are sitting on a park bench and I am walking by with my chin on my chest, mumbling to myself "The cat is

---

6. See Chapter Two, pp. 91-92.

on the mat." I make a statement, you receive it, and the concept you get is the same as the concept I have. Yet it is not a communication from either my viewpoint or yours, because I do not intend to communicate, and you know it. One could imagine other cases where one person thinks he has received a communication, but the other person does not think he has communicated to the first person. For instance, if I am at the train station and a beautiful stranger looks at me and says, "Hi!", I may be very happy at the thought that my sterling qualities are so recognizable to a total stranger, while the stranger might actually be talking to the man behind me, as I may soon be disappointed to find out.

This factor of *intention* is crucial to the success of a communication, as it is to the success of any act. Communications delivered with strong intention tend to be successful, whereas communications delivered in a listless sort of way tend not to go through. The receiver must also intend to receive the communication in order for it to be successful. If she is trying to think about something else, or if she has a strong intention *not* to receive the communication, the act of communicating will be impeded or prevented.

The other item implicit in this definition is *attention*. In order to perform the receptive action of perception, awareness or attention is required. If I'm not paying attention to someone who is trying to communicate to me, then communication does not occur. If I come off a train and, spotting a beautiful stranger, I say, "Hi!", that communication will not go through if the stranger is looking at the younger, more handsome man behind me. I may think I've communicated, but I will not have unless I really have the other person's attention. Of course, the originator of the communication must also have her attention on the recipient in order for the action to be a bona fide communication. It is difficult, in any case, to imagine how one could intend to communicate to a person without being aware of the existence of that person.[7]

Another way of expressing these ideas is to say that communication requires *interest*:

Definition: Interest is directed attention.

A person's interest may be other-directed by being *attracted* to various entities without the person's having *decided* to place her attention on those entities. But a person is also capable of consciously directing her own attention. The ability to be interested *at will* is crucial to one's ability to communicate — or to engage in any other activity, for that matter. Some people spend a great deal of time trying to be interest*ing* to other people, but such people are typically poor communicators. It is far more important to be interest*ed* than to be interest*ing*.[8]

The many different components of the act of communication that I have teased out of the definition given above are of more than academic interest. Again, short of telepathy — which might be a form of communication anyway — communication is the only way to make contact with other people, the only way to arrive at a concurrence with them, creating thereby a common reality. Without communication, each of us is alone in our own world. Communication is the key to sharing experience with others and to having affection for them.

---

7. In the case of a lecturer or a TV news commentator, although she doesn't generally know *everyone* she is communicating to, she knows that *someone* will receive her message.

8. The ability to direct one's attention toward — to be interested in — another person at will can easily be taught by means of an exercise called "Communication Exercise 2" ("CE-2"), which is part of a series of exercises designed to improve a person's expertise in performing all the different parts of the communication cycle. Being interested is just one part, albeit a crucial one.

Two-Way Communication

I have now described the anatomy of communication and given the bare bones of what constitutes a communication — namely, the sharing of a concept or experience by means of the transfer of a token from one person to another. In the normal course of things, however, data are transferred in both directions. One person (say, Marsha) communicates to another (say, George) and then George communicates back to Marsha.

In fact, if a two-way flow of communication does not occur, the originator of a communication has trouble being sure that she has actually communicated at all. If Marsha says, "The cat is on the mat," and George does not respond at all, she will not be sure that a communication has occurred. So, while George, from his viewpoint, may have received a communication, for Marsha, the communication cycle that began with her intention to communicate and continued while she was speaking the words "The cat is on the mat," has not ended. This is because she has no way of being sure that her words have been heard or comprehended. It is actually *George's* responsibility to end Marsha's communication cycle for her by giving some sort of indication that he has heard and comprehended. Such an indication is called an "acknowledgement". The person-centered viewpoint is especially useful in understanding communication. Marsha and George will often be found to have different realities (especially insofar as the communication cycle is concerned), until an acknowledgement occurs — in his world, the communication has definitely occurred, while in her world, it might or might not have:

> **Definition**: An acknowledgement is an indication given by the receiver of a communication to the originator of the communication that is intended to convey the datum that the communication was received and comprehended.

An acknowledgement can take many forms. What all these forms have in common is that they are all ways of letting the other person know that she has been heard and comprehended. Some common acknowledgements are: "OK", "Fine", "Got that", "Thanks", or "I understand." Or an acknowledgement may be included in a more extensive communication. If, for instance, Marsha says, "The cat is on the mat," George may say, "And he looks hungry." In this case. he has given her an *implicit* acknowledgement, whereas the other forms of acknowledgement mentioned are *explicit*.

Since a communication cycle is not complete until the originator knows it has been received and comprehended, it might seem that we could get into an infinite regress, because the acknowledgement itself begins a communication cycle and, as such, would not be complete until its originator was sure of *its* being received. Thus it would, in turn, require an acknowledgement and so on to infinity. Fortunately, this infinite regress is not necessary. When George gives a simple explicit acknowledgement, like "OK", Marsha does not normally then have to acknowledge this acknowledgement. An acknowledgement is assumed to be comprehended unless there are indications to the contrary. In fact, it is easy to tell when a person has not received an acknowledgement. Such a person has not completed her communication cycle and will endeavor to complete it by repeating her communication, explaining or rephrasing it, asking, "Did you hear me?", or in other ways. So, if the originator *does not* do these things, the receiver will know that his acknowledgement was received, and the *receiver's* communication cycle, which consists of an acknowledgement, will be complete as well.

Looking back on our discussion about the dimensions of an activity in Chapter Three, pp. 132-134, we can better understand why we must be punctilious about acknowledging. A communication cycle is just one type of activity cycle, like any other. And no activity cycle can end until the actor gets receptive feedback that her activity has been completed, which allows her to accept that fact and thus end the cycle. Otherwise, the cycle is likely to continue indefinitely. In the case of communication, an acknowledgment is just the feedback she needs.

A person can become a compulsive talker when she does not perceive herself to be properly acknowledged. She does not really feel her communication has been comprehended, so she keeps repeating it, explaining, and elaborating in the hope that her viewpoint will eventually be shared. The way to handle such a person is to figure out how you can adequately convince her that you do fully comprehend what she is saying. This may involve giving her a very strong, forceful acknowledgement or saying something like: "Let me see — what it seems to me you're saying is _____ . Am I right?" Then, if it isn't right, you can have her clarify it until you really do comprehend.

The over-talkative person may not be thinking particularly clearly. That is, he may not have a very clear concept of what he is trying to express. So he may talk on and on because what he is saying is fundamentally not really comprehensible and at some level he knows it. In such a case, you might have difficulty helping him to complete his communication cycle because even if you repeat back exactly the words he gave you, it may sound unclear to him (because it *is* unclear). If he says something vague like "People are funny," *he* may not know exactly what he means by this statement. You might have to get him to clarify (for you and possibly for himself) which people he is talking about and what he means by "funny". Two kinds of clarification may be involved: The first is getting more data and explanation so that you can get a clear concept of what he is saying; the second is helping him to clarify his own concepts. Often, these two steps go on simultaneously.

If you are successful, then:

1. You may have helped him clarify his thinking, which can be quite beneficial to him.
2. You have helped him to complete his communication cycle.
3. He may well regard you as a remarkable person because you will be one of the very few people to whom he has been able to communicate.
4. His compulsive communication will cease (at least for the time being).

It is actually quite hard on a person not to complete a communication cycle. As with any incomplete cycle, it leaves the person with a period of past time being carried forward into present time — thus using up a portion of the person's "intention units". As I noted in Chapter Three (pp. 107-119), a person creates a period of time — a cycle — by formulating an intention. Present time spans the length of that intention, and that cycle, with its intention, remains as part of present time until it is completed or unmade. Helping to unclutter another's present time gives her more personal power. So you can help a person considerably simply by letting her know that what she is saying or thinking has been comprehended. Carl Rogers, with *his* "person-centered therapy", uses simple comprehension ("active listening") quite effectively as his major therapeutic tool. In so doing, he has rightfully earned a high degree of respect amongst therapists. But, of course, this principle should not apply only to therapeutic situations. Acknowledgement, broadly applied, improves the quality of one's life considerably.

One kind of two-way communication, then, is simply a communication followed by an acknowledgement. But a person usually has a further intention behind an act of communication, beyond the intention to communicate itself: she intends to get *concurrence* on something. Most communication is actually a demand for agreement on some point, despite the *apparent* form of the communication.

There are three forms that a sentence can take in ordinary discourse:

1. Imperative
2. Interrogative
3. Declarative[9]

An imperative sentence (like "Open the door!" or "Pass the sugar!") is used to ask another person to do something. An interrogative sentence commands another to provide data and is functionally equivalent to an imperative. "Where is the cat?" is equivalent to "Tell me where the cat is." What might not be quite so obvious is that a declarative sentence is also a command:

---

9. I prefer this term to the grammatical term "indicative", because I am describing *functions*, of sentences, not grammatical forms. Note also that rhetorical questions are grammatically questions but functionally declarations.

it commands or invites another to accept the existence of some entity. Polanyi makes the excellent point that a declarative sentence contains a hidden component: an affirmation of belief in what is being said.[10] If the other person does not feel that I intend to communicate a belief, then she will not view the sentence I am uttering as a legitimate statement. She may view it, for instance, as a quotation or as a "test" of some kind (as when I am saying something only to shock someone). Without the element of expressed belief, an utterance is not really a statement or assertion at all. I must, however, add to Polanyi's formulation one more necessary component: a statement or declaration must contain not only an implied assertion of belief but also a demand that the person to whom it is delivered must *also* believe the statement. In other words, to use our terminology, a statement:

1. Asserts a reality and
2. Commands concurrence.

When I make a declaration or statement, I want another to concur in a particular view of the world. If I say, "Glass is a liquid," you can assume that I intend that you concur with my opinion that glass is a liquid. If I say, "Glass is a liquid," and I give indications (such as by rolling my eyes or uttering a guffaw), that I do not believe that glass is a liquid or that I do not intend that you concur with this belief, you are justified in claiming that I have not made a real assertion. Sarcastic utterances, for example, are not meant to be taken as normal assertions. If I say "The moon is made of green cheese," I can hardly expect you to take that at its face value as a genuine declaration. You would say something to me like: "You do not really mean that. What are you driving at?" You might assume that I am speaking in some sort of code, and the real declaration I am making is: "The assassination is to take place at 12:00," or some such thing. Or you might assume I

---

10. Polanyi, Michael, *Personal Knowledge* (University of Chicago Press, 1962), pp. 27-30.

am trying to do something entirely different, such as to confuse or amuse you. But you will not assume I mean literally what I say.

If I say to you "I have the belief that glass is a liquid," or "I believe in God," I am not asking you to concur in the belief that glass is a liquid or that God exists. I *am* requesting concurrence in the fact that *I* have a certain opinion concerning glass, or God. The statement is a command that you concur on the existence of my *opinion*. The imperative function of statements is well illustrated in the field of hypnosis, where most of the commands are commands to believe or accept concepts as true. These commands are issued as declarative sentences (e.g., "Your eyelids are getting very heavy."). All sentences that mean what they say, then, are commands, either to *do* something or to *have* something (i.e., to concur with something).

Exceptions that prove this rule abound in the fields of literature and drama. Sentences in poetry that appear to be declarative may in fact only be word-painting or a celebration of the author's delight in the sound of words. It depends whether the author intends the reader to have some particular view of reality as a result of reading a poem. Thus, poems and works of art or literature that speak for some political system or for some social cause are declarative, while others, such as the poems of Dylan Thomas or the novels of James Joyce, may be primarily evocative (stimulative of an experience of some kind), despite the indicative form of the sentences contained therein. Consider again this line from Dylan Thomas:

"This world is half the Devil's and my own,
Daft with the drug that's smoking in a girl
And curling round the bud that forks her eye."

Grammatically, this is a perfectly constructed indicative sentence, yet I would not say that Thomas is making a definite statement, nor declaring something to be true, in the normal sense of the word "declare". Furthermore, sentences whose declarative meaning is entirely clear (as the above example's is not) may be *quoted* without constituting declarations in their own right. Shakespeare's *King Lear* is replete with indicative, interrogative, and declarative sentences that are far from meaningless. Yet they are not binding on an audience because although they are *uttered*, often with great force, they are not *declared*. That is, they are not intended as statements of fact directed at the audience.

All types of sentences that "mean what they say" — assertions, questions and orders — are commands of one type or another. And a person makes an assertion to another person in order to get the other person to agree. A declaration made by Marsha to George, such as "The cat is on the mat," also contains a command and an intention that he agree with it. But he can comprehend the communication *without* agreeing with it. So if he says (verbally or otherwise), "I comprehend, but I do not agree," she *does* feel she has communicated. But another cycle is embedded in the communication — namely, the cycle created by her intention that he agree. And this other cycle is incomplete. So in this case, she feels only partly satisfied by the acknowledgement. The conversation may be prolonged at this point, while she tries to persuade him to agree with what she has said. This is another reason why a person can become over-talkative — the person does not feel he has succeeded in getting the other person to *agree* with what he is saying. To let Marsha end her communication cycle, George will either have to end up convincing her that he agrees with her, or he will have to get her to stop intending his agreement, e.g., by saying "Let's agree to disagree," or by getting her to agree to redefine her declaration as a statement about her feelings or opinions. George can usually agree that what Marsha said is indeed her opinion (unless he feels that she is lying). So he could say, "I feel you have a right to your opinion," and if she is willing to unmake her intention that he *agree* with her, then she has implicitly agreed to modify her statement to a statement of the form: "My opinion is that the cat is on the mat," or "The cat is on the mat — for me." This kind of modification will allow the communication cycle to end for her, whereas if she continues to assert, "The cat is on the mat," a long argument might ensue.

In some situations, such as in certain forms of counseling or facilitation[11], it is implicitly assumed that "I believe that ... " or "I feel that ..." is *automatically* prefixed to each statement made by a person. In such person-centered contexts, if the client says,

"My father is a real bastard," he does not expect the facilitator to *agree* that his dad is *actually* a bastard. He might, in fact, get quite upset if the facilitator said, "You're right. Your father actually *is* a bastard." Rather, he expects the facilitator to agree that he, the client, *feels* that his father is a bastard. In other words, he expects the facilitator to agree that he is not lying or mistaken in reporting his feelings and beliefs. It is often the case in personal enhancement that the moment a person has expressed a thought, he changes his mind and thinks something entirely differently. If the facilitator gets sucked into actually *agreeing* with the client, she may very shortly find herself regretting having done so.

Note that setting up a person-centered context is not the same as humoring someone. You humor someone when you do not agree with that person's assertions but pretend to agree in order to end a communication cycle or avoid an argument. In this case, you are trying to deceive the person into thinking you agree with him, whereas in a person-centered context both parties agree that "I think that ..." or "I feel that ..." is implicitly prefixed to all statements made.

The person-centered viewpoint is thus very well adapted to facilitation. In adopting this viewpoint, I have made the assumption that a thing can be true only for a *person*, not *absolutely* true. When a person says something to me, barring the possibility that she is lying, I automatically assume that:

1. Her statement is true for her.
2. She wants me to agree that it is true.

In the person-centered context, (2) would be modified to read: "She wants me to agree that it is true for her." In this context, then, I can automatically take statements of fact and regard them as statements about what is true for the other person. Thus I can help the other person view her own world without obtruding with

---

11. A preferable term, because there are other ways of helping a person beside giving him counsel. I will henceforth use this term instead of terms like "counseling" or "therapy" to describe the act of helping.

elements of my own. This "non-interference" policy (absence of evaluation) is crucial for effective facilitation.[12]

When a person asks a question, a cycle starts which is partly a communication cycle and partly a command cycle. The command part of the cycle is a demand for information. This cycle is complete when the questioner receives the information he asked for, when he decides he does not want the information after all, or when he finds that the information is definitely not available. If George says, "Where is the cat?", Marsha *could* answer, "I understand. You are asking me where the cat is." This acknowledgement would leave him quite unsatisfied, even though he realizes that she comprehends his question. In order to really complete this cycle for George, Marsha would have to say, "On the mat," "I don't know," "I will not tell you," "Please do not ask me that question," or something of that nature.

A cycle ends when its goal is fulfilled or when the intention behind it is unmade for some other reason. One such reason might be that there is no hope of successful completion. Another might be that something else has become more important.

The same is true for imperative communication, except that, in this case, what completes the cycle for the person giving the command might not be a communication. For instance, George says to Marsha "Put out the cat." If she puts out the cat, then his intention is satisfied, and that ends the cycle without her having to give him a verbal acknowledgement. If Marsha simply answered "OK" and did nothing, that would end the communication part of the cycle, but not the command part. George would justifiably feel frustrated in this case and would probably pursue the issue, trying to complete the command cycle.

So, to reiterate, all communication cycles are also command cycles, and the communication part can be satisfied without the command part being satisfied.

---

12. See the section on evaluation in "The Rules of Facilitation", Chapter Eight, pp. 387-388.

I have said that, in order for person **A** (say, George) to complete a cycle started by a statement or command, a second cycle must be started by person **B** (Marsha), as a compliance with the command that is implicit or explicit in George's communication. But now this *second* cycle needs to be complete for Marsha. This cycle may be a communication cycle, in the case of a question; perhaps an action, in the case of another type of command; or an agreement, in the case of an assertion. Normally, a simple, explicit acknowledgement by Marsha to an assertion by George does not need any particular response from him in order to be complete for her. But other types of cycles that Marsha initiates do require an acknowledgement from George, so that she can feel *her* cycle is complete. So if Marsha, on command, puts out the cat, he should acknowledge her for doing so. And if she says, "On the mat," as a response to his question, he must acknowledge her for her cycle to be complete. In the latter case, where her assertion is just a response to his question, Marsha intends that George must agree with her (as in any declaration), but given that George asked the question, Marsha can often just assume, if he acknowledges, that he agrees with the answer. Of course, if he gives signs that he does not agree (e.g., by shaking his head or otherwise looking dubious, or by saying, "I do not know about that..."), then she will have to go on communicating in order to convince him to agree with what she has said, e.g., by saying "But I'm not lying, and I'm not mistaken — the cat actually *is* on the mat."

In the case of a simple declaration, then, there is often a *presumption* of belief that makes it unnecessary for the other person to specifically communicate his belief. So here a simple acknowledgement often suffices. But in the case of a question or command, a second communication or action cycle (itself necessitating an acknowledgement) will have to occur in order for both parties to get their cycles completed. The ultimate acknowledgement for an assertion, then, is "I believe you," "I agree," or "You're right." The ultimate acknowledgement for a question is its answer, and the ultimate acknowledgement for a command is the action commanded. The latter two themselves require acknowledgement.

The reader might wonder why it should be necessary to acknowledge the carrying out of a command. If George says to Marsha, "Put out the cat," and she does so, surely she knows she has done so. So why would George have to acknowledge her, in order for her to know his cycle is complete? The reason lies in the person-centered viewpoint. George is commanding that *his* intention be fulfilled. While Marsha may know she has done what he wanted her to do, she also knows that the cycle is not complete for him unless *he* knows that it is done. Therefore, Marsha does not know for sure whether or not George has really completed his command cycle, so far as *he* is concerned, unless he lets her know that he knows it is completed. When she is assured of this, she can relax, knowing she has created the desired effect in his world. It appears, in other words, that the person-centered viewpoint is rather ingrained into the everyday communication pattern of most people, because we *do* usually feel a need to inform others when we comply with their commands. A failure to acknowledge, apart from its leaving the other person with an incomplete cycle, also betokens a lack of regard for the other person. Punctilious acknowledgements are regarded as indicative of respect for the validity of another's world.

The following exercise should illustrate the importance of acknowledgement:

Exercise 16. Acknowledging and Not Acknowledging

1. Get in a conversation or interaction with someone and try *not* acknowledging anything they say or do for a period of time (not too long!).
2. Observe what happens.
3. Ask the other person how it felt.
4. Be careful to acknowledge everything she says, as she finishes saying it (not before).
5. Continue being careful to acknowledge everything that the person says or does.
6. Observe the results and compare them with those obtained in Step (1).

You may find that you created quite an upset in Step (1). Make sure it gets fully handled by telling the person what you have been doing and then letting her tell you how she feels about it, being careful to acknowledge her when she does so.

If a person starts a question or command cycle, she often has to use a fair degree of persistence in order to get it completed. She does not always get instant compliance with her commands, but if she forgets what she was trying to do or gives up easily, she can, again, get left with an incomplete cycle. It is often necessary to repeat questions or commands several times in order to get them replied to or complied with. A person with an incomplete question or command cycle can get trapped indefinitely in the period of time defined by that cycle, unless it gets completed. If the person is easily distracted or turned away from completing what she wanted to complete, she can stop working on carrying out an intention and put it "on the back burner" indefinitely, thus leaving herself with a period of present time that includes a sizable part of the past. Incomplete communication and command cycles are very common sources of difficulty for a person.[13] A person can learn, by doing certain exercises, to be persistent in getting questions answered and commands complied with.

Finally, the situation can arise where person **A** starts a question or command cycle and before person **B** complies, **B** starts a communication cycle of his own that also needs to be handled. For instance, a mother says to her son, "Put out the garbage," and her son says, "I had a *lousy* day at school today!". The mother needs to exercise some judgment at this point so that the collision of communication cycles does not cause an upset. She must judge the relative importance and urgency of her son's need to communicate about his rough day, relative to her own desire to get him to put out the garbage. She must then either hold her own cycle in abeyance until his cycle is completed or skillfully

---

13. See Chapter Three (pp. 117-119) for a further discussion of incomplete cycles.

negotiate with him to arrange how *both* cycles can be completed in the proper order. She could say, "I want to hear all about your day, dear, but first put out the garbage and then you can tell me all about it. The garbage is really smelling up the place and we have guests coming." Or she could say, "Tell me all about it," and then *later* come back and say, "Please put out the garbage." If the situation with the garbage is really urgent, she is not going to be able to really listen to what he has to say about his troubles at school. On the other hand, if he is desperately wanting to get his upset off his chest, he will not want to be bothered with putting out the garbage first. Part of the skill involved in communication lies in this kind of negotiation; part lies in being able to distinguish between a cycle that has to be completed right away and one that can wait; part lies in keeping track of the cycle that cannot be completed right away. The failure to smoothly negotiate such a clash in communication cycles — and failures to acknowledge — account for most upsets that occur between people. A person's skill in handling all aspects of communication can be greatly enhanced by specific exercises.[14]

Communication, Comprehension, and Affection

I have discussed the rules by which a person generally decides on the nature of the world he lives in, and how he relates to the various entities in his world.[15] A person relates to entities so as to maximize power, i.e., drive, control, and understanding, and when he is successful an ascending power triad occurs, while if he is unsuccessful a descending debilitation triad occurs.

---

14. These "Communication Exercises" ("CE's") form a very important part of the training of a metapsychology practitioner and, in fact, constitute an excellent "basic training for life" for anyone.
15. See Chapter Four.

But there are presences in the person's world that are not *things* — namely, other persons. Other people are not entities — objects, events, or states of affairs. No one ever *perceives* a person. One only perceives a person's *body*[16], some of the other perceivable identities he assumes, and the effects he creates. Further, people cannot be *understood*, strictly speaking, in the sense that a datum could be understood to be indicative of an underlying reality. What a person *can* do with other people is to share their viewpoints and concepts, which, to some degree, entails a willingness and an ability to *be* them. In other words, the communications of other people can be *comprehended*, which results in a sharing of a viewpoint:

> **Definition**: Comprehension is a co-experiencing or sharing of one or more elements of experience between two persons, such as phenomena or concepts. Comprehension is the result of communication; it need not involve agreement or concurrence.

So, with respect to other people, we do not have a power triad. Instead, in a relationship between two people, there is, inevitably, a relationship between their communication, their sharing of experience, and their affection for each other.

The act of successful communication involves comprehension of what is communicated, i.e., a conceptual or phenomenal sharing. George comprehends Marsha's communication if the concept or phenomenon she intends to convey to him is the same as the concept or phenomenon he actually receives. It is important to mention that agreement is irrelevant to the sharing of phenomena and not needed in order for there to be a sharing of concepts. Comprehension involves one iteration of the learning cycle. Agreement requires a second iteration. Though George may comprehend that Marsha said, "The cat is on the mat," and may

---

16. Which, as we have seen, is not necessarily the person himself but an identity he may assume.

get the concept of a cat being on the mat (which was what Marsha intended him to get), he need not *agree* that the cat is *actually* on the mat in order for the communication to be successful. Often — perhaps even usually — communication does lead to concurrence, but it need not. When successful, however, it always leads to comprehension.

It is also a known fact that, when a person comprehends the viewpoint of another person, she tends to *like* that person, even if she disapproves of the person's actions or disagrees with her concepts. *"Tout comprendre, c'est tout pardonner."* — "To comprehend everything is to forgive everything."[17] Certainly, the more of a person's viewpoint one acquaints oneself with, the easier it is to assume that viewpoint and thus the more willing one may become to share that viewpoint. The method acting school of Stanislavski takes advantage of this fact. A method actor learns to practice *thinking* like her character, so when she acts the part of the character she does so "naturally". Her ability to see entities from the viewpoint of her character improves markedly with practice. In general, we enjoy doing things that are easy for us, and actions grow easier with practice. Comprehension is a perceptual and conceptual skill that is usually a challenge to acquire but rewarding when finally acquired. Also, irrespective of whether or not concurrence occurs, if comprehension occurs, there is, to a degree, a convergence of viewpoint. Person **B** may not *agree* with person A's viewpoint, but **B** does *see* it. So **B** is, *de facto*, sharing A's viewpoint to some degree and therefore must be willing or inclined to do so to that degree.

Therefore, the definition of affinity was given as:

Definition: Affinity is a willingness to be close to, or to assume the viewpoint of, something or someone.

---

17. Attributed to Madame de Staël, a French Baroness of the early 19th Century.

Note that although, with both entities and people, affinity is the willingness or inclination to share a space, there is a difference in the way in which one shares space with an entity and the way in which one shares space with a person. With an entity, one shares space by *having* it in one's vicinity. Since a person is not an entity, however, there is nothing there to *have* in one's vicinity[18] So one shares space with another person by sharing the *viewpoint* of the other person, by looking at entities from her viewpoint — i.e., by conceptual, phenomenal, and factual sharing, or comprehending. One partially assumes the identity or viewpoint that another person has at a particular moment and sees what the world looks like from that viewpoint. So the quality of the affinity one has for another person is different from the quality of affinity one has for an entity. As was mentioned in Chapter Four (pp. 179-182), affinity directed toward entities is "desire", whereas affinity directed toward *people* is "affection":

> **Definition**: Affection is the wish to be close to another person, to share a common space, viewpoint, and identity. It is an impulse toward communion.

Since comprehension leads to the willingness to do more sharing of viewpoints, comprehension leads to more affection (see Figure 29).

Communication ·······➤ Comprehension ·······➤ Affection

Figure 29. Relationship between communication, comprehension, and affection.

Affection, in turn, "wraps around" by leading to more communication. If a person were completely unwilling or averse to sharing another's viewpoint, he would not be willing to communicate.

---

18. One might have a person's body, her car, or her writings, but these are not "her", strictly speaking, but only identities she has assumed.

Conversely, the more inclined one is to share a viewpoint or identity with another person, the easier it is to comprehend a concept, so the easier communication becomes. Communication is the means by which the sharing of viewpoints occurs. Therefore a willingness to share a viewpoint entails a willingness to communicate. Besides, it is necessary to get relatively close to another person in order to communicate effectively with him. In the absence of a reasonable degree of affection, therefore, communication does not occur readily. If the affection is very small, the quantity and quality of the communication will be correspondingly small. On the other hand, if the affection is very strong, chances are that the communication will be correspondingly high in quantity and quality.

Like drive, understanding, and control (power), communication, comprehension, and affection tend to follow an ascending triad (see Figure 30).

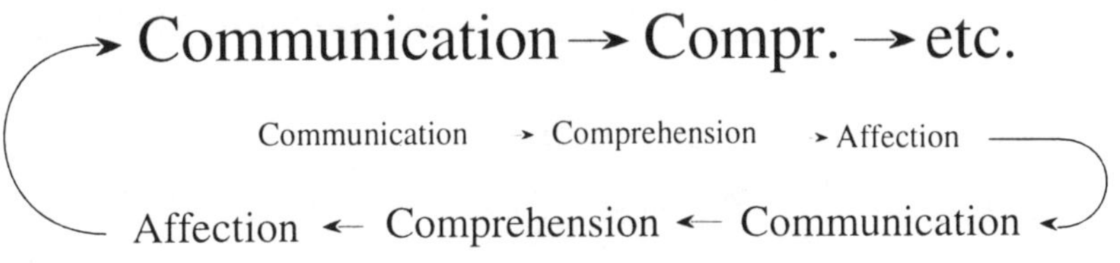

Communication→ Compr. →etc.

Communication ➤ Comprehension ➤ Affection

Affection ← Comprehension ← Communication

Figure 30. The triad of communion.

If two people communicate more, they comprehend more; if they comprehend more, they have more affection for each other. If they have more affection, they communicate more easily, and so forth. On the other hand, one can also get a descending triad (see Figure 31). If two people communicate less or miscommunicate, they comprehend less, and they become disaffected, which, in turn, amounts to an unwillingness to approach each other to communicate.

Therefore — like drive, understanding, and control — communication, comprehension, and affection are closely related as part of an ascending or descending triad. For this reason, it is

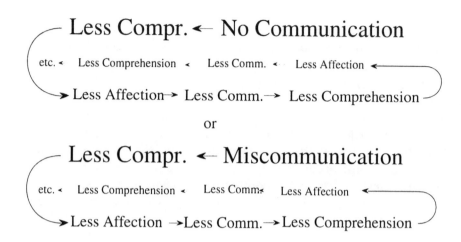

Figure 31. The triad of alienation.

useful to use a single term to describe the combination of the three, and I have chosen the term "communion" to serve this purpose:[19]

> **Definition:** Communion is a combination of communication, comprehension, and affection, which together form an ascending triad: more communication leads to more comprehension and more affection, more comprehension leads to more affection and more communication, and more affection leads to more communication and more comprehension. The easiest entry point to this triad is through communication.

Two people, then, can be thought of as having a certain degree or level of communion at any given time. That level can be said to consist of a triad that is either ascending or descending, depending on where their relationship stands. Generally, if they are above

---

19. "Communion" may be a problematic term because of its religious overtones, but I am using it in a secular manner to mean a combination of love, fellow feeling, communication, and sharing of experience.

the emotional level of ambivalence with respect to each other, they will experience an ascending triad, whereas if they are below ambivalence, they will be experience a descending triad of alienation:

> **Definition:** Alienation is a low degree of communication, comprehension, and affection which, together, form a descending triad, with less communication leading to less comprehension and less affection, less comprehension leading to less affection and less communication, and less affection leading to less communication and less comprehension. The easiest way out of this descending triad is by communicating.

The *intensity* of affection (not the *level* of affection) is related to the importance, or cardinality, of the person in question. If a person is not very important to me — for instance, if I hardly know the person — then a failure to communicate or a lack of affection or comprehension is not very significant or upsetting. But if the person in question is important to me for some reason, disaffection with her can be quite intense and significant. Thus, if a stranger says she doesn't like me, that may only be mildly disturbing, whereas if my daughter says *she* doesn't like me, that might be quite upsetting. It is possible to have a very high level of communication with a total stranger (such as a person sitting on a plane next to you), and to genuinely share the other person's world and like her, and yet not have the relationship between the two of you be a very intense one.

But having issued this caveat, I should add that when a strong communion exists between two people over a considerable period of time, the two people tend to *become* important or cardinal to each other, because a person values communion — just as a person who discovers that he is very good at a particular sport will tend to make that sport an important part of his life. Because a given act of communication involves two and only two persons[20], it is customary for a person to have one other person who is the *main* person he communicates with. In time, these two people come to rely more and more on each other. In the current vernacular, they become "significant others" for each other. When so much communing has occurred that two people consider each other their main cardinal points, the relationship may become a sexual one, bodily communication having been added in as an expression of exceptionally strong affection of an exceptional intensity. If not sexual, such a relationship is at least a close, familial-like relationship.

In such a case, if communication or some other component of communion drops off, then because of their cardinality for each other, the lowering of affection — perhaps to a level of ambivalence, or even to a point of hatred or fear — is felt as a severe and highly upsetting shock. Conversely, if the affection remains strong, equally intense positive feelings (love, passion) may exist. But in any case, the feelings will not be bland.

Of the three elements that make up communion, the one over which a person can most readily exercise control is communication. It is difficult for a person who has an aversion to another person to change that aversion by simply deciding to do so. Out of politeness or other motives, people often pretend not to have aversions that they do in fact have. But it is rather difficult to genuinely stop having an aversion for no reason. Likewise, it is possible for a person to consider past communications that another person has issued, in the absence of any present communication, and acquire a greater sharing of the other person's viewpoint. That may be easier than affection by fiat, but it still requires a prior communication to have taken place. Given anything except the most intense aversion, however, a person *can* communicate with another person, and thus comprehend, have more affection, and start an ascending triad of communion.

---

20. A person can, e.g., in a lecture, communicate to a number of people at the same time, but in this case, there are many acts of communication happening simultaneously.

I earlier stated (pp. 198-201) that the relationship between a person and the entities that make up his world is a bipolar one in which drive on the person side of the person-world polarity corresponds to beauty or pleasure on the world side, control corresponds to order, and understanding corresponds to heuristics. A person-to-person relationship, however, is not bipolar but reciprocal. Thus, with *entities* we have:

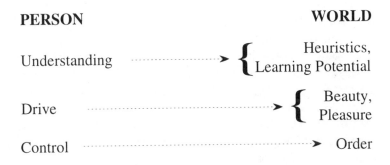

Figure 32. A person's bipolar relationship to entities.

Whereas with *persons*, we have:

Figure 33. Reciprocal person-to-person relationships.

To the degree a person has affection for another person, he is willing or inclined to *be* that other person. In looking at another person, one sees a reflection of oneself. I have affinity for another person to the degree that I conceive that person to be someone who, himself, has affinity — someone who creates beauty and pleasure in his own life, as I do in mine. It is not the *person* that is beautiful or pleasurable. The person *brings about* beauty or pleasure by having affinity (or positive emotion) toward something or someone. Nor is the *person* ugly or painful. The person may cause and experience pain and ugliness by having aversion for (or negative emotion toward) something or someone. My affection for another person *is* my willingness or inclination to share his pain or pleasure — my willingness to put myself in his shoes, to *be* him. My level of communication with another person is likewise a mirroring. I am in communication with him to the same degree that I perceive him to be in communication with me. Finally, in sharing the viewpoint of another person, I am not comprehending *him*; I am comprehending his concepts and perceptions.

Since all these interactions occur between equals, they are symmetrical. And because where there is affection a person cares about the quality of others' relationships, she is easily affected by the quality of relationships amongst others, especially significant others. A can have affection for B, and B can have affection for A. Also, B can have affection for C, as seen from A's viewpoint. People naturally try to maximize all forms of affection — affection received, affection given, and affection existing amongst others. I shall show that the interpersonal upsets a person experiences all result from a failure to commune with others or to promote or observe communion amongst others.

The major difference between the relationship a person has with an entity and the relationship a person has with another person is that a person exercises her power to *control or understand* entities, whereas she achieves communion by *communicating with* and *comprehending the concepts and experiences of* other persons. Another person is not an entity and therefore cannot be controlled, strictly speaking. It may be possible to control another's *body* (e.g., by pushing it around). But in so doing, it is *you* who have done the action, not the other person. And it may be possible to give another person strong reasons for doing a certain thing. But, strictly speaking, another person cannot be *forced* to act. The person can only be requested or commanded to do something. She need not accept the invitation nor obey the command. Nor can the person herself be analyzed or understood. The person is that which analyzes and understands her environment (including her mind); she is not the object of these actions. Unlike a control cycle or a perception cycle, a communication cycle has as its object something that is not really an entity, but that *transcends* entities — namely, a relationship of communication, comprehension, and affection between persons, a communion. This transcendent character of communication gives communication a special status amongst the actions of a person.

Flows

Causation, to, from, and amongst people, and between people and entities, goes in various directions, or "flows". All aspects of power and communion: drive, control, understanding, communication, comprehension, affection — in fact, any effect caused by one person on another, by an entity on a person, or by a person on an entity — proceeds in one of four directions, from the viewpoint of a particular person:[21]

---

21. Because the person-centered viewpoint is only concerned with persons and their worlds, I am not concerned with the effects of objects on other objects except insofar as these objects affect one or more persons.

Definition: Inflow is the receipt of some kind of effect by a person.

Definition: Outflow is the creation of some kind of effect by a person.

Definition: Crossflow is the causation of some kind of effect between two or more persons, or between one or more persons and one or more entities, as viewed by another person who is not directly involved.

Definition: Reflexive flow is causation from self to self (also called "Reflexion").

Let us examine these flows from the viewpoint of person **A**. If **A** gets a present from **B** (or from **C**, **D**, etc.) that is an inflow. If **A** gives a present to **B** (or **C** or **D**, etc.), that is an outflow. If **B**, **C**, or **D** give one or more presents to each other and **A** knows about it, that is a crossflow. People are also able to cause effects on themselves. Auto-hypnosis would be one example; pinching oneself, buying oneself a present, or drinking a glass of water would be others. These are reflexive flows.

Although people seem to understand intuitively what reflexion is all about, it has some puzzling aspects. The riddle is: When person **A** is talking to himself, who is talking to whom? The definition of communication[22] requires two persons and a space between them, so in what sense can reflexive communication occur?

A possible answer to this riddle is the following: A person seems to be able to "be" more than one identity at the same time. For instance, I am a father, but at the same time I can have a second identity as a Monopoly player. Let us say I am visiting a friend and having an intense game of Monopoly. It is getting late, and I have a baby sitter who needs to get home very

---

22. "Communication is the transfer of a token from one person or being to another, where the concept or phenomenon received is the same as that intended by the originator."

soon. As the father, I suddenly realize that I should be getting home. As the Monopoly player, I am about to have an opportunity to acquire Boardwalk, a long-awaited piece of real estate. Since, in this particular situation, the two identities have opposing intentions, I must make a decision. So I "step back" from both identities and allow the "father" to enter into a dialogue with the "Monopoly player". These two identities are separate, so there is something like a "space" across which they can communicate, negotiate, make compromises with each other, and finally reach an agreement. Or, from my "senior" position, I can arbitrate.

What is really happening when a person "does something to himself" is that two different identities that he has assumed are interacting. Since he is, in some sense, "being" these identities, it could be considered an interaction of "self" with "self". It is often useful, when a person is talking or otherwise interacting with himself, for him to know precisely which identity is interacting with which other identity. Freud touched on this question in his discussion of id, ego, and superego, all of which seemed to cause effects on each other. Eric Berne goes into this point at length. His school of transactional analysis is based on a (simplified) analysis of the different identities a person assumes and how they interact with each other and with others' identities.[23]

In a person's attempt to promote communion, all four flows are involved. It is hard to have affection for another person when that affection is not reciprocated. If person **B** does not have affection for person **A**, then **B** will not be willing to communicate with **A**, and **A** cannot improve her communion with **B**. Since a person has a primary goal to increase communion, she will want others to have affection for her and she will also seek to have affection for others. Furthermore, it is possible (but often uncomfortable) to have affection for two people who do not have affection for each other. If it is hard for them to be in each other's

---

23. See Berne, E. *Transactional Analysis in Psychotherapy* (Grove Press, New York, 1961).

space, then it is hard for a third person to share space with both. So, sometimes one must choose to be with one *or* the other, and this limits one's ability to commune with both. For instance, a parent wants her children to get along with each other because if the children find it hard to share a space with each other and are always arguing or antagonistic, it will be hard for the parent to share a space with both of them. A more poignant example is that of a child with parents who hate each other. The child wants to enjoy being with both of them but cannot do so. In such situations, it is almost universal for the child to have an intense wish that her parents would restore their affection for each other. It is, of course, not at all impossible to love someone who does not love you, or to love two people who dislike each other, but it is easier on a person if there is affection all around. A person will therefore naturally attempt to achieve a condition of widespread affection amongst associates. She will also attempt to do this because of her affection for them and her desire for them to be happy.

A person also wants to achieve "internal" affection. She wants the different identities she assumes to be compatible with each other, a condition known as "integrity":

Definition: Integrity is congruity of intention and identity.

Her ability to make ethical decisions depends on harmony amongst her intentions and identities.[24] A person will attempt to create communion on all four flows.

---

24. See the discussion of ethics and integrity later in this chapter, pp. 258-261.

Causation and Responsibility

Since a person transcends the world of entities, he cannot genuinely be controlled[25], just as he cannot genuinely be located in space and time. He can, however, *agree* to assume a location or viewpoint in time and space, he can agree to comply with commands given by other persons, and he can agree or decide to respond in certain ways to changes in his world. For instance, if Marsha says, "Pass me the salt," George may agree to comply — or he may not. George might also make a blanket decision to take orders from Marsha. One might say that he is then agreeing to be "controlled" by her. But, strictly speaking, he is only agreeing to *comply* with her demands. If he makes such an agreement and thereafter it becomes a habit, he may feel that she is "running his life" and that she is responsible for his actions, where "responsibility" is defined as follows:

Definition: Responsibility is causativeness.[26]

So if George continues to be aware that he is causatively complying with Marsha's orders, he continues to be responsible — from his viewpoint, he is still causative. But when he decides that he has no choice, that she is controlling him, i.e., that *she* is the cause of his actions, then he does not consider himself responsible for (causative over) his actions.[27]

---

25. The person's body or his possessions may be controlled, but not the person himself.

26. When I say a person is responsible for something, I mean that he caused that thing or helped to cause it. There is a difference between responsibility and *blame*, although the two are related. Blame is assignment of causation with intent to punish; praise is assignment of causation with intent to reward, and responsibility is simple assignment of causation. Responsibility can be retrospective or prospective. If retrospective, it is a recognition that a person has caused something. If prospective, it is the intention that a person be causative with respect to something in the future.

27. As a matter of fact, George does not really see himself as *acting*, in this case.

Two more definitions are useful, here:

Definition: Other-determinism is the consideration that someone else is responsible for one's actions.

Definition: Self-determinism is the consideration that one is responsible for one own actions.[28]

Other-Determinism

A person who gives someone else the credit or the blame for her own actions is other-determined. A person who feels she has no choice about something because she is "under orders" is other-determined concerning that thing. Other-determinism is responsible for all major atrocities that have occurred in the history of the human race. Since people have fundamentally good intentions towards others, it does not come naturally to people to perform atrocities. In order to bring themselves to do so, they must assign responsibility (i.e., causation) elsewhere. That way, they can avoid intense guilt and horror by holding to the view that they didn't actually *do* these things, that they were merely an instrument of someone else's causativeness. Of course, it is not true that they didn't do these things, but they can't afford to let themselves see that fact. The German officials who were personally involved in the incarceration and murder of millions of Jews felt, characteristically, that they were "under orders" and had no choice. If these officials had been self-determined, rather than other-determined, the Holocaust could never have happened.[29]

---

28. These concepts are similar to the concepts of "outer-directed" and "inner-directed", put forward by David Riesman in *The Lonely Crowd* (Yale University Press, 1958), and are also discussed in recent psychological literature as the "locus of control".

29. Hitler himself, of course, felt that *his* actions in ordering the Holocaust were caused — i.e., necessitated — by what he considered to be the pernicious and evil nature of those against whom they were directed.

To the degree that a person is other-determined, she considers herself a "victim of circumstances". She feels as though her life is "out of her control", that other people are responsible for the condition in which she finds herself. Dependency relationships are in this category. In a dependency relationship, a person has abrogated her ability to cause effects in many areas and has assigned the responsibility (or causativeness) to another. Having done so, she must wait for the other person to do things for her or to order her to do things. A person who has committed harmful acts or misdeeds — or is afraid of doing so — will tend to refuse to take responsibility for the person or area harmed and will try to assign the responsibility to someone else. An employee who makes mistakes — or is afraid of making them — will try to get her boss to give her orders so that she can view the boss, not herself, as responsible for her actions and their consequences.

Being other-determined can, in that way, relieve guilt and anxiety. But recall: control over one's world is a cardinal principle of life. And an other-determined person feels that she does not control her world. It may *be* controlled. It may, in fact, seem *more* orderly than if someone else were *not* controlling it. But in reality that world is not really under control. If the "authority" — or other cardinal person on whom the person is dependent — should disappear, turn against her, or just get tired of running her life and stop doing it, that apparent orderliness would shatter. An other-determined person, in other words, has other people as aberrated cardinal points.

Self-Determinism

With respect to causativeness over his own world, the person's best cardinal point is himself. This is the viewpoint of the self-determined person. He has taken control over his own universe. Such a person is usually in good shape.

But there is still room for improvement. I have described how a person may widen his scope of identity to include a larger and larger portion of his world. This ability is reflected in the fact that a person is not just concerned about inflow (things happening to him), or reflexion (what he is doing to himself). He is also concerned about outflow (things that he does to others) and crossflow (things that others do to others). Since he is concerned about these other flows, when he is doing well in life, he takes responsibility for others as well as himself. When he is other-determined, he considers himself to be the effect of others' intentions. When he is self-determined, he takes responsibility for his own intentions. When he improves still further, he takes responsibility for others' intentions as well — in other words, in any given situation, he acts to maximize pleasure, order, and heuristics for all persons in that situation. He acts to empower all participants. When he is merely self-determined, he tends to find himself butting up against the intentions of others; often he finds himself in opposition to others. He finds himself in a competitive "zero-sum" game, a game where the more there is for one of the players the less there is for the rest, where if one wins the others lose. Mere self-determinism, then, tends to result in a lifetime of zero-sum games and struggles.[30] A merely self-determined person is very concerned with being "strong", "forceful", "intelligent", and, generally, "superior". He wants to be "a winner". If someone else's intentions prevail against his — or even if someone else does better than he — he may feel quite upset.

Multi-Determinism

A *truly* superior person (or, rather, a truly *powerful* person) can take responsibility for the well-being of all concerned. I must define another term to describe the orientation of such a person:

---

30. Schopenhauer's pessimistic view of "the world as will and idea" assumes a universal self-determinism. See Schopenhauer, A. *The World as Will and Idea* (Routledge and Kegan Paul, London, 1964) Haldane, R.B and Kemp, J., Translators.

Definition: Multi-Determinism is the consideration, in a certain situation, that one shares responsibility for the intentions and actions of all persons involved in that situation.

A person who plays a game of tennis just to win is being self-determined. She is happy if she wins and unhappy if the other person wins. A person who plays a game of tennis in order to provide an enjoyable experience for both players transcends her self-determinism and is multi-determined. The self-determined person will get upset if she loses a point; she will tend to argue about whether a ball is in or out. A multi-determined person will congratulate the other person on a good play and will be happy for the other person if the other person wins.

There is a progression, then, from other-determinism to self-determinism and from self-determinism to multi-determinism. It is first necessary to bring a person up to the point where she can take responsibility for her own actions and intentions and stop being a victim or a robot. Then it is necessary to get her to a point where she can also take responsibility for others' intentions and actions without taking away the causativeness or responsibility others have as well and without making them dependent.

A Cause and *the* Cause

Just because one entity or person causes something does not mean other entities or persons cannot cause the same thing at the same time. There may be multiple causes for a single situation, any one of which could be regarded as *the* cause, depending on one's viewpoint. Let us consider the "cause of death", in the case of a homicide. It depends on the viewpoint one is taking. The coroner says the cause of death was cyanide poisoning. The police, judge, and jury say the cause of death was Bill, the accused murderer. A biochemist says that the cause of death was an inhibition of the respiratory enzyme, cytochrome oxidase, leading to a failure of cellular metabolism. A sociologist says the cause of the murder consisted of various social forces; the psychologist says it is hostility toward a parental figure transferred onto the murder victim. The defense attorney says the cause is insanity. The prosecuting attorney says it is malicious intent. A right-wing politician attributes the murder to the abolition of the death penalty.

What a person perceives to be *the* cause of a situation depends on the identity she has assumed at the time and its ruling intentions. A person will select a cause that is relevant to her identity and its intentions. So it is meaningless to ask, "Which is the *real* cause?" *All* are real causes. We adopt one or another cause as "the cause" depending on what we intend to accomplish by making an assignment of cause. The coroner wishes to establish the means of the murder; the biochemist's job is to clarify the biochemical mechanisms caused by cyanide; the detective wants to get the "whodunit". So there is really no contradiction involved in having multiple causes for the same entity, as seen from different viewpoints. And, in fact, many different people and entities can all be causative in contributing to the existence of an entity.

In fact, it is not the multi-determined person, but the wholly *self*-determined person — concerned with being "one-up" on others or more powerful than they — who tries to take away the causativeness of others, to overwhelm their self-determinism or to make them dependent on him. Multi-determinism is a reflection of the basic ability to love, a reflection of such a high degree of affection that, to a degree, the multi-determined person *becomes* others, shares viewpoints with others, and does what he can to *help* them organize their worlds, in addition to trying to organize his own. He acts *with* the intentions and actions of others, not against them. The following definitions are useful, in this context:

Definition: Help is action that furthers the intentions of a person.

Definition: Harm is action that opposes the intentions of a person.

A truly multi-determined person transcends any particular game he is playing. He sees any such game as a subsidiary action, as a means of winning a higher-level game — the game of maximizing power in oneself, validity and value (empowerment) in one's world and communion with all persons — the game called "high ethics", "compassion", or "love". That is, indeed, the "master game", the traditional goal of the major religions and psychotherapies. If one person wins that game, all win it. And that is the goal, the optimal state, toward which we are striving in applied metapsychology.

The Six Domains

Other-determinism, self-determinism, and multi-determinism make up a gradient of increasing responsibility, increasing causativeness. But another way of increasing responsibility is to increase one's scope of activities. A person may undertake a very small task or a very large one. Her task may involve finding the right kind of chewing gum in a candy store or trying to prevent World War III. She may even decide to work unceasingly until "the last blade of grass attains Buddhahood."

When the scope of causativeness is considered, it is convenient to divide this scope into six concentric spheres of responsibility, or "domains":

Definition: A domain is a sphere of responsibility. There are six domains: self, intimates, groups, mankind, life, and the Infinite. These domains are concentric; each successive domain contains the previous ones, with the self at the center. Each domain has a subjective or mental side and an objective or physical side, reflecting the polar relationship between a person and his world.[31]

---

31. I am indebted to my friend Marian Volkman, director of the Center for Applied Metapsychology at Ann Arbor, for pointing out the two-poled nature of each domain.

The First Domain — The Self

On the physical side, the first domain contains one's body, clothes, tools, and other personal property — things with which one tends to identify oneself. On the subjective side, it includes oneself as a person, and one's thoughts, hopes, abilities, emotions, and mental pictures. A person who takes responsibility only for herself is at a relatively low level of causativeness. She is concerned only with self-improvement and with her own survival.

The Second Domain — Intimates

This includes sexual partners and other people to whom the person is very close, including family members and close friends. It may also include pets. The objective side of the second domain includes the physical characteristics of close friends and family, their bodies, sexual acts, physical nurturing and caretaking, their house, and other shared property. On the subjective side, it includes those individuals as beings, their personal characteristics and abilities, and their state of mind. A person operating in this domain is concerned with improving her close personal, familial, and sexual relationships and with the physical and mental well-being of her friends, family, and household.

The Third Domain — Groups

This includes all groups other than close family or intimate groups with which the person associates and identifies himself. These may include racial, business, social and political groups. Groups can be very large or very small. The objective side of this domain includes the bodies of group members, the property owned or used by each group, and the physical activities and products of the group. The subjective side includes the persons who comprise these groups and their subjective characteristics, as well as group agreements, policies, and culture. A person operating in the third domain is concerned with the survival and well-being of one or more groups and with furthering the purposes of the groups of which he is a part.

The Fourth Domain — Mankind

This includes all of the human race as a group. On the objective side lie all human bodies, all the physical products of Man's endeavors, and all the physical tools and physical aspects of Man's civilization and technology. On the subjective side lie basic aspects of human nature, including any spiritual characteristics, and all human aspirations and ideas. A person operating in this domain is concerned with the survival of the human race — with eliminating war, poverty, and disease, and with the education and enlightenment of all people.

The Fifth Domain — Life

This domain includes all forms of life. On an objective level, it includes all the flora and fauna of the planet and possibly extraterrestrial life as well, if such is conceived to exist. At a subjective level, it includes all consciousness and intention, all thoughts and experiences of all beings. A person operating in this domain is very concerned with ecology (on a physical level) and harmony (on a subjective level) of all forms of life.

The Sixth Domain — The Infinite

This domain includes everything in the universe, the "All-That-Is". On the objective side, it includes the entire physical universe, and, on the subjective side, it includes Universal Consciousness or God, if such is conceived to exist. There is no limit to what this domain contains, so it is called the "Infinite" domain. A person operating in this domain is concerned with her relationship to God and to the universe as a whole.

The Domains as a Hypersphere

I cannot forbear to indulge in a little speculation, at this point. As I mentioned in Chapter One (pp. 27-29), it has been said that, as one steps further and further back, renouncing identities, aspects of the "ego", and seeking one's "True Self", one can reach a point of ultimate enlightenment where one sees no separation between oneself and the entire universe because all particular identity is eliminated and only the universe exists as an identity. On the other hand, it is said that if one is able to expand one's identity to include the whole universe, there is likewise no point of separation between the self and the Infinite. Many Eastern religions teach that the "Self", in the truest meaning of the word, is God; others teach that one reaches one's true self by attaining unity with the universe.

Therefore, it might be said that the concentric spheres of responsibility and identity that comprise the domains actually form not an ordinary sphere but a hypersphere, a sphere whose outside surface ultimately turns around and becomes its center. Like a Moebius strip or a Klein bottle, its outside becomes its inside.

Inverted Domains

In order to operate effectively in a given domain, one must operate effectively in the domains that lie below it. A person cannot truly have a good marriage and family life until she herself is in reasonably good condition. Moreover, one is unlikely to have good work relationships when one's intimate relationships are in a state of turmoil. And one has to be able to function well as a group member in order to be effective in creating any meaningful beneficial effect on mankind or on planetary ecology. As a person's condition begins to deteriorate, she begins to retreat from the upper domains toward the lower ones. When a person is failing at her job, she can then, perhaps, only function as a friend and family member. Failing as a family member, she is thrown back on a concern with her own survival. But what happens when she begins to fail in her goals for herself?

At this point, the person's concerns may become "inverted". When a person has given up on herself, she may become obsessed with and dependent on sex, family, and friends. But now, instead of being interested in what she can *cause* in the second domain, she is concerned with needing to receive certain *effects* from that domain. When she fails to receive the wanted effects from the second domain, she may seek effects from the third domain. She may become a "workaholic". Since she is unable to function as a friend or family member, she may dive into her work or into other groups as an escape from her first and second domain failures. If she fails at her work or ceases to be accepted as a group member, she may obsessively become interested in achieving recognition as a benefactor of mankind. Here is the person who hates people but has an abstract "love of mankind". In an inverted fifth domain, a person, having given up on people, may be obsessed with pets or plants. Finally, a person may escape even from those concerns to an obsession with religion, where her only hope lies in receiving some kind of effect from a Supreme Being.

It is easy to distinguish a person in an inverted domain from a person who is truly functioning in that domain. A person functioning in a domain, as I mentioned, will be mainly concerned with *causing* effects, instead of being *affected*. His activities will tend to further well-being in that domain. A person in an inverted domain will be primarily concerned with receiving effects from that domain, and his efforts will tend to be destructive to the well-being of that domain, or at least not constructive. A person operating in a non-inverted domain will also be operating well in the lower domains whereas a person who is in an inverted domain will be inoperative or operating poorly in lower domains.[32]

Using the Domains to Help People

If a person is found to be operating in an inverted domain, it is important to begin by helping him attain functionality in the first domain, even though his attention may be elsewhere. Most people with marital problems are, in fact, suffering from first domain problems. These problems need to be addressed before the marital problems can be adequately addressed.

The domains also function as a useful way of categorizing experience with a view to handling it. One can address the domains individually, using various procedures, and handle each thoroughly in numerical order from first to sixth.

In mastering the domains, one is, in effect, mastering one's life.

Ethics

Although some, with Nietsche, have exhorted humankind to rise above considerations of good and evil, most of us live in a world in which we perceive that both exist. So it is necessary to address these issues.

From the person-centered viewpoint, we must decide what the necessary and sufficient conditions are, under which we attri-

---

32. A friend and colleague, Julie Grimes, pointed out to me that it is also possible that a person who had been able to operate successfully in the sixth domain might "evert" (instead of inverting) and take up the first, the second, and each of the lower domains on a completely new and more positive basis. In discovering God, one could have new realizations about oneself and about one's relationships to others. There is possibly no limit to the number of eversions of the domains one might enjoy.

bute goodness and badness to entities and people. In traditional philosophy,[33] goodness is divided into two types:

1. Instrumental goodness
2. Intrinsic goodness

We may think of something as good because it is useful as a *means* toward something else. A screwdriver is "good", in this sense, if it is useful for turning screws. Likewise, we may talk of a "good" barber, or a "good" plumber — one that does a good job. Or, we may think of something as good *in itself*. In this sense, we might think of a work of art as intrinsically good.[34] Some seem to regard life in general as intrinsically good; others are mainly concerned with the "purpose of life". The former tend to be preoccupied with the intrinsic goodness of things and ignore instrumental goodness to a large degree. These people seem to drift through life, living for the moment, never seeming to "go anywhere" or to have any purpose. People who go through life looking for immediate enjoyment, leisure activities, or "kicks" or who take an aesthetic pleasure in the process of living belong to this category. People who concentrate exclusively on instrumental goodness tend to have difficulty appreciating the intrinsic goodness of things. They give the impression of being "driven". They are always doing something for some purpose, rather than simply enjoying the doing of it.[35] People who are very career-oriented might fall into this category.

A person regards something as "good" if it is:

1. An *end*: Something that the person intends to bring about or create.

or

---

33. For instance, in Aristotle's *Nicomachean Ethics*, I, vii, 3-4.
34. If we are a proponent, with Metro Goldwyn Mayer, of *"Ars gratia artis"* — "Art for art's sake".
35. I am indebted to Michael Hanau for this observation.

2. A *means*: Something that enables a person to carry out his intentions.

The first corresponds to intrinsic goodness, and the second to instrumental goodness. In the act of lighting a fire, the fire is the intrinsic good I am seeking, and the match is the instrumental good I am using to achieve that intrinsic good.

Nowhere is it more important than in a discussion of ethics to remember that I am speaking from the person-centered viewpoint. If the statements I make seem to be outrageous, I urge the reader to look at them again from the viewpoint of an individual person at a particular moment in time. Having given this caveat, I will go on to assert that *no one ever intends something which, at the moment of intending it, he does not conceive to be good*, either instrumentally or intrinsically. Conversely, a person does not view or contemplate something he conceives to be good at a certain moment without desiring or intending it at that moment. In other words, a person intends to bring about whatever he conceives to be good at any particular moment. So, for a particular person at a particular time (i.e., from a person-centered viewpoint), what is good *is* what is intended, and vice versa. The two are coextensive. Everything we seek, we seek because at the moment we seek it we think it is good or right, and, on the other hand, we always seek good or right things, *as we conceive them at a particular time*. Even people like Hitler and Stalin, who committed what any sane person regards as atrocities, were, in their own view at the time, performing high acts of heroism that the rest of humanity did not have the vision to perceive as such or the guts to perform. I most emphatically do not condone these atrocious actions because they conflict not only with my own value system but also with values that are almost universally held. However, no one — not even Hitler or Stalin — does something he thinks is wrong at the time. If he really thought it was wrong, he would not do it. The ethical code that people live by is their *real* ethical code, not necessarily the one they talk about or the one they may *think* they are espousing. I think it clarifies our thoughts to decide that that is true by definition.

A person may, of course, be in conflict about whether an action that he is doing is right or wrong. For instance, if I eat an ice cream cone when I know I should be minding my cholesterol intake, I may feel that it is wrong. *But* I will also have success-fully rationalized it to a point where I believe, at that exact moment, that eating the cone is more right than wrong, e.g., because I think it is OK to have some pleasure in life, or because it *tastes* good, and "a little bit of cholesterol cannot hurt". I may regret my action immediately afterward, especially if I have a sud-den attack of angina, heartburn, or toothache, but *at the time*, it will be found that I thought the action was right, or at least justifi-able. Otherwise, I would not have done it. A person, at the instant of doing something, has the action justified to the point where it is considered at least *slightly* better to do that act than not to do it. Often, a person seems to expend the minimum amount of effort required to justify an action — just enough to tip the balance in favor of acceptability. It would seem to be "waste-ful" to try to justify an act more strongly![36]

This concept *does* allow for self-deception. One can be deceived, or one can deceive oneself, into thinking that something is good when, in one's more sober or reflective moments, one realizes it is not. Nevertheless, at the time one does it, one thinks it is good. Obversely, a person may avoid doing something (as when he procrastinates about going to the dentist) that he "knows" is right. But this, again, is an act of self-deception, in which something else seems more important (or a better thing to do) at any given moment, such as visiting a friend, mailing a

---

36. Leon Festinger [*A Theory of Cognitive Dissonance* (Stanford University Press, 1962)] did some interesting work on how "cognitive dissonance" is eliminated *after* the fact of having made a decision. What I would find even more interesting would be a similar study of how people "sell" themselves and others on making certain decisions, *before* the fact, or *in* the act of deciding. Why should a person try to "sell" herself on something, before the fact? The real purpose of the act she is trying to sell herself on is to avoid the emergence of repressed pain. But if she allowed herself to become aware of the real reason for the action, she would have to confront the pain she is trying to avoid. Hence she must invent a fallacious reason for acting in that way, much as a person acting on a post-hypnotic suggestion tries to justify her acts.

letter, or almost *anything*. It is only when these self-deceptions
and rationalizations break down that he overcomes his aversion
and goes to the dentist. Then and only then does he feel that his
procrastination was "wrong" and going to the dentist is right.
This parallels the momentary infallibility of beliefs and intentions.
Recall:

> A person never *has* a false belief; he only *had* false
> beliefs.[37]

and

> A person never *does* something he does not intend to do;
> he only *did* things that resulted in unforeseen and unin-
> tended consequences.

to which I can now add:

> In his own view, a person never *does* anything wrong; he
> only *did* wrong things.[38]

Since the possibilities of higher or lower hierarchies of identity and intention are virtually limitless, it is hard to conceive of
anything that could not be at certain times intrinsically good, from
the viewpoint of a limited intention, and at other times instrumentally good, from the viewpoint of a more extended intention. The
terms "intrinsic" and "instrumental" only describe a *relationship*
between two things contained in the hierarchy of intentions, not
an absolute position in that hierarchy. Saying that something is

---

37. See Chapter Four, pp. 169-172.

38. Because of this fact, it is relatively useless to try to get a person to change
his behavior by telling him it is wrong, or by getting him to tell you what is
wrong with it. From his viewpoint it is *not* wrong, and he will simply assert
this rightness all the more strongly, overtly or covertly. A much better
tactic is (without being to any degree sarcastic) to get the person to tell you
all the reasons why it was a *right* thing to do. This tactic will allow the
person to examine his reasons for doing the action, whereupon he will tend
to spot the flaws in his thinking.

"intrinsically good" is equivalent to saying that it is an end towards which something else is a means. Saying that something is "instrumentally good" is equivalent to saying that it is a means towards some other end. If something is good as a *means* to something else, then it is the object of a lower-level intention or subsidiary intention, provided that one is aware of it at all. If I intend to paint an oil painting, then I will probably need a palate knife to do the job. We would say, then, that a palate knife is *instrumentally* good toward this goal of doing an oil painting. But in a context where my present goal is to find a palate knife, finding the palate knife may become the *intrinsically* good thing toward which other goods are instrumental, such as having money in my wallet, having gas in my car so I can drive to the art store, etc. And the oil painting could, from a different perspective, be regarded as merely instrumental toward providing pleasure for others or money for me.

When we tell someone to be "task-oriented", we are asking her to view the goodness of entities as instrumental toward a certain task. In other words, we are telling her to expand her identity to include her tools. On the other hand, when we exhort people to be more "process-oriented" — to enjoy or appreciate the process of doing things, rather than becoming "attached to the fruits of their labors" — we are asking them to *shed* a more extended identity and now to regard things that were formerly seen as instrumentally good as being intrinsically good. When art is regarded as intrinsically good, we see it from the viewpoint of "art for art's sake" or "the medium is the message", whereas when art is regarded as instrumentally good, we see it (for example) as a means of communication. Both forms of goodness are, however, ruled by intention.

Looking at this issue from a person-centered viewpoint also has practical implications. To convince someone else that an entity is good, it is necessary to get her to intend that that entity should exist, or continue to exist — i.e., to *assent* to it. One does this by showing her that she "really wants" that entity to exist.

Statements made to others (or to oneself) about what is good or bad, like other statements, are, in fact, functionally the same as commands. If I tell you, "It is good for you to get lots of exercise," I am doing the same thing as if I say, "Get lots of exercise," or (as I have just mentioned) "You really want to get lots of exercise." All the arguments I can give you to prove that exercise is good are the same arguments I would give to get you to *want* to exercise. Conversely, any time I want you to intend something or support an intention of mine, the arguments I give you to get you to intend that thing will also be arguments to prove to you that that thing is good.

Commands can also be regarded as ethical exhortations. Even a declarative statement, which is a command to agree or concur (in believing something), could be considered to be an ethical exhortation. Stating "The cat is on the mat," is equivalent to saying, "Accept (or assent to) the concept that the cat is on the mat!", which is, in turn, equivalent to "You really want to accept the fact that the cat is on the mat," which, in turn is equivalent to, "It would be good if you accepted the fact that the cat is on the mat."

When you give a command (including that kind of command called a "question"), you are trying to get someone to do something. More to the point, you want him to *intend* something. Since people do not do what they do not intend, to get someone to do something, you must first get him to *intend* to do that thing.[39]

In deciding for yourself what is good, you are deciding which intentions to have. In telling someone else what is good, you are asking him to have certain intentions.

So the definition of good — *from the person-centered viewpoint* — is:

Definition: Good is that which is intended.[40]

and conversely:

---

39. Intention is the beginning of an activity, as discussed in Chapter Two, p. 94, and Chapter 3, pp. 132-133.
40. See Aristotle's beginning statement in the *Nicomachean Ethics*, "Every art and every investigation, and likewise every practical pursuit or undertaking, seems to aim at some good; hence it had been well said that the Good is

Definition: Evil is that which is counter-intended.

where

Definition: Counter-intention is the intention that some
entity *not* exist. The entity opposed may be an object,
an event, a state of affairs, or another intention.[41]

The word "ethics" actually has two quite separate definitions,
which makes ethics a little hard to talk about. "Ethics" is used,
first of all, to mean the study of, the knowledge of, or the act of
deciding, what is good or evil, or — equivalently, from the
person-centered viewpoint — the process of studying, deciding, or
knowing what intentions to have. An "ethical" decision, in this
sense of the word, is a decision to intend a certain thing. In fact,
any decision is an "ethical" decision, in this sense of the word
"ethics". The second meaning of "ethics" is "goodness". In this
sense, some of a person's decisions may be said to be "ethical"
and others "unethical". I will use "ethics" and "ethical" in the
first sense of the word. "Good" and "goodness" will serve in
place of the other meaning of "ethics".

Ethics is thought of as being confined to sapient beings; non-
sapient beings are not considered to be moral or immoral. One
definition of "sapient being" is "a being who is aware of being
aware." Animals (if they are viewed as not sapient) may be *very*
aware of and responsive to their environment. Yet (unless we
regard them as sapient) we do not think of these animals as being
aware that they are aware. One who is aware of being aware can
direct his own awareness, rather than merely *reacting* to his

---

That at which all things aim."

41. It should be obvious that in giving these definitions I have by-passed the
question of what is "absolutely good", whether or not it is recognized to be
so by anyone, just as I earlier by-passed the question of what *exists*
absolutely, whether or not anyone knows it exists. See Chapter One, pp.
55-56. Adherence to the person-centered viewpoint requires that these
issues be bypassed.

environment. His awareness or attention becomes an *instrument* for him; he can "step back" from it and regard it as such.

Similarly, a sapient being is capable of "intending to intend". If one conceives of animals as having intentions but as being incapable of *controlling* their intentions (e.g., as being "ruled by instinct" or the like, which may or may not be true of some or all animals), then one is conceiving of them as neither ethical agents nor sapient beings. If one regards animals as capable of making ethical choices, then one cannot conceive of them as being any more (or less) "innocent" than humans. They are either responsible for their intentions and therefore capable of right or wrong conduct or not responsible for their actions and incapable of such conduct. Therefore I assert:

> **Definition**: Ethics is control of intention. It is intending to intend, the action of choosing amongst different intentions.

It is because people are viewed as being in control of their impulses and intentions that they are held responsible for their actions — i.e., held to be ethical agents. If they had no control over their impulses and intentions, they would also have no control over their actions and could not be held responsible for them.

Integrity and Identity

A major facet of ethics has to do with integrity:

> **Definition**: Integrity is congruity of intention and identity.

If one has assumed a given identity, one is constrained to intend certain things and not to intend others, in carrying out the activities of that identity.[42] When I am being a classical guitarist, I

---

42. I am indebted to Dr. Harold Puthoff for this observation.

must control any impulses to stand up, jump around, or play non-classical riffs. All these actions are incompatible with creating the effects that a classical guitarist is supposed to create. If I did these things, I would be a "bad" classical guitarist, though I might be a "good" rock guitarist. As a parent, I am supposed to care for my children. The basic intention of a parent is to nurture and protect his children; if I decide to abandon them or to beat them, I am a "bad" parent. If, as a boxer, I am supposed to disable my opponent or render him unconscious, a decision not to hurt my opponent makes me a "bad" boxer. Deliberately "throwing" a fight is considered very bad form. But if I do intend to inflict damage, I am a "good" boxer.

A person who lacks integrity has "incomposssible"[43] intentions and cannot control them so as to make them align with each other. As a student, a person has an intention to do well and learn. But, swayed by biological urges, addictions, habits, or peer-pressure, he may also have other incongruent intentions, such as an urge to go to the movies, to take drugs, or to engage in unrestrained sexual activities. His failure to control these intentions results in his acting in an inconsistent, unintegrated manner. The result of this lack of control is that he tends not to be successful or happy because he cannot concentrate sufficiently on his major tasks in life.[44]

For a person, what is good depends on the identity that he has assumed at any given moment. Inflicting physical damage on another's body is "good" for a person who is being a boxer or a soldier but "bad" for the same person when he is being a spouse or parent. Lecturing on entomology is "good" for a person who has assumed the identity of a professor but "bad" for the same person when he is at a cocktail party or making love to his wife.

---

43. Mutually conflicting and incapable of co-existing.
44. Certain techniques of applied metapsychology can improve integrity by helping a person:

   1. Find incongruencies of intention and resolve them.
   2. Eliminate uncontrollable intentions or bring them under control.

It is the identity a person has at a particular time that determines what is good or bad for him at that time.[45]

A person making an ethical choice always takes the viewpoint of a "senior" identity, looking at the various sub-identities and sub-intentions that further its basic purposes and allowing an internal dialogue to occur between them. We now see that such dialogues are crucial to the ethical life of the person. The current identity and its purposes are paramount to a person at any given moment, but since the person can also "be" senior identities, he has the ability to "step back" from the identity he is in at any particular time and look at the identity he has just been "being". Without this ability to "step back", a person would be fixed in the identity he is currently being and would be unable to make ethical choices. So the basic action of ethics is stepping back from what a person was being and intending a moment ago, examining that identity and the overall situation, and deciding which intention and identity to choose now. Ethics, then, is the action of deciding which intentions to have, which identities to select, which activities to engage in, and which activities to abandon, for a "higher" good — i.e., in furtherance of the intentions of a "senior" identity.

We see now that versatility — the ability to be "flexible" in expanding, contracting, and shifting identities — has a great deal to do with a person's ability to make ethical decisions. In fact, the ability to make such decisions *is* the ability to control which intentions and identities one assumes. A person fixed in an identity will find it very difficult to make them. Hence it is understandable that meekness and humility (in the Christian system) and "eliminating the ego" (in Eastern practices) are cardinal

---

45. This is not to say that I think that all *identities* are of equal ethical value. A major task a person has is that of deciding what to *be* in any given situation. And it is definitely better to assume certain identities than to assume others. I can see no circumstance, for instance, in which it would be appropriate to make a career of being a tyrant or a torturer. Such identities, and their associated intentions, violate the basic nature and intentions of a person.

virtues, since egoism and pride are just inflexibility in the assumption of identity, whether the person is unwilling to step back from some approved-of identity or unwilling to assume some non-approved-of (but necessary) identity.

Worldly Good and Evil

The major criteria that a person will use in making ethical decisions have to do with the intentions of the "senior" identities she steps back to. But perhaps a person's most fundamental goal, with respect to her world, is to increase her power, i.e., to have a world containing maximum value and validity — empowerment.

As was outlined in Chapter Four (pp. 195-197), power is composed of a proper balance of drive, control, and understanding. Personal power corresponds to empowerment in the person's world (value and validity), which are composed of a proper balance of pleasure, order and heuristics. Maximum value is what a person strives to produce by her creative actions; maximum validity is what she strives to produce by her receptive actions. The hedonists, then, are only one-third right in their view of basic goodness — order and heuristics are also basic goods. Aristotle, in stating that the basic good is knowledge,[46] is only one-third right — order and beauty (and pleasure) are equally basic. And those — such as Thomas Hobbes[47] and B.F. Skinner[48] — to whom an orderly world is paramount and who would be in favor of a "controlled society", are only one-third right.

The work of Bruno Bettelheim,[49] Viktor Frankl,[50] and others

46. *Nicomachean Ethics* X, vii-viii.
47. Hobbes, Thomas *Leviathan*, in *The English Philosophers from Bacon to Mill* Burtt, E.A., Ed. (Modern Library, New York, 1939) pp. 129-234.
48. Skinner, Burrhus F. *Walden Two* (Macmillan, London, 1969).
49. Bettelheim, B. "Trauma and Reintegration" in *Surviving and Other Essays* (Knopf, New York, 1979) p. 34ff.
50. Frankl, Victor, *Man's Search for Meaning* (Simon and Schuster, New York, 1984).

has demonstrated how an experience like that of a Nazi death-camp can be near-ultimate in painfulness and chaos and yet lead to a great deal of knowledge and wisdom, so that the person can look back on the experience and see that some "good" has come of it. A commonly expressed "optimistic" view of life is that any kind of experience can be beneficial, because it is bound to pro-mote aesthetics, pleasure, order, learning, or some combination of the above. I agree that, in this sense, there is, at least poten-tially, some good in any experience. But the person always has to balance one good against another so as to maximize pleasure, order, and heuristics. Certainly, if one *has* to have an experience, it is best to make the most of it. But that does not mean that all experiences are equally good for a person to have. By her choices, a person attempts to bring into existence the experiences she values and to avoid unwanted experiences.

Personal and Interpersonal Good and Evil

What I have said above concerns a person's relation to the world of *things*. In his dealings with *people*, a person has a high-level goal to maximize the degree of communion between himself and others. In this effort, he may regard some people as "good", or more worthy of communion, and others as "bad", or less worthy of communion. But in what sense could a *person* be said to be "good" or "bad"? As I have earlier emphasized (p. 15), a person is not just a thing, an entity. He *lives*. A person is not an object or state of affairs that can be created or brought about. Recall our definition of "good":

Definition: Good is that which is intended.

By this definition, a person cannot be intrinsically or instrumen-tally good, because a person is not something that can be intended![51] A person's *actions* can be good or bad, intrinsically or instrumentally, because they can be the object of an intention (either his or another's), and a person can be moral or immoral — he can make good or bad ethical choices.

To make sense of this tricky subject, we must remember that what is good *for a person* is what either constitutes or leads to success in the carrying out of his intentions. So, in a vague sense, a person is "good", for himself, to the degree that he is successful in carrying out his own intentions. A person regards himself as "bad" when he accumulates a lot of failures. Likewise, a person regards another person as "good", in this same sense, when the other person intends to help him — i.e., when the other person has intentions and actions that are congruent or in agreement with his. This is the "instrumental goodness" that a person has for another.

Another way of looking at the idea that people are "good" is the concept that a "good" person is one who intends to do good deeds. In some ethical systems, a person is judged for his intentions rather than for the final outcome of acting on these intentions. If a person is misinformed and so actually commits a harmful act when he thinks he is doing something laudable, he is not regarded as evil. By this definition, everyone would have to be judged "good" because, as I have shown, everyone intends what he considers to be good at the time he intends it.

Finally, we tend to regard as "good" those people whom we like. Goodness, pleasure, and beauty are what, in the world, correspond to affinity in the person. One could therefore say, loosely, that people would be seen as basically "good" or "bad", depending on one's basic affinity for them. But a person's

---

51. Except, perhaps, by his Creator! Again, this is not to say that an *identity* (such as that of a torturer or a mass murderer) cannot be evil. By saying that Hitler and Torquemada are basically "good", I do not mean to condone or recommend these identities but only to reaffirm that even these individuals, in their distorted way, were trying to accomplish what they considered to be good deeds.

tendency to have affection for others is more fundamental than his tendency to dislike them, however twisted or blunted the former tendency may be for one who is low on the Emotional Scale. Therefore, people regard each other as basically "good", in some sense.

In actual fact, however, we regard a person as good or bad when we see him as an object, an entity. But when thought of — correctly — as a living being, a person can be neither good nor bad in the same sense that an entity can. She simply *lives*.[52] A person is ethically transcendent in the same way that she is existentially or ontologically transcendent. She transcends existence, because, by her activities and her agreements, she *causes* existence. She transcends goodness and badness, because, by controlling her intentions, she *brings about* goodness and badness. The way to regard other people is not to judge them as good or evil but to have affection for them — to love them, to communicate with them, and to comprehend their communication.

From the person-centered viewpoint, good is that which is intended by the person and evil is that which is counter-intended by her. Harm is action that opposes her intentions; help is action that furthers them. A basically good or helpful act, performed by one person and affecting another, is an act that the second person perceives as furthering her intentions. A harmful act creates an effect that the second person perceives as *countering* her intentions. As with her own acts, a person may change her mind about the goodness or badness of another person's actions. That is, she

---

52. This point is also made by Dr. Albert Ellis [in a lecture given in the conference on the Evolution of Psychotherapy, Phoenix, 1985], who disagrees with Carl Roger's view that people are basically good and should be treated with "unconditional positive regard". Ellis makes the point that if a therapist validates her client, it may make the client nervous, because of the possibility of *not* being validated later. So Ellis advocates a completely non-judgmental position, in which the client is regarded as neither good nor bad but only "alive". Ellis thus reaches the same conclusion as mine, but for different reasons.

may initially feel another's act is against her intentions (bad) and eventually (through becoming aware of certain things, or possibly by becoming *un*aware of certain things) reach the conclusion that it aligns with her intentions and therefore was "really" good. For instance, you may tackle a stranger and push her down on the ground. She may feel that you have done something bad, since she probably intended to remain upright. But when, a second later, a rain of machine-gun bullets crosses the space that she formerly occupied, she will probably change her mind, and — in the light of her more important intention to stay alive and unharmed — will feel that it was a very good act indeed. Conversely, you may do something for someone that she initially regards as good but eventually perceives as having been bad. A con artist who sells phony stocks to old ladies may be thought of by her clients as doing them a great favor. Six months later, when they discover she has absconded with their money, they will consider that she has harmed them.

We judge a past action, as we judge everything, by our *current* intentions and knowledge, rather than by the knowledge and intentions we had at the time of the action. Even if we believe that the person whom our proposed action will affect is likely to change his knowledge and intentions later to align with our actions, it is nevertheless generally a good rule to get the other person's agreement *before* doing something that affects him in any significant way. That way, one avoids any *temporary* evil, which, though temporary, is still evil to the other person. There are emergency situations, such as the machine-gun attack mentioned above, where one does not have time to explain and get the other person's agreement. Outside of combat and child-rearing in dangerous environments, such situations are extremely rare. It is tempting, sometimes, to say or assume that an emergency exists, in order to avoid having to explain to others or get their agreement. This is an extremely risky practice if one hopes to act for the benefit of all concerned.

There are other situations where several people's different intentions are involved. In such cases, a person still has the duty to explain to the parties concerned why he is acting as he is. In such a situation, *someone's* intentions are likely to be thwarted.

But the actor should judge the propriety of his deed by predicting the effect it will have on all the persons it affects, including himself. In other words, he must be multi-determined. A proper act is that which takes into account all the relevant intentions of affected persons, each intention being multiplied by its appropriate cardinality or intensity factor. If something is very important (e.g., a life-and-death matter) to one person and unwanted but of minor importance to a few others, it may be correct to decide in favor of the one, because the cardinality tips the balance. On the other hand, if one or two (e.g., a "vocal minority") feel quite strongly about something and a much greater number of others feel only *fairly* strongly about it, it might be correct to decide in favor of the majority.

In arriving at a proper ethical decision according to what furthers the sum of (intention × importance) for all concerned persons, it is important to realize that people can reconsider and remake their intentions. It should not be assumed that others' — or one's own — intentions and importances are cast in concrete. In making an optimal ethical decision, part of what needs to be done may well consist of insisting on full communication amongst those involved. One must not only find out what they want and how much they want it, but also make sure they get as much data as they need to ensure that their intentions and importances can be informed and aligned. One does not simply do a survey and then apply a kind of calculus to it. The result of omitting communication and sharing of information would be to make a *less* ethical decision than one could make if all were allowed to communicate about the issues, because, in the absence of communication and agreement, the sum of (intention × importance) would be less in favor of the final decision than in the presence of such discussion. One of the factors that helps people to thus reach a consensus is their natural tendency to commune with each other. Another is that the rule of pleasure-order-heuristics amounts to a universally understood and agreed-upon ethical standard since it could fairly be said that the ultimate intention of any person is to enhance these three factors along with communion with one's fellows. As I have shown, enhancing these characteristics of a world for one person tends to enhance them for others as well.

A person's innate sense of justice is equivalent to his tendency to maximize communication, comprehension, and affection to, from, and amongst others and himself.[53]

These criteria must also be considered in making ethical decisions. As John Donne observed, "No man is an island." People seem to have a very high-level intention to share their viewpoints and their worlds with others and to share others' worlds. A person who is unable to do so is extremely unhappy. It is an often-observed fact that a person who has at least one close, loving relationship — who has someone to talk to, someone who can comprehend his viewpoint — will not commit suicide. It is (to me) a mystery and a miracle that people can love each other, communicate with each other, and share worlds with each other. And it is this miracle that gives meaning to life. The entire physical universe, with all its wonders, and the care with which we interpret and change our experience so as to maximize pleasure, order and heuristics, appears to be merely a stage that we are continually setting for the living drama of love and communication.

---

53. A person wants to do this on all four "flows", as discussed earlier in this chapter, pp. 237-238.

PART II

BASIC DISABILITIES

Chapter Six

Types of Disability

I have spent the first part of this book outlining a person's basic abilities and the nature of her world as she sees it. In the second part, I shall focus on various disabilities and the undesirable conditions that result from them. My decision to present the material in this order has been quite deliberate. It is not possible to either address or understand disabilities without first understanding the corresponding abilities. The practice of psychotherapy has often tried to talk about mental "diseases" and "disorders", without really defining clearly what constitutes a *desirable* mental condition. But trying to help someone, without first having a clear conception of what you are trying to help her *toward*, is a very difficult business. In the discussion of disabilities that follows, therefore, I will define each disability as a failure in a corresponding ability, and the general condition of being "disabled" will be contrasted with the goal of being "fully realized".

Categorizing Disabilities

Naturally, as there is no end to the magnitude or variety of abilities a person could conceivably have, there is no end to the number of different disabilities she may have. Nevertheless, it *is* useful to classify these disabilities — in a way that enables us to *do* something about them.

In using the term "disabilities", I wish most emphatically to avoid the medical model. I have tried to be very careful to avoid words like "illness", "disease", or even "disorders", which have a medical flavor. Also, I do not refer to people as "patients", nor to people who render help to other people as "therapists". I concur fully with Thomas Szasz, who has brilliantly shown that the concept of "mental illness" is a mere metaphor, and a useless and destructive one at that.[1] It is destructive because it imparts a stigma to the person to whom it is applied. This model, in fact, is worse than useless because the difficulties a person has are *not* illnesses; it clouds our thinking to refer to them as such. It is painful enough to be unhappy and confused without having one's burdens added to by being stigmatized as "sick", "neurotic", or "psychotic".[2]

The basic principles an extremely upset person uses to organize her experience are the same as those any other person uses. It is just that the upset person has had a number of losses and failures and can more easily recover from her upset with the help and companionship of another person than she can by herself. To help others in this way is highly legitimate, even if you are not

---

1. Szasz, Thomas *The Myth of Mental Illness* (Dell Publishing, New York, 1961).

2. Besides, *persons* cannot be ill; their *bodies* may be. A body may become ill when its owner is unhappy, uncomfortable, or confused in certain ways. And people do tend to become unhappy when their bodies are ill. But the two should not be equated. In equating them, the medical model violates the person-centered viewpoint since a person experiences herself only *sometimes* as co-extensive with the body.

being a "doctor", treating the "sick". Shamans, priests, ministers, bartenders, friends, and relatives have fulfilled this function for millenia — and still do, in most parts of the world.[3] It is only in the past two hundred years and in the western world that the medical model has obtruded into the personal lives of people.

Fixation of Identity

A person has a basic ability to *be* various things. Optimally, a person is able to extend, contract, or shift his identity at will to suit the circumstances. The corresponding disability is a fixation of identity — an inability to shed an identity, as in the "Great Person Syndrome", or an inability to extend an identity, as in self-deprecatory identities. More specifically, an unwillingness or inability to *assume* a larger identity causes a person to become depressed, to feel inferior, or to be unable to handle power or assume responsibility, whereas an inability to *shed* identities and assume senior, less specialized identities produces arrogance or conceit, a "superiority complex". An inability to shift to a *different* identity results in getting "stuck in a rut" in life; it is an inability to change the course of life when necessary. All of these disabilities prevent a person from having a full range of ethical choices in any given situation since an ethical choice is basically a choice of identity or intention.[4] A person with a disability related to identities will tend to do things he regrets later because he has difficulty selecting the correct intention or identity to fit the occasion. Teenagers commonly feel they must engage in destructive acts in order to be "cool". The "being cool" is just a fixed identity. Some adults feel they must always be "sociable". It might

---

3. In the movie "Crocodile Dundee", upon being told that a woman is seeing a psychiatrist, the Australian hero asks, "Why? Doesn't she have any mates?"

4. Again, I am using "ethical" to mean "pertaining to the act of deciding what is good or bad", not to mean "good". See Chapter Five, p. 257.

sometimes be appropriate to be "cool" or "sociable", but if the same identity is applied to all circumstances it will prove inappropriate to many of them.

Disabilities of Creating and Receiving

As the first set of abilities just discussed has to do with *being*, so the second set has to do with *doing* — creating and receiving — i.e., with our ability to do what we want, and to *have* the kind of experience we want, structured in the way we want it to be.

As I noted earlier (pp. 163-169), a person endeavors to maximize the combination of pleasure, order, and heuristics (i.e., empowerment) in his world. Stated from the person side of the person-world polarity, he wishes to maximize his own power: drive, control, and understanding and minimize the corresponding disabilities: aversion; overwhelm, helplessness, irresponsibility; bafflement, ignorance and boredom. (See Figure 34).

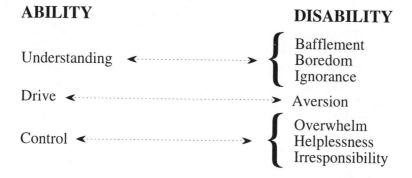

ABILITY	DISABILITY

Understanding ⟷ { Bafflement / Boredom / Ignorance

Drive ⟷ Aversion

Control ⟷ { Overwhelm / Helplessness / Irresponsibility

Figure 34. Subjective view: basic powers and disabilities.

Stated objectively, a person wishes to maximize validity and value: pleasure, order, and heuristics; he wishes to minimize loss of value and lack of validity: pain/ugliness, disorder, and monotony/tedium. (See Figure 35). Some forms of help (such as making environmental changes, providing jobs, money, and entertainment for a person) directly enhance the quality of a person's

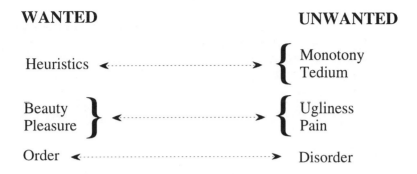

Figure 35. Objective view: basic wanted/unwanted conditions.

life by making changes in his *objective* environment. The actions of applied metapsychology, on the other hand, mostly concentrate on enabling a person to change his *subjective* environment. The focus is on enhancement of *power*, rather than direct enhancement of *empowerment*. When the person becomes more powerful or gets rid of disabilities, he will produce a better world for himself.

People seek communion; they are devoted — perhaps *primarily* — to maximizing communication, comprehension, and affection with other people. The corresponding disabilities are inability or unwillingness to communicate, isolation or loneliness, and aversion.[5]

---

5. All of these abilities and disabilities are manifested along the four flows: inflow, outflow, crossflow, and reflexive flow (or reflexion). The reflexive disabilities tend to add up to:

   1. A lack of contact with aspects of oneself; perhaps a fragmentation of different identities within the self.
   2. Lack of control and coordination of one's own intentions and actions.
   3. Internecine warfare within the self.
   4. Self-hate.

   See Chapter Five (pp. 235-238) for a discussion of the four flows.

Some dislikes or aversions are completely idiosyncratic, aesthetic, or culturally determined. Of these, one can only say, *"De gustibus non disputandum"*.[6] Others are peculiar to an individual but explainable by an analysis of her past experiences. Still others are intrinsic and universal. These are the ones that are of most interest because it is out of these intrinsic aversions that all others are built.

Intrinsic aversions fall into two categories:

1. Entities for which people just "naturally" have an aversion — certain specific "built-in" aversions common to people.
2. Aversions determined by the rules and principles people universally use to organize their worlds.

In the category of "natural aversions" lie certain physical sensations for which we appear to have a "built-in" aversion. These include the various sensations called "physical pain", most types of sensory overload (such as overly bright lights or loud noises), and certain other sensations, including itching, the feeling of hunger, and nausea. These sensations mostly have to do with preserving the body, and they appear to be constant as long as a person identifies herself with her body. For practical purposes, the average person does appear to have her body as a fixed part of her identity. Except under extraordinary circumstances — such as masochistic delight, religious ecstasy, or sagehood — these various bodily phenomena are universally viewed as painful or unpleasant.

Other common aversions can be understood from an examination of the basic ways in which a person seems to organize her experience. These would exist whether a person had a body or not. A person seeks to maximize empowerment in her world and communion in her relationships with other people. In discussing aversions and pain, I have been talking about the opposite of affinity, which is present in both the ability and the communion triads. So I could generalize to state that a person has an

---

6. "There is no accounting for tastes."

aversion to aversion, in much the same way that I could say that a person has affinity for affinity, because she seeks to experience pleasure and beauty.[7]

The fact that a person has aversion to something is *itself* something to which she has an aversion, a fact that tends to lead to some unpleasant "vicious circles": Person **X**, say, has a strong aversion to entity **A**. Let us call the fact that person **X** has this aversion "fact **B**". Then **X** has a *further* aversion to being aware of fact **B** (the fact that she has an aversion to entity **A**). This complicates, reinforces, and *makes less accessible* the original aversion to entity **A**. The aversion **X** has to fact **B** can *itself* be unpleasant, which can lead to an aversion — fact **C** — to fact **B**. And so forth. For instance, a person gets up to speak in front of an audience (fact **A**). She has an aversion to public speaking (feels afraid — wants to run away — fact **B**). Then (fact **C**) she hates herself for wanting to run away. And maybe (fact **D**) she even feels she is bad for hating herself for being nervous.[8]

Scolding someone is counter-productive; it only reinforces her tendency to a vicious circle of aversion. If I want to help someone, I must (as a first step) be *accepting* of any aversion she presents to me and non-judgmentally make it safe for her to be aware of and talk about the aversion. It is this acceptance that breaks the vicious circle. That is one reason why a facilitator *must* be non-judgmental.[9]

People also have a natural aversion to feeling helpless, trapped, or overwhelmed, towards entities or conditions that tend to nullify their power and freedom. This aversion is based on the universal tendency people have toward wanting to bring order into their environment.

---

7. Hence the Rodgers and Hart song, "Falling in Love with Love".
8. I deal with some of the other effects of a person's aversion to aversion in Chapter Seven, pp. 331-334.
9. Other reasons are given in Part III, pp. 387-388.

People naturally dislike entities that are unintelligible or situations that are boring, in which they cannot learn anything further. This aversion is the counterpart of the universal tendency toward wanting to understand one's world. People want their surroundings to be intelligible, and to be able to learn from them.[10]

A person must balance his desire for control and predictability with his desire for learning. A completely ordered world would be sterile and boring because of its anti-heuristic quality,[11] whereas an overly disordered world would be overwhelming. People have a natural aversion for either extreme.

In their dealings with others, people naturally tend to avoid situations where too little communication occurs, or where they are cut off from sharing with other people. In other words, they do not like to be lonely, isolated, or misunderstood. This aversion is the counterpart of the universal tendency to seek communion — communication, comprehension, and affection — with others. But communication and comprehension must also be balanced against the need for stability and order. A person can be averse to an *excess* of contact with other people because such contact may be overwhelming to him. He may, therefore, seek a degree of isolation as a remedy for excessive disorder.[12]

---

10. A good, (though extreme) example of a naturally aversive situation is a condition of sensory deprivation. A person in a sensory deprivation tank, with all his various sensory inputs nullified, may eventually become very uncomfortable or even psychotic. He will strive to escape from the boredom into an inner world of fantasy. It has also been found that people subjected to sensory deprivation become extremely suggestible, because *any* new datum is desperately seized upon as at least one intelligible factor in the person's experience. This may, indeed, be one of the mechanisms of hypnosis. The hypnotist induces a state of sensory deprivation by getting the subject to concentrate only on him or on his voice. The hypnotist becomes the only source of new data for the subject and so becomes a cardinal point for him.

11. This is the subject of many anti-Utopian novels, such as Huxley's *Brave New World* and Orwell's *1984*)

12. A "catatonic" is perhaps a person whose universe has too much disorder in it already. For him, virtually *any* additional randomness or communication from another person can be intolerable. So he tries to find a quiet location in which to sit or lie quietly and tune everything out. But others of us also

I have tried to separate the various disabilities into useful categories and thus to produce an inventory of the ways in which conditions can be sub-optimal for a person. The different disabilities or inabilities relate to each other in a variety of ways, however. We have already seen how drive, control, and understanding interrelate, and how communication, comprehension, and affection relate to each other. There are likewise many interactions among the corresponding disabilities. Although I will attempt to present things in as logical an order as possible, I will have to refer forward as well as backward in discussing the many interconnections. For this reason, the reader might be well advised to read through Part II twice.

Upsets

We have seen that people seek communion with others. They also want to be able to control and understand entities. As long as a person is progressing toward a greater degree of personal power and communion, she is relatively content. But when she suffers a lowering of power or communion, particularly a sudden or unexpected one, she becomes upset.

If Marsha has no particular affection for George, that fact may be something she wants to change, but it does not, in itself, create an upset. But if she has a high degree of affection for him and something happens to dramatically lower it, that *does* result in an upset. For instance, let us say that George goes out with Susan. Marsha may perceive this as a lowering of communication, of sharing, and of affection with herself. She thinks that if George still had a very high affection for her, he would not feel a need to be with someone else. His communicating or sharing of experience with Susan may appear to her as a turning away from

---

feel the need to retreat from the world at times and be by ourselves.

communication and sharing with herself. The above considerations can apply to any close second-domain relationship, not just sexual ones.[13] Non-sexual friendships can be extremely intense, especially in pre-adolescence, and if one of the friends becomes "best friends" with someone else, that can occasion extreme upset and jealousy, especially if possessiveness is involved, or the consideration that the relationship should be exclusive.

The intensity of an upset depends on the degree of cardinality of the entity or person that is the object of the upset. If I make a date with a woman who is not particularly important to me and she rejects me, my upset will probably be quite mild. But if she is important to me, my upset is likely to be quite severe. If someone for whom I have no particular respect attacks me, I will probably be somewhat annoyed, although I might be amused. But if someone whose opinion I value attacks me, I am likely to be very upset.

People endeavor to promote communion along each of the four flows.[14] Therefore, a person can have a reversal of communion (i.e., an upset) along any of them. Some of the more intense upsets a person has, in fact, are those she has on behalf of another person (crossflow upsets). Gerald French, a colleague of mine, introduced the apt term "The Mother Bear Syndrome" to denote this phenomenon. If someone does something mean to my daughter, I am likely to become more upset about it than she is, and vice versa. People also often have more attention on receiving affection than giving it. They are often more concerned with being unlov*ed* (inflow) than with being unlov*ing* (outflow). And often a person has very severe upsets with herself (reflexive flow). A person often reserves her most extreme criticisms for herself; she often has much harsher standards by which she metes out

---

13. The second domain is the domain of intimate relationships. See Chapter Five, p. 246.
14. As discussed in Chapter Five, pp. 237-238.

affection for herself than she does for granting affection to others. Hence, all four flows are very important to a person. Yet the outflow (affection for others) is the fundamental one.

A person can also have upsets about entities (instead of persons). Here, the upset is a sudden or unpredicted lowering of drive, control, or understanding (power) or pleasure, order, or heuristics (empowerment). If I have a lovely painting and someone scribbles all over it in ball-point ink, I will be upset because something that was a significant source of pleasure to me is no longer a source of pleasure. A person can also be upset about the demolition of a beautiful house or the destruction of forests, or at meeting an old flame after many years and finding him to have become ugly. Physical pain in any form is also something to which most people have a natural aversion. The sudden appearance of pain in any form is upsetting (apart from being painful), including the appearance of a sudden aversion, since we are averse to aversion as well.

Losses of various kinds are often upsetting because of the lowering of power or communion that occurs as a result. The loss of a close friend removes the possibility of continuing to commune with that friend. A loss of a major piece of property is upsetting because of the loss of the value of that property.

One can be upset at a sudden appearance of disorder: loss of control or predictability. If I am using a tool or instrument, to have it malfunction or break can cause an upset. Physical illness or injury is upsetting for the same reason. A car's (or body's) breaking down, running out of gas (or food), or otherwise going out of control virtually guarantees a significant upset of some sort. The *degree* of the upset depends on the degree of importance the person places on using the car (or the body).

It is also generally upsetting to find that things did not turn out as predicted. All these untoward events cause some degree of upset because they demonstrate that one's world is not as orderly and in control as one thought and that one's powers of prediction are faulty. Thus, for instance, a failure to keep a promise is very likely to upset the person to whom the promise was made, even if it leads to no great inconvenience, because of the failure of prediction. A person can get upset when he finds out that he was wrong about something if he experiences being wrong as a lack of control over his world (or as a lack of understanding). Such an invalidation of his world-view brings up the possibility that other ideas and predictions could turn out to be false and thus lower the empowerment of his world. If the entity predicted is a cardinal one, then the upset is all the more intense. That is why invalidating another's cardinal points is likely to upset him.

An "obsessive-compulsive" person is easily upset by even tiny lapses of control or prediction; he feels a need for an excessive degree of control over his world. Such a person tries to so control the actions of others as to have everything absolutely neat and tidy. The slightest degree of disorder is very disturbing to such a person. Other people who value learning or pleasure to a greater degree may be less easily upset by lapses of control. They may, indeed, even seek them out (through drugs, adventures, or other relatively uncontrolled experiences) for the pleasure or learning experiences they provide.

Finally, people do not like to be bored, to be in situations where there is nothing new to learn. Certain kinds of losses are upsetting for this reason. For instance, being forced to stop playing a game one is enjoying, being interrupted in one's reading or study, having someone turn off the TV while one is watching something that is intensely interesting, not getting into the college of one's choice — all these are mainly upsetting because of the loss of heuristic opportunities.[15]

A large number of upsets are centered around studying and learning. It can be quite upsetting not to be able to understand a textbook or resolve a problem. The consideration or decision that one is not very intelligent can be devastating because it appears to

---

15. Fear of death may exist because life, with all its changes and games, is a learning experience. Perhaps it is the possibility of being stuck in a forever-unchanging situation (one in which one cannot discover anything new) that is horrifying. This possibility is brilliantly portrayed by Jean Paul Sartre in his play, *No Exit.*

put a limit on any future potential for major discovery. Any invalidation of intelligence or learning ability, such as flunking a test, can be extremely upsetting for this reason.

Upsets related to a lowering of power, validity, or value are, like upsets related to a lowering of communion, equally applicable to each of the four flows. One does not just want to have power and empowering conditions for oneself. One wants to create these conditions for others. A person is not happy when surrounded by other people who are upset for any reason, because of his basic capacity for comprehension and because of his affection. If someone close to us is in pain or suffering from aesthetic revulsion or discomfort, we tend to experience his discomfort as well. Others' capacity for communing with us is lowered when they are preoccupied by upsets. What is disorderly for another is also disorderly for us, to the degree that we share our experience. Because of our ties with others, we naturally wish to increase the order in others' universes and will avoid, as much as possible, creating disorder for others. Finally, we love to reveal ourself and our world to others and to make it possible for others to learn because:

1. The action of imparting data to another is basic to the act of communing.
2. If someone else learns something, then that gives me an opportunity, via communication, to learn it as well.

An unhappy person in my surroundings adds to my unhappiness; an ignorant or stupid person detracts from my potential knowledge of the world, and disorder in others' worlds adds to the disorder in mine.

Along the reflexive flow, the above considerations can be expressed as a matter of internal harmony and integrity. One sub-identity, optimally, will not act in such a way as to make life difficult for another sub-identity.

Misdeeds

A person naturally desires the well-being of others, if only to make the world a better place for *her* to live in. Yet, she inevitably does some things that she considers (after the fact, of course — never at the time she does them) to be wrong. These actions occur either inadvertently or because of aversion, false information, or upset.

There are really two kinds of wrongdoing:

1. Actions that are against the greater number and intensity of intentions.
2. Actions that are against the moral code of a group of which the person is a member.

The first type of misdeed is an unethical act; the second is immoral. Adherence to morality ultimately rests on the notion (sometimes ill-thought-out or outmoded) that a breach of a group moral code is more or less automatically guaranteed to be against the interests of the majority of the group. So, the simplest definition of a misdeed is:

> **Definition:** A misdeed is an action that runs counter to the important intentions of the majority of people affected by the action.

And a "good deed" can be defined as follows:

> **Definition:** A good deed is an action that aligns with the important intentions of the majority of people affected by the action.[16]

---

16. It is interesting to note that, though there are many terms for an *evil* deed: "sin", "iniquity", "wrongdoing", "crime", etc., there seems to be no single English word for a *good* deed. Evidently good deeds do not occupy much of our attention since it is the misdeeds that need to be handled. We can simply *admire* good deeds without having either to classify them or to *do* anything about them.

In thinking about these matters, we must always remember to adhere to the person-centered viewpoint. Different people have different opinions concerning what is intended by and important to others, and they have differing moral standards. Therefore the same act may be a good deed for one person and a misdeed for another. In helping a client, it is important not to impose one's own viewpoints and standards on her. Since *she* is the client, one should be concerned with helping her improve the quality of *her* world, not one's own.

Because a person does, basically, wish to improve conditions all around, when she finds out (after the fact, of course) that she has worsened them by some misdeed, an incongruity exists that can be painful for her. She will therefore apply various mechanisms in an effort to resolve the incongruity, such as:

1. Suppressing her own awareness of the occurrence.
2. Justifying the action.
3. Punishing or attacking herself in an attempt to prevent recurrences.
4. Rendering herself powerless.

Justifications

The tendency to rationalize or justify a misdeed often takes the form of devaluing the importance of (or denying) the intentions that are violated. A thief will tend to believe that the person or organization she is robbing is "very rich anyway, so they will not notice the loss or care about it." This might be called the "shoplifter" justification, or the justification from unimportance.

A second type of justification is to explain how the misdeed really constituted doing a favor for the other person. Violent parents justify their actions on the ground that it helps their children to discipline them. Actually, such violence is usually not the result of a considered judgment but merely a manifestation of frustration, of negative emotion. Others have justified hostile actions toward others on the ground that surviving a hostile environment is salutary to the person, e.g., that it makes him hardy, makes a man out of him. This is the "character-building" or "disciplinary" justification.

A third type is "revenge" — the claim that, in acting against the person, you are merely "paying him back" for what he has done to you, thereby "evening the score". This justification is characteristic of the emotional level of antagonism.

A fourth is *argumentum ad hominem*. This type of justification devalues the importance, worth, or goodness of the person injured by the misdeed. It is considered acceptable to attack or destroy people who are thought of as evil, degraded, or "subhuman". Wartime propaganda commonly uses *argumentum ad hominem*. Racial and religious bigots use it. So do proponents of conflicting scientific beliefs, when these beliefs acquire the flavor of religious dogma.

Then there is justification based on the argument that a misdeed was inadvertent or unintentional or was an action beyond the control of the perpetrator, or that he was too weak to prevent the action and therefore did not really *act* in that situation but was, rather, a victim of circumstances. This is the argument from weakness.

To summarize the principal forms of justification, we have:

1. Relative unimportance of the act to the other person (the "shoplifter" justification).
2. Discipline/Education (Doing a "favor" for the other person).
3. Revenge (Evening the score — retributive justice).
4. Unimportance (or evilness) of the other person (*Argumentum ad hominem*).
5. Weakness (of the one committing the misdeed).

Actually, since human ingenuity knows no bounds, the number of possible justifications is virtually infinite, but many will be found to be combinations and variations of the above.

The Function of Justifications

The very existence and universality of the act of justifying is evidence for the fact that people are basically good. Justifications are used to explain one's actions to others, but, more importantly, they are used to explain these acts to *oneself.* Since a justification comes on the heels of a perception of a person's own past or future wrongdoing, it is a falsehood introduced to make it unnecessary for her to confront what she has actually done or is about to do. At some level, she *knows* she has done (or is about to do) wrong, but the justification overlies that knowledge. The stronger the underlying knowledge of wrongdoing is, the stronger the justification must be, in order for the person to remain unaware of wrongdoing. As a result, justification is deleterious to a person's functioning in a variety of ways:

1. The falsehoods involved are injurious to the person's ability to see her world clearly or accurately, so, to that degree, she is disabled.
2. The need to see certain other people as evil or as in need of punishment tends to populate the person's world with other people whom she does not like. This makes life unpleasant for her and violates her natural tendency to commune with others.
3. The need to explain her deeds as arising out of weakness tends to give the person a lessened view of her own power or potentiality, the viewpoint that she is a victim instead of being causative.
4. A demand for retribution against — or forceful "education" of — other people who are thought to have done wrong often ties up a person's energies in destructive activities, instead of leaving her free to apply them to the furtherance of her own goals toward more power and communion.

Having once used a justification to mask an awareness of her own wrongdoing, a person must adhere to it in order to avoid an unpleasant awareness crashing in on her. So, having committed one misdeed and having decided it was right for some reason, she is then bound to go on committing the same kind of misdeed, because the former justification now becomes a *rationale* for future similar actions. Once having decided that beatings have a useful disciplinary function, the wife-beater feels that it is his "duty" to go on beating his wife. Each misdeed of a particular type thus tends to reinforce its justifiers, and the justifiers reinforce the misdeeds, so a whole pattern of destructive behavior can set in.

Furthermore, the person, at some level, still knows, despite his justifications, that he is doing wrong. Therefore, since he is basically good and does not *really* want to harm others, he will eventually take action to render himself powerless to commit more misdeeds. He will do one or more of the following:

- Injure or attack himself (make himself guilty, or punish himself)
- Solicit, expect, or invite injury from others
- Try to lessen, or prevent himself from having, contact with the person he has harmed. He will try either to make the person go away or to avoid him.

The Vicious Circle of Misdeeds and Justifications

None of these methods works; each, paradoxically, makes the situation worse. Strategem 1 has effects similar to those of the argument from weakness — "I couldn't help it" — and can reinforce this argument, thus prolonging the misdeeds. The person becomes committed to being weak and at the mercy of "external" forces. So she "cannot control herself" and commits more misdeeds. Strategem 2 reinforces the person's perception of being out of control and provides a revenge justification for further misdeeds. Strategem 3 makes it hard for the person to make the contacts that would enable her to handle the situation. All tend to *reinforce* the pattern of wrongdoing and thus create a vicious circle of wrongdoing and justification.

A major limitation on a person's potential lies in her unwillingness to allow herself to have power or responsibility because she is afraid of abusing it. That may be why confessions and penances have been effective helping techniques in the Catholic

Church. If there is a method of confronting one's wrongdoings without justifying them, and of regaining a sense of control over one's actions, this method must surely be a powerful tool for enhancing human potential.[17]

Withholds

Obviously, withholding communication from other people violates a person's basic intention to commune with his fellows. If people did not keep secrets from each other, the level of communion would greatly increase.

Some instances of withheld communications ("withholds"), of course, are benign. When I give someone a Christmas present, I do not tell him what it is beforehand because I want him to have the pleasure of anticipating a surprise. Other benign withholds exist, such as when I do not tell someone something out of a desire to spare his feelings. If I run across a person I find physically unattractive, I usually keep my opinion to myself. A misguided effort toward "honesty" can lead to communications that are very destructive in their effects. In fact, it is safe to say that "honesty" is the most common justification for the misdeed of indulging in the expression of negative emotions and saying hurtful things to others.[18] "Benign" withholds may exist to spare

---

17. Such methods do, in fact, exist, as will be seen in Part III, pp. 463-464, 479-480.

18. Things said in anger or out of antagonism tend *not* to be truthful, despite the fact that one often considers one is "merely being honest". It is usually laudable *not* to express secret negativity felt toward another, except, perhaps, in special contexts such as the person-centered context, in which it is understood that everything said is just the opinion of the person speaking and not a request for agreement. Since the sixties, it has become fashionable amongst some people to "let their aggressions out", under all circumstances. No one actually does this, and if they did, the world would be a disastrous place to live in.

someone's feelings, to keep the confidence of a friend, or simply because the data are irrelevant or would not be understood. People who compulsively confess their innermost secrets on a continuous basis become tiresome very quickly. Others may not need or want to know their secrets.

Apart from such "benign" withholds, the quality of your life is greatly enhanced if you can share it with at least one other person from whom you do not have to withhold anything. Often, a sexual partner or a good friend serves this function. The highest levels of communion are achieved in such relationships, where the sharing of information is complete in both directions. Anything less than complete comprehension is in itself less than optimal for a person, but he can easily live with it if the secrets are of a benign sort.

However, where a person has committed a misdeed and then withholds it, or if for any reason he knows something which, if known to others, could result in some harm happening to him, having to withhold that information can have adverse effects on him.

Harmful Effects of Withholds

Withheld information is dangerous if revealed *and* dangerous if kept secret. If it is revealed, the person may be penalized, at least to the extent of incurring some disapproval for violating a moral code, or for being "undesirable". If it is *not* revealed, the person is to that degree unable to communicate with others. There are certain topics she will have to avoid, and she may have to mislead or side-track other people to keep them from discovering the information. Such efforts have the net effect of making her communication cautious and reticent. Often (not always) the content of a withhold is a misdeed done by the person withholding it. A person will often expect or even invite attack when she does something she thinks is wrong, and she may easily interpret the actions of others as punishment or retribution of some kind.[19] So, when she has committed what she considers to be a misdeed, she will tend, in her own mind, to exaggerate the dangerousness of having people find out what she has done. She tends to attribute to the withheld datum an importance that it may not have for other people. A person who feels that premarital sex is immoral will, if she engages in it, withhold it from many people who do not think it is immoral. But the person, in her guilt, thinks they share her views and consequently will disapprove of her if they find out. So in many cases the person will withhold things that, if known, would not actually cause any ill effects. As a person becomes more aware and as she experiments with being more open, she typically discovers many such non-dangerous "dangerous" withholds. These discoveries can be very helpful to her.

Reduction of Comprehension

A person does not like having to act against his natural tendency to enhance comprehension by trying to deceive others or to keep them in the dark, especially in a relationship that is supposed to be intimate. The basic action and intent behind withholding something is to avoid sharing it, so a lie is just another type of withhold — another attempt to avoid comprehension. Since communion comes as a package, a person starts a descending triad of alienation when he becomes secretive. By reducing comprehension, he reduces affection. This, in itself, leads to a lesser amount of communication, and hence less comprehension, less trust, and more need for secrecy. Marital partners can fall into this descending triad when they have significant withholds from each other (such as extramarital affairs).[20] If one finds a low

---

19. Partially because such interpretations serve to justify the person's misdeeds.
20. People think that a bad relationship leads to, or justifies, extramarital affairs and a failure of communication. In fact, the exact reverse is usually the case. By committing misdeeds and failing to acknowledge and communicate them, a descending triad of alienation begins, and a bad relationship results.

affection in a relationship, one can often trace it back to a failure
to communicate about something important (not necessarily an
affair). If one can convince both spouses that it is better to communicate and risk disapproval than to withhold communication
and jeopardize the survival of their relationship, then one can get
each of them to make it safe for the other to communicate. In so
doing, one can cause very dramatic improvements in relationships.

Erosion of Others' Reality

Another harmful effect of being secretive or untruthful, especially in a close relationship, is that it can undermine the cardinal
points of others or reduce their sense of reality. People are normally quite perceptive. Even though they do not always report
what they perceive or sense, they usually have a very good idea of
what is really going on with close friends and lovers, whether
because of some kind of "telepathy" or because of unusual sensitivity to subtle indicators. If one tries to deceive them or lie to
them, they may become upset because their intuition tells them
something *is* going on. And when they are told that something
else is going on that doesn't fit their intuitions or that *nothing* is
going on, they may start distrusting their own perceptions and
thinking of themselves as paranoid. People have often been
known to seek psychiatric help because their intuitions and perceptions do not match up with the deceptions and untruths that
they are being told by others. R.D. Laing makes this point quite
forcefully in his work.

Losing One's Own Sense of Reality

Finally, since people have a need to justify their actions, and
since no one likes to think of himself as a liar, someone who has
been consistently practicing deceptions may eventually come to
believe his own untruths. This is the classical manifestation in
pathological liars, but it can apply to anyone. The person tends

to lose track of his own reality when he attempts consistently to deceive others. It is very easy to "forget" an inconvenient truth or to invent and then accept a convenient, acceptable falsehood. The motive for this kind of self-deception is the painfulness of admitting the real truth and of admitting that one has been a liar. But the price is excessive. In order to accomplish this deception, one must introduce false information and clouded perception. The result is that one introduces more complexity,[21] incongruity (disorder), alienation, and decreased reality into one's life. This is usually too high a price to pay, but since it is usually paid gradually on the "installment plan" it can happen quite insidiously.

Try the following exercises:

Exercise 17. Conceiving of Speaking the Truth

a. Think of a recent situation in which you told a "white lie" or a half-truth.
b. Now imagine handling that situation in a different way, without engaging in any lying, deceiving, or misleading.
c. Did you think of a way to do it?[22]

If you did well on the above exercise, try this one:

Exercise 18. Speaking the Truth

a. Tell only the exact truth and do not deceive anyone (including yourself) in any way for 24 hours.
b. Could you do it?
c. What happened as you did, or attempted to do, this exercise?

To the degree that you were successful in doing either of these exercises, you probably observed that part of the process involved

---

21. To quote Sir Walter Scott, "Oh, what a tangled web we weave, / When first we practice to deceive!"
22. I am indebted to Michael Hanau for suggesting this exercise.

peeling off layers of forgetfulness, inventiveness, and justification from your own view of the world. This should result in a pleasurably heightened awareness of the world around you.

To Communicate or Not to Communicate?

Although, as I mentioned earlier (pp. 290-291), many — perhaps most — withholds are unnecessary, it is sometimes better *not* to communicate something. A person does not need to tell her office mates about all the times she masturbated or played around with her siblings, or about the time she was arrested for being drunk and disorderly, because the subject is unlikely to come up or to have any importance. Also, if I am amongst others who regard me as an enemy or an undesirable (as was the case with Jews in World War II Germany), I may have to lie in order to prevent a major wrongdoing to myself and others. But when a person feels she has to be deceptive with friends or colleagues, she has probably stepped over the line into wrongdoing. What happens in such a situation is that, having withholds from these people, she begins to justify the deceptions — as one would justify any wrongdoing — by adopting negative attitudes toward these friends and associates. And if what she is withholding is a wrongdoing against them, she has a double reason to view them as enemies. If, as is likely to happen, she then starts *treating* them as enemies, her misperception of these people may become a self-fulfilling prophecy.

In most (not all) cases, a person who has many enemies or who feels that many people are against her is someone who has committed harmful acts against the people in question and who has many withholds from them. One can usually tell when complaints and critical remarks about others are valid and when they are indicative of the *critic's* misdeeds and withholds. If the critic is not merely criticizing but also trying to do something constructive to rectify the situation, then the criticism is probably valid. If she is merely continuing to criticize without actually doing anything constructive about the situation she is complaining about (despite being *able* to do so), then one can pretty safely assume that the criticism and the perception of wrongness in the other person or people serves a *purpose* for the critic — namely, that of justifying her own misdeeds and deceptions. These expectations of hostility may become a self-fulfilling prophecy, the people who are thus regarded as enemies may become *actual* enemies. One will usually find, however, that they are *created* enemies. Fortunately, the fact that enemies can thus be created also implies that they can be uncreated as enemies and recreated as friends.

On balance, the liabilities of withholding communication from others greatly outweigh the liabilities of communicating. Yet people often withhold compulsively even when it is unnecessary. This habit can be broken. There are several ways of addressing the subject of withholds using applied metapsychology. These procedures help to bring a person to the realization that it is generally safe to tell the truth, to get into honest communication with others. When a person has handled the subject of misdeeds, withholds, and justifications, her level of communion with others — and, indeed, her enjoyment of *all* aspects of life — will be found to be greatly improved.

Incongruities and Problems

A person organizes his experience in such as way as to maximize learning, pleasure or beauty, and order. Congruity is a sub-category of order. Although congruity is not the be-all and end-all of what the person is trying to achieve in his world, it does have considerable desirability for him. Therefore, it is worthwhile to spend some time on the topic of what happens when congruity breaks down. When the congruity of a person's world breaks down in important respects, the person acquires problems:

> **Definition:** A <u>problem</u> is an incongruity that is of concern or importance to a person at a particular time.

Some entities are incongruous with other entities. As previously discussed, this could be because of logical contradiction. A burner, for instance, cannot be both hot and not hot.[23] But there are other forms of incongruity. The entire field of aesthetics is concerned with congruities and incongruities. If you are listening to a nice Baroque piece, and suddenly the horn player starts playing Dixieland, the incongruity becomes immediately apparent. Mozart's "Musical Joke" is a good example of deliberate aesthetic incongruity. City planners are quite concerned with aesthetic incongruities such as ugly buildings, billboards, or urban sprawl. More subtle aesthetic congruities and incongruities are the subject of good and bad taste, respectively, and here the skill of the observer is involved in detecting the incongruity. To a professional musician or experienced music appreciator, even a slight lapse in rhythm or intonation can be a painful incongruity.

Awareness of Incongruity

People have a varying degree of ability to perceive an existing incongruity. The great human ability known as "explaining" helps us to order our experience and resolve apparent incongruities. Like any ability, however, it can be misused, at which point it becomes rationalization or justification.[24] It is actually very useful to know when something *does not* really fit the rest of our experience and should *not* be explained away. In order to be able *not* to explain something away, however, one has to have a

---

23. When I say that something cannot be both hot *and* cold at the same time, I mean, "when looked at from the same point of reference." This does not necessarily mean that something could not be hot from one viewpoint and cold from another. A red dwarf is a "cold" star, but with reference to room temperature, it is quite toasty. Is it difficult or easy to play a cello? It is difficult if you've just started cello lessons; it is easy if you are Pablo Casals. But logical contradiction is not allowed from the same viewpoint at the same time.

24. As I discussed at greater length in Chapter Two (pp. 88-91), it is just as important to be able *not* to exercise an ability as it is to be able to exercise it.

certain tolerance for the incongruity that remains unexplained. A person who does something he (later) thinks is wrong, automatically experiences an incongruity between his sense of rightness and what he perceives himself as having done. If he cannot confront that incongruity, he will try to explain it away. But it is not only misdeeds that are inappropriately rationalized. A wife, confronted with evidence of her husband's infidelity, may "explain it away" because of its incongruity with her affection for him. Unfortunately, after rationalizing, one is left with a less valid world-view, because the rationalization, while apparently "solving" the incongruity, introduces greater complexity into the world and eventually leads to other incongruities.

When one does recognize an incongruity as such, one's tendency is often to laugh. Humor depends on the perception and rejection of an incongruity. Laughter is an expression of relief at not having to be burdened with an excessively complex explanation of something, because instead of trying to *explain* an incongruity, one has just confronted it and seen it for what it is. A humorless person has a low tolerance for incongruity, so he will try to explain it away instead of appreciating it.[25]

Sometimes incongruity appears as an incompatibility of frames of reference, where behavior is inappropriate to the context. If a student regards her professor as a teacher, not as a prospective mate, flirtation by the professor can introduce a painful incongruity into her life.

Or something can be incompatible with an intention or purpose. A rat is incongruent in an operating room during an operation because the intention, during an operation, is to keep a sterile space in order to avoid infection, and a rat is most decid-

---

25. Mark Twain said, "It's easy to stop smoking. I've done it hundreds of times." If one tried to make *sense* out of this, one would have to say that Mark Twain had invented a new kind of therapy that involved "practice quitting" of smoking and that he had become good at doing this therapy.

edly not a sterile object. A college professor in a birthday cake or a belly dancer at a board meeting are similarly incongruous.

Spotting an incongruity for what it is makes it possible to find an acceptable resolution of the incongruity whereas not spotting it leaves it unresolved, or "resolved" incorrectly. A rat is out of place in an operating room. If I notice it, I can remove it before the patient gets infected; if I notice a cockroach in my soup, I can avoid eating it. If politicians can confront the real global danger of nuclear weapons, then there is a chance of eliminating them.

Problems

The world is full of incongruities, but at any particular time some are more relevant to a person than others. These are *problems*:

Definition: A <u>problem</u> is an incongruity that is of concern to a person at a particular time .

Or, equivalently:

Definition: A <u>problem</u> is an entity that conflicts with a person's intention.

Note that *any* incongruity can be a problem for a person if she intends to solve it, as she often does. But often the person is not particularly interested in resolving a particular incongruity, so the incongruity is not a problem for her at that time. Almost any legal case contains many incongruities, some of which a certain person may be aware of. But unless she is a lawyer, a judge, or otherwise connected with a particular lawsuit, she is unlikely to consider the various incongruities in the suit to be problems for her. They will be "none of her concern".

What constitutes a problem for a person at any particular time depends on the intention she is operating on and the identity she has assumed to fulfill that intention. Entities are not *in themselves* problems. They only *become* so by conflicting with our intentions. A brick wall is not in itself a problem, but it becomes a problem to a person who is trying to get to the other side of the wall.

An intention or purpose can conflict with another intention or purpose, as when I want to study but also wish to go to the movies. This is really a special kind of problem in which the entity that conflicts with a person's intention is another of her intentions:

Definition: A dilemma is a conflict between two or more of a person's current intentions.

An incongruity may be an inappropriateness, a misalignment, a puzzle, a problem, or a dilemma. It involves two or more incompatible elements in a person's world, two or more parts of her world that do not fit with each other. When I have a dilemma, I have two intentions that are "incompossible" — i.e., both cannot be realized. Thus, I may be puzzled about what to do. The answer to a dilemma is to assume the viewpoint of a higher identity, to understand the situation thoroughly, and then to see which intention best furthers the realization of the higher goal. Suppose I cannot decide whether to study or go to the movies. To resolve this dilemma, I must look at the two conflicting intentions from the viewpoint of a higher goal, such as that of living a full and happy life. I must then decide which intention, if fulfilled, would best lead to *that* goal. From this viewpoint, which is "multi-determined" with respect to the two conflicting intentions, I can decide whether I am being too much of a "bookworm" for my own good or whether I will be happier in the long run if I get my assignment done. The essence of making a correct ethical choice is this ability to "step back" and assume a higher identity. Other types of incongruities can be resolved by:

- Carefully observing the situation.
- Selecting the most valid explanation or the most valuable outcome by applying the principles outlined in Chapter Four (pp. 156-166).
- If necessary, taking physical action to resolve the problem (such as *removing* the rat from the operating room).

The Value of Problems

Generally, people like to have problems to solve. Although they always try to eliminate incongruity where it concerns them, they like to have *some* problems to work on at any particular time. If, for some reason, a person has a scarcity of problems to resolve or a scarcity of incongruities that he can confront well enough to resolve, he will tend to hang onto the ones he has and to regard them as difficult or insoluble because if he does solve them, he will have nothing to do (or he will have to confront something else he does not want to confront).

An incongruity or conflict can act as a wonderful distraction from other things that are unconfrontable. A person who is too shy or timid to generate conflicts with most people may generate very complicated conflicts with the people that are safe for him, such as a spouse or child. If a company cannot get enough business, or if any group cannot find enough external problems to solve, its members will start creating "games" and conflicts amongst themselves. Office politics and administrative details become all-important in such a circumstance.

Problems are also valuable as heuristic elements in a person's life. As long as there are problems to resolve, people will continue to learn. When there are no more problems, life becomes boring, and a person will *invent* and cling to problems in order to avoid the boredom.[26]

---

26. The "games people play" are mainly a distraction from their failures in life or a remedy for boredom. The reason there was so much court intrigue during medieval and renaissance times was, no doubt, that the nobles had a great deal of ability but nothing much to use it for in the way of constructive action. So they used their abilities scheming against each other and thus acquired an acceptable number of problems in their lives. Rulers have sometimes recognized this fact and when threatened by internal disunity, have contrived to create an outside enemy to focus on, thus giving everybody enough to do.

There are two reasons, therefore, why problems are valuable:

1. As a remedy for boredom.
2. As a distraction from things that are unconfrontable.

The mechanism of seizing on a problem to repress something that seems unconfrontable bears further discussion because it gives us a clue to the way in which unwanted problems arise, and to the connection between problems and misdeeds.

False Solutions

When the world becomes too confusing, ingongruous, or overwhelming for a person to even *begin* to handle it, a person can begin to introduce order by finding one or more cardinal points around which the confusion can be aligned. If a person is able to confront the confusion and really handle it, she will find that not only order, but also pleasure and heuristics, are maximized. But if she cannot confront the confusion, she is apt to seize on something rather arbitrarily to try to align the confusion quickly, and *that* aberrated cardinal point may eventually cause more confusion than it "solves":

> **Definition**: An aberrated cardinal point is an arbitrary stable point — a person or entity selected as a reference point in a confusion because one is not willing or able to confront the confusion. This unwillingness tends to cause one to cling to that person or entity as a fixed idea because otherwise one would have to confront the confusion. An aberrated cardinal point serves to hide the repressed confusion rather than to align it.

Situation comedies are full of these fixed "solutions" that, in themselves, become problems. A person pretends to be someone else in order to avoid an embarrassing situation, and then, in carrying out the pretense, runs into an escalating series of ever more embarrassing situations. Actually, most misdeeds can be traced back, not to a desire to inflict evil on another, but to a need to find a rapid solution to a confusing and overwhelming situation. After a misdeed is committed, *then* the mechanism of justification sets in, and the person becomes committed to a pattern of misdeeds, as discussed earlier (pp. 288-289). But the first in a sequence of misdeeds will generally be found to be a response to an inability to confront an overwhelming situation; the misdeed is simply a bad solution. If the person feels she is able to confront a given situation well and has time to figure it out, she will arrive at a more optimal solution than if she feels rushed and overwhelmed.

The various strategies found on the lower emotional levels are examples of "built-in" bad solutions to overwhelming situations. Rather than confront the situation, a person goes on an attack, tries to destroy something, tries to run away, and so forth. Her actions may seem to handle the acute situation, but they often lead to worse situations later. The person may run away from a situation by taking drugs. She may handle an acute need for money by theft, or she may lie and deceive others in order to gain something perceived as acutely needed. All the various misdeeds can fall into this category. A person who is able to confront well and keeps her head in a crisis rarely commits misdeeds. One good way of resolving misdeeds is to trace back a sequence of similar misdeeds to the first one, and then to find the confusion, problem, or overwhelm that predated this first misdeed, for which the misdeed was a solution.

Apart from committing misdeeds, a person may seize upon a problem or incongruity that is relatively comfortable and make it a cardinal point that so occupies his attention that he need not confront the larger, more overwhelming situation. This is the second basic mechanism by which problems or incongruities become valuable. The person comes to depend on a small group of problems to hold a great deal of confusion at bay. He cannot afford to solve the problems because that will cause the confusion to come crashing in on him. So he tries to make them as complex and long-lived as possible. They become "valuable" to him, and he will vigorously resist any attempts to help him resolve them (if one is so foolish as to be drawn into making such an attempt). A person who cannot confront the enormity of the task of writing a book will find himself running into various problems doing research, finding a proper typewriter, or finding the time to do the writing. If, without handling the factors that make writing the book unconfrontable, I try to advise him on getting a typewriter or help him to organize his time, he will resist my help, or he will become very ingenious at finding other problems and barriers to doing the writing. But these logistical problems are not the real issue, so trying to resolve them will not help the person. It is better to direct his attention to his negative feelings about writing the book and to help him confront his confusion on this larger subject. Once the larger issue is resolved, the logistical problems will vanish "magically".

So one is really not doing someone a favor by taking away his problems or conflicts. What one *can* do for him is:

1. To improve the *quality* of the problems he selects to place his attention on.
2. To help him attain the ability to select interesting and pleasant problems to work on.
3. To make it safe for him to take on a wider range of problems.

If one can accomplish these goals in helping another person, the person will readily resolve problems that he earlier perceived as far too complicated ever to be resolved.

The Ability to Have Larger Problems

A person who is doing well will generally have *more* problems than a person who is in bad shape, but the problems will be much more interesting and enjoyable to her. As she improves her ability to extend her identity, her area of concern will extend to wider and wider circles and the scope of her problems will also become wider. Although her concerns may extend initially only to the first domain — her own health and mental state — as her condition improves, she will begin to have second-domain concerns, then wider concerns, as outlined in the section on the domains (pp. 245-250, above). A person must be in reasonably good condition to genuinely have the well-being of mankind as a problem. People are not going to readily take the viewpoint of helping the whole world if they are introverted and tied up in myriad personal problems.[27] Conversely, as a person's condition deteriorates, she retreats from wider concerns to narrower ones and, eventually, to inverted domains. Her problems will match the domains (inverted or otherwise) on which she is operating.

Boredom and Education

A person naturally has an aversion to situations that are boring or anti-heuristic — that do not contain a sufficient potential for learning and personal expansion. Aristotle and many others have said that the "Master Game" is the game of improving one's ability, awareness, and understanding.[28] A person does not like to be trapped in a situation where his ability to play this game — or other games — is blunted. A person likes to have a game to play, new worlds to conquer, new things to learn. He likes the opportunity for advancement, for variety, for personal expansion. Lacking that opportunity, he feels bored and stultified.

Boredom is inevitable in a situation where one is supposed to be learning and is not. Actually, from a certain viewpoint, all of life is a learning situation, but one has a particular tendency to get bored in situations that are supposed to be mainly learning situations. People often become bored while studying. Students commonly go into a learning situation with a "know it all", blasé, jaded — in other words bored — attitude. They think they know it all, even though from the teacher's viewpoint they usually do

---

27. The route to the type of planetary thinking recommended by Buckminster Fuller and others thus lies through improving the condition of individual persons.

28. See DeRopp, Robert S. *The Master Game* (Delacorte Press, New York, 1968).

not. Often, students become bored because they are not being given new material fast enough. Elementary school arithmetic programs often progress in a painfully slow manner. Children could become interested if they were allowed to learn new material at an acceptable rate. But spending years and years on monotonous addition and subtraction problems can ruin a child's interest in mathematics. Generally, children's ability to learn is grossly underestimated by adults who have forgotten the intensity of the thirst for knowledge that they themselves had as children.

But boredom can also occur when the student does *not* know it all. When the student is having a hard time grasping the material, the sense of boredom can be even more excruciating. If enough such incidents occur, a person can develop an intense aversion for that subject of study or even an aversion to studying at all or to anything like study. Such an aversion is crippling to a person and can itself lead to a vicious circle of boredom, no study, no tools for further understanding, inability to understand, more boredom, and so forth (See Figure 36).

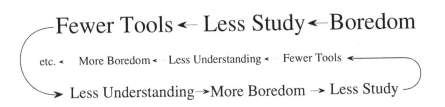

Figure 36. The vicious circle of boredom.

A person is fortunate if, in early years, his teachers can make study exciting because the circle can — and should — be an *ascending* circle of study, more understanding, more tools for further study, more affinity for studying, more study, and so forth (See Figure 37).

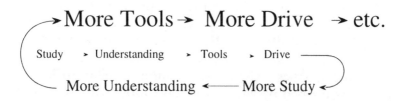

Figure 37. The ascending circle of learning.

Boredom and the Learning Cycle

The learning cycle proceeds from data to interpretations, which are verified (or disproved), and then accepted (or rejected). Certain criteria make one interpretation more valid than another, namely, those with which we have become familiar as the principles for organizing experience: pleasure, order, and heuristics. These criteria are the objective poles that correspond to drive, control, and understanding. In the learning cycle, the transition from interpretation to belief or acceptance involves several "checks" on the different possible interpretations to see which are acceptable. Broadly speaking, there are checks for:

1. Hedonic or aesthetic value.
2. The degree to which the interpretation increases or decreases order, which includes checks on:
   a. Simplicity
   b. Stability, including past precedents
   c. Congruity
3. Heuristic value

At least *two* such learning cycles must take place in order for learning to occur via communication, where what is communicated is a concept, rather than a phenomenon.[29] The first such cycle takes the physical communication — the token, such as the sentence uttered — and arrives at knowledge of what the concept is that the communicator intended to communicate. The second starts from the concept communicated as a datum and proceeds by a process of verification to the knowledge of whether that concept is true or not.[30] Often, the checks performed in the verification step require further creative or receptive (or learning) cycles. If someone tells me there is a rat in the closet, I am likely to go and open the door of the closet to see for myself before necessarily accepting the concept as true.

If any part of the learning cycle is prevented or inhibited, a person will be bored and frustrated, because people have an intense, fundamental intention to learn. Sensory deprivation can be very disagreeable precisely because perception is interrupted. And any situation in which a person is not allowed access to data can be disagreeable. It is also true that if a person is not allowed to make his own interpretations of data but is always spoon-fed data and told how to interpret it — or told that he must *not* interpret it in certain ways — he will be unhappy. The same is true if, for some other reason such as some moral or political consideration, he is told that he must not look at certain things or consider certain interpretations. Nothing is as boring as listening to a "party line". Finally, if a person is told that he must believe a concept that he is not allowed to verify for himself, he will never fully complete the learning cycle. In such a case, the concept or interpretation received will be much less useful to him than if he were allowed to conduct various mental or physical checks to ascertain its truth or falsity.

---

29. As we have seen (pp. 209, 226) one cycle suffices when it is an *experience* that is communicated.
30. See Chapter Five (pp. 209-210) for more data on these cycles.

Barriers to Learning

In looking for the cause of boredom, then, one should look for a point where the learning cycle has been interrupted. The following are some of the barriers that can prevent the completion of a learning cycle:

1. **Pain** — The person may not be able to bear the pain of confronting, thinking about, or being aware of certain subjects or certain perceptions, concepts, or interpretations. The pain barrier, if present, must be handled first, before a person can make suitable progress in learning.[31]

2. **Lack of Intention** — A person may not wish to learn a certain subject. Any receptive or creative cycle involves intention. If a person does not intend to carry out a cycle, the cycle will not occur. If a person wants to learn subject A and you force her to study subject B, she will not learn well because her intention is not behind the learning cycle. And she will be bored because she is actually being *kept* from learning something else that she *wants* to learn. People do not become bored because they are forced to learn but because they are not *allowed* to learn.[32]

3. **Omitted Data** — Conceivably, a person may not be free to receive data fully or at all. If a person is not allowed to study when she wants to, she can become bored. Or she may be allowed to study but may have a physical disability that prevents perception, in which case the answer may be

---

31. The topic of pain and its effects is discussed at greater length in Chapter Seven.

32. A person who wants to learn about life by living life will be bored in school. A person with intellectual interests will be bored when she is just living life without formal study. So getting students to learn sometimes involves a certain amount of salesmanship. A good teacher must be able to arouse her students' interest in learning the material she has to offer. You cannot force learning.

glasses or a hearing aid (A small child will become very bored at a parade if she is not allowed to see what is happening!).

4. **Omitted Interpretation** — The person may not be allowed, or may not be able, to interpret the data in various ways. If a person cannot understand the material of a subject, if she cannot find any meaning or "point" in it, or if she cannot find any relevance to her life in it, she will become bored with it.

5. **Omitted Verification** — A person, pressured to accept a particular datum without an opportunity to test it against the various entities that compose her world, doesn't really *learn* it. Trying to absorb a "party line" is surely one of the most boring situations a person can encounter.

The last three items given above are caused by defective teaching methods. If the student is not exposed to the data she needs, if she is not allowed to really think about the data (explain it or interpret it), or if she is not allowed to experiment with it, verify it, and decide about it for herself, her response will be a failure to learn.

I have mentioned sensory deprivation as one example of omitted data,[33] but there are many other forms of data deprivation. One is simply a failure to educate a person at all! John Dewey's ideas concerning "progressive education", with its emphasis on the importance of developing "social skills", caused many elementary schools to be converted into something resembling therapeutic communities. Falling scores on reading and other intellectual skills resulted from this practice. The children were simply not exposed to enough data. Consequently, many of them did not learn some very basic skills, such as how to read and write. If you look back to the 18th or 19th centuries and read a representative letter from those days, you will find that those people expressed themselves extraordinarily well and were able to

---

33. See footnote on p. 278.

think with a great deal of sophistication, compared to the inarticulateness and lack of sophistication present today in the average product of progressive education. The reason is that most people today have been exposed to much less information concerning the skills of reading and thinking. More to the point, they have had much less practice in applying these data. Hence they are more easily bored in school and in life.

Another form of omitted data occurs when data are presented too slowly. Learning must occur at an optimal pace. When a person progresses too slowly, he gets bored because he is not learning as rapidly as he can.

Under "omitted interpretation" I include various categories of failure to comprehend data. One is bored when confronted with incomprehensible data — phenomena that are seen as nonsense. Incomprehensible data may take the form of words, phrases, or symbols that are not understood or incorrectly understood. If a person runs across a phenomenon that is supposed to mean something but he cannot make out the meaning, learning can cease at that point. It does not matter a great deal whether the phenomenon is verbal or non-verbal. I can look at a photograph of a motor or an X-ray and fail to be able to interpret it. Someone must tell me or show me the meaning or correct interpretation of something if I do not understand it despite my best efforts to do so. So in viewing an X-ray, my tutor can say, "This shadow is the kidney. This is the heart," and so forth. In a verbal context, we must often consult dictionaries (or a teacher or friend) to determine the meaning of a word or phrase.

If a person cannot get a clear meaning, then he is prevented from making further progress because the remainder of the material he is being taught will probably depend on his having successfully completed the learning cycle with respect to the material containing the unclear word or phrase. That is, contained in the current material are facts that will be needed for understanding later material. These facts (being the *meaning* of the current material, when accepted by the student) will then be taken as data from which *other* facts are to be derived later. But if the current material is not comprehended, the later material cannot be comprehended either and so the student's progress rapidly comes to a standstill. A good way of preventing this eventuality is to make sure that the student does not try to continue studying after encountering a misunderstood or uncomprehended word, phrase, symbol, picture, or situation without first clearing it.[34]

A word is usually misunderstood (or not understood) because the student has no understanding — or an incorrect understanding — of the word. Sometimes, however, the author or teacher is misusing it, having, herself, an incorrect understanding. Authors do not *usually* use words incorrectly; being able to use something usually implies a *correct* understanding of it. Such mistakes do happen, however.

A more common fault of writers is unclear syntax. The study of grammar and usage is supposed to prevent such situations from arising, but unfortunately grammar has not been heavily emphasized in recent years, so many people do not know how to write clearly. The result is a great deal of misery for their readers. A student who fails to get misinterpretations clarified for herself, whether they are her own or the writer's, will find herself hindered and eventually stopped on a course of study or learning. She will henceforth be bored with that subject because it is unintelligible to her.

Using several different means of understanding something can be much more effective than relying on only one. This has partly to do with interpretation but is mostly a form of verification. "One picture is worth more than a thousand words", according to the Chinese proverb. But a few words may also be worth a great many pictures. And actually having the object there to look at, feel, and use may be worth several thousand

---

34. A failure to understand what is going on in life can have an effect similar to that of a failure to understand in a study context. But since life is generally not programmed linearly like a course, with a gradiently increasing expectancy of knowledge, a person can often find her way around points in life where something is not understood without her progress being prevented in the same way as it would be on a linear course.

words *and* pictures. *Doing* something with data is almost guaranteed to be helpful in conceptualizing it. For instance, diagramming the data or making a model of it will help. But especially helpful is *applying* the data in some way. According to the power triad, greater control leads to greater understanding. If a person can fully use a concept, then she can be said to understand it, and vice versa. And applying a concept and seeing that it works is the ultimate way of verifying it.

The ultimate test of a concept is thus a pragmatic one. A person can fully integrate a datum into his world when he can apply the datum in some way; conversely, he can apply it when he can integrate it. The two really go together. Therefore, rote learning does not usually result in real understanding and is, consequently, boring.[35]

Application should be a central part of education. Even in teaching a student the meaning of words, he must be made to *use* them — in sentences. To learn the game of golf, the student must actually *play* golf. Whenever one helps a person acquire ability or knowledge — one must make sure he has an opportunity to *apply* it.

Having material presented at too fast a pace can also be classified under omitted verification. When a person is given material too fast, he has insufficient time to understand all the words, figure out the syntax, use other auxiliary modes of perception and

---

35. It is no accident, then, that I am presenting metapsychology as a pragmatic and a phenomenological discipline. The only way that someone can really accept and integrate metapsychological ideas is by applying them. Therefore, I must make sure that I express ideas that *can* be applied — as statements about an unknowable "absolute reality" or "unconscious psychological entities" cannot.

The role of application in certainty has also been discussed in the earlier section on "Quasi-Entities", pp. 37-41, where I stated that something could be accepted as a real entity (as opposed to a quasi entity) at the point where a person has sufficient certainty to act as if it were a real entity.

activity, and verify the data for himself by application, by reasoning, or by other means. So he does not get the data and:

1. It does not help him construct or expand his view of the world, nor to become more competent at managing it.
2. He quickly becomes mired in multiple layers of incomprehensible data and becomes bored.

Many people are in this condition with respect to a wide variety of subjects, or even with respect to the subject of study itself.

In summary, study difficulties could be said to fall into five major categories:

1. Inability to confront the subject matter.
2. Lack of interest in the subject matter.
3. Omitted data
    a. Nothing offered for study.
    b. Data presented too slowly.
    c. Incomplete data
        i. Missing prerequisites.
        ii. Gaps in reasoning or omitted steps.
4. Omitted interpretation (incomprehensible data)
    a. Misunderstood or misused words or phrases.
    b. Faulty or misunderstood syntax.
5. Omitted verification
    a. Data presented too rapidly.
    b. Lack of opportunity to test data.
    c. Lack of opportunity to use data.
    d. Misprogramming of study — lack of other data to relate it to.
    e. False information
        i. Inconsistent data.
        ii. Incorrect data.

If any of these problems are present, learning is prevented or inhibited. If all these barriers are successfully overcome, there will be no difficulties with study. Pain connected with study, or inability to confront the subject matter, is remedied by using various personal enhancement techniques, such as those given in Part III of this book. Lack of interest is handled by either finding a subject that *does* interest the student or inspiring his interest in the subject at hand by an adequate job of salesmanship. Omitted data, interpretation, and verification are remedied or prevented by using correct teaching methods.

Cumulative Effects of Learning Failures

A failure to understand and assimilate data has a cumulative effect on later learning in that it leads to further such failures. This is true of any course or acquisition of knowledge, but it is especially true of "linear" disciplines like mathematics in which each datum acts as a strict prerequisite for acquiring later data. The concept of a number is a prerequisite for arithmetic. A child who does not understand that the concept of "two" is different from two specific apples she sees on a table will be unable to understand or assimilate the idea of adding or subtracting. A person who does not understand what adding and subtracting are will not be able to understand algebra and trigonometry. A person who does not understand the basic concepts of algebra and trigonometry will not be able to do calculus.

At the point where one fails to understand a section of a mathematics textbook (at whatever level), one feels a "blankness". This blankness is not a failure of perception. One is generally fully aware of the symbols one is reading — perhaps painfully aware of them — but there is a blankness where a corresponding concept should be:

> **Definition:** Blankness is an experience encountered in study when there is a failure of comprehension. It is a feeling of emptiness or stupidity that results from the absence of a concept that should be there.

The material "means nothing" to the person, where it should "mean something". No concept exists, and therefore one feels blank after passing a section of the material one has not understood. If the student carries on despite this failure of understanding, then every time that symbol or concept is referenced in the material, a further blankness will occur. If one does not understand the concept of a fraction, one will get a blankness when one sees a symbol like "3/4" or "1/3". And, of course, if one goes on to algebra, expressions like x/y or 3x/9z will generate more blankness.

Sometimes, the *initial* step in such a sequence of blanks is not itself felt as a blank, but is simply an incorrect concept (wrong idea). In this case, one has made an interpretation of the material, but the verification and assimilation steps are missing or faulty. Since the student *thinks* she understands the word or concept, she may not be bothered by it — in fact, she may have no attention on it whatsoever. On reading that a minus sign outside a parenthesis changes the sign of whatever is inside the parenthesis, a student might think that one only changes whatever *signs* are inside to their opposites. She might think, for instance, that:

$$-(a + b - c) = (a - b + c),$$

when in fact:

$$-(a + b - c) = (-a - b + c).$$

Later, she may not be able to understand why her teachers mark her answer wrong when she says that:

$$-(5 + 3 - 2) = (5 - 3 + 2) = 4,$$

instead of

$$-(5 + 3 - 2) = (-5 - 3 + 2) = -6.$$

She will feel confused and "blank" and will remain so until her *original* conceptual error is discovered and corrected.

Similar problems can also arise in a non-mathematical, non-linear subject, however. A person might read a book and, seeing the word "fractious", might think it means "fragmented" (instead of "irritable" or "troublesome"). If the book contains the sentence, "His mother was fractious," this reader might get the concept that the mother was scatterbrained or schizophrenic. The reader later feels she is missing something when the mother turns out to be very organized and capable but bad-tempered. She then experiences a certain blankness because she cannot understand why the mother is supposed to be schizophrenic but does not show any of the signs of schizophrenia. So to that degree the book is not assimilable; her whole appreciation of the book is marred by the original misconception. She feels a continuous conceptual blankness with regard to the mother. Eventually, she might abandon the book altogether as incomprehensible. She does not necessarily have any way of knowing that the difficulty started with a misunderstanding of the word "fractious". She does not necessarily even remember or think about that word.

These ideas:

1. Blankness is based on the failure to successfully complete a learning cycle.
2. These blanknesses can be cumulative.

are useful as powerful tools for resolving learning problems. Many such problems can be resolved by taking the following steps:

1. Retracing the steps the student took in studying the material to a point just *before* the point where he was first aware of feeling blank, frustrated, bored, or puzzled with the material.
2. Moving forward slowly to find the initial point at which the misunderstanding or failure to verify or assimilate occurred, such as (in my first example) the point where the statement about signs inside parentheses first appears or (in my second example) where "fractious" first appears.
3. Doing whatever is needed to complete the incomplete learning cycle on that point. This action would include clearing up any misunderstood words, phrases, or syntax, possibly doing one or more practical exercises to help assimilate the data, or using a word in some sentences until the student can apply the word, giving examples of fractious people, and the like. The action would be continued until the learning cycle on that point has been fully completed and the data fully assimilated.
4. Restudying from that point forward, and clearing up any further blanks.

If one were to design an ideal course, then, it would have the following elements:

1. A safe, non-traumatic environment in which to learn.
2. A clear reason why the student should learn the course material, one that makes sense to him.
3. Well-presented, clear lectures or written materials.
4. A logical sequence in giving data, so that there are no omitted data or undefined terms.
5. A thorough glossary of any specialized or technical terms.
6. An opportunity for the student tō verify and apply the data as he goes along without being rushed.
7. The policy of being alert for "blankness" or other indications of having gone past a misconception, and, if such an indication is encountered:
   a. Tracing it back promptly to its source — the original misconception — just before the first point of blankness.
   b. Handling the failure to understand by clarifying the meaning of any unclear words, phrases, or syntax.
   c. Restudying the material from that point.

A thorough understanding of the learning cycle and the various points at which it can break down is extremely important. It is through some form of learning that all extension of identity and all increase of ability occurs.

Fixed Identities

The ideal state with respect to identity was given in Chapter One (p. 29) as a high degree of ability to move into and out of identities, i.e., versatility. The corresponding disability is the condition of being *fixed* in one or more identities. Fixations of identity fall into two types;

1. An inability to extend one's identity in a certain direction.
2. An inability to shed or "step back" from a particular identity to a senior identity.[36]

I spoke of the "Great Person Syndrome" as an inability to shed an identity. Here, a person seems to feel that her success depends on being in a certain identity and that if she were to step back from it, she would fail. We speak of this as "arrogance" — assuming a scope that is overextended or overspecialized for a particular situation. When one is around good friends, family, or children, it is really counterproductive to have the identity of a "big shot", a "Big Man on Campus", or an "Executive". If one does maintain such an identity, one will be viewed as arrogant or conceited. Arrogance, then, is not only a vice but also a manifestation of a disability. The corresponding virtue, "humility", is also a manifestation of an ability — the ability to step back from identities.

It may be inappropriate or even injurious to display an ability when it really is not necessary to do so. A champion tennis player, when she is playing with ordinary players, should be able to tone down her game. She should not retain the identity of a champion competitor under these circumstances but should assume a more appropriate identity — that of a coach or rallying partner. If she always plays like a champion, she will be rightly regarded as uncouth or thoughtless.

The obverse disability is the inability to extend oneself into an identity of greater scope. We see this disability in people who are anxious, phobic, or depressed. They cannot assert themselves. They cannot assume an identity extended enough to fit the occasion. So instead of taking responsibility and taking causative action, they act very meek, mild, and self-deprecatory under

---

36. The ability to shift identities horizontally amounts to the ability to move up in the hierarchy of identity and then to move down again in a different direction, so the ability to shift horizontally should be viewed as a special case of the ability to shed and assume identities (i.e., versatility).

all circumstances. In this form of self-limitation, the person has decided that if she tries to assume a larger identity, she will somehow make mistakes and fail or that she will be "being a phony", so she avoids extended identities.

The ground common to both self-deprecation and arrogance — to the inability to extend into, and the inability to step back from, identities — is being fixed in one or a few "safe" or "successful" identities. One feels unable to move out of these identities for fear of failure. An arrogant person is afraid of *shedding* a more extended identity; a depressed person fears failure should he *assume* one. So both arrogance and self-deprecation are sides of the same coin: a fixation in a relatively "safe" or "successful" identity. It has often been correctly observed that just beneath the skin of an arrogant person is a person who feels undeserving, unloved, and inferior. And just beneath the skin of a self-deprecatory person is contempt for those who claim to be superior and an unwillingness to "make a fool of himself" as they do. The core disability concerning identity, then, is having one or more fixed identities:

> **Definition**: A fixed identity is an identity a person has assumed in an effort to avoid pain or unpleasantness, one which the person does not feel completely free to shed or extend.

Some teenage males most emphatically do not want to be like their fathers; some young women don't want to be like their mothers. And, indeed, it may take effort to avoid the phenomenon of "identification with the aggressor" or "what you resist being, you become" that I discussed in Chapter Four (pp. 185-186). An unwillingness to assume an identity can be problematic when some of the abilities, intentions, perceptions, or characteristics of the hated identity are necessary for success. A man may be compulsively meek and mild because he does not want to be like his aggressive father. Another may be chronically aggressive because he does not want to be a "wimp", like his father; a woman who views her mother as excessively strict may find herself unable to discipline her own children. A parent, even though hated, may have a great deal of influence on an adolescent precisely *because* the adolescent is determined *not* to become a carbon copy of the parent. Hence, where adolescents are striving to "be themselves" — i.e., *not* to be their parents — we can see extreme "pendulum swings" from generation to generation.

What can cause a person to become fixed in an identity? One circumstance is that of being "trapped" in a success. If a person has had a fair number of failures in various identities and then has a spectacular success in one identity, he may decide henceforth to stay in that one. If a person fails to win the affection and admiration of others (does not succeed in communing with them) and then assumes an identity for which he is accorded respect, honor, or notoriety, he may become fixed in that identity. A girl who has not been very popular may one day discover that acting "sexy" attracts a great deal of attention. She may then become fixed in this sexy identity even when it is inappropriate and damaging to her self-esteem. A boy who has been able to attract attention in high school only by acts of bravery or effrontery may retain a "macho" persona. A child who does not get enough attention or affection when engaged in her normal activities may discover that people are nice to her when she is sick and so can become chronically "sickly".

Any identity, if continued long enough, becomes a habit pattern. The person simply has not learned to cope with life in any other way. She has become like a musician with a very small repertoire, a "character actor" who always finds herself cast in one particular kind of role.

Debarment from an identity is usually caused by some degree of boredom, pain, incongruity, or confusion connected with that identity. Actually, fixation in an identity could be viewed as a special case of debarment — it is a debarment from *other* identities.[37] Some debarments are culturally sex-related. A girl may feel that it is inconsistent with a feminine identity to be a

---

37. Debarment from an identity could also be viewed as a fixation in one or more identities that are incompatible with the debarred identity.

mechanic or an electrician. So she will not be able to fix a flat tire or check the oil in her car because it is "unfeminine" to do so. Her male counterpart may refuse to sew on a button, cook, feed a baby, or cry, because it is not "macho" to do these things. Such debarments may be enforced by social disapproval or ridicule, though they are usually also based on painful past experiences. In other cases, painful past experiences may *enforce* an identity. It is an observable fact that people under strain may start acting like parents or other significant past or present figures in their lives — especially punitive figures.[38]

The issue of identities has to do with "phoniness". We think of a person as "phony" when she is pretending to be something she is not or claiming an ability or possessions that she does not really have, in order to influence, beguile, or impress people, or otherwise to do something that does not align with the intention of that identity. If the identity in question is an identity that is *effective* in handling the present situation, the person is not regarded as a phony. In other words, a person is viewed as "phony" when she tries unsuccessfully to assume an identity that is appropriate to the situation she is in. The "sincerity" or "phoniness" of an identity, of course, has nothing to do with having or not having credentials. There are famous cases of people who masqueraded for years as physicians with no formal training. Yet after a certain period of time, some of these people were fully functional as physicians and did, in fact, help and cure patients. From the person-centered viewpoint, intentions, abilities, and

---

38. In all cases, in fact, it will be found that there are traumatic incidents connected with particular identities that have caused the person to debar herself from, or force herself into, those identities. It is true that social forces or disapproval can help to create such debarments and enforcements, but these forces are only effective if they are themselves traumatic or reactivate past traumas. A person cannot otherwise be forced into or out of an identity. Thus, eliminating or weakening the effects of traumatic incidents will tend to restore a person's power of choice over her selection of identities. A highly effective means of handling traumatic incidents (Traumatic Incident Reduction) is presented in Part III of this book (pp. 433-452).

actions — not credentials — define an identity. A person may have a Ph.D. in physics, but if she is laying bricks, then she is a brick-layer. A person who claims to be a physicist because of her Ph.D. but who makes a living laying bricks and does not actually do any teaching or research in the field of physics is a phony. But a person without credentials (like Einstein, who was employed in a patent office and lacked an academic title) who nevertheless makes a significant contribution to the subject of physics *is* a physicist, regardless of his lack of academic position.

If a person takes on the identity of a therapist without credentials and handles a client with great skill and effectiveness, he is not a "phony". He is a "lay therapist". But if a person pretends to be a great pianist and then sits down at the piano and is unable to play a fairly simple piece properly, he is rightly regarded as a phony. He has assumed an identity without integrity:

Definition: Integrity is congruity of intention and identity.

Anyone who is a "phony" lacks integrity and vice versa. Since ethics is control of intention, it is also control of identity. Often, a person in a fixed identity will appear to lack integrity, or to be "phony" — and so he is. When a person does "evil" deeds or has "evil" intentions, he will usually be found to have assumed some fixed identity that is doing or intending these things. In a way, assuming a "bad" identity enfranchises him to have those intentions and perform those actions, which he would never allow himself to do when he is "being himself". So he can rationalize to himself and feel that, as he was "not himself", he did not really do those things.[39] People often take alcohol or drugs in order to "become someone else" so they do not have to take responsibility for their actions. But, of course, it is not really true that the

---

39. The explanation that one is "not being oneself" could be added to the list of common justifications given earlier in this chapter (pp. 285-286).

person is being "someone else". A person cannot help but be himself, regardless of the identity he has assumed. He is himself, operating as that identity.

Chapter Seven

Pain and Aberration

If irrational behavior and chronic unhappiness are caused by certain basic mechanisms, then finding these mechanisms could provide the key to helping people resolve these conditions. Such mechanisms do appear to exist, and this chapter is devoted to describing them.

Pain, Aversion, and Repression

Pain is a central factor behind unhappiness and inability; no discussion of human potential is complete without addressing this issue. Unless we are able to understand and handle pain, all our efforts to gain positive abilities and states of being will fail. Besides, as we shall see, pain has a great deal to do with unconsciousness. If we seek more awareness, we will have to confront the issue of pain head-on.

Pain

"Pain", as I use the term, does not just denote a physical sensation. Under varying circumstances, the same physical sensation can be felt as sometimes painful, sometimes intensely pleasurable. In a state of sexual or religious ecstasy, physical sensations normally thought of as painful appear sometimes to be ecstatic. Exercise is painful for some and pleasurable for others. Heroin addicts undergoing withdrawal may gain exquisite pleasure from pricking themselves with needles, an activity that most regard as a minor form of torture one has to put up with in doctors' offices. Sexual intercourse is exceedingly painful when it is involuntary and exceedingly pleasurable when voluntary.

What appears to convert a mere sensation or perception into pain is one's unwillingness to experience it. The nature of pain is to be undesirable. If an experience is tolerable or pleasant, it is not painful. Under most circumstances, people are unwilling to experience injury to their bodies, so injury is normally experienced as painful. Masochists, however, may experience certain kinds of injury as pleasurable.

Pain, in other words, is basically intolerance of experience. It exists in the *flinch*, not in what is being flinched *from*. If there were no flinch, there would be no pain, in the full sense of the word. But a flinch is simply an aversion, so it is now possible to tie this concept into the concept of the affinity scale and to venture the following definition of pain:

Definition: <u>Pain</u> is the presence of an entity to which a person has aversion.

Or, conversely:

Definition: <u>Pain</u> is aversion to an entity that is present.

In other words, if something is nearby and I have an aversion to it, I experience pain. I may have an intense aversion to something but not experience pain, provided the thing is sufficiently distant. The presence of people or entities we dislike is, to a varying degree, painful to us. Pain can range from mild discomfort to intense agony. The *quality* of the pain is determined by our position on the Emotional Scale (anger, grief, ambivalence, etc.) and the nature of the situation in which the pain occurs; the *quantity* of the pain varies with the cardinality of the entity, activity, or identity to which we have an aversion. We say things like: "He is a real pain." Although such statements are perhaps meant to be metaphorical, it is quite literally true that such a person's presence is felt as painful, to a degree.

The term "pain", however, seems to embrace two different things:

1. Physical pain.
2. Situational (or emotional) pain.

Both kinds of pain involve aversion. The degree of pain in both cases can vary from a mild discomfort to intense agony.

Physical Pain

Physical pain often seems to result from an intolerance to too high an intensity of sensory input — an intensity that threatens to damage sensory organs or to overwhelm the person. Very bright lights, loud sounds, strong smells, and other strong physical sensations are usually painful. Often, too, physical pain seems to be related to certain *types* of sensory input, such as nausea, certain odors, itching, the feeling of a full bladder or bowels, the feeling of hunger (apart from actual hunger pains), or the sensation of "physical pain" in its various forms (such as aches, burning sensations, and sharp sensations). These aversions appear to be genetically "built in" to our bodily identity, and most are clearly conducive to organismic survival. A person with leprosy, for instance, does not lose extremities only because of the disease. She loses them mainly because of the loss of sensation in these extremities, which therefore do not warn her when a physical injury has taken place. Infections may go unnoticed until it is too late to save the extremity. The physical pain associated with appendicitis can be life-saving in that it gives warning before a fatal rupture and massive infection can occur. In the absence of knowledge (as in young children and animals), physical pain also aids survival by causing an aversion to things that are physically damaging to the organism. A dog bitten by a raccoon will (rightly) avoid raccoons in the future. So physical pain does have real usefulness.

But painful sensations are often counter-productive for a reasoning person. Once the warning function has been served, it would be better for the person not to have to continue to flinch from the sensation of physical pain. It would be better if she were able to take effective action without being distracted or constrained by a continued need to flinch. Persistent physical pain is like an alarm clock that continues to go off long after it has served its purpose of awakening a person. As long as a person is more or less fixed in a bodily identity, however, she cannot nullify physical flinches entirely. The ability to experience physical pain without flinching is perhaps possessed only by rare individuals — sages who have completely disentangled themselves from their self-identification with the body. The rest of us continue to have these built-in physical aversions, and the best way to handle them is to stay healthy and avoid injury.

Situational Pain

Situational pain is associated with the various types of situations discussed in Chapter Six — discomforts connected with such things as upsets, misdeeds, withheld communications, problems, and boredom. It is based on the intolerability of non-physically-painful experiences. Although not physically based, it is often at least as intense as physical pain. People spend far more time avoiding situational pain than they spend avoiding physical pain. Severe failures or losses, extreme confusion, extreme negative emotion — all these can cause severe situational pain. Like physical pain, situational pain has a tendency to go on beyond the point at which it might be useful. A severe feeling of anxiety may alert me to the fact that I am in danger of falling off a cliff, and for this reason it may serve a useful purpose. But if the anxiety continues for days — or years — after the danger has passed, it is counter-productive.

Pain and Unawareness

Pain and unconsciousness are closely related. A flinch, or an aversion, is an "averting" of one's attention, a lowering of awareness, a turning away from something. So pain and unconsciousness are actually two sides of the same coin. In order to clarify this point, I should mention that there are, in fact, two kinds of unconsciousness or unawareness:

1. Simple unawareness
2. Directed unawareness

Simple Unawareness

Simple unawareness is the "normal" form of unawareness we have of things we take for granted or that we do automatically. It has various different forms:

1. Unawareness of things that we have not found out about yet.
2. Forgetfulness caused by the passage of time. If I have not thought of something in a long time, I may not remember it under normal circumstances unless there is some extraordinary reason to do so.
3. Unawareness of subsidiary actions done to accomplish a task on which we are focused. If I learn to wiggle my ears or to ride a bicycle, that does not necessarily mean that I am aware of the muscular movements I am doing to perform these actions, nor of what I am doing to get the muscles to move.
4. Unawareness of things that are irrelevant to a particular purpose or identity. After assuming a particular identity, a person tends more or less automatically to screen out awareness of things that do not have to do with that identity. This kind of unawareness is quite salutary. While driving a car, it is to be hoped that one is *not* attending to the various aesthetic qualities of one's passengers. While making love, one should not be attending to the relative state of balance

or imbalance of one's bank account. Generally speaking, this type of unawareness consists of unawareness caused by a decision to attend to something else, along with the fact that there is a limit to how much we can attend to at the same time.

If we shift identities, we can become aware of things we ignored previously. By choosing to be aware of the figure, we become relatively unaware of the ground, and by attending to the ground, what was the ground becomes the current figure and the former figure becomes the current ground (and we become relatively unaware of it).

Exercise 19. Figure and Ground — II

a. Look at the following figure/ground example in Figure 38 (the same one used in Chapter One):
b. Note the goblet, then the two faces, and note what happens to your awareness as you switch back and forth a few times.

Figure 38. Example of a figure and ground.

You will note that you cannot be *primarily* aware of both the faces and the goblet at the same time. One or the other always recedes.

Directed Unawareness

The other form of unawareness — *directed* unawareness — is unawareness based on aversion, on a flinch from pain. It is unconsciousness *of* a specific entity, and it is brought about by the presence of that entity or by the presence of a related (similar) entity.[1] Whereas simple unawareness is caused by turning *toward* something else, directed unawareness is caused by pointedly turning *away from* the thing of which one is unconscious. There is a more or less automatic paradox associated with directed unawareness: the person has to be aware of something in order to know where to direct his unawareness! At some level, one has to know or suspect that something is present in order to know that one must turn off one's awareness of it. One has to know that something is there in order to know where *not* to look. In order to understand how difficult this is, try the following classic exercise:

Exercise 20. Pink Elephant

a. Try *not* to think of a pink elephant.
b. Can you do it?
c. If so, how? If not, why not?

It is *this* kind of unawareness — directed unawareness — that can be profoundly detrimental to a person's achievement of the kind of world he wants to have. Following Freud, I will refer to directed unawareness as "repression".

---

1. Harry S. Sullivan used the term "selective inattention" with a similar meaning. See *The Psychiatric Interview* (W.W. Norton, New York, 1954) p. 218.

Repression and Aversion

In order to help a person become more aware of a situation that she has repressed, one must handle her aversion to the various underlying truths about that situation. Aversion or pain can be regarded as a transition stage from consciousness of something to a directed unawareness or repression of that thing. It is a transition, because while the pain exists, one is still in contact with the thing and one still has a choice of whether to move toward it or back away. Flinching is an attempt to avoid experiencing — to reject or separate from — an entity, activity, or identity. Of course, repression is not the only means a person has of escaping. She can also run away from, hide from, throw away, resist, destroy, or throw out a hated object or person. In short, she can remove it from her space in a variety of ways. These are the *physical* equivalents of the process of repression, which is just a *mental* attempt to throw away something that is unwanted.

In looking at the Emotional Scale,[2] we can see that from around hidden hostility on up, the person's strategy involves moving *toward* the entity in question, with destructive purpose at the lower levels and with constructive purpose at the higher levels. This could mean *creatively* moving toward or reaching for the entity (by approaching it, changing it, doing something about it — exercising creativity in its direction), or *receptively* reaching for the entity (by perceiving it, interpreting it, understanding it). At these higher levels of the Emotional Scale, the person is being *causative* toward the entity, to a greater or lesser degree; she is confronting it and handling it:

Definition: Confronting is engaging in receptive action with respect to an entity, being aware of that entity.

---

2. Which could be described as a scale of emotion, success, or closeness (See Chapters Three , pp. 141-144, Four, pp. 183-187, and Nine, pp. 517-528).

Definition: <u>Handling</u> is engaging in creative action with respect to an entity.

Each is an exercise of causativeness toward an entity.

In the upper range of the Emotional Scale, the aversion is not sufficient to cause a person to turn away from the entity toward which it is directed. His awareness may not be wholly accurate, but he is aware of that entity. His handling might not be perfect, but he is doing something about it. Below hidden hostility, however, the direction of motion reverses, and we find a motion *away* from the entity in question; the person is mostly being the *effect* of it, instead of handling it (being causative over it), and he is mostly avoiding it — failing to be receptive to it — instead of confronting it.

The various modes of directed unawareness or repression are ways of mentally escaping from entities that one cannot run away from physically or handle through activity.

The process of running away from an object, activity, or identity (mentally or physically) should not be confused with the process of deciding to choose one activity or identity over another or to choose one concept rather than another as factual. A person is always making choices about what to do, what to have, and what to be, and there is nothing wrong with that. If a person chooses to read a book, that does not mean that he is aberrated because he is not going to a movie, dancing, or flying a plane. Nor does it imply that he has an aversion to these other activities. I shall call this kind of "pristine" choice, not made as a reaction to some prior choice, a "first consideration":

Definition: A <u>first consideration</u> is the first decision a person makes on a particular topic. By definition, it cannot be a contradiction of another, earlier consideration on the same subject. It is possible, however, for the person to add a layer of delusion on top of the first consideration — a second consideration that is incongruent with the first — and then to add a third that is incongruent with the second, and so forth.

In contradistinction to the first consideration is the situation in which the person has made a decision that something exists and is now trying to get rid of it mentally *without "unmaking" the prior decision that it exists* and without doing anything to handle it. If I mentally reject something hard enough, I can cease to be aware of it, but it is still there and I may well find myself running into it later because it still exists, unconfronted, as a repressed entity.

In other words, the problem with a person's attempt to throw away entities by repression is that no one ever empties the garbage! It just piles up, and it, as well as the effort to keep it repressed, consumes the person's personal power. If I shove garbage under the beds, it may "disappear", but I will start to smell it after awhile, and I might wonder what it was that I was smelling. Or I might move the bed, and suddenly — there's the garbage! The force of my unchanged agreement on the existence of something that I have rejected or repressed — rather than actually removed, destroyed, or knowingly ceased to accept — causes it to continue to exist and to affect me, apparently without my consent.

In the mental realm, aversion or rejection is repression — a refusal to be aware of something. One manifestation of mental aversion is forgetting. Repression is the mental equivalent of losing something or sweeping it under the carpet. Like physical garbage, mental garbage may eventually have an untoward effect on a person. I can never get rid of something I cannot or will not admit is there. The only way to get rid of it is to overcome my aversion for it, become fully aware of it, and accept it — at which point I can *understand* it. At the point of understanding it, I also stand at the point of knowing that I have accepted it as true. At that point, I can choose consciously to change my opinion to conform better with my observations. Or, recognizing that it exists, I can do something constructive about it. Then, like a problem that has been truly solved, it will be gone. We are probably all familiar with the relief of having completed or deliberately abandoned an important but onerous task. This is the type of feeling one gets from eliminating mental garbage. Since there is no other garbage collector for repressed refuse, a person must burn all his own garbage in the fire of his perception, acceptance, understanding, and constructive action. When he does that, he finds that the power that was tied up in the garbage has been reclaimed for more useful purposes.

Strategies of Repression

When a person represses something, she *starts* to become aware of it, but this cycle of receiving knowledge is interrupted. Thus an incomplete learning cycle is created. Any part of the cycle of becoming aware may be affected: perception, interpretation, verification, or acceptance. The net result is that the person does not learn (remains unaware of) the thing that she would learn if the cycle were completed.

Failure to Perceive

The learning cycle may be interrupted at the point of perception. A person may start to perceive something and then flinch from the perception, leaving the cycle of perception incomplete. A person who cannot stand the sight of blood but is required to watch a surgical operation will try not to see what she is looking at or may even faint in order to avoid the perception. The classic Victorian "vapors" is another instance of using physical unconsciousness as a way of avoiding perception of something unwanted.

But a person does not have to become completely unconscious. More often, she just "dims down" her ability to perceive to a degree. People have "the vapors" all the time without actually being so dramatic about it as to faint. They may just "space out".

Failure to Interpret

The person may successfully perceive something but refuse to try to interpret it or to think about it. He refuses to make the "obvious" interpretation, the one he would make in the absence of aversion and repression. A parent who dotes on his son, who feels that his son can "do no wrong", may see the boy staggering in the door late at night, notice that he has a smelly breath, and yet fail to make the interpretation that he is drunk. A woman may have a lump on her breast but fail to think of the possibility that it might be a malignancy.

Failure to Verify

Next, the person, while having in mind a possible interpretation, may refuse to verify (or disprove) it. The wife knows that the lump in her breast *might* be a malignancy, but because she cannot confront finding out whether it is true or not, she doesn't go to a doctor.

Failure to Decide

Finally, a person may have a correct interpretation and may start to accept it as factual, and then interrupt this cycle. The result is that he fails to accept something he "knows" is true. This receptive disability can take the form of saying that the "correct" interpretation is false. In psychoanalytic language, this strategy is called the "defense mechanism of denial". The woman who feels a lump in her breast may say, "It's the sort of thing that could be cancer, but that can't be true because I'm not old enough and cancer doesn't run in my family," or the doting father might say, "My son looks as if he's drunk, but he's not the type." Sometimes denial goes beyond a mere negation of a fact to a positive controversion of it.[3] A woman who thinks her husband is a contemptible toady but can't admit it to herself may well be found to assert loudly that "he doesn't take any BS from anyone." Alternatively, a person may resort to chronic indecision. She procrastinates the decision that could end the learning cycle. She may feel herself unable to choose amongst two or more interpretations, one of which is the "correct" one: "That lump might just be a cyst, or it might be cancer. I just don't know". "He might be drunk, or he might be tired, or sick. It could be anything. I can't decide." It is, of course, acceptable not to decide something if there is insufficient data. But when the indecisive person does not take any effective steps to resolve the indecision yet continues to worry about it, she is acting in the service of repression.

Delusion

Repression is often aided by the introduction of delusion. A delusion is a concept that is accepted for its "anesthetic" value, rather than for its validity. The purpose of a delusion is to make it unnecessary for the person to feel the pain or discomfort that a valid fact would cause. Repression can exist without delusion, of course. I have just given some examples where perception, interpretation, verification, or acceptance are simply interrupted without being distorted. Commonly, however, there is an altered (or substituted) interpretation or acceptance, backed up, perhaps, by a fallacious "verification", as a way of derailing the receptive cycle.[4] For instance, the wife may interpret the lump in her breast

---

3. In psychoanalysis, this is called "reaction formation".

4. Note that I do not include misperception as a category. Since phenomena are a person's primary data, when a phenomenon is seen as such, it is indubitable. Something a person *perceives* is a primary source of knowledge. As a phenomenon, it is not right or wrong. It simply is what it is. A radiologist looks at a chest X-ray and sees viral pneumonia. A senior radiologist, if she disagrees, does not say, "You do not see viral pneumonia; you see bacterial pneumonia!" No. The radiologist saw viral pneumonia. In order to resolve the issue, the senior radiologist must get the radiologist to back off from his identity as a radiologist to his identity as a student and

as a "gland" or a "cyst", or the doting father may interpret his son's staggering and bad breath as indicative of tiredness or illness.

Rationalization is a form of delusion. It is a combination of denial or uncertainty and misinterpretation or misverification: "I know lumps like this ought to be reported to my doctor, but it's probably just a swollen gland," or "He looks drunk, but he must be tired or sick."

So repression comes in five "flavors" that can be combined in several different ways, but which all add up to an incomplete or distorted learning cycle. These forms of repression are:

1. Failed perception
2. Failed interpretation
3. Failed verification
4. Failed acceptance
    a. Denial
    b. Uncertainty
5. Delusion

---

take another look. Now he sees shadows on an X-ray film, which he *interprets* as viral pneumonia. The senior radiologist can now show him how he is applying the wrong rules of inference and that therefore to say the person has viral pneumonia is a wrong interpretation of the data. Now the student can "re-expand" his identity correctly and see bacterial pneumonia, which, again, as a perception, is indubitable. So from the person-centered viewpoint a person cannot really have an incorrect perception as such. If a person knows she is looking at an illusion, she considers she is perceiving an illusion, not that she is having an incorrect perception. It *is* possible to "step back" from a phenomenon and view it as an interpretation of *another* phenomenon that is "closer" to the person — in the polar dimension, on the causal chain between the person and his world. See Chapter Three, pp. 126-133, for a discussion of the "polar dimension". In this case, the interpretation, formerly seen as a phenomenon, can be viewed as false. But now the person has assumed a "senior" identity from which the former *phenomenon* is seen as just an interpretation and has therefore become doubtable.

The consequence of having directed unawareness or repression — of not completing receptive cycles (or learning cycles) — is that a person has many old, incompletely received incidents persisting in present time, waiting to be fully perceived and understood. But because an alteration or contrary assertion can be introduced to aid the process of repression, repression has the additional liability of introducing false or delusory data:

> **Definition**: A <u>delusion</u> is a falsehood introduced in the act of repression in order to help hide the repressed material.

Layers of Delusion

Delusions come in layers, where delusions are used to repress other delusions. Let us say George starts out thinking that Marsha is a good person, then commits a misdeed against her, such as doing something, in a fit of anger, to injure her reputation. He may find it hard or impossible to confront the fact that he has harmed an innocent person, one that he likes. So he represses the fact that Marsha is a good person and decides that she is obnoxious. Now he can feel his action was justified. Suppose, though, that George is a devout member of a church that disapproves of having negative thoughts about others. Then he might not be able to confront the "fact" that Marsha is obnoxious, because he faces possible social disapproval for having that opinion. So he represses *that* concept and decides that she is "really OK". Here, we see the following lineup of concepts or decisions that George has about Marsha:

3. She is really OK.

2. She is obnoxious.

1. She is a good person.

Later on, George may start feeling unhappy at the thought that other people are really OK, because he thinks he, himself, is *not* "really OK". Thinking that other people *are* OK just makes him feel worse. Therefore, he may now decide that everyone, including Marsha, is "looking out for Number One" So now we get the following lineup of decisions:

4. She is looking out for Number One.

3. She is really OK

2. She is obnoxious.

1. Marsha is a good person

Now we have three layers of delusion on top of the first consideration that George made about Marsha. As we use various means[5] to help George become more aware, he will initially discover that the concept that Marsha is looking out for Number One is just something he used to make himself feel better, and that she is really OK. Here, A has indeed arrived at an underlying truth, an insight. If we continue to raise his awareness, he will next realize, with a great feeling of relief, that he does not have to go around thinking that Marsha is really OK — that that concept was just Pollyanna-ish nonsense enforced by group pressure — the "truth" being that she is obnoxious. If he becomes still *more* aware, he will realize that it was just his inability to confront his own misdeed that caused him to justify it (by deciding that Marsha was obnoxious) and that she *is* actually a good person. At that point, having arrived at his first consideration, he will have cleared off the various layers of delusion and will have no more layers to pick off on this subject.

Delusions are thus formed in layers. A person decides something. Then, for some reason, the fact he has decided on causes him pain so he becomes directedly unaware of it — he represses it — and makes a second decision that contradicts the first and is therefore a falsehood, a delusion. Since the first decision is only repressed and not unmade, it remains, but the

---

5. Such as those discussed in Part III of this book.

person is only aware of the second decision. This decision, in turn, can be repressed and overlaid by a third decision, the third by a fourth, to an indefinite number of layers of delusion.[6]

Reaching Underlying Truths

If we are able to raise the level of awareness, we can peel off these layers of falsehood and arrive at the relative truth that underlies each one. As we move toward the first decision, each layer is "truer" or more "fundamental" than the one that overlies it. The third layer is truer than the fourth, the second is truer than the third, and the first is truest of all. In peeling off these layers, we are arriving at the underlying truths:

Definition: An underlying truth is a concept that is closer to a first consideration than the relative falsehood or falsehoods that it underlies.

A person increasing in awareness on a certain subject will have a series of new cognitions or "realizations":

Definition: A cognition is a prehended fact, one of which a person is currently aware, or the act of prehending a fact. (verb: cognize)

Definition: A realization is a new cognition — an acquisition of new knowledge.

An insight is a particular kind of realization:

Definition: An insight is a realization of an underlying truth.

---

6. The reader may recognize, here, shades of the Freudian theory of repression and defense mechanisms. What is defended against, however, is nothing so abstruse as the "Id" or the "Superego". It is pain and overwhelm.

Insight is the opposite of delusion. In both insight and delusion, the person changes her idea of what is true. In becoming deluded, the person introduces a layer of untruth; in acquiring insight, she *removes* a layer of untruth to uncover the underlying truth.

In order to help a person become more aware of a situation that she has repressed, the person's aversion to the various underlying truths in the situation — i.e., the repressed pain on that subject — must be handled. It does little good to adopt a strategy of trying to find underlying truths if the *reason* for the introduction of falsehood remains unhandled because that reason will then be a reason for resisting the method you are using to increase awareness. The person must be brought to the point of being able to confront the painful subject sufficiently to perceive the truth. Then insight will come spontaneously. Otherwise, it is likely that more layers of delusion will be introduced. The way in which these principles are used to help a person to confront her pain and to acquire insight and ability is called "viewing":[7]

> **Definition**: Viewing is an activity in which a person systematically examines his world in such a way as to gain insight and personal power by undoing repression.

Stress

A concept akin to that of pain is stress. What is stressful for one person is not necessarily stressful for another. One person finds speaking in front of groups very stressful; another belongs to a public speaking club and does it regularly for relaxation. One person feels under extreme stress when going out on a date; another considers it a form of relaxation. Clearly, what determines the nature of stress for a certain person has a great deal more to do with the nature of that person than with external

---

7. I discuss viewing more fully in Part III of this book.

factors.[8]

The common denominator of all forms of stress is that the person considers herself to be in danger of being driven downward on the Emotional Scale, rendered less able to carry out her intentions, and made less aware. A stress is a challenge that a person feels she cannot handle. If she feels capable of confronting a situation, she can find it invigorating, and she regards it as a challenge, rather than as a stress. In fact, anyone will rapidly come to regard a complete lack of challenge as quite boring (anti-heuristic). Life is a series of challenges, and happiness consists in mastering them. But certain entities or situations are of such a nature (whether because of intensity or because of subject matter) that people often feel they cannot fully confront them. Such entities or situations often result in a person's feeling overwhelmed. Therefore, I offer the following definition:

> **Definition**: A stress is an entity that a person thinks might be capable of overwhelming her or that she considers she may be incapable of fully confronting or handling.

This definition should be seen from the person-centered viewpoint as expressing the way the stressed person looks at a situation. Another person looking at the same situation might feel that no one should have any problem confronting and handling the situation. Nevertheless, such is not the view of the person under stress. To her, the stress is real.

---

8. Some things are pretty much guaranteed to be stressful, however. Certain physical conditions — such as sleep deprivation, certain drugs, certain physical sensations, hunger, illness, and injury — fall into this category, especially if one closely identifies oneself with the body. It is said that there are persons (such as mystics and adepts) who can endure such things without feeling under stress. Such individuals probably do *not* tend to identify themselves with their bodies. In addition to physical stress, the loss of a person to whom one is close is very likely to be stressful, as are other actual or threatened losses and failures. Other forms of stress are highly idiosyncratic.

The definition of stress is very similar to that of pain. When a person encounters a stress, she is at a decision point. She can decide to confront it — at which point it becomes a challenge — or she can decide that it is too much for her and that she cannot confront it, at which point it becomes painful and the mechanisms of repression start to operate.

As a person's condition deteriorates with respect to a particular entity or situation, what may have started out as a challenge becomes a stress. Then, if she does not confront the stress, the situation becomes painful to her, and eventually she avoids the pain by repression. As she becomes more aware, a person comes out of a state of unconsciousness to find herself faced with a painful situation. As she confronts the situation still more, she perceives it as stressful but no longer painful. Finally, it becomes a challenge, and then, handled or fully confronted, it ceases to be of interest or concern to the person.

Traumatic Incidents

Many schools of psychotherapy and many spiritual disciplines have recognized that past harmful acts, given or received, can adversely affect a person's present and future condition, even when they have no direct objective effect on that condition. Some schools explain these effects as the "law of karma"; others as "conditioning"; still others, such as certain followers of Freud, believe that past trauma adversely affects the person because it causes an inhibition of psychosexual maturation, thus fixing the person in an immature phase of growth. A few schools, such as various cognitive therapies, also include a consideration of self-damaging acts. Few address the effects of crossflow harmful acts, done by others to others.[9]

---

9. See the discussion of "flows" in Chapter Five (pp. 235-238). Crossflow effects are mainly encountered in discussions of "role modeling", but severe

The Effects of Incomplete Cycles

The effects of past traumatic experiences — given, received, or observed — are caused by incomplete cycles.[10] end" A cycle, as I have said (p. 110), is an expanded piece of present time, defined by the existence of an (unrealized) intention. "Normally", when we start a cycle, it continues until it is completed or unmade. A third outcome is possible, though, and that is *repression* of the intention and the cycle. This occurs when a person has descended, for whatever reason, down the Emotional Scale to a point where he has enough aversion toward the cycle to want to blot it out. But when we repress something, we are also, paradoxically, continually *aware* of it, because we need to know in which direction *not* to look. This effort *not* to be aware of something of which one *is* aware can be quite a drain on one's personal power.[11] Some of our attention and some of our volition is tied up in the repressed cycle, and more power is tied up in our effort not to be aware of it. As Fritz Perls stated, our energy is doubly drained by this paradoxical act.[12] In other words, this piece of time, defined by the repressed cycle, is not entirely relegated to the past; it continues to have a "present time" feel about it, and it can affect our perceptions of present time. In attempting to perceive present time, we can find ourselves attempting to perceive

---

effects observed happening to others can be traumatic. For instance, Post-Traumatic Stress Disorder victims may be severely traumatized by witnessing horrible combat incidents, e.g., a friend being set on fire or horribly injured. Even observing a relatively mild event such as a severe scolding can be somewhat traumatic for an observer.

10. That is, incomplete (and therefore ongoing) receptive or creative actions. See Chapter Three, pp. 107-110.

11. This effort might be said to use up one's "intention units". See Chapter Four, p. 194.

12. Perls, F., Hefferline, R.F., and Goodman, P., *Gestalt Therapy*, Ch. IX (Dell Publishing Co., New York, 1951) pp. 353-368.

what is here and now "through" the other "present times" defined by our incomplete cycles. Thus, we can get a perception of present time that is a mish-mash of actual present time perceptions and past incomplete cycles.

In recalling past incidents, we "go back in time" and see what happened. Similarly, when we have a repressed incomplete cycle, we are perceiving the past but confusing it with the present. When we have something unconfrontable like a dental appointment we have tried to forget about, we can be "reminded" of that cycle by something that happens in present time such as hearing a friend talking about going to the dentist, seeing someone that looks like our dentist, or driving by the dental office. In the same way, we can be reminded by some environmental (or even mental) stimulus of other things we have repressed. When that happens, the balance of power between the tendency to be reminded and the effort to repress becomes unbalanced, and the hidden material begins to come to awareness. Then the person has a choice of allowing himself to become aware of the repressed material or making a further effort at repression. Usually, he elects the latter course, thus leaving himself with yet another incomplete cycle: the receptive cycle of knowing that he has been reminded (for instance) of the appointment. Let's say he sees a set of false teeth and is reminded of his appointment. At the same time, perhaps, his sister is in the room and makes some remark about the teeth. He does not want to think about it, so he represses the incident of being reminded. His sister can now also become an item that can remind him of the incomplete cycle of being reminded and thus, indirectly, of the original incomplete cycle. If he eats strawberry ice cream, starts to think of a dental appointment, and then represses the thought, the next time he eats something with the same strawberry flavor, he may be reminded again of the appointment (by being reminded of the last time he started thinking about it). Then he will again have to make an effort to repress the thought.

The outcome will be either that he ties up a large number of intention units in not thinking about the appointment or confronts completing the original cycle. If the latter happens and he does go to the dentist, then he feels considerable relief — not just because his teeth feel better but also because all the incidents he had started and "put on hold" through repression are now automatically ended since the original cycle upon which they were based is completed. Going to the dentist, in this case, is the "root" cycle — the first of a sequence of related incomplete cycles.

Remembering and Repressing Traumatic Incidents

The more recently one has been reminded of an incomplete cycle, the easier it is to be reminded of it again. The longer it has been since one was last reminded of it, the harder it is to be reminded of it again. The full reason why we are more easily reminded of some things than others awaits further research. But we do know that events appear to be arranged and interconnected by:

1. Similarity of content or context.
2. Temporal proximity.

In Pavlov's classical conditioning experiments, he observed that events occurring at the same time become associated. If a bell is rung every time a dog is fed, the dog comes to associate the sound of the bell with being fed and so salivates when he hears the bell, even in the absence of food.

Things closer to a person in time appear to be more easily remembered and more easily predicted, just as events closer to a person in space are more easily perceived. Things can get lost in the obscurity of time *or* distance. It isn't precisely known what happens when we are "reminded" of a past incident by experiencing a similar context or content in present time. All we know is that such reminders occur.

If a person has a large number of incomplete receptive cycles or persisting incidents related to a root incident, and if she has been successful in repressing the root incident, she can find herself no longer able to recall the root incident at all, even if she wishes to. Someone could come up to her and say, "Isn't there something you should be doing?", and the person would not think of the dental appointment. In this state, all she knows is that the sight of false teeth is disagreeable or that her sister sometimes makes her feel uncomfortable. People who continually remind others of things tend to be disliked. They are called "nags". The disagreeableness of the original incident "rubs off" on those things and people who remind us of them, deliberately or otherwise. Mark Twain once quipped, "Few things are harder to put up with than the annoyance of a good example." "Good examples" irritate us because they remind us of all of our deficiencies, unpleasant things that are as yet unremedied about ourselves. Hence, in reminding us of incomplete cycles, they bear the brunt of our ire.

In the example given of the dental appointment, the first incomplete cycle seems to be a creative cycle or task, which is then added to by receptive cycles, or incidents. Often, however, the root cycle is also an incident, a *receptive* cycle. And even in the case of the dental appointment, the initial reluctance to go to the dentist is probably a reflection of the fact that the person had some earlier, unconfrontable experience with a doctor or dentist that started an incomplete receptive cycle. In other words, the dentist is unconfrontable mainly because she serves as a reminder of some earlier unpleasant experience.

A person "naturally" has certain basic types of aversions.[13] Any one of them, if sufficiently cardinal and inescapable, can drive a person down the Emotional Scale into negative emotion and cause her to experience pain. At this point she decides not to become aware of the thing to which she has an aversion. That is, she represses it, develops a "directed unconsciousness" of it. And so the act of receiving this thing is not completed. This receptive cycle or incident is an incomplete cycle and, as such, *it remains part of present time as an incomplete or undischarged incident.* I will call an incident that is undischarged because of repression a "traumatic incident" or "trauma".

---

13. See Chapter Six, pp. 276-279.

Sequences of Traumatic Incidents

By the mechanism outlined above, a root trauma, or "root" can lead to further, secondary or derivative traumas, or "sequents". Obviously, "traumatic incidents" contain a variable degree of pain and negative emotion; they can be severe or mild. Some earlier definitions are relevant, here:

Definition: An incident is a receptive cycle or activity.

Definition: Pain is the presence of an entity to which a person has aversion, or aversion to an entity that is present. It can vary from mild discomfort to intense agony.

Definition: Physical pain is a type of physical sensation to which most people have a "built-in aversion", including various aches, burning sensations, sharp sensations, and the like. The "painfulness" of physical pain, however, lies in the person's aversion to the sensation, not in the sensation itself.

Definition: Situational pain is pain that is non-physical but derived from the presence of a situation (such as a misdeed, a withheld communication a problem, disorder, lack of control, boredom, etc.) for which a person has a natural aversion because it violates the principles of pleasure, order, and heuristics by which a person organizes his experience.[14]

---

14. See Chapter Four, pp. 156-166, for an explanation of these principles.

To these definitions, I now add the following:

Definition: A <u>traumatic incident</u> (trauma) is an incident that is wholly or partially repressed and that contains a greater or lesser degree of pain — felt, created, or observed.

Definition: <u>Charge</u> is repressed, unfulfilled intention.

Definition: <u>Discharge</u> is the bringing to awareness of the contents of a traumatic incident and the intention behind it, with a consequent fulfillment or cancellation of the intention and a movement of the traumatic incident out of present time into the past as a completed (and no longer traumatic) incident.

"Traumatic incident" can now be given an alternate definition:

Definition: A <u>traumatic incident</u> is a receptive cycle that is undischarged because of repression.

Further:

Definition: To <u>restimulate</u> a traumatic incident or sequence is to remind a person of it, knowingly or unknowingly, so that it can now have an adverse effect on him. Restimulation activates a traumatic incident or sequence, thus enabling the person to be reminded of it more easily.

Definition: A <u>restimulator</u> is an entity that reminds a person, knowingly or unknowingly, of a traumatic incident or sequence.

Definition: <u>Restimulation</u> is an instance of being restimulated or the act of restimulating.

A person who has incidents restimulated is "disturbed"; that which disturbs him is a "disturbance", and his state after being disturbed is one of "turbidity":

Definition: To <u>disturb</u> a person is to cause his traumatic incidents or sequences to be restimulated or to put his attention on an upset, problem, withheld communication, or misdeed. To create turbidity.

Definition: A <u>disturbance</u> is a subject, situation, or item that is currently in a state of restimulation. Such items include upsets, problems, withheld communications, misdeeds, and traumatic incidents. A disturbance is an area of charge on which the viewer has his attention fixed.

Definition: <u>Turbidity</u> is the state of having one's attention fixed on one or more disturbances. A person in this state is said to be "disturbed".

Further:

Definition: <u>Primary pain</u> is physical or situational pain, based on "natural" aversion. It is not derived from restimulation of a traumatic incident.

Definition: <u>Secondary pain</u> is pain derived from restimulation of an earlier traumatic incident or sequence.

Definition: A <u>negative feeling</u> is negative emotion or some other unwanted phenomenon resulting from the restimulation of one or more traumatic incidents.

Definition: A <u>sequence</u> is a group of one or more related or associated traumatic incidents, connected by one or more types of restimulators, in which later traumatic incidents contain restimulators of earlier ones.

Definition: A <u>theme</u> is a common restimulator that links different traumas in a sequence. The same theme need not be present in the entire sequence.

Definition: The <u>root</u> is the traumatic incident that is earliest in a sequence and on which the entire sequence relies for its existence. It contains natural aversion (primary pain). It does not merely contain aversion based on a reminder of an earlier incident (secondary pain).

Definition: A <u>sequent</u> is a trauma that is not the root for a particular sequence, but is based on restimulation of a root or another sequent. Besides a restimulator of an earlier traumatic incident in the sequence, it may also contain primary pain, as well as one or more other restimulators that fit a different sequence.

The Traumatic Incident Network (Net)

A sequence need not necessarily be a simple chain of events, as in the example of the dental appointment. A sequence *may* contain one incident (the simplest case), or a simple chain of incidents. More often, however, a sequence has a "tree" structure (Figure 39).

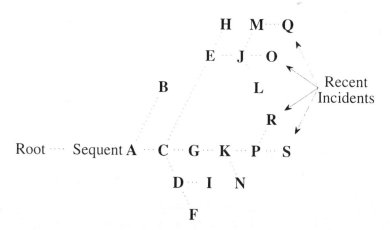

Figure 39. Tree structure of a sequence of traumatic incidents.

Here, the root is incident **A**. Incident **A** is restimulated in incident **B** and in incident **C**. Incident **C** is restimulated in incident **E** and in incident **D**, and so forth. This is how the situation looks if we look from the past toward the present.

Starting from the present and working back, we find a similar branching out backward in time (Figure 40).

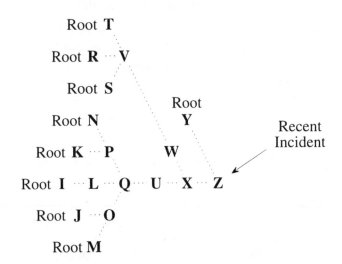

Figure 40. Backward branching of traumatic incidents.

Here, recent incident **Z** contains a restimulation of **Y**, but **Z** also contains a restimulation of **X**. **X**, in turn, contains restimulations of **W** *and* **U**. We will find that **Z** and **Y** have a common theme, and **Z**, **X**, **U**, **Q**, **L** and **I** have a common theme, as do **X**, **W**, **V**, and **T**. Starting from **Z**, we could conceivably find many roots, just as a root could result in many offshoots of sequents.

Although we will retain the notion of a sequence as being a tree structure, in actual fact, since different sequences interact with each other, the whole picture is that of a *network* of incidents, with both common roots and common sequents (Figure 41).

One sequence in this Net consists of nodes (or incidents) **A**, **E**, **G**, **J**, **L**, **M**, **O**, **P**, **Q**, **R**, **S**, **T**, and **U**; another (starting at **B**) consists of all the nodes except **A** and **C**; the third consists of **C**, **F**, **H**, **K**, **N**, **O**, **R**, **T**, and **U**. So, I will define yet another term:

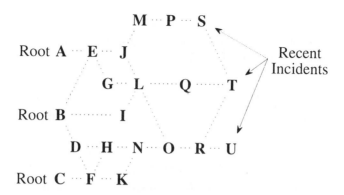

Figure 41. The traumatic incident network (Net).

Definition: The <u>traumatic incident network</u> (or "Net") is the network composed of all of the person's traumatic incidents, with their various interconnections.

As an example of how a sequence is formed, let us say that, at an early age, a child is severely beaten by a bully with red hair (Incident 1). The pain and negative emotion in this incident is primary pain, not a restimulation of an earlier incident. The pain is too intense for the child, so he represses the incident: he does not allow himself to become fully aware of it. Two months later (Incident 2) he is in school when a different red-headed boy says something to him in a loud voice, and he has a violent emotional reaction. Now, if Incident 2 were not preceded by Incident 1, perhaps the child could have tolerated being yelled at without it having any permanent effect. In other words, being yelled at would not be an unconfrontable or traumatic incident for him. But because of the similarity in theme (a boy with red hair), the child is unknowingly reminded of Incident 1 by Incident 2. That is, Incident 2 restimulates Incident 1, which, being incompletely confronted, is still undischarged and therefore stuck as part of his present time. Because of the reminder in Incident 2, Incident 1 begins to come to mind.[15] If the child allows himself to be fully aware of Incident 2, he will also have to deal with Incident 1, since awareness of the one awakens the other because of the common theme. The child begins to experience Incident 2 *and* Incident 1 at the same time. At this point, the situation can go in one of two directions:

1.   The child can complete the receptive cycle — confront Incident 2 and Incident 1, become fully aware of what happened in both incidents, and thus discharge the incidents. This can occur in the course of personal enhancement procedures, by letting the child talk about it. Sometimes it can also happen when the child simply allows himself to be aware of what happened. Since an intention creates a piece of time that remains in the present only so long as the intention exists, fulfilling an intention causes a task or incident to move from present time into the past. In discharging the incidents, the child thereby eliminates them from his present and makes them "things of the past".
2.   The child can repress Incident 1 *and* Incident 2, thus adding Incident 2 as a sequent to Incident 1.

If this second eventuality happens, then the charge of Incident 2 is added to that of Incident 1, and more content is also added to the sequence, so now it is easier for the child to be reminded of the sequence. The red-headed boy and the classroom where Incident 2 took place can now both be restimulators. Incident 3 could consist of the red-headed boy simply walking up and saying "Hello", or of the child simply walking into the classroom. Incident 3 is then added to the sequence in a similar way. Another incident of being yelled at or bullied may be added to the sequence, with more content being added — say a swing the child happened to be swinging on at the time. It now becomes increasingly easier for the child to be reminded of the various traumas in the sequence. But because of the increased charge

15. This is sometimes called a "flashback".

and the increased repression, it becomes harder and harder for the child to opt for completing all the receptive cycles. There are so many traumas in the sequence by this time that it would be too overwhelming to be aware of them or complete them all at once. So the child goes on repressing them. Eventually, he may have a chronic school phobia, a dislike of playgrounds, and a distrust of red-heads.

Fortunately, when a person has not been reminded of something for awhile, it becomes harder for her to be reminded of it. The traumas are still there, still undischarged, still tying up some intention units, and still capable of affecting her with undiminished force, but they are currently inactive. They do not affect her now to any great degree. To return to our example, if the child moves to a new environment or otherwise successfully avoids restimulating the sequence for some time, he may cease to be reminded of the traumas in the sequence. He may eventually lose his school phobia and acquire an ability to be on good terms with red-heads. This is the "healing" effect of time. Nevertheless, even traumas that have been "healed" in this way can again become restimulated under certain circumstances.

This situation differs from that in which a person has managed to confront areas that are disturbing to her, to overcome the effects of charged incidents, and to handle these areas effectively — where she "gets back on the horse that threw her". It seems that if one persists on a course of action despite negative feelings, the feelings eventually tend to disappear. Here, what is happening is that one is *not* repressing the feelings and so is not building up a longer series of traumatic incidents. Confronting negative feelings as they arise seems to have the same destimulative effect as the passage of time. The ability to confront in this way is highly valued and goes by various names, such as "courage" or "fortitude".

At this point we will add a few more definitions to our armamentarium:

Definition: An active sequence or trauma is one that is easily restimulated.

Definition: An <u>inactive</u> sequence or trauma is one that (because of the passage of time, a change of environment, or some other reason) is not easily restimulated.

Definition: <u>Reactivation</u> occurs when restimulation of an inactive sequence or traumatic incident makes it easier for the person to be disturbed by it again.

Definition: <u>Deactivation</u> occurs when, because of passage of time, change of environment, or some other reason (such as the application of a viewing technique), an active sequence or traumatic incident becomes inactive.

Deactivation is different from *discharge*. If a trauma is fully *discharged*, it can no longer be reactivated, *because it is no longer traumatic*. It no longer exists as an incomplete cycle. On the other hand, if a trauma is only *deactivated*, the person may feel relieved but the trauma can be reactivated again later on and can then affect the person as strongly as ever.

A change of environment can be (temporarily) helpful. Taking a vacation does help a person feel better. The reason may be, in part, that she stops being sleep-deprived and gets some rest. The *major* reason, though, is that many of the restimulators that were in the person's usual environment are not usually present in the location where the person is taking a vacation. She does not get telephone calls or visits from people who upset her or who are upset with her. She is not constantly reminded of her inadequacy as an employee or as a professional. When the child goes on vacation (to use the above example), he is no longer around the dreaded classroom, he does not see the red-headed boy, nor is he around noisy children. So that sequence is not restimulated, and it gradually or rapidly becomes inactive.

What a person considers to be a good vacation spot will depend on what the environment is like that she normally inhabits. A New Yorker might go to Vermont to enjoy the peace and quiet of the country and to escape the fast pace of the the big city; a Vermont farmer may go to New York to get away from the boredom of being isolated and communing with cows all day and to *enjoy* the fast pace and excitement of the city. Europeans come to America, and Americans go to Europe. Of course, one point of taking a vacation is that a change of surroundings has heuristic value ("Travel is broadening."). But part of a vacation also consists in *vacating the surroundings that contain restimulators*.[16]

Some people repeatedly "vacate" — run away from — *relationships*. As soon as a relationship becomes too restimulative, a person feels she must flee. She may feel better after she has run away, but then the loss of the other person is likely to be, in itself, restimulative, so she may return to the relationship — or to another, similar, relationship — to try to escape *that* restimulation. She may, again, feel temporary relief, but then the original restimulation in the relationship returns and she feels she must flee again. Such relationships have a characteristically destructive, oscillatory pattern.

One of the saddest and most striking examples of the effects of restimulation is the condition known as "Post-Traumatic Stress Disorder" (PTSD). Perhaps the most striking example of PTSD is found in veterans who have had severe traumatic experiences during combat duty. They may find themselves almost constantly reliving these experiences, constantly re-experiencing the anxiety and guilt contained in their wartime traumas. They also find themselves acting as though they are in a combat situation. These individuals are greatly helped when the charge contained in these traumatic incidents is reduced.[17]

There are certain circumstances under which a person seems to be more easily disturbed than usual. These are all circumstances in which his level of awareness or awakeness — or his

---

16. Some people seem, in fact, to make a life career of moving from one environment to another in order to try to achieve relief from pain and negative emotion. They are sometimes said to be "running away from themselves". More accurately, they are trying to run away from their traumas by running away from restimulators. The problem with this strategy is that in each new location, a person is bound, eventually, to find restimulators that can reactivate her traumas and sequences.

17. The procedure for doing this, "Traumatic Incident Reduction", is discussed in some detail in Chapter Eight, pp. 433-452.

personal power — is diminished for some reason. Intention units are required to maintain *both* sides of a repression — the repressed material *and* the act of repression. When one's power is low for any reason, one becomes less aware and more easily overwhelmed and one also becomes less adept at repressing material. The effect of the decreased ability to repress material is that repressed material becomes more easily restimulated.[18]

Returning to our example of the child beaten up by a bully, let us imagine the following scenario: the person, now in his twenties, who has had no problem with red-headed people for many years, has a low personal power because of having taken drugs or alcohol, being sleep deprived, or upset about something. Under these circumstances, a red-headed colleague speaks to him angrily. Perhaps, too, the setting is similar to the setting that existed at the time of the original incident or to that of a later incident on the sequence (a sequent). Let us say that he happens to be drinking a particular kind of herb tea. Because of his low power, he is easier to disturb, and one or more incidents in the sequence are once again restimulated. Since his power is low, he cannot confront the charge contained in the sequence and so represses it. This sequence is now reactivated. He has added another sequent to it, and, having been recently reminded of (or disturbed by) it, it can now more easily be restimulated again.

---

18. Empirically, people tend to have low personal power when they have taken drugs of various kinds, when they are sleep-deprived, ill, malnourished, upset, or overwhelmed. Why these various physical factors should lower power is not entirely clear. Perhaps it has to do with the identification the person has with the body: the physical energy reserves of the body may be considered one's own energy reserves (power). Again, some extraordinary persons are able, apparently, to overcome or ignore physical conditions such as drug intoxication, sleep deprivation, hunger, and illness and remain fully alert and functional. These are probably the same people (sages and saints) who are apparently able to confront physical pain sensations without aversion because they can move out of a fixed bodily identity. Most of us, however, are affected by these factors. On a non-physical level, if a person is already overwhelmed or has negative emotion, her power is certain to be diminished. So it is not surprising to find that people in this condition are easily disturbed.

Now, drinking that kind of herb tea — or perhaps drinking *any* kind of tea — can reactivate the sequence. As the sequence grows, more and more stimuli can reactivate it, until he may once again find himself in a more or less continual state of turbidity. In other words, he may once again fall victim to chronic fears similar to those he felt as a child.

In describing this state of affairs, I am not describing "neurosis" or anything that is abnormal. The normal, average person has a dense network composed of a very large number (probably thousands) of very highly charged traumatic incidents and sequences in varying states of activation, and there are a large number of potential or actual restimulators. I am, in fact, describing the *usual human condition*. A person with relatively few active traumatic incidents and sequences appears to be in very good shape indeed, yet even she is likely to have many inactive traumatic incidents and sequences that could be activated under certain circumstances.

A major goal of applied metapsychology is the systematic discharging of a person's Net (traumatic incident network). As a person discharges past traumas, her condition improves progressively and markedly. It is unclear at this time whether a person could ever discharge *all* the traumas in the Net. As she progresses toward this goal, however, she will be found to be progressing toward the traditional goals of personal enhancement: toward being enlightened, fully conscious, fully unrepressed, fully able, fully self-actualizing (to use Maslow's term), fully functioning (to use Carl Rogers' term), or fully rational (to use Albert Ellis's term). These desired states of being are expressed as absolutes and, as such, are unlikely ever to be *fully* achieved, but they are worth keeping in mind, in that they give a direction to our work. I believe that, starting from a state of "normality", we can progress a long way toward these traditional goals by applying the principles of metapsychology.

Aberration

In finding a term to describe what can be wrong with a person, I shall begin with a consideration of what the ideal state is. I define the ideal state, not as "mental health" but as an absence of a Net. The state of not having a Net is ideal from the point of view of the person, because she would rather not have to repress the exercise of her receptive abilities. She would rather have all the personal power that is tied up in the repressed material available for her use in achieving her goals and in organizing her world. Such a fully-realized person would tend to be multi-determined, highly ethical, able, successful and high on the Emotional Scale. She would have a full ability to be aware, to perceive, interpret her perceptions, and verify these interpretations. In other words, such a person would be extremely capable of learning and growing.

Having described the ideal state, it is now my task to describe its opposite: the state of aberration — which I define as follows:

Definition: Aberration is distortion of thought, perception, intention, identity, and behavior, caused by the traumatic incident network.

I have already defined one of the forms of aberration:

Definition: A delusion is a falsehood introduced in the act of repression in order to help hide the repressed material.

This is a distortion of thought. I have also defined "negative feeling":

Definition: A negative feeling is negative emotion or some other unwanted phenomenon stemming from the restimulation of one or more traumatic incidents.

This is a distortion of perception. For instance, if a person has "free-floating anxiety" or a diffuse sense of guilt without any definite present-time cause, that would be called a "negative feeling".

Finally, aberration can also be a distortion of behavior, in which the person "acts out" behaviors that were part of an earlier traumatic incident.

Definition: A <u>dramatization</u> is behavior that is caused by the restimulation of one or more traumatic incidents and is an unconscious re-enactment of the behavior that occurred at the time of the traumatic incident or incidents.

Dramatization is directed toward present-time objects or people. The behavior involved may have been appropriate to the past incident or incidents, but it is usually not appropriate to the present situation, although often rationalized to *seem* appropriate in some way. Therefore it often has destructive consequences. An eating compulsion or inhibition can be a dramatization, as can biting one's nails, yelling at one's wife, or being accident-prone. A woman who acts like a disapproving parent when she goes out with a particular man may be engaged in a dramatization of an earlier incident in which her mother was punishing her for being naughty and dramatizing the role of the mother in that traumatic incident. A person engaged in such behavior is usually completely unaware that she is dramatizing a past incident. She attributes her actions to the present-time situation.

Reliving a Past Trauma

When a past traumatic incident is restimulated, a person *relives* that incident to a greater or lesser degree, usually without realizing that he is doing so:

Definition: <u>Reliving</u> is the unconscious re-experiencing of one or more traumatic incidents that have been restimulated but not discharged. It can cause aberrations, i.e., delusions, negative feelings, or dramatizations.

He experiences the feelings he had at that time and may behave as he or others in the traumatic incident behaved at that time, directing this behavior to his present surroundings. By "reliving",

I do not mean to suggest that there is a *conscious* re-experiencing or re-enactment of a past incident. Reliving has three different forms: the re-experiencing of the various uncomfortable phenomena or perceptions in a traumatic incident (negative feelings), the re-experiencing of thought patterns contained in a traumatic incident (delusions), and the re-enactment of the actions of the traumatic incident (dramatization).[19]

The presence of the Net not only robs a person of power but also causes him to think, feel, and behave in certain ways that, to him — and often to others — are undesirable, because of the charge it contains and the aberrations it causes. Bear in mind, however, that a facilitator should have no interest whatsoever in getting a person to change things *others* do not like or cannot cope with about him. A facilitator should only be interested in improving the condition of the client's world, as seen from the *client's* viewpoint. This focus of interest fits well with the person-centered viewpoint. It is also true, generally, that when a person's world becomes better for him, it also turns out to be better for those around him.

Paradoxically, although repression is intended to eliminate undesired feelings, emotions, sensations, attitudes, and pains, it actually causes the person to suffer *more* from these unwanted experiences than he would if he had not repressed them in the first place. An incomplete creative or receptive cycle — an incomplete task or a "stuck" incident — remains with the person as part of his present time, and thus continues to affect him to a greater or lesser degree until it is completed. In the following section, I will consider some of the ways in which the Net affects the person.

---

19. Again, a particularly debilitating example of the reliving of a traumatic incident occurs in victims of Post-Traumatic Stress Disorder (PTSD). Vietnam veterans, for instance, find themselves having "flashbacks" in which they re-experience thought patterns and feelings they experienced under combat conditions (e.g., anxiety, rage, guilt, or numbness) and also often behave as they did in combat situations (engaging in violent expressions of rage, avoiding open spaces, being excessively vigilant).

Dealing with Restimulation

Empirically, we can observe that when a sequence is activated, one has three choices:

1. To discharge by inspection — to confront the sequence in its entirety, and complete the receptive cycles contained therein, thus discharging the sequence.
2. To notice the presence of the sequence or of the fact of restimulation without handling it right away.
3. To repress and relive the trauma — to become directedly unaware of the activating incident (the incident containing the restimulation) — thus adding another traumatic incident to the sequence, and, at the same time, unconsciously re-experiencing or dramatizing one or more traumatic incidents in the sequence.

Alternative (1) is unusual but possible if the person is relatively unaberrated and if the sequence is not too heavily charged. If it does occur, the aberrative force of the sequence is eliminated. Alternative (2) can afford temporary relief and does not add to the sequence, but also does not eliminate it. Alternative (3) is the more usual response and the only one that concerns us in our discussion of aberration.

Repressing and Reliving

Along with repression, there is usually some degree of reliving of the sequence. In other words, the person re-experiences or dramatizes one or more incidents in the sequence. Because of the repression, she does so without realizing that that is what is going on. She fails to recognize that the feelings she is feeling and the behavior she is manifesting actually constitute a reliving of one or more traumatic incidents. Instead, she misinterprets the source of her feelings and the objects of her behaviors as being caused by, or directed toward, some part of her *current* experience — especially the part that disturbed her.

Let us say that, as a child, George was often severely punished by his mother, who told him he was "an idiot" and "good for nothing". Later in life, he meets Marsha, who bears a physical resemblance to his mother or who has some of her mannerisms. Marsha, then, can serve to restimulate the sequence of traumatic incidents from his childhood. When he sees her, he is unknowingly reminded of these incidents. There is a remote possibility that he could simply look back at all the childhood incidents in the sequence and fully confront them — complete them as receptive cycles. Or, instead of just being upset, he could recognize that certain earlier similar incidents had been restimulated by Marsha. Such a recognition would, itself, usually suffice to prevent him from being majorly disturbed. More likely, however, he will repress a full awareness of the sequence and instead look at Marsha and feel inadequate (or "no good") or stupid ("idiotic"), as he did when he was a child. He may even behave toward her the same way he used to behave toward his mother. But he will think that there is something about Marsha, *here in present time*, that is causing his negative feelings, and he will be completely unaware of the true nature and origin of his own behavior.[20] His powers of rationalization will come to the fore to "protect" him against an awareness of the sequence from the past.

Or let us say a person has a severe emotional shock such as the loss of a parent. Let us suppose that at the time she received the news, she was walking out of a church and the church bells were ringing. A pastor, dressed in clerical garb, told her the news. Later in life, this person may tend to avoid churches and ministers because of a feeling of melancholy that comes over her in their presence. Church bells may make her feel sad. She will probably not be aware of why this is so.

---

20. If a person could understand *completely* (not just intellectually) the reason for one of her aberrations, she would no longer have that aberration because the traumatic incidents that lay behind it would no longer be repressed and hence would no longer be aberrative.

Married couples often trigger each other's past traumas. For one thing, being husband and wife, father and mother, creates a "built-in" similarity to situations that occurred in childhood. Secondly, mates seem often to choose each other because of their (unconscious) resemblance to parents. Finally, any two people who stay together long enough eventually have upsets with each other or shared traumatic incidents. It is easy, then, for them to serve as reminders to each other of these traumatic incidents. Early in a relationship a couple may have a great deal of affection for each other, but as the number of shared traumatic incidents increases, charge in these incidents accumulates and contact with each other can become increasingly painful. Such couples finally need but see each other to trigger a number of uncomfortable restimulations, leading to various negative feelings and delusions. Furthermore, they tend to dramatize their past shared traumatic incidents. So we often find married couples repeatedly playing out precisely the same scenes with each other and responding to each other with pat phrases that actually arise out of past incidents. Such couples, however, are surprisingly unaware that this is what is happening. To them it seems that each argument or upset arises freshly, while to an outside observer it is quite obvious that they are like a broken record, repeating and repeating the same phrases and reliving the same situations.[21]

Identification with the Winning Identity

One of the more interesting forms of misinterpretation is a delusion concerning identity. Suppose a person has a traumatic incident in which he is being punished by his father. If something happens to restimulate this traumatic incident, he can dramatize it from his own viewpoint and feel the grief or hurt. Or he can

---

21. Much of traditional family and marital therapy consists in attempting to give members of such a family group an objective view of their own behavior so that they can modify it.

misinterpret the experience by misidentifying or switching around its *dramatis personae* and, in his dramatization, "become" his father. A past trauma is often an incident in which the person considered himself to be "losing" — in which he was driven down the emotional scale by someone else who was "winning". In reliving it, he misidentifies himself in the incident as the one who is "winning". This delusion is introduced to help make it possible for him to repress the uncomfortable feelings that exist in the incident, as seen from his own point of view. In psychoanalytic terms, he "identifies with the aggressor", and he will now tend to dramatize the actions the aggressor took at the time of the incident. When he does that, he will feel what he perceived to be his father's feelings at the time and he will tend to act as his father did. So, for instance, he will feel angry and disappointed instead of sad and guilty, and he will scold his own son, his wife, or somebody else, using just the language his father used on him. Since his father, though angry, was feeling better than *he* was at the time, he can avoid more uncomfortable feelings by reliving his father's role in the incident than by reliving his own. This adds another dimension to the observation, "What you resist, you tend to get." Now we can see that "Whom you resist, you tend to become."

This tendency to choose the "winning" identity is a source of a great deal of unhappiness, though its short-term effect is an improvement in how the person feels. When a person is in a traumatic incident in which someone else is winning and she is losing, the other person is usually doing most of the *acting* while she is doing most of the *feeling*. If a person is reliving her *own* role in that incident, she tends to experience negative *feelings*, whereas if she is reliving the winning identity she is mainly *behaving*. An angry or contemptuous person is often dramatizing a traumatic incident in which someone else behaved angrily or contemptuously toward her. If she stops acting angry or contemptuous, she will have to feel what she felt in her own identity at that time — a great deal of physical or situational pain. Underlying the angry, conceited, pompous, or contemptuous identity she has assumed for the time being lies a little child in pain or in tears. Typically, however, she is unaware of having assumed *any* identity, or of reliving any past incident.

When a person assumes a "winning" identity, she usually dramatizes the worst characteristics of the other person. A woman may generally be mild-mannered and pleasant. Her associates, however, will not have traumatic incidents containing this person when she is in her usual state. In her usual state, after all, she does not traumatize others! Any *traumatic* incidents they may have involving her will contain those (relatively rare) moments when she loses control of herself. These are undoubtedly moments when she *herself* is dramatizing a winning identity and gets angry, sarcastic, etc. So when her associates dramatize incidents containing this person, they will act as she does when she is at her worst. Aberration is thus contagious, and the worst characteristics of people tend to be propagated to their associates, who in turn propagate them to others. The result is a world in which there is much brutality and unhappiness.

The Dark Side of Human Nature

The traumatic incident network (Net), and the various aberrations that result from it, constitute the "dark side" of humanity. The negative feelings resulting from the Net account for most of the suffering that occurs in the world, while the dramatizations account for what has been labeled "evil" in human nature. These are the manifestations that religions, governments, and therapies have tried, with varying degrees of success, to alleviate or suppress. No theory or technique that fails to come to terms with and handle this dark side of human nature and experience can hope to be effective in the long run. Yet there is a natural tendency to try to ignore this side of life. People tend to be phobic or superstitious about confronting it because they are somehow afraid they will give it power or become contaminated by it. A person naturally has an aversion to aversion, to pain and suffering; such things are difficult to confront, whether in oneself or in others.

The same tendency that causes us to repress negativity in ourselves also tends to make us want to ignore it or avoid it in others. During the optimism of the mid-sixties, many felt that by denying the negative side of life or accentuating and developing the positive side, one could circumvent these dark feelings and actions. Although I agree wholeheartedly with the goal of negating the effects of the "dark side" of human nature and human experience and of allying ourselves with the positive side, the Net and human aberration cannot be ignored or side-stepped. They must be confronted head-on and definitively handled by anyone who hopes to be of real assistance to his fellow man. When so confronted, it will be found that they *can* be understood and handled. Confronting the Net is the only way *not* to be affected by it, the only way to *avoid* contamination, because the Net exists and has power only because of repression. Negative feelings and dramatizations are manifestations of charge. The way to handle them is to make it possible for a person to find, confront, and eliminate the charge that is causing them.

Automaticities

In talking about things that are "unconsciously" or "subconsciously" known, conceived, pictured, perceived, or done, I am talking about "automaticities":

Definition: An automaticity is an action done by a person without his being focally aware, at the time, of doing it. He has only a *subsidiary* awareness of doing it. He may be aware that the action is *happening* but, if so, he does not see himself as the originator of that action. It seems to be "just happening".

Automaticities are needed in order for a person to function at all. If a person had to pay attention to the details of every assumption that lay behind every thought, every subsidiary perception and action that lay behind every focal perception and action, he would find that he did not have enough personal power to do it — his attention and intention would be too dispersed for him to be able to get anything done. He would undoubtedly become psychotic. In fact, he would die. Putting a large number of actions, perceptions, and thoughts "on automatic" is part of the extension of identity discussed earlier (pp. 183-185). The person extends his identity to incorporate abilities or skills, both creative and receptive, as part of himself. This is not the same as repression, or *directed* unawareness. Rather, it is a beneficial form of *simple* unawareness that enables the person to focus on what is relevant to the task at hand. If he finds that there are falsehoods or limiting characteristics in the subliminal actions, perceptions, and conceptions that are part of the skills of an identity, he can fairly easily "step back" from his extended state and learn new skills, then re-extend by incorporating these revised skills. Anyone who is striving to improve his performance in any activity goes through this cycle regularly. It takes a certain amount of work, but it is not painful. In fact, it is often experienced as pleasurable. We can define "skill" as follows:

Definition: A skill is an ability of which a person has a simple (not directed) unawareness: the ability has been incorporated as part of an identity the person has assumed.

In contradistinction to this benign form of learned automaticity, the person has other automaticities that are aberrations. As you recall:

Definition: Aberration is distortion of thought, perception, intention, identity, and behavior caused by the effects of the traumatic incident network.

Although it might seem odd to describe an aberration as the manifestation of an ability, nevertheless it is just that. Aberration depends on a person's ability to *create* — to conceive or picture something that is different from what is actually there — and to act. Aberration depends on the ability to conceive a thought (delusion), to picture a phenomenon (negative feeling), or to perform an action (dramatization) that is incongruent with what is going on in present time.

Whereas skills are based on *simple* unawareness resulting from personal growth, aberrations are based on — and part of the process of — *directed* unawareness, or repression. Unlike skills, aberrations are difficult to eliminate because of the repression involved and because of the *reason* for the repression — the pain that is being avoided by pointedly being unaware of aberrations — and because the repression itself makes awareness of aberrations and their sources difficult.

Automatisms and Skills

Since aberration can be viewed as a repressed, automatic exercise of ability, it is useful to have a term to denote aberration, from the viewpoint of its being a form of automaticity. So I am going to conscript the word "automatism" to carry this meaning:

Definition: An <u>automatism</u> is an aberrated automaticity, a conditioned automaticity.

We can also redefine "skill":

Definition: A <u>skill</u> is a learned automaticity.

The first can be eliminated; the second can be improved.

Automatisms can be either receptive or creative. If a person has an automatic feeling of anxiety that "turns on" whenever she has to talk to a stranger, that is a *receptive* automatism. If a person has a handwashing compulsion or a compulsion to smoke, that is a *creative* automatism. Although a person generally has many automatisms, some stand out as being rather more significant and habitual than others, and it is useful to have special terms for these major automatisms, since they are the ones we are going to be especially concerned with. The following definitions will serve:

Definition: A <u>compulsion</u> is a significant and habitual creative automatism.

Definition: A <u>fixation</u> is a significant and habitual receptive automatism.[22]

Compulsions include addictions and other unwanted but habitual behavior patterns over which a person appears to have little or no control. Fixations include chronic negative feelings and fixed ideas over which she similarly lacks control.

When she has a traumatic incident in restimulation, a person often seems to have a choice between:

1. Having negative feelings stemming from the traumatic incident.
2. Dramatizing the incident, generally from the viewpoint of the "winning" identity in the incident.

A dramatization, as a compulsion or set of compulsions, serves the purpose of shielding the person from uncomfortable negative feelings. If a person is prevented from exercising a compulsion, she usually feels very uncomfortable. It is the threatened discomfort that "compels" her to exercise the compulsion. The "force" of the Net consists of negative, painful feelings.

Secondary Gain

Although automatisms are "useful" in facilitating repression, they are sometimes "useful" in other ways as well. I will adopt the psychoanalytic term "secondary gain" to describe these other "uses":

---

22. I do not mean to use the word "fixation" in its psychoanalytic sense of "a state of being arrested at an immature phase of development". Rather, I use it to mean fixed perceptions or ideas.

Definition: Secondary gain is the "usefulness" of aberration, apart from its function in facilitating repression. For instance, a person may cultivate or exaggerate an upset or a psychosomatic condition in order to get help or attention from others.

A justification of a misdeed, originally adopted to relieve the discomfort of thinking one has harmed another, can later serve to allow one to feel superior to or dominate others and win self-determined or zero-sum games. If a man harms a woman and then adopts as a justification the concept that women are inferior, he may later use that fixed idea to avoid feelings of inferiority toward certain other women, or to gain an advantage over female competitors. A compulsion, such as a tendency to fly into a rage when thwarted, can be useful in gaining mastery over others. A chronic negative feeling (such as a psychosomatic backache or neckache) can allow a person to collect disability payments, win judgments in lawsuits, get people to pay attention to and care for her, and so forth. So a person may be doubly motivated to cling to her automatisms:

1. To avoid the underlying pain that the automatisms are meant to repress and
2. To provide secondary gain.

Some (perhaps most) forms of secondary gain are really illusory. An automatism (like a handwashing compulsion or compulsive neatness) that appears to give a person a useful ability can quite easily be replaced by a learned habit or skill that does not have the liability of being based on traumatic incidents. A person can *learn* to be careful and neat; he can *learn* to scrub thoroughly, when appropriate; he doesn't need a handwashing *compulsion*. I can, in fact, make this flat assertion:

Any ability a person has as an automatism he can have better as a skill.[23]

Although the notion that aberration leads to artistic or scientific productivity is a common one, it is unsubstantiated by observation. The vast majority of highly productive scientists and artists are extraordinarily stable people.[24] The vast majority of highly aberrated people are extraordinarily unproductive. A person who is not chronically disturbed does better in every sense, because he has available to spend, in his productions, the power he does *not* have to spend on maintaining his aberrations.

Just as compulsions sometimes appear to be useful, so do fixations (significant and habitual *receptive* automatisms). Besides providing secondary gain, a fixation may also serve as an aberrated cardinal point for a person; clinging to it may seem to shield him from a great deal of unpleasantness or pain. Such a cardinal point is a falsehood or misperception, but it can also be "useful" for its anesthetic or repressive qualities, as well as for any secondary gain it may provide. A fixation may develop from a fear of confronting some fact or part of life, and it may serve as a justification for not confronting it. If I am afraid of public speaking, I may decide that I am really a poor speaker, that it is not really that important for me to speak, or that only arrogant people speak in public. Or I may develop a psychosomatic throat condition. Similarly, if I'm afraid of sex, I may decide that sex is really

---

23. The concept of "learning" has been muddied somewhat by behavioristic thinking, though there are elements of truth in the behaviorist formulation. The behaviorist model is correct in pointing out that learning involves the establishment of an automaticity, but it fails to distinguish between *skills* — which are more or less beneficial and under the control of the person — and *automatisms*, which are generally not beneficial (or only *secondarily* so) and are not under the control of the person. I think it best to apply the term "conditioning" to the creation of automatisms, since these are based on "deficiency motivation", or an attempt to avoid pain. In a conditioning situation, a person has a "choice" of either performing the conditioned action or experiencing pain, and if the pain is not confrontable, the choice has to be to act. We should reserve the term "learning" for a process that results in knowledge and skill, not delusion and compulsions.

24. Or they produce the work for which they are known during periods of stability.

degraded or evil or I may become impotent or frigid. If I am confused about which direction to take in life and cannot confront fully sorting out the confusion for myself, I may seize upon some authority, guru, or fixed belief system to order my world for me. This belief system may then become a fixation, an aberrated cardinal point, for me, based on its "usefulness" in repressing the elements of the confusion.

Automatisms and Fixed Identities

Automatisms and fixed identities are very closely interwoven. A compulsion is one of the creative activities of a fixed identity. It is normal, for instance, for a performer to interest and entertain others. A dull performer is a bad performer. If, however, a person becomes *fixed* in the identity of a performer, then he may feel compelled to be interesting *all* the time, even in situations where such behavior is counter-productive. In fact, in *most* situations, it is more effective to be interest*ed* than to be interest*ing*. Yet to the degree a person is trapped in the identity of a performer, he will have the compulsion to entertain and interest others.

A fixation is one of the *receptive* activities of a fixed identity, one of the ways in which that identity interprets, thinks about, or understands the world. When fixed in an identity, a performer may have the fixed idea that all other people are his "audience"; a doctor may look on others exclusively as patients; a con-man may be stuck with the idea that others are "suckers" or "marks" or that "You have to be trickier than the other guy." Fixed identities, in short, lead to fixations and compulsions, and any fixation or compulsion can be related or assigned to a fixed or aberrated identity. The one is really the obverse of the other.

Automatisms are "useful" because they appear to help avoid pain, create a sort of order, and provide a form of knowledge. They thus appear to provide the three basic elements one seeks in organizing experience — pleasure, order, and heuristics. But they are actually much more of a liability than a help. They can appear to provide useful skills, and certain fixations can make it seem as though one has arrived at an important truth — such as the "truth" that "there's a sucker born every minute". But this "knowledge" actually amounts to fixed ideas; it prevents *real* learning and is, in fact, a major barrier to study. The "order" they provide is equally illusory — an aberrated stable datum that only masks confusion, instead of resolving it. And the relief from pain they appear to provide actually causes repressed pain to persist indefinitely by preventing its discharge.

Automatisms as Resistance to Help

Because of the apparent "usefulness" of automatisms, a person may resist eliminating them. Although a person is usually quite willing to examine and change those habit patterns of hers that are skills, she will strongly resist a direct effort to get rid of her automatisms because of the threatened loss of secondary gain. In helping a person give them up, it may be necessary first to help her become aware of the ways in which they seem to help her. It is also useful to recall that, although automatisms seem to be out of a person's control, they are in fact being caused by her but the causation is repressed. If she becomes *aware* of causing them, then they are no longer automatisms; in fact, they are no longer aberrations, since aberration depends on repression. When the person knows exactly what is going on in a given area, she has no more aberration in that area. So we will see that rather than encouraging a person to resist her automatisms, one encourages her to "take them over", to do consciously what she was previously doing unconsciously. Another useful technique is to address the areas of pain that underlie automatisms. Once a person has confronted this pain, she has no further reason to cling to the automatism that overlies it, and it can then be seen to vanish spontaneously or to be replaced by a learned skill.

PART III

APPLIED METAPSYCHOLOGY

Chapter Eight

Viewing:
An Effective Enhancement Method

By applying the principles of metapsychology, it has been possible to arrive at very effective methods for helping people handle disabilities and unwanted conditions in their lives. Having outlined, in Part II, what those basic disabilities and unwanted conditions are, I will now turn to a discussion of a number of tools with which they can be handled. These tools form part of an approach to personal enhancement called "viewing":

> **Definition:** Viewing is the action of a person systematically examining his world in such a way as to gain insight and personal power by undoing repression.

Viewing consists of a group of procedures designed to enhance personal ability. It usually takes place in a one-to-one session in which one person (the facilitator) helps another person (the viewer) take those steps that are necessary to improve the quality of his life. The *viewer* does the procedures; the facilitator helps him do them.

Before I discuss viewing in more detail, I would like to review certain definitions:

Definition: A delusion is a falsehood introduced in the act of repression in order to help hide the repressed material.

Definition: An underlying truth is a concept that is "closer" to a first consideration than the relative falsehood or falsehoods that it underlies.

Definition: A cognition is a prehended fact, one of which a person is currently aware, or the act of prehending a fact. (verb: cognize)

Definition: A realization is a *new* cognition — an acquisition of new knowledge.

Definition: An insight is a realization of an underlying truth.

Viewing is intended to increase awareness, provide insight, and reduce aberration. It is a very powerful method for resolving or reducing disturbances, compulsions, inhibitions, negative feelings, fixed ideas, delusions, and other forms of aberration or charge. To give an exhaustive account of the many methods that comprise viewing would be beyond the scope of this introductory book. I must therefore content myself with presenting the general principles of viewing, a classification of the different viewing procedures, and a description of a sampling of commonly-used viewing techniques.[1]

It should not — and need not — take years of expensive schooling and training to learn how to help someone effectively. Wholesale reduction of aberration requires an inexpensive method that can be easily learned and applied by any person of good will and reasonable intelligence. Some years back, a study was done

---

1. If a person wishes to learn techniques well enough to use them to help others in an actual viewing situation, training is available in a number of places. A list of metapsychology centers is given in Appendix 3 (pp. 553-556), some of which offer training as well as viewing.

that showed that housewives, subjected to a minimal training period, could outperform therapists with years of experience because of their "enthusiasm".[2] If these individuals had been given some of the simple techniques outlined later in this chapter, their effectiveness, I submit, would have been spectacular. A few weeks of full-time training or a few months part-time should enable an interested person to master the necessary material well enough to conduct effective viewing sessions with another person. And, of course, the principles involved are applicable to a wide variety of situations in life, outside of the viewing session.

The Facilitator

A person using the process of viewing to help another is called a "facilitator". I avoid the term "therapist", both because I am trying to avoid the medical model and because that term implies that something is *done* by one person to another, which is not the case in viewing. I also avoid the term "counselor", because the facilitator does not *counsel* the viewer. Her function is only to help the viewer to view his world and thereby to alleviate the charge and aberration contained therein.[3] I use the term "viewer", instead of "patient" or "client", because "patient" has the same disadvantages as "therapist", and "client" emphasizes the financially contractual nature of the relationship instead of the functional one.

Barring telepathy, no one has direct access to another person's world. A facilitator can only find out about what a

---

2. Truax, C.B. and Carkhuff, R.R. *Towards Effective Counseling and Psychotherapy* (Aldine Publishing Company, Chicago, 1967).

3. The term "facilitator", in current usage, sometimes means a person who runs group meetings and helps facilitate the group process. Our usage is similar except that what is facilitated is generally an *individual* process of gaining insight.

viewer is viewing via the viewer's communications. And a facilitator cannot change anything in a viewer's private world except via the viewer. A facilitator can merely help, or *guide*, the process of insight and charge reduction.[4] He does this by getting the viewer to apply various techniques to assess his situation and handle it.

Some might object to the notion of "using techniques", on the ground that doing so is anti-humanistic. There is somewhat of a bias amongst humanists in the helping professions against "using techniques on a person", as those engaged in behavior modification are said to do. This distrust of technique is, I feel, based on the idea that the person to whom the techniques are being applied is thereby being manipulated, dehumanized, and treated like an object.

Even the most dedicated behaviorist does not really perceive *himself* to be a machine, and any method that attempts to deal with a person as though he were a machine is doomed to failure, since:

1. The technique is based on a perceived falsehood.
2. A person resents terribly being thought of as an object. He knows he is a living, perceiving, acting person and will resist manipulations predicated on the idea that he is a mere object.

It is possible to produce behavioral changes in a client by using various manipulations or even by using his *resistance* to manipulations, but changes so produced are often of more benefit to the surrounding society than to the person himself. A person may, in other words, manifest correct social behavior but feel miserable or frustrated. Many people, perhaps most, need to work very hard in order to free themselves from social machinery, to overcome social conditioning or programming. It takes work to become

---

4. See the analogy of a facilitator as a "long-distance car mechanic" given in the introduction, p. 6.

aware of their thoughts and feelings and to regain control of their actions and their lives. The last thing they need is to have another layer of conditioning and machinery plastered on top of what they already have, and they will resist any effort to do so. People need to be *de*-conditioned, not conditioned.[5]

I share this distrust of technique, but there are conditions under which techniques are acceptable.[6] In viewing, it is the person herself, not the facilitator, who is using the techniques; the facilitator merely *provides* them. But just because the person is not herself a mechanism does not mean that she cannot be *surrounded* by an environment that operates by certain mechanical laws. The mind is not the person, nor is it *inside* the person; it is part of the person's *environment*. It does not detract from the power and causativeness of a person to say that the physical universe surrounding her can be understood in terms of various mechanical laws. On the contrary, a knowledge of these laws helps her gain mastery over her world. In the same way, a person is not her disabilities; her disabilities are part of her environment. They operate by definite principles, presented in Part II. A knowledge of the nature of her disabilities and their causes adds to, rather than detracting from, her ability to control her environment. It does not dignify a person to consider her disabilities to be part of her, nor to disregard the principles by which they operate and refuse to help her to use methods that will handle them.

When a person has handled a significant amount of charge and has been well-trained in the skill of facilitation, she can actually become her own facilitator.[7] Up to that point, however, she

---

5. See Chapter Seven, pp. 372-373, for more on the distinction between learning and conditioning.

6. Even one of the least technique-oriented schools of psychotherapy — the Rogerians — has an extensive program to train therapists in the techniques of being non-directive.

7. This possibility is inherent in the notion of viewing as an action done *by* the viewer, not *to* the viewer. Solo viewing is also possible because it is both unnecessary and highly undesirable for another person to evaluate for the

needs another person to get her through the process. The reason why a facilitator is needed initially is that the mechanics of restimulation distract a viewer's attention and may throw her off the task of viewing, especially because the whole action of restimulation involves repression — an inhibition of awareness. The action of viewing runs directly counter to that of repression and the Net. In such an encounter with the Net, the unassisted viewer who is not in excellent psychological condition will almost certainly be the loser, and instead of being successful in viewing something and gaining insight, the person will most likely just add another traumatic incident to a sequence and introduce a new layer of aberration on top of what was already there. The presence of a facilitator is crucial to viewing, because she is not (or should not be) disturbed by the material the viewer is trying to look at and can remain undistracted. The facilitator can therefore keep the viewing process on the right track — or return it there when it is sidetracked by restimulation. She is responsible for seeing to it that no incomplete viewing cycles are left behind and that each action of viewing is carried out to a satisfactory conclusion.

In viewing, the role of the facilitator and that of the viewer are specifically defined, and the viewing session itself — by agreement between the participants — is sharply compartmentalized off from the rest of life. It is begun and ended precisely, and the agreement between viewer and facilitator is that, for the duration of the session, the viewer is being a viewer and the facilitator is being a facilitator. There is no use of transference or countertransference in viewing, so there is no need for the facilitator to protect a "neutral image" outside of the session. Therefore the viewer can have other relationships with the facilitator when he is not being a viewer. The only restriction is that the facilitator *must* refrain from making comments about the viewer's case, *in or out of a viewing session*. Two people can have a session and then

---

viewer. The viewer can and should reach her *own* conclusions about her world.

go out to a movie together, or they can reverse roles and do "co-facilitation": the former viewer becomes a facilitator and the former facilitator becomes a viewer.

The above characteristics of viewing allow the conditions under which it can be done to be much more flexible than those that are necessary for many other forms of personal enhancement. With the appropriate training, it is possible for a person to act quite successfully as a facilitator for friends and relatives.[8]

Viewing techniques have the additional advantage of being discrete, well-defined, and easy to learn. It is possible to learn to be a facilitator in a relatively short time. Prolonged training periods are needed only when a discipline has not graduated to the stage of being clear, concise, and definite in its actions, but remains an "art" that is difficult to master. Although I cannot boast that applied metapsychology has fully achieved this state of simplicity, it has made significant progress in this direction. In a few days or weeks, a moderately competent and motivated person can become quite effective as a facilitator, well-versed in some of the simpler (but still effective) techniques. Of course, it is possible to spend months training and thereby to become skilled in the more advanced techniques. And, of course, years of experience as a facilitator refine one's skill considerably. But a facilitator can get excellent results without extensive training. In a world where there is much pain, aberration, and unawareness to overcome, this is a great advantage.

If a significant number of people are ever to be relieved of their suffering, simple economics demands that there be a relatively inexpensive and readily available method of raising

---

8. The only caveat is that people who are very intimate with each other, such as close family members or significant others, may find it difficult to co-facilitate. They can be quite disturbing to each other because having spent a great deal of time together, they may have many past traumatic incidents in common. So when the viewer describes a trauma, he can restimulate the same trauma in the facilitator. The facilitator can then get distracted or fail to maintain her role as a facilitator, at which point viewing ceases to occur and the session becomes yet another traumatic incident.

awareness and handling aberration. The various ills to which the world is prone can be solved only by handling the individual aberrations of a great number of people. Unawareness and aberration are not a group or national matter; they are a *personal* matter. It is the person, not the state, that must look into her own world and repair its deficiencies. Therefore a method that is widely accessible to many individuals is much needed. It is toward that end that we are striving.

Creating a Safe Environment

A facilitator wishing to help others to change unwanted conditions in their lives must adhere to certain definite rules in running a viewing session. Much of her skill has nothing to do with her knowledge of the theory or techniques of metapsychology. The greatest skill lies in creating a suitable environment in which viewing, with its various techniques, can take place, and in expertly managing communication cycles. Once the proper environment exists and communication is occurring, the process of viewing proceeds in a very simple manner. A special environment is needed because viewing involves intense concentration on material that is often elusive or difficult to confront. If a person's awareness is dispersed in several different directions, she will be overwhelmed and will not be able to do anything well. The first requisite to viewing, then, is a calm and safe environment in which to work. In order for such an environment to exist, the viewer must have:

1. Confidence and trust in the facilitator.
2. Confidence in the way the session is being run.
3. A calm and distraction-free environment.
4. No duress and no time pressure.

Rules of Facilitation

Certain policies must be strictly followed in order to create a safe viewing environment. Although some or all of them may seem obvious or simplistic, their importance cannot be overstressed. Every one of them is vital to successful facilitation. Years of experience have convinced me and many others that *the vast majority of all failures in facilitation — and in personal enhancement techniques of all kinds — can be traced directly to violations, often "trivial", of one or more of these rules.* Therefore the following is a strict code the facilitator must abide by in order to be successful:

1. **The facilitator must not interpret for the viewer.**

   She must not tell him what he is viewing or what it means. In this respect, facilitators differ radically from psychoanalysts or psychotherapists who offer interpretations. The viewer must be regarded as an authority on his own experience. This does not mean that the facilitator should take orders from the viewer or give the viewer the responsibility for running the session. But the session must be conducted in a person-centered context. The facilitator must accept the viewer's data without interpreting it for the viewer. The viewer makes his own interpretations. It is understood from the outset, in the viewing process, that all statements made by the viewer are assumed to be prefixed by "It is my opinion (or observation) that ...." Therefore the facilitator need not agree with the content of what is said; she simply agrees to accept the communication as a communication about the viewer's world.

2. **The facilitator must not evaluate for the viewer.**

   She must not attack, punish, or invalidate the viewer or his concepts, perceptions, or actions, *nor must she praise or validate them.* By "evaluate" is meant suggesting in any way that the viewer is right or wrong for something he has said or done. This may require some skill on the part of the facilitator, since even a minor comment, grunt, gesture, or change of facial expression can be interpreted as a sign of approval or disapproval. Obviously, if the viewer feels threatened or made to feel wrong, his attention will be distracted to the facilitator, and he will no longer feel safe in the viewing session. Even if he is praised, the viewer may take this as an indication that the facilitator is judging his performance, and that the next judgment might not be so favorable. If a facilitator praises or expresses agreement with the viewer even occasionally, the viewer will feel invalidated at those times when he does *not*. Some schools of therapy encourage the therapist to express her feelings about what the client is saying or doing, or to tell the client when he is doing right or wrong. This involves the client in trying to please the therapist or facilitator or avoid her disapproval. Approval and disapproval might be appropriate in a context where one is trying to control behavior, but where the goal is to increase self-reliance, perception, ability, and awareness, it is completely counter-productive. The viewer should be *viewing*, not trying to cause an effect on the facilitator. And the facilitator should be *facilitating*, not trying to create an effect on the viewer.

3. **The facilitator must agree not to reveal or use anything the viewer says to her in a session for any purpose except to help the viewer and to enhance the process of viewing.**

   If the material is to be used as an illustration to train or educate others, the consent of the viewer must first be obtained, and suitable steps must be taken to protect the privacy of the viewer. If the viewer feels that certain material should not be recorded because of its potentially damaging or embarrassing nature, then that material should not be recorded. The facilitator can usually put down all data necessary to continuing the process of viewing without recording those items.

4. **The facilitator must control the session and take complete responsibility for it without dominating or overwhelming the viewer.**

This makes it unnecessary for the viewer to worry about running the session and allows him put all of his attention on viewing. If he is concerned about what the agenda should be for the session, his attention will be distracted from its proper object: the material he is viewing. Conceptually, the facilitator is like a personal secretary or office manager who handles and screens all phone calls, keeps the files, and informs the executive of his appointments, so that the executive (in this case, the viewer) can smoothly do his job. Like a secretary, the facilitator keeps records of the session, keeps the agenda straight, and informs the viewer when he needs to take the next action. But it is the *viewer* who takes the action.

5. **The facilitator must make sure that he comprehends what the viewer is saying.**

A viewer knows right away when he is not being comprehended. When that happens, he feels alone and unsupported. If the facilitator does not comprehend, she must seek clarification by admitting her lack of comprehension as something having to do with *her*, not with the viewer. So she would say, "I'm sorry — I did not get what you said. Could you give it to me again?" She would *not* say: "You are being unclear," or: "That sounds like nonsense," or even: "Please clarify what you mean." In other words, the *facilitator* must take responsibility for not comprehending. She must never blame the viewer. At the same time, she must not interrupt or stop the viewer from reporting, explaining, or making himself understood. Such interruptions can be quite distressing or distracting to a viewer.

6. **The facilitator must be interested in the viewer and what he is saying, instead of being interesting to the viewer.**

If the facilitator becomes interesting, she will act as a distraction, pulling the viewer's attention to the facilitator instead of allowing the viewer to place his attention on the material he is viewing. The facilitator's interest reinforces the viewer's willingness to view and report on the material he is viewing. A viewer generally knows immediately whether or not the facilitator is really interested.

7. **The facilitator must have a firm and primary intention to help the viewer.**

If the facilitator has such an intention, she will be interested in what is going on, per (6), above. On the other hand, if the facilitator is, for instance, mainly interested in improving her skill or in making money, even if she *also* has the intention to help the viewer, the viewer will pick up the fact that his well-being is of only secondary importance or interest to the facilitator, and the session will go awry. This does not mean that the facilitator could not *also* have other intentions, but they must be secondary to a genuine, *primary* intention to help the viewer.

8. **The facilitator must ensure that the viewer is in optimum physical condition for the viewing session.**

She must ensure that the viewer has had enough sleep, and that he is not hungry or under the influence of alcohol or psychoactive drugs (except when drugs are medically prescribed as an absolute necessity)[9], and that he is not physically tired. If the viewer is in urgent need of immediate help, this rule can be relaxed. It is better to help in an emergency under less-than-optimal conditions than not to help at all. Nevertheless, drugs, tiredness, and hunger tend to lower a person's awareness, and a lowered awareness is counter-productive in a viewing session. Sometimes a

---

9. When a person is taking psychoactive drugs, one should not necessarily forbid viewing since when a person needs to take such drugs, she often urgently needs personal help as well. It is sometimes better for a viewer to take pain killers, for instance, than to be too distracted by physical discomfort to concentrate on the session. One should try to get the viewer to avoid tranquilizers and pain-killers if she can, though, or to refrain from taking a dosage that would make viewing difficult.

person must delay viewing (except for minor emergency remedies) for periods of from a day to two or three weeks, until the effects of exhaustion, drugs, or medication have fully worn off. The precise amount of time one must wait is a matter of judgment, but in most cases seems to be around 24 hours for alcohol or aspirin and longer for drugs with longer-lasting or more potent effects. The exact amount of time depends on the dosage and on the way in which an individual viewer is affected by a particular drug. To make sure the viewer is not tired or hungry, the facilitator may have to get him to take a nap or eat something before starting a session.

9. **The facilitator must ensure that the session is being given in a suitable space and at a suitable time.**

She ensures that the viewing environment is safe, private, quiet, a comfortable temperature, and comfortably lighted. The space need not be exquisite or magnificent, but it should be pleasant — not messy or smelly, nor overly distracting. The viewer should have a comfortable chair (so should the facilitator). The door should, of course, be closed, preferably with a very noticeable sign on it stating that a session is in progress and no one is to disturb it. Any distracting external noise must be dealt with before starting the session.

The facilitator also ensures that the *time* is safe. She makes sure that the viewer is not pressed for time and that suitable precautions have been taken against any need to interrupt the session for any reason. Thus the facilitator ensures that she has all necessary materials (such as paper and pens) ready to hand, so she will not have to interrupt the session to get anything. She also goes into the session with a written agenda for that session so that, during the session, she does not lose track of what she intended to do with the viewer. Neither the viewer nor the facilitator should have conflicting appointments or be under time pressure that could cut the session short before it reaches a suitable stopping point[10] or cause worry about time that would be distracting.[11]

10. **The facilitator should act in a predictable way so as not to surprise the viewer**.

If the facilitator engages in unpredictable actions, the viewer can become distracted by wondering what is going to happen next. Part of being predictable is that the facilitator must keep any session appointments she has made.[12]

11. **The facilitator should not try to work with someone against that person's will or in the presence of any protest**.

Sometimes a relative or friend can persuade a person to do viewing even when he does not really want to, or other pressures can be brought to bear on a person to do viewing

---

10. The classic "fifty-minute hour" used in many therapies is often quite counter-productive because the time may not be sufficient to complete certain actions. The concept of an end point is crucial to timing the ending of a session. I recall with intense regret the many psychotherapeutic sessions in which I sent away a client in a state of intense restimulation because I had not encountered the concept of an end point. I hated sending people home in such a state, but within that structure there seemed to be no other choice. A case in point was a woman who, during the session, started re-enacting an early childhood experience of being beaten by her mother. She probably would have needed another hour to finish re-enacting the incident and come out the other side, having reduced its charge. Nevertheless, I had to send her away at the end of fifty minutes in order to see my next patient. I shall never forget the crushed expression on her face, nor the way she had to walk down the hallway, touching the walls to restore her contact with present time. That kind of thing shouldn't have to happen to anyone.

11. Also, as an elementary precaution, one should make sure the viewer is not going to have to use the toilet before the session has progressed very far.

12. Again, this may seem a trivial point, but experience has shown that even the inadvertent breaking of an appointment can have disastrous effects on the facilitator-viewer relationship. When a facilitator breaks an appointment, she conveys the message that the viewer is not very important to her. Being "stood up" for viewing sessions can therefore do serious damage to a viewer's confidence in his facilitator. Also, one should try not to change facilitators frequently. It usually takes a while for a viewer to "get used to" a facilitator, for the facilitator to become safe and predictable to the viewer.

against his wishes. Under such circumstances, viewing does not work well or at all. A major purpose of viewing is to reduce the stress in a person's life. Being *forced* to do viewing *increases* stress. What applies to the whole process of viewing also applies to each step of the process. Once a session has started, the facilitator must not force or rush the viewer. The facilitator must allow the viewer to take as much time as he wants to answer a question or execute a viewing direction. If the viewer feels that a quick response is being demanded, he will not take the time to do the major beneficial action in viewing — the action of viewing itself. Also, the facilitator must always consult the viewer's interest and must not try to force the viewer to run a particular procedure when the viewer is not really interested in doing so.

12. **The facilitator must not do anything in a session that is not directly conducive to the viewing process.**

A facilitator who, during a viewing session, engages in social chit-chat, talks about herself, makes random comments, gives lectures or advice, laughs excessively or inappropriately, or indulges in emotional reactions toward the viewer, such as anger or expressions of anxiety, is distracting the viewer and destroying the safe space. It has not proven workable for the facilitator to be "honest" about her own feelings during the session. The viewer has enough to do when engaged in the viewing process without also having to cope with extraneous actions or displays of emotion on the part of the facilitator.

13. **The facilitator must carry each viewing action to a success for the viewer.**

She must not leave the viewer at a point of failure, incompleteness or unresolvedness. For this reason, as stated in the footnote on page 373, viewing sessions must *not* be fixed in length. Both the viewer and the facilitator must have somewhat flexible schedules. The facilitator must take responsibility for ending the session when she decides that an appropriate end point has been reached. When viewing becomes embarrassing, difficult, or painful, the viewer may feel like leaving the session. Should this occur, the job of the facilitator is to encourage the viewer to stick with it and confront and handle the difficulty to a good point of resolution. One of the major functions of a facilitator is to help the viewer find the courage and confidence to confront difficult material that he has not been able to confront alone. The facilitator, then, must also be courageous and confident. Fortunately, the "tools of the trade" are sufficiently powerful and effective to warrant such confidence on the part of an experienced facilitator.

Following the above rules will help to ensure that a "safe space" exists in which viewing can occur.

Avoiding Dependence

The facilitator must resist all temptations and invitations to do things for the viewer (except to run the session). Only the person himself can be aware or conscious for himself; no one else can be aware of something *for* him. No one else can intend things for a person; he must intend things for himself, and he must act for himself. If someone else acts *for* him, *he* is not acting, and neither the scope of his activity nor his ability has been increased.[13] Paradoxically, some well-meaning attempts to help

---

13. This does not mean, of course, that one should never do anything for another person, explain anything to him, or show him anything. Nevertheless, in a context where the intention is to increase conceptual, perceptual, or instrumental ability, the person must be *allowed* to do what he can, understand what he can, and perceive what he can. One cannot improve a person's skill in violin playing without letting him play a violin. If someone else plays the violin for him, he will never learn to play it. In fact, when someone else acts *for* a person in any way, both his scope and his ability will at best not be enhanced and at worst may be diminished. If a person relies on others' perceptions and interpretations instead of perceiving

achieve the opposite of what is intended. Overprotective parents make life *more* dangerous for a child by not giving her the opportunity to confront and handle danger for herself. The overzealous psychoanalyst who is very free with her interpretations may find herself confronted with an analysand whose view of his own mental contents is clouded or distorted because instead of seeing what is there, he is trying to see what the analyst says or suggests *should* be there. If a person has a preconceived notion of what he is looking for, he is likely to find it, whether it is really there or not. It is all too easy for the viewer to *create* the mental pictures, thoughts, or feelings that the psychoanalyst or other facilitator suggests should be there and then to mistake these creations for *received* data. In so doing, he may miss what is really there. Freudian patients may have Freudian dreams and Jungian patients may have Jungian dreams, but it is better for a person to perceive and interpret his dreams according to his own belief system.

A facilitator who expresses disagreement — verbally or non-verbally — with what a viewer is saying or who says that the viewer is wrong about something he is perceiving or understanding may cause the viewer to distrust his own ability to perceive or understand. In this way, the facilitator can inadvertently make the viewer dependent upon others to do his perceiving and understanding for him.

Similarly, a facilitator must not let herself be seduced into giving advice about how the viewer should run his life. While apparently helpful, such advice may actually tend to make the viewer dependent on the facilitator, and the viewer's capacity for decision and action may thereby be reduced.

---

and interpreting for himself, the scope of his own perception and interpretation may be diminished.

The basic principle is that a facilitator must not do anything that actually *interferes* with the exercise of ability on the part of the viewer. It is a cardinal rule of viewing, therefore, that the facilitator must *not*:

1. Tell the viewer what he is looking at or what he is to find.
2. Tell him the *meaning* of what he is perceiving.
3. Tell him how to run his life.
4. Tell him that he is wrong.
5. Tell him that he is right.

(1) and (2), above are called "interpretation"; (3), (4) and (5) are called "evaluation". (4) is a special kind of negative evaluation called "invalidation", and (5) is a positive evaluation called "validation". Validation is less destructive to the process of viewing than invalidation or evaluation, but it can still make the viewer dependent on the practitioner for praise and fearful that it will cease.

But how can one use special knowledge to help another person without interpreting or evaluating for that person? Some forms of psychotherapy attempt a very permissive approach, such as that used in Rogerian person-centered therapy or certain free-associational therapies. Such therapies tend to be quite long and of uncertain outcome. The problem is that if the client were able to arrive at the answers to her own problems without guidance, she would not need a therapist. It can, of course, be quite helpful just to be available to a person as a good listener. If a person is able to feel safe enough to talk about her problems, she can make progress on resolving them. This is an important feature of the helping relationship. But, although merely listening well and creating a safe space is a *necessary* condition for helping someone, it is not a *sufficient* condition because talking to a safe, good listener usually does not, in itself, produce rapid enough improvement. On the other hand, if one does more than just listen, there is always the danger that what one says will be taken as an evaluation or an interpretation and thus be counter-productive.

One approach would be simply to avoid making any assertions at all about the viewer's experience. If I ask you to pass the salt, or if I say, "Tell me what happened today." (both imperatives), I am not making any statements about how you ought to live your life, nor about how you should look at something or what you should see. If I ask a question, such as "What happened at the office?", that is not an assertion either. It does not tell you what the answer is or what I think it should be. This strategy is not infallible because some imperative statements might tell the person how to run his life ("Learn to be more aggressive toward your boss."), and some questions might be leading questions ("Don't you think your dislike of your father could be based on an Oedipus complex?"). In each of these cases, however, there is an implied assertion embedded in the question or direction ("You are not aggressive enough toward your boss.", and "Your dislike of your father is based on your Oedipus complex."). Good facilitators are trained to avoid such utterances.

The non-assertive approach requires considerable judgment. If the facilitator says, "Tell me about your relationship with your father," the viewer may take this to mean that the facilitator thinks that she is having trouble getting along with her father. This is a tricky point, and it appears that one cannot, after all, altogether eliminate implicit evaluation and still take any action as a facilitator. But one can and should avoid explicit assertions about the viewer or her experience and minimize implicit ones. One way to avoid harmful assertions is to follow a pattern in one's actions such that the viewer can see how these actions grow out of, or result from, the viewer's own thoughts and statements. For instance, one could ask, "What would you like to have handled?" Suppose the viewer said, "I want to handle my anxiety." Then the facilitator might say, "Can you recall a time when you were anxious?". And the viewer can go to work.

Another guideline is that it is safe to make assertions (implicit or explicit) about entities that are already completely accepted by the viewer. For instance, some procedures involve getting the viewer to look at various physical objects. Since there is no doubt in the viewer's mind about the existence of these objects, it does no harm to point them out, even though in so doing you are implicitly asserting that they exist. At times, too, a viewer may be genuinely stumped or unable to continue. Under these circumstances, the facilitator may use a biomonitoring device or other means to help the viewer find charged subjects.

Part of the contract between viewer and facilitator is that the facilitator is entirely responsible for running the session and deciding which topics will be addressed, in which order, and which procedures will be used. The viewer should not be burdened with the need to make such decisions, because he needs to keep his attention on the action of viewing. Therefore, the facilitator is within her rights to assert what she thinks the correct next action should be, even though that could be regarded as an implicit interpretation or evaluation.

As a viewer gains experience and becomes more aware, more and more decisions can be left to her concerning which areas of her life need to be addressed in viewing. The ability to spot areas of charge without external assistance is one of the most important abilities enhanced in the course of viewing. Therefore as a viewer progresses, the facilitator should rely less and less on external means of assessment such as biomonitoring and more and more on the viewer's own assessments. The basic criterion for deciding whether an action constitutes a harmful assertion, then, is whether it assists the action of viewing or inhibits, disturbs, or replaces it. Generally, we can say that an assertion is harmful if it takes the place of the viewer's own perceptive, interpretive, and evaluative processes. In other words, assertion itself may not be bad, but asserting *for* the viewer, when the viewer could do it for herself, is undesirable.

A facilitator has a variety of tools or methods for helping the viewer to explore and expand her experience. These tools work well when used in a session governed by the above principles.

The Viewing Session

Before starting a viewing session, the facilitator must make sure that all the session prerequisites are met. She must also make sure that the viewer is willing to have her as a facilitator. Any reluctance on the part of the viewer is an indication that the session should not be started until it has been fully communicated about and handled. Some viewers do not get along with some facilitators, and it is better to know about a mismatch early on, before putting a viewer into the situation of trying to address sensitive material with someone whom he does not find congenial.

Before starting the session, the facilitator should also have worked out the various topics to be addressed in the session and the procedures to be used. This information should be written down before the session as the "session agenda":

Definition: The <u>session agenda</u> is a written list of the actions the facilitator plans to take in the next viewing session.

The facilitator then starts the session by giving a definite and precise statement, such as, "Start of Session," or "We are starting now." This is rather like the phrase, "Play ball!" in a baseball game. From the moment those words are uttered, both parties understand that the normal rules of social communication and interaction are suspended for the duration of the session, and that nothing will be said or done by the facilitator that is not directly relevant to facilitating the process of viewing. By having a definite session start, the facilitator also implicitly agrees that anything the viewer says thereafter will be held in strictest confidence and not commented on, evaluated, or invalidated by the facilitator, during the session or *ever*. As far as the facilitator is concerned, things said in a viewing session were never said and will never be used for any purpose except to facilitate the viewing process in that session or in future ones.

After starting the session but before the facilitator launches into her agenda for the session, she checks to see if the viewer has his attention on anything in particular that, if not addressed, will inhibit his ability to concentrate on the material to be addressed in the agenda. Such items are called "disturbances". To reiterate the definitions given in Chapter 7:

> **Definition**: To <u>disturb</u> a person is to cause his traumatic incidents or sequences to be restimulated or to put his attention on an upset, problem, withheld communication, or misdeed. To create turbidity.

> **Definition**: A <u>disturbance</u> is a subject, situation, or item that is currently in a state of restimulation. Such items include upsets, problems, withheld communications, misdeeds, and traumatic incidents. A disturbance is an area of charge on which the viewer has his attention fixed.

> **Definition**: <u>Turbidity</u> is the state of having one's attention fixed on one or more disturbances. A person in this state is said to be "disturbed".

A disturbance, then, is an area of charge on which the viewer has his attention fixed. This area may not be one of the major issues that were supposed to be addressed in the session. Nevertheless, it needs to be handled first (at the start of a session or as part of a remedial plan) so that the viewer can free his attention from it and thus be ready for major actions. If the facilitator simply ignores or attempts to override such disturbances, the viewer is likely to become upset, either immediately or within a few minutes, because of the unhandled charge contained in them. Normally the facilitator selectively restimulates charged material, but the viewer has enough available attention to be fully aware of this material and thus to complete receptive cycles. In other words, the facilitator helps the viewer to reduce or eliminate the charge in the restimulated material, instead of just leaving it restimulated. But when the viewer has his attention fixed on something else, he does not have enough free awareness to confront and handle the charge and becomes overwhelmed. He then either dramatizes by acting upset, feels uncomfortable emotions or sensations, or both. The session itself thus becomes another traumatic incident that will have to be handled later. So disturbances must be checked for and "cleared" first:

> **Definition:** Pre-session clearing is the handling of any disturbances to a point where the viewer's attention is relatively unfixed and can be directed toward more fundamental case issues. It is a remedial viewing action, done at the beginning of a session or when a person is unable to continue a session because of some disturbance. It is an action taken to free a person's attention from material that is already inadvertently or accidently restimulated in life or in session. The point at which pre-session clearing is complete is when the viewer is free of the disturbance and ready to move on to the body of the session.

where:

> **Definition:** The body of a session is the part of the session that comes after the pre-session clearing. It contains the major actions of that session.

and:

> **Definition:** A major action is a procedure, contained in the case plan and the session agenda, that is done as part of the body of a session.

It is a general rule of facilitation that one must clear what is *already* restimulated before taking up items that are not currently restimulated:

> **Definition:** Clearing is the action of reducing or eliminating turbidity by destimulating, deactivating, or discharging restimulated items. A person who is free of turbidity is said to be "clear".

Note that there are three degrees of thoroughness in handling disturbances or restimulated material:

1. <u>Destimulation</u> — simply enabling the viewer to take his attention off the restimulated material.
2. <u>Deactivation</u> — putting the disturbance at considerable distance from the viewer, so it is not easily restimulated.
3. <u>Discharge</u> — eliminating the root of the disturbance so that it cannot be restimulated at all.

Clearing can encompass any of the above actions, applied to material that is in a state of restimulation.

The most common forms of disturbances found at the start of a session are:

1. Upsets
2. Problems
3. Misdeeds
4. Withheld communications
5. Traumatic incidents

If the viewer presently has his attention fixed on any of these, it will be difficult or impossible for him to concentrate on something else, particularly a charged topic. If the viewer's wife has just stunned him with the announcement that she has had an affair, it will prove impossible to get much done on an agenda designed to handle problems with his work or the effects of childhood traumas. If the viewer is disturbed by worries about a recent exam he has taken, if he has just done something he feels guilty about, or if he is beginning to suspect that his wife knows about an affair *he* is having, that will also make it impossible for him to address any other subject until the disturbance has been addressed sufficiently to release the viewer's attention from it. If the disturbance is very severe, a completely new agenda will probably have to be worked out. Otherwise, certain short clearing procedures will probably suffice.

So, the first step of any session is to check for disturbances and clear any that are found. Pre-session clearing may be temporary, because a person who is clear of disturbances could become disturbed again at any time. The purpose of pre-session clearing is not necessarily to resolve these disturbances for all time — they may be quite deep-rooted — but rapid and profound beneficial effects often occur anyway. It is common for a viewer who is severely upset at the start of a session to resolve the upset in one or two minutes with a short clearing procedure. The same upset could occupy one or more entire therapeutic hours in "conventional" psychotherapy.[14]

When all agenda items have been completed, or when a suitable stopping point has been reached (generally *between* major actions), the facilitator asks the viewer whether there is anything she wants to say or ask before ending the session. This is an important question; it gives the viewer a chance to comment on the session and, if anything has been left incomplete, for the viewer to point it out so that he can complete it before ending the session, or so that it can be added to the agenda for the next session.

The facilitator then ends the session with a definite, precise statement, such as "End of session," or "That's all for this session." The practice of having a definite session end, like the practice of having a definite session start, has a real and significant purpose: it helps keep the viewer from continuing to mull over the material dealt with in the session. When a person has completed something, it is better for her to turn her attention to something else than to keep her attention fixed on what she has just completed. So after a viewing session, it is best for the viewer to get involved with some other activity. Otherwise she might restimulate related material that has *not* been handled in the session and thus remain in a disturbed state until her next ses-

---

14. As a psychiatrist, I once worked with a client for an entire *year*, with very modest results. Then she finally told me something she had been withholding all that time. Only then did she begin to make adequate progress in her therapy. Had I done a little pre-session clearing in the first session, she could have started her work a year earlier! Another client kept coming back, session after session, with the same upset about her husband, which precluded working on anything else. With the appropriate clearing procedure, her attention could have been released from that upset rapidly and we could have addressed more fundamental case issues.

sion. The precise termination of a session also serves to reinforce the idea that a viewing session is an island of calm and safety in an ocean of busy life.

The Process of Viewing

The basic action of viewing is that of getting the viewer to examine her world in such a way as to increase her ability and awareness:

> **Definition:** Viewing is the action of systematically examining one's world in such a way as to gain insight and increased ability.

Its focus is on regaining an ability to be aware (i.e., a receptive ability) that was lost or prevented because of repression, traumatic incidents, charge, and other difficulties. Because of the close relationship between receptive and creative abilities, having a new receptive ability often enables a person to acquire one or more new creative abilities. If, for instance, a person obtains genuine insight into the nature and origin of her fear of communicating, this fear lessens and she becomes better able to communicate. So the net effect of viewing is a general enhancement of awareness and ability.

The basic viewing cycle is as follows:

1. The facilitator asks the viewer to do something.
2. The viewer does it.
3. The facilitator acknowledges her for having done it.

For instance, in a "recall" procedure, the facilitator may ask the viewer to "Recall a time when you were happy." The viewer views the material she needs to view in order to carry out the request, then informs the facilitator, "OK. I was happy on my twelfth birthday," or just "OK".[15] The facilitator then acknowledges the viewer's answer and gives the next direction. The session proceeds in this way until the viewer has obtained a favorable result from the procedure. The request may be in the form of a question, in which case carrying it out consists of answering the question. Note that each viewing question (or request) and its answer (or compliance) by the viewer constitutes a single viewing cycle. On a higher level, an entire *procedure* is itself a cycle, made up of a number of individual viewing cycles.

End Points and Overruns

Certain phenomena characteristically appear at the successful completion, or end point, of any procedure:

> **Definition**: The end point is the point at which the cycle connected with an activity has been successfully completed. This is the point at which the activity should be ended. It is manifested by a set of phenomena that indicate the successful termination of the activity. These phenomena vary from activity to activity.

The end point of fixing a car is the point at which the car operates normally. The end point of eating is a full stomach or the disappearance of hunger. The end point of any process manifests those phenomena that indicate it is time to *stop* that procedure and start doing something else.

The concept of an end point is not commonly found in religious or psychotherapeutic literature (Zen koans, Focusing, and Hakomi therapy are exceptions),[16] but it is an essential one.

---

15. Obviously, if there is no visible evidence of compliance to the request (as where the viewer has been directed to perform a mental act), the viewer will have to inform the facilitator that she has done it.

16. Gendlin, E. *Focusing* (Bantam Books, New York, 1982) pp. 45, 49, 57-61. Kurtz, R. *Hakomi Therapy* (Hakomi Institute, Boulder CO, 1985) Ch. 10, p. 4.

Everything a person does is a cycle and, as such, has a proper starting point, continuation period, and end point. It is just as useful to know when to *end* a cycle or activity as it is to know when to begin one or to continue one. Failing to end an activity at the appropriate time usually has unwanted consequences. If a person does not know when she has had enough to drink, she can wreak havoc. If I exceed the attention span of someone to whom I am talking, I can waste my time. If one does not know when to stop spending money, one can become poor.

The same is true in a viewing procedure. Continuing past the end point results in almost immediate protest on the part of the viewer, who may experience an acute feeling of boredom, and often a shift of attention to an entirely different area of his world that usually has little to do with the procedure being run.[17] Sometimes, the result may be a massive restimulation of an area of the person's case. Such an incorrect continuation is called an "overrun":

> **Definition**: An <u>overrun</u> is the action of continuing an activity beyond its proper end point, or the fact of having done so.

In order to avoid such untoward effects, it is very important to recognize an end point when you see one, whether in facilitation or elsewhere.

For this reason, the "fifty-minute hour" generally used in psychotherapeutic sessions is not workable as a time-frame for a viewing session.[18] A viewing procedure or set of procedures may reach its end point in ten or twenty minutes or it may take two or three hours or — rarely — longer. So session times must be flexible. If one has not obtained a full end point for a procedure and

---

17. The viewer may not *voice* his protest, so a facilitator needs to be very sensitive to subtle indicators, such as the viewer's tone of voice or facial expression. Biomonitoring can help pick up such unvoiced protests; it will be covered later in this chapter (pp. 413-421).

18. See footnote, p. 392.

time is limited or the viewer is getting tired, one may be able to find a relatively acceptable ending point — say, when the viewer has not yet attained the end point but is feeling comfortable. The procedure can then be completed fully in the near future. This approach is workable but less desirable than completing an entire procedure or set of procedures in one session. Even if the viewer feels comfortable at the end of the session, he may find his attention somewhat fixed on the area being handled until the full end point is reached.

The end point of a properly-run viewing procedure should include *at least* a relatively happy or content viewer. The facilitator can be quite certain that when the viewer is heavily embroiled in negative feelings, it is not a good time to end the procedure he is doing.

The nature of the end point varies from one type of procedure to another. When doing pre-session clearing, the aim is only to unfix the viewer's attention from such events as minor upsets, problems, and withheld communications, so that it can be directed elsewhere. Therefore the end point of pre-session clearing occurs when the viewer simply feels better and can, for the time being, take his attention off the area addressed in clearing. For instance, if the viewer was insulted by a fellow employee just before the session, a brief discussion of the upset (and perhaps a few earlier similar upsets) will usually provide relief from the feeling of upset. The viewer may have some small realization, such as: "I didn't realize he was having a bad day." In contrast, the end point of a major viewing procedure includes a major realization (or insight), a high level on the Emotional Scale (often enthusiasm or elation), and sometimes an ability gained or regained. For example, after running a number of communication procedures, the viewer may exclaim, "You know, I feel as though I could actually *talk* to people now, and they would really understand what I was saying!"

Planning the Viewing Session

Apart from knowing various viewing procedures, a facilitator must have a means of deciding:

1. Which procedures to use with a particular viewer, and in which order.
2. To what part of the viewer's world these procedures should be addressed.

In short, she must know which tools to use and where to use them. Just as a screwdriver may screw or unscrew any number of different screws, so a viewing procedure may be applied to different areas of the viewer's world. Deciding which procedures to use, and in which order, is the activity known as "case planning":

> **Definition:** Case planning is the action of deciding which procedures should be used with a viewer and the order in which they should be done.

Case planning is done *before* the session; the facilitator always has a written agenda, based on a plan, when she starts a session. Often, and ideally, it is not the facilitator herself who writes out the plan but another person who is not dealing face-to-face with the viewer but is familiar with the case and expert in the application of viewing procedures. This person has the advantage of being able to look objectively at the viewing process because she has some distance from it. The person who works out the viewing plan is called the "technical director":

> **Definition:** The technical director is the person in charge of planning individual curricula and session agendas. She is also responsible for ensuring that the facilitators are doing their jobs correctly, and she makes sure they get help promptly if they get into difficulties.[19]

---

19. One technical director can accomodate several facilitators.

An experienced facilitator may function as her own technical director, but if she does so, she should very sharply separate the two functions. She does not do case planning while running a viewing session.

Assessing

Deciding which area of the viewer's world to address with a procedure is called "assessing":

> **Definition:** Assessing is the action of finding areas of the viewer's life to which one or more viewing procedures can be fruitfully applied. It is always done with the viewer, during a viewing session or interview.

Assessing follows the general rule that, in viewing, you are getting the person to do what he *is* able to do in order to gain an ability to do something he *has not* been able to do.[20] Since viewing deals mainly with receptive abilities — abilities to perceive and understand — it consists mainly of getting the viewer to look at something of which he *is* aware in order to gain an awareness of something of which he *has not* been aware. In other words, the areas of the viewer's world that should be addressed are those of which he is not currently aware, but of which he can *become* aware using a certain procedure. These fruitful areas are only slightly below his level of awareness — just below his "awareness threshold" (see Figure 42).

> **Definition:** The awareness threshold is the dividing line that separates those entities of which a person can be readily aware from those that are repressed. A person can only become aware of the latter by using a special procedure (if at all).

---

20. This rule holds for any form of personal enhancement, including education.

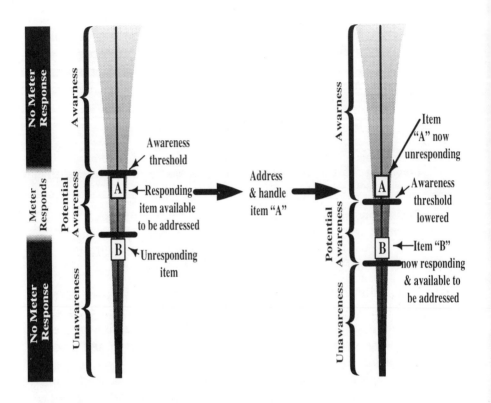

Figure 42. The awareness threshold

If a person is completely aware of some aspect of his world, he will not gain anything new from addressing it. But if an area is too far below his awareness threshhold, he will not be able to find it. As a person's level of awareness increases, however, his awareness threshold "descends"; entities that were previously too far below it to be approachable now lie close to it and so can be addressed fruitfully. The ultimate goal of viewing is to lower the awareness threshold all the way to the "bottom" so that the person is fully aware of the contents of his world. Though such a state is probably not attainable, it gives us a direction in which to move.

In order to determine what to handle, then, we must determine what lies *just below* the awareness threshold. This determination *is* the action of assessment, so we can also say:

Definition: Assessing is the action of finding charged areas of a viewer's case that lie just below his awareness threshold.

To assess is to examine and analyze various phenomena relating to a viewer in order to decide what it would be most fruitful to view at a particular time. Assessments may or may not be intermingled with viewing procedures. Perhaps the most common form of assessment in various forms of helping procedures is an interview. By asking various questions, a skilled interviewer can reach conclusions concerning what particular issues (entities) a viewer needs to look at. There are also more formal kinds of assessment, such as psychological tests (e.g., Rorschach, TAT, MMPI). These methods have a varying degree of accuracy and are highly dependent upon the skill and intuition of the assessor.[21]

Various biomonitoring devices have been used in assessing, such as wave detectors, EEG, voice stress analyzers, and the polygraph, although the latter is rather too cumbersome for everyday use. The most venerable of these methods (dating from the 19th century) is the galvanic skin response (GSR) meter (now called the "electrodermometer"), a simple device that measures baseline skin resistance and fluctuations therefrom. In working with viewers, facilitators make extensive use of the electrodermometer, in a more modern form, for assessing and for other purposes.

---

21. One interesting form of assessment used in Hakomi therapy, is called "probing". Probing consists of asking the viewer, "What happens for you when I ... ?" and then doing a physical action (such as touching a person) or making a statement. The viewer gives her subjective response to the stimulus. This appears to be quite a sensitive method for finding charged (but accessible) areas.

One of the principal signs that viewing something will result
in greater awareness is that the viewer is *interested* in it. A person is strongly attracted to heuristic situations. He seems to
"know", at some level, what will lead to more knowledge.[22]
Often, then, if a facilitator has a choice of going in several directions, he can simply ask the viewer which interests him the most,
and that will most likely be the correct area to pursue.

Various physical indicators are useful in detecting contact
with a charged subject that lies close to the awareness threshold.
Often, the viewer will blush or flush, smile or laugh, or show or
report some other emotional response. Sometimes, the pupils will
dilate. Experientially, when a fruitful subject is contacted, a
person's attention becomes attracted to it, or the person feels
warm or slightly relieved when it is contacted. Some viewers
experience a slight feeling of anticipation, tinged, for some, with
nervousness, for others with pleasure. If a person protests
addressing a subject, that is usually a good indication that the subject is not going to be fruitful at that time, and, as stated earlier
(pp. 392-393), it is not a good idea to try to override a protest.

It is, in any case, never a good idea to try to *force* a viewer
to do anything or look at anything. To do so creates an unsafe
space, and future progress will be severely hampered. Facilitating
must be completely nonviolent and non-forceful. By doing a
correct assessment, the facilitator can always find something fruitful that the viewer will be interested in pursuing without being
forced to do so.

---

22. This "knowing" should not be too surprising, when we consider that, in
    talking about viewing, we are generally talking about areas toward which a
    person has a directed unawareness. Recall that a person has to be "aware"
    of something at *some* level in order to know where *not* to look. At a
    subliminal level, therefore, a person "knows" what she has repressed, so she
    "knows" that she can become aware of something in that area.

Biomonitoring

Biomonitoring and biofeedback can play an important role in viewing. The electrodermometer (also called, simply, "meter") is useful for this purpose (See Figure 43). First described in 1888 by C.S. Féré, a French physician, it is probably the earliest biomonitoring device. It has been extensively used in psychotherapy.[23] It has also been used as one of the measurements taken in a polygraph recording ("lie detector").

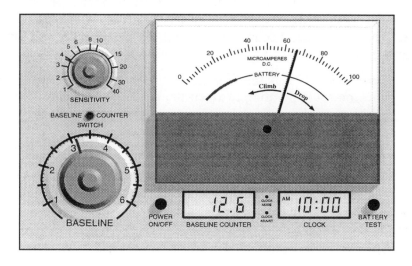

Figure 43. An electrodermometer.

The meter works by measuring the electrical resistance between two electrodes on different parts of the skin surface. The palms are commonly used as contact points. The version often used in viewing uses hand-held electrodes. These electrodes (or "contacts") are cylindrical, about 4-5 inches long and have a

23. For instance, Carl G. Jung used it in connection with word-association tests.

diameter of 1-2 inches. A low voltage (about 0.5-3.0 volts) is applied to the contacts, sending a tiny, imperceptible, and harmless current through the body, and the resistance between the two contacts is measured. The resistance measured in this way varies from about 2000 ohms to over 30000 ohms, depending on a variety of factors. In most people under ordinary circumstances, the resistance will be found to be in the range of 5000-20000 ohms. The meter commonly used has a control that compensates for the baseline resistance, numbered rather arbitrarily from 1 to 6, to indicate the different possible baseline values. The meter also has a galvanometer circuit that drives a needle to display moment-to-moment fluctuations in resistance from the baseline. The baseline value is found by rotating the baseline control until the needle is pointing to a "set" position on the dial:

> **Definition**: The baseline value is the number the baseline control is pointing to when the needle is at the "set" position on the dial. It gives the level of skin resistance around which fluctuations of the needle occur.

Movements of the needle then indicate fluctuations around this baseline value. There is a sensitivity control that determines the breadth of the needle movement in response to fluctuations in resistance. At a high sensitivity, the needle will swing widely on a very small change of resistance; at a low sensitivity, it takes a much greater change in resistance to affect the needle in the same way.[24]

---

24. Examples of such meters are the "Omega 1" and "Omega 2" meters used by C. Maxwell Cade, as described in Cade, C.M. and Coxhead, N. *The Awakened Mind* (Element Books, Longmead, England, 1979) and Cade, C.M. and Blundell, G. *Self-Awareness and E.S.R.* (The Evolving Institute, Boulder CO, 1985). An excellent meter, the "Ability Meter", is available from The Society for Metapsychology, U.K., 9 Portland Rd., East Grinstead, Sussex RH19 4EB, England. It is also possible to use non-mechanical displays (such as CRT's or LED's) in place of a physical needle movement. For historical reasons, however, I will use the term "needle" to describe such electronic displays as well.

By squeezing the contacts, or by making various bodily motions, the needle and the baseline can be made to fluctuate. Some people have speculated that needle responses are caused by slight "subliminal" squeezes of the contacts. With training, however, a facilitator can easily learn to distinguish between needle movements that reflect a genuine change in resistance and those caused by physical motion. Such "false" reactions can be minimized by teaching the viewer how to hold the contacts properly and by using contacts that fit comfortably in the hands of a particular viewer.[25]

The meter is extremely useful as an assessing tool, to find charged "items" that are below the awareness threshold but accessible to the person. Such an item, when "presented" to the viewer, causes a change in resistance:

Definition: An item is an entity or topic that is possibly or actually charged for the viewer. Also, a word, phrase, or sentence that communicates such an entity or topic.

Definition: Presentation is the appearance of an item in the viewer's awareness, the *prehension* of an item.[26]

This change in resistance is reflected in various needle actions. Presentation occurs when the *viewer* thinks about (or prehends) an item — whether or not he mentions it — or when the *facilitator* mentions an item or calls it off from a list of items and the viewer comprehends what the facilitator is saying. An item is not necessarily *presented* simply because the facilitator mentions it. The viewer must actually *comprehend* what the facilitator meant. When he finally "gets" the concept mentioned or stated by the

---

25. Further research is needed to verify various conclusions that have been arrived at empirically concerning the meter and the meaning of its various reactions. The description that follows, however, is based on the experience of a large number of people who have used the meter in this way.

26. See Chapter Two, pp. 60-67, for a full discussion of prehension and having.

facilitator, then, and only then, can the item be said to be "presented" to him. It sometimes happens that the facilitator thinks she has presented a certain item to the viewer, but the viewer has misunderstood what she meant, and so a different item, or no item, has actually been presented. A British facilitator might ask, "Did Sam knock you up?", meaning "Did Sam wake you up by knocking on your door?"; if the viewer is American, she may think the facilitator is asking (crudely) whether Sam impregnated her. Any reaction on the meter would reflect charge she had on the latter item rather than on the former.

Needle Actions

The actions of the needle and the baseline give the facilitator many valuable clues concerning the viewer's condition. Needle actions fall into two categories — patterns and reactions:

Definition: A pattern is an ongoing type of needle behavior that reflects the mental status of the viewer.

Definition: A reaction is a *change* of needle pattern caused by a mental change in the viewer.

Different needle patterns indicate different physical or mental conditions. Some of the more useful ones are:

Definition: A climbing needle is a needle that is moving to the left because skin resistance is increasing.

Definition: A dropping needle is a needle that is moving to the right because skin resistance is decreasing.

Definition: A still needle is a needle that barely moves or moves not at all. It often accompanies a high baseline and indicates that the viewer has too much material in restimulation or has his attention solidly fixed on something.

Definition: A rough needle is a needle that is moving in a jerky, uneven manner, not as a response to a presented item. It often indicates that the viewer has a withheld communication. A rough needle can make it hard to read the meter properly. The undelivered communication can also get in the way of viewing. Generally, a rough needle can be made smooth by simply asking the viewer for undelivered communications. When the viewer has told the facilitator what his attention is on, the needle action will become smooth.

Definition: A smooth needle is a needle that is not rough and that does not change in pattern (usually slowly climbing or slowly dropping).

Definition: A free needle is a needle that moves smoothly backward and forward at steadily varying and not overly rapid rates of speed, with no particular directionality. When accompanied by good indicators, it indicates unfixed attention, as when a person is clear (free of restimulation) or when he has successfully completed a cycle or procedure.

In viewing, the free needle is one of the cardinal indicators that something has been completed and, as such, is something with which every facilitator should become so familiar that she can recognize it without hesitation.[27]

In speaking of needle reactions (changes of pattern), we are primarily concerned with those that are a response to some known item:

Definition: A response is a reaction that occurs almost instantaneously after a charged item is presented to the viewer.

---

27. Its further significance will be discussed later in this chapter, pp. 429-433.

Definition: A <u>delayed reaction</u> is a reaction that is not instantaneous.

A delayed reaction is usually disregarded because it is not obvious to *what* it is a response, if anything. It is not possible to say just how instantaneous a response needs to be. Sometimes, as when a viewer is not using his native language, the response may be somewhat delayed while he puzzles out the meaning of what the facilitator has said. This can also happen if the concept presented is not instantly clear to the viewer for any other reason. The facilitator must judge when the item was *presented*, i.e., when the viewer got the concept. If a response is going to occur, *that* is when it will occur. There is no purpose in waiting for a response beyond this point.

Needle responses vary in magnitude and in significance. The degree of fruitfulness of a particular item is positively correlated with the size of the response obtained when the item is presented. Responses include the following:

Definition: A <u>drop</u> is a response (dropping needle) of moderate size (over 1/8").

Definition: A <u>baseline drop</u> is a drop that is so large and of such duration that it requires an adjustment of the baseline control to keep the needle on the dial.

Definition: A <u>stopped free needle</u> is a response in which a free needle stops being free and starts manifesting some other pattern. It indicates the presence of charge.

Definition: An <u>instantaneous free needle</u> is a response in which a needle that was not free frees up when an item is presented to the viewer. It is also a major indicator of charge.

Definition: A <u>no response</u> is a lack of needle response to a given item; it generally indicates that the item presented should not be addressed at this time, either because it is too heavily charged to be dealt with readily or because it is completely uncharged.

Generally speaking, the greater the response to an item, the closer that item is to the awareness threshold and the more fruitful it will be to take it up. If an item elicits no response on a meter, it may still be heavily charged, but if so, it lies too far below the awareness threshold to be dealt with at present. When the viewer's general level of awareness increases, the item will be found closer to the awareness threshold and will now generate a meter response when presented to the viewer. Thus a needle response often indicates the presence of a certain condition in the viewer *before* the viewer becomes aware of it.

The Baseline Value

The baseline value is of interest in itself. Each viewer has a usual or customary baseline value.[28] Various physical or mechanical conditions can affect this value; these should be dealt with before the session. Cold hands or feet, dry hands, contacts that are too big or too small to be held comfortably, or contacts that do not make adequate electrical contact with the hands can result in an artificially high baseline and a relative insensitivity of response. So can fatigue, hunger, tight shoes or clothing, drugs or alcohol, or even improper nutrition. An excessively hot room or sweaty hands may cause an artificially low baseline.[29] Other factors affecting the baseline can be assumed to be intrapsychic or psychosomatic.

A drop in resistance is generally correlated with confronting and discharging charge or with becoming aware of something, perhaps momentarily or subliminally. It seems to be indicative of an alerting or awakening response, an increase in awareness. It is

---

28. Usually between 5000 ohms and 20,000 ohms, for hand-held contacts.

29. There is a great deal of individual variation in baselines, so a certain amount of judgment is needed in interpreting baseline levels. Some people, for instance, tend to maintain a low baseline value at all times and almost never get into higher ranges of baseline resistance.

logical to assume, then, that a climb should be correlated with a lowering of awareness or getting into contact with something of which one has not yet become fully aware, and that assumption is borne out in practice. A very high, immovable baseline (high in relation to the viewer's usual baseline) generally indicates over-restimulation: too much has been restimulated; too few of the restimulated items have been handled. A rapid climb in baseline, when accompanied by negative emotions, uncomfortable feelings, or other unpleasantness, often indicates an overrun (something that has gone past its proper ending point) or protest. Often what one becomes aware of when there is a drop in resistance is some charge that was previously contacted but bypassed instead of being handled. For instance, if the viewer is avoiding thinking about going to the dentist, the baseline may climb, but at the point where the viewer realizes or remembers that he has to go, the meter is likely to show a drop or baseline drop. A rapidly climbing baseline, then, is useful in allowing the facilitator to spot when the viewer is running into difficulty, protesting, having too much going on at once, or when a procedure is overrun. By observing a "soaring baseline", a facilitator may become aware of a protest or overrun before the viewer does.

Assessing with an Electrodermometer

Falls and baseline drops are useful mainly in assessing. Their magnitude is noted during the session, and thus different items can be rated according to the size of the response. Generally an item that gives a large response is easier to address than one that gives a smaller one.[30] An item that gives no response, regardless of how "obvious" it may seem to the facilitator as a charged item, is seldom useful to pursue and does not usually have the viewer's

---

30. Although stopped free needles and instantaneous free needles are counted as large responses.

interest.[31] For instance, though it may be obvious to the facilitator that the viewer has difficulty communicating, the subject of communication might not cause a response on the meter, whereas the subject of, say, his sister might give a major response. In this case, despite appearances, the facilitator is better off addressing the sister than communication, unless the *viewer's* interest lies in the area of communication. After the charge on the sister is reduced — the awareness threshold having been lowered somewhat — the area of communication will now, perhaps, respond on the meter and thus be accessible to viewing.

Assessing can be done by observing certain physical characteristics of the viewer. But it is often helpful or essential to use a meter if the viewer is not adept at gauging his own bodily or emotional responses. Specific assessment techniques include:

1. Exploration
2. Inquiry
3. Listing
4. Selecting
5. Calling

Exploring

The most informal of viewing procedures is called "Exploring". Here, you select a particular charged topic, such as an interpersonal relationship, that the viewer is interested in handling. The facilitator asks the viewer to tell her about the topic and listens to what he has to say. She may also ask for any perceptions, considerations, decisions, or thoughts the viewer may have about the subject. If some part of the topic generates a sizable meter response, an emotional response, or a great deal of

---

31. Rarely, the viewer's strongest interest lies in an area that does not cause a response on the meter. In such a case, addressing the item will very often "awaken" a meter response, and the area will prove fruitful after all.

interest, it is noted as a charged subject, and, if appropriate, Explored as a subsection of the topic. If, for instance, the viewer flushes when her husband is mentioned, or if she talks excitedly about him, the facilitator may say, "Tell me more about your husband." As in all viewing, Exploration questions are *non-evaluative* and *non-interpretive*. They serve only to "draw out" the viewer. If Exploring a certain topic and associated sub-topics does not lead to relief, a realization, and very good indicators, then it is permissible to ask for earlier similar considerations, decisions, etc., or for an earlier similar topic, to open up a new subject for Exploration, which can be similarly "milked" for charge. One version of Exploring, called "guiding", is done by simply watching for a meter response and then querying what the viewer is looking at. Guiding should be used sparingly since it tends to cause the viewer to become dependent on the meter.

Exploring resembles what is commonly done in psychotherapy in that the facilitator asks a few questions to draw out the viewer and mostly keeps quiet and listens. There are, however, major differences between the two:

1. **Close adherence to the topic at hand**. The viewer is not permitted to wander into unrelated topics. The Exploration is of a particular topic, not just a general Exploration.
2. **Strict avoidance of evaluation or interpretation**. Whatever the viewer says is accepted and acknowledged without comment.
3. **Recognizing an end point and stopping the procedure at that point**.

Exploring can be used to effect a quick destimulation on a particular subject. It often produces a dramatic improvement.

Inquiring

Inquiring is really an interviewing technique rather than a viewing procedure, but it bears some similarity to an Exploration. An Inquiry is a relatively informal means of obtaining more information about a particular subject. As in an Exploration, the facilitator or interviewer tries to draw the viewer out on a particular subject and inquires more closely into topics that give meter responses or seem to have the viewer's interest. In an Inquiry, however, one is not trying to reduce charge on a subject, and one does not need to bring an Inquiry to an end point. One is merely gathering information in a systematic way. Consequently, the facilitator does not *have* to ask the viewer to give her his ideas, considerations, or decisions about the subject at hand (though the facilitator might want to, to get more data), nor does she need to ask him about earlier similar incidents or topics. Of course, she will very often — "by accident" as it were — reduce charge and reach end points. But an Inquiry need not go to a viewing-type end point, nor need it necessarily end when such an end point occurs. The end point of an Inquiry occurs when all the information is collected that the Inquiry was intended to collect.

All viewing procedures except Exploring and Inquiring are very tightly patterned.

Listing

Listing and selecting both involve asking the viewer a question and getting him to give a list of items, while observing the response to each as he gives it. When listing, one expects the viewer to find several items, none of which is particularly "right" or "wrong". For instance, if the viewer complains of compulsions, the facilitator may ask him, "What compulsions do you have?" The viewer then gives a list of items, such as "a compulsion to wash my hands", "a compulsion to be neat", and so forth. The facilitator records the items and their meter responses (or lack of response). These are then used to determine which items should be addressed and in which order.

Selecting

In selecting, the facilitator asks a question for which there are correct and incorrect answers — from the viewer's viewpoint, of course. The list (or "selection") obtained from the viewer tends to be "convergent", in the sense that it tends to narrow down to one item. For instance, if the facilitator asks a question like, "Who is giving you the most trouble?", the viewer may give several responses (like "John ... Sue ... Betty ...") while she is looking for the most appropriate answer. Finally she finds it. Let us say the "correct" item is "Paul". The facilitator can tell from the meter responses and the appearance of the viewer that "Paul" is the right answer and gives that item to the viewer by saying "Your item is 'Paul'," " 'Paul' was the one," or something of the sort. If the viewer confirms that it is the right item and manifests good indicators, the facilitator ends the procedure.[32]

Calling

In calling, the facilitator starts out with an item (sentence, question, phrase, or word) or a list of items and calls these off, noting the meter responses. The ones that respond are either addressed as they come up or taken up after the whole list has been called, generally in descending order of size of response. The lists may be a standard list of commonly-charged items, a list tailored for an individual viewer, or a list of items obtained earlier from the viewer.

These different forms of assessment are often combined in various ways. Selecting may also involve some calling, in order to help find the central item or items.

---

32. Selecting is a specialized procedure, discussed further in Chapter Nine, pp. 499-502.

Having done an assessment, either in the current session or in an earlier session, the facilitator then proceeds to use various procedures to handle the charged areas found. Some of these procedures involve doing further assessments along the way.[33]

One general caveat: I reiterate that it is important not to make the viewer dependent on the facilitator by evaluating. In the case of a conflict between the viewer's data and what the meter shows, the facilitator should always take the viewer's data. As a general rule, too, the facilitator should try to consult the viewer before resorting to a meter assessment. Early in viewing, the facilitator will tend to rely heavily on the meter.[34] Later, after the viewer knows what it feels like to have a free needle, a climbing needle, a response, etc., he can usually tell the facilitator what is happening.[35] If so, the facilitator may be able to work effectively without needing to rely so heavily on the meter. A major purpose of viewing is to enhance the viewer's ability to spot (view) what is going on in his mind, so that he can *change* it. The facilitator is always safe in taking the following as a guideline: *actions that enhance an ability are valid; actions that substitute for or inhibit an ability are not.*

---

33. I shall discuss some of these procedures and their associated forms of assessment later in this chapter and in the next.

34. Experienced, highly-trained facilitators tend to use the meter a great deal, but by using the many procedures that don't require a meter, a less highly-trained facilitator can accomplish a great deal.

35. Some experienced viewers can even produce many of the various meter phenomena at will.

Indicators

A person tends to fix her attention on aspects of the environment that are sub-optimal or problematic because these are the entities that need to be handled. Aspects of the environment that are positive or beneficial can safely be ignored in most circumstances. They are "taken for granted".[36]

In running a viewing session, however, the facilitator must school herself to be as aware of things that are *right* with the viewer as she is of those that are *wrong*. If the facilitator fails to notice or acknowledge things that are right and constantly searches for things that are wrong, the effect can be disastrous for the viewer, who can get quite discouraged because he feels that he is not accomplishing anything. Of course, the facilitator should not express approval or praise the viewer, any more than she should express disapproval or blame. That would be evaluation. Rather, when something happens — good or bad — and both the viewer and the facilitator are aware of it, the facilitator should take the appropriate action. When something bad happens, the facilitator should take the appropriate corrective action. If good things are happening, she should continue the successful action; if something *especially* good happens, the facilitator should end the procedure she is running, or even end the session.

Various phenomena (indicators), perceptible to the facilitator, indicate whether things are going well or poorly. These are called good and bad indicators:

Definition: A good indicator is a phenomenon that indicates (implies, means, signifies, or suggests) that a person is being successful in carrying out some activity.

---

36. A person with a car that runs well or a body that is healthy does not particularly notice the well-running car or the healthy body. She incorporates these as tools and focuses her attention outward to do what she needs to do in a broader sphere.

Definition: A bad indicator is a phenomenon that indicates that a person is not being successful in carrying out some activity.

For a boxer, a puffy eye or staggering gait are bad indicators, whereas rapid, precise punches and a springy gait are good indicators. Bad indicators for a heart patient include abnormal blood pressure, shortness of breath, and swollen ankles; good cardiac indicators include normal breathing, a normal blood pressure, and unswollen ankles. The indicators listed below are those that show how well or poorly viewing is going. Bad indicators, for a viewer, include:

1. Persistent negative emotions, negative feelings, or dramatizations, in session or in life.
2. Pallor and poor skin tone.
3. Physical coldness.
4. Inability to concentrate.
5. Lack of interest in viewing.
6. Trying to manage the session herself or to dictate her own viewing plan.
7. Illness or injury after a session.
8. Missing or being late for sessions.
9. Trying to get a plan or procedure "over with" as quickly as possible.
10. Not having any insights.
11. Not feeling better after sessions or rapidly losing gains made in session.
12. Becoming less happy or successful in life.

Good indicators would include:

1. Freedom from negative emotions, negative feelings, and dramatization in life, and effective handling of them when they appear in session.
2. Good skin tone and color.
3. Physical warmth.
4. Ability to concentrate and handle distractions.
5. Being very interested in viewing.

6. Attention on the material she is viewing rather than on the facilitator or the mechanics of the session.
7. Remaining physically well after a session.
8. Coming to sessions regularly and on time. Finding time for sessions.
9. Being willing to spend time and attention on procedures to get the most out of them.
10. Having many insights and successes.
11. Making stable gains that last over the long term.
12. Becoming happier and more successful in life.

What constitutes a good indicator or a bad indicator varies from person to person, from time to time, and from situation to situation. Judging indicators requires experience and a certain perceptiveness on the part of the facilitator. For a very reserved viewer, a smile or a little laugh might be a very good indicator; for a very volatile person, a smile or laugh might be an immediate prelude to violent grief. For one person, a frown might be a bad indicator; for another, it might be an indication that she is about to have a significant insight.

Recognizing the End Point

A major reason why a facilitator — or anyone who wants to help another person — should be very familiar with good indicators is so that she can recognize when an end point has been reached. The definition of "end point" is:

Definition: The end point is the point at which the cycle connected with an activity has been successfully completed and the activity should therefore be ended. It is manifested by a set of phenomena that indicate successful termination. These phenomena vary from activity to activity.

In viewing, an end point occurs when a subject that was charged is now at least partially discharged, destimulated, or deactivated. A part of the traumatic incident network (Net) such as a trauma or sequence can be deactivated so that it is not currently affecting the person. Or it can be discharged so that that part of the Net is eradicated — no longer there to affect the person. Certain metapsychological techniques, such as those used for handling current restimulation, are most likely to result in deactivation whereas others, such as Traumatic Incident Reduction (See pp. 433-452, below), result in a more complete discharge.

The components of an end point reflect how major an end point it is, i.e., what degree of deactivation or discharge has been achieved. In order of significance, they are:

1. Very good indicators
2. Realization or insight
3. Free needle (if a meter is used)
4. Extroversion

And, sometimes

5. Disappearance of unwanted conditions
6. Abilities gained or regained

At a certain point in a procedure, the facilitator (if she is using a meter) may observe a free needle. Then the viewer may express a realization (such as: "I just realized that I was looking at my girlfriend the way I used to regard my mother!", or "I see now that I brought on that difficulty myself."). Usually, he will then smile or laugh, and show good skin color — all good indicators. At this point, his attention, which was introverted while he was looking at his difficulties, will extrovert. Now he is aware of present time, the facilitator, and the room. If some unwanted condition manifests itself during the session, such as a headache or a feeling of nervousness, it should be gone or greatly relieved at the end point. Major disabilities (long-term anxiety, guilt, or hostility) may disappear and not return. And finally, abilities, new or regained, such as "the ability to forgive" or "the ability to communicate", may suddenly become apparent.

A facilitator must be *very* familiar with the different phenomena that indicate the presence of an end point. When using a meter, she must be able to recognize a free needle without hesitation. She must also familiarize herself with the forms end points take for a particular viewer, since there are many individual variations in style and content. One person may have very dramatic end points, in which he begins uncontrollably laughing or shedding tears of joy. Another may have end points that are merely interesting or entertaining to him and not earth-shattering. The insights that the viewer expresses may sound quite mundane ("I can see the room more clearly now."), or they may constitute major, life-changing revelations.

Precise timing is important in indicating to the viewer that a procedure is complete. The process of completion must not be interrupted when only some of the indicators of an end point are present. On the other hand, a procedure must not be overrun past its proper end point. Often, the viewer is looking at something and the needle begins to free up, perhaps only slightly at first. The viewer is *in the process* of becoming aware of something. If the facilitator interrupts this process, the viewer is distracted and the coming awareness may not occur. In other words, a receptive cycle may be left incomplete and charge may be restimulated and left unhandled.[37] If instead of interrupting, the facilitator simply remains silent and observes, the viewer's needle will start to swing more widely, and (usually) he will eventually voice his realization: *"Now* I see why I have always hated flowers!". Next, he will show very good indicators, usually smiling or laughing, or becoming flushed in the face. At this point, his attention, which up to now has been directed toward the material he is viewing, is freed up. He extroverts and often looks at the facilitator or the room. Only at *this* point does the facilitator indicate that the procedure is complete. She does this simply by saying something like: "We are done with that procedure now," or "That's all we are going to do with that item."[38] This

---

37. Charge is unfulfilled intention, and, in the case of an interrupted end point, the viewer has an intention to reach an insight that is thwarted when the cycle is interrupted.

38. It is *not* done by making evaluative statements, such as "That's wonderful! You've come a long way!".

more or less formal step of indicating the successful completion of a procedure serves the same purpose as does the formal ending of a session: it completes the cycle and allows the viewer to take his attention off that subject and put it elsewhere.

After a full end point, if the facilitator were to say, "Uh huh?" or indicate in any way that she wanted to know *more* about the subject of the procedure, the viewer would probably start searching for more when there is nothing more to be had at this time on this subject. In other words, the facilitator will have overrun the procedure past its proper end point. When an overrun occurs, the viewer starts looking at other areas of the Net that are not really handleable with this procedure. These, then, become restimulated, and the viewer is likely to protest and can become quite upset. So the facilitator must be vigilant and end the procedure at exactly the right moment, so as neither to overrun nor to interrupt the viewer before the full end point is reached.[39]

Failing to indicate an end point may be just as damaging an evaluation as indicating one when it has not occurred. If the viewer feels he has reached an end point and the facilitator fails to indicate it, a great deal of upset may ensue. In order to avoid ill effects, the facilitator must be alert for signs of an end point and also for signs of overrun and protest.

Viewers do not always voice their realizations. Some viewers may become rather coy about them. They may have a free needle, very good indicators, and extroversion but not say anything. A facilitator needs to get to know a viewer and to know what she looks like when she has had a realization. It is OK to ask whether the viewer has had a "thought" (not a "realization" — that would be evaluative). This follows a general rule of viewing that the facilitator must stay in close communication with the

---

39. A free needle is the first sign of an impending end point. If the facilitator is good at spotting free needles, she is put on alert, when she sees one, to look for the rest of the indicators of an end point.

viewer and may always inquire to find out what's going on in the
viewer's mind. The facilitator can usually get the viewer to voice
a realization if she has had one.

The indicators of an end point, after all, are only indicators.
What the facilitator must judge by observing them is whether or
not a deactivation or discharge has occurred and whether the procedure has therefore reached a suitable end point. The facilitator
ends a procedure when the viewer has experienced some kind of
success. If the success is a very major one, the facilitator ends
the whole *session* at that point. A viewer who has just had a
major success tends to become quite clear and may lose interest
in — or, indeed, all contact with — his Net for the time being.
This generalized deactivation of the Net sometimes lasts days,
weeks, or even months. During this time, the viewer does not
like to be forced back into the Net by further sessions, nor should
he be. The facilitator must judge whether to continue or not.
Often, the right thing to do is for the viewer to go live his life and
enjoy and apply his successes and abilities. He can come back
when he is interested in doing more viewing.

Even if overrun phenomena such as protest or a soaring baseline do not occur when a person has continued past a major success, such a success, if persistent, can interfere with a proper
assessment. If a major success in handling a part of the Net has
caused the viewer to lose contact with the Net, he is not really
interested in doing any further viewing for the time being because
he does not see anything there to handle. It all looks quite rosy.
Most of us are familiar with the intoxication of a big success, such
as a wonderful new love relationship or a major success in a
career. Similar effects are observable in viewing and must be
watched for. Going beyond such a point can be experienced by
the viewer as an invalidation of his success. Furthermore,
because the viewer has lost contact with the Net, subjects that are
actually charged may fail to respond or arouse the viewer's
interest. This can lead to errors in case planning: charged items
can be overlooked.

One sign of a major success (if the viewer is on a meter) is a
persistent free needle — a needle that just remains free regardless
of what you try to address. An even more extreme manifestation

is a "free baseline", where the needle is swinging so widely that the facilitator has to almost continually adjust the baseline control to keep the needle on the dial. It is useless and counter-productive to continue with viewing when these phenomena occur.

The facilitator, then, must keep a close watch on the viewer and — if she is using one — the meter, and must take cognizance of all indicators — both good and bad — as they appear.

Traumatic Incident Reduction

I would now like to present an outline of the procedure called "Traumatic Incident Reduction" (TIR).[40] TIR serves as a good example of how the various different concepts presented in earlier chapters can be fit together into a workable procedure. TIR is the viewing procedure that is most akin to traditional psychoanalytical procedures. It involves tracing back sequences of traumatic incidents to their roots while completing the incomplete receptive cycles that have accumulated in the sequences. I do not intend to give a complete account of how to do TIR. For that, a person should take a course in applied metapsychology, which will give more detail and practical exercises and experience. But I will give enough data so that the reader can get a good idea of how viewing in general (and TIR in particular) works.

Freud was perhaps the first to employ a type of TIR. He describes the procedure as follows:

> "What left the symptom behind was not always a *single* experience. On the contrary, the result was usually

---

40. The current procedure for traumatic incident reduction was developed, in part, by David Mayo, former Director of Research at the Institute for Research in Metapsychology.

brought about by the convergence of several traumas, and often by the repetition of a great number of similar ones. Thus it was necessary to reproduce the whole chain of pathogenic memories in chronological order, or rather in reversed order, the latest ones first and the earliest ones last; and it was quite impossible to jump over the later traumas in order to get back more quickly to the first, which was often the most potent one."[41]

Freud gave up this technique in favor of free association, presumably because he had difficulty making it work. Any difficulties he may have had probably stemmed from the fact that he did not know how to do a proper assessment or when to *stop* working on something, as well as from violating the rules of facilitation given earlier in this chapter (pp. 387-394). He lacked a suitable biomonitoring device and did not seem to use physiological signs such as pupillary dilation or flushing[42], and so he mainly relied on interest as a method of assessing.[43]

---

41. Freud, Sigmund "Two Short Accounts of Psycho-Analysis" Tr. James Strachey (Penguin Books, Singapore, 1984) p. 37.

42. It is, in my view, a basic weakness of Freud's method — and many other methods — that physical indicators are almost never used in determining when a point of resolution has occurred. The only exception I could find in Freud was in *Psychotherapy of Hysteria*, where Freud mentions that he can tell from the presence of facial tension that a person has as-yet-undisclosed material. [*The Complete Psychological Works of Sigmund Freud* (Hogarth Press, London, 1966) v.II, p. 294,301.]

43. Free association might be regarded as a type of viewing in which one simply follows the line of the viewer's interest wherever it leads. This method has a certain workability but takes too long because it is too dispersed as a method. The mechanics of the Net tend to send the viewer on a wild goose chase. Free association is further hampered by the use of psychoanalytic interpretations, which act as evaluations and so tend to inhibit the viewer from viewing freely and making her *own* interpretations. Carl Rogers' method is better than Freud's in avoiding interpretations, but the Rogerian method would be stronger if it used methods of assessing other than simply following the interest of the viewer. Freud's method — as presented in his later works — also suffered from being based on a theory that was both incomplete and excessively arbitrary and complex. The theory did not lead to a systematic method. Nor did it lead to a method that was focused on

What Traumatic Incident Reduction Does

Traumatic incidents cause a wide variety of unwanted emotional, psychological, and psychosomatic conditions. Traumatic Incident Reduction is a powerful, though simple, method for handling these conditions. It addresses incidents of loss, failure, upset, emotional shock, injury, accident, or illness and reduces the emotional shock caused by these incidents. After a traumatic incident, a person may have an aversion for certain areas of life and a tendency to withdraw from them because they are restimulative. TIR reduces this aversion by discharging (or "reducing") the charge contained in past traumatic incidents, thus making it easier for the person to recontact and cope with those areas of life.

In addition to specific handling of acute trauma and restimulations, TIR can also be used in a more general way to address more chronic forms of restimulation and, in general, to handle charge contained in the Net.

---

the exact action needed to resolve the person's aberrations. It imposed a structure that did not necessarily fit the individual viewer, however much it may have fit the typical hysterical patient that Freud originally dealt with. This is not to detract from Freud's contributions to the subject of metapsychology, perhaps the most major of which was his concept of the therapeutic alliance. He realized, as many others have not, that the analysand would have to be an active participant in the process. And if the Freudian system was far from perfect, at least it offered some structure and workability.

How TIR Works

A traumatic incident includes a person's *reactions* (thoughts, sensations, and feelings) as well as her *perceptions* of the event itself. Part or all of a traumatic incident is *uninspected*. That is, there is an incomplete receptive cycle holding the incident in place, consisting of the incomplete act of fully perceiving and understanding what happened at the time. Viewing the incident thoroughly enables the viewer to regain the missing data and thereby to complete the repressed incomplete receptive cycle by coming to understand what was going on at the time and how she was reacting to the ongoing event. And by becoming aware of the incident, she also becomes aware of and can (if she so chooses) complete or unmake any intentions that she had during the incident. When this awareness occurs, the charge (repressed, unfulfilled intention) contained in the incident is reduced or eliminated, and it no longer has the power to affect her adversely.

If you want to become thoroughly familiar with an object, you must look at it carefully for a period of time, from different angles. If, however, what you want to become aware of is an *event*, it is necessary to *go through it* sequentially a number of times. One cannot usually become aware of it in a glance, as one might with an object. If you want to become thoroughly familiar with a movie, you have to review it several times, each time from the beginning to the end. Since the aim of TIR is to familiarize the viewer thoroughly with the contents of incidents, the procedure of TIR prescribes a thorough sequential review of each incident.

Usually, more than one incident must be reviewed in order to resolve a sequence. Theoretically, the viewer could simply find the root incident, review it a number of times, and resolve all the incidents that are dependent on that root incident. In practice, however, the viewer usually cannot find the root at first because of the layers of charge and repression that lie between him and it, contained in more recent similar incidents (sequents). Each restimulation that occurs adds yet another layer of repression and an additional increment of pain on top of what was already there. If he attempts to find the root without having addressed the sequents, he cannot do so. He can, however, find a relatively recent sequent. When he reviews one of these recent incidents a few times, *some* of the pain and repression is discharged and his awareness increases somewhat. He can now find an *earlier* incident on the sequence which he previously might not have been able to locate. He then runs through *that* incident a few times, discharging more pain and repression, so that now he can find yet an *earlier* incident, and so on, until eventually he can find the root. When the root is discharged or reduced, the particular sequence that depended on that root ceases to exist, its charge is no longer there to affect the viewer, and the end point of the procedure has been attained.

Sequences and Roots

What all incidents in a sequence have in common is a *theme* of some kind — some similar or apparently similar *response* the viewer makes in each incident. Whenever the root incident — or *any* incident on the sequence — is restimulated, the theme appears — as the viewer's response. A sequence of such incidents can be traced back to its root. The definitions of "sequence" and "root" were introduced earlier:

> **Definition**: A sequence is a group containing one or more related or associated traumatic incidents, all containing a common theme. Incidents later in a sequence contain restimulators of earlier ones.

> **Definition**: The root of a sequence is the traumatic incident that is earliest in the sequence and on which the entire sequence relies for its existence. It contains primary pain. It does not merely contain secondary pain, based on a reminder of an earlier incident.

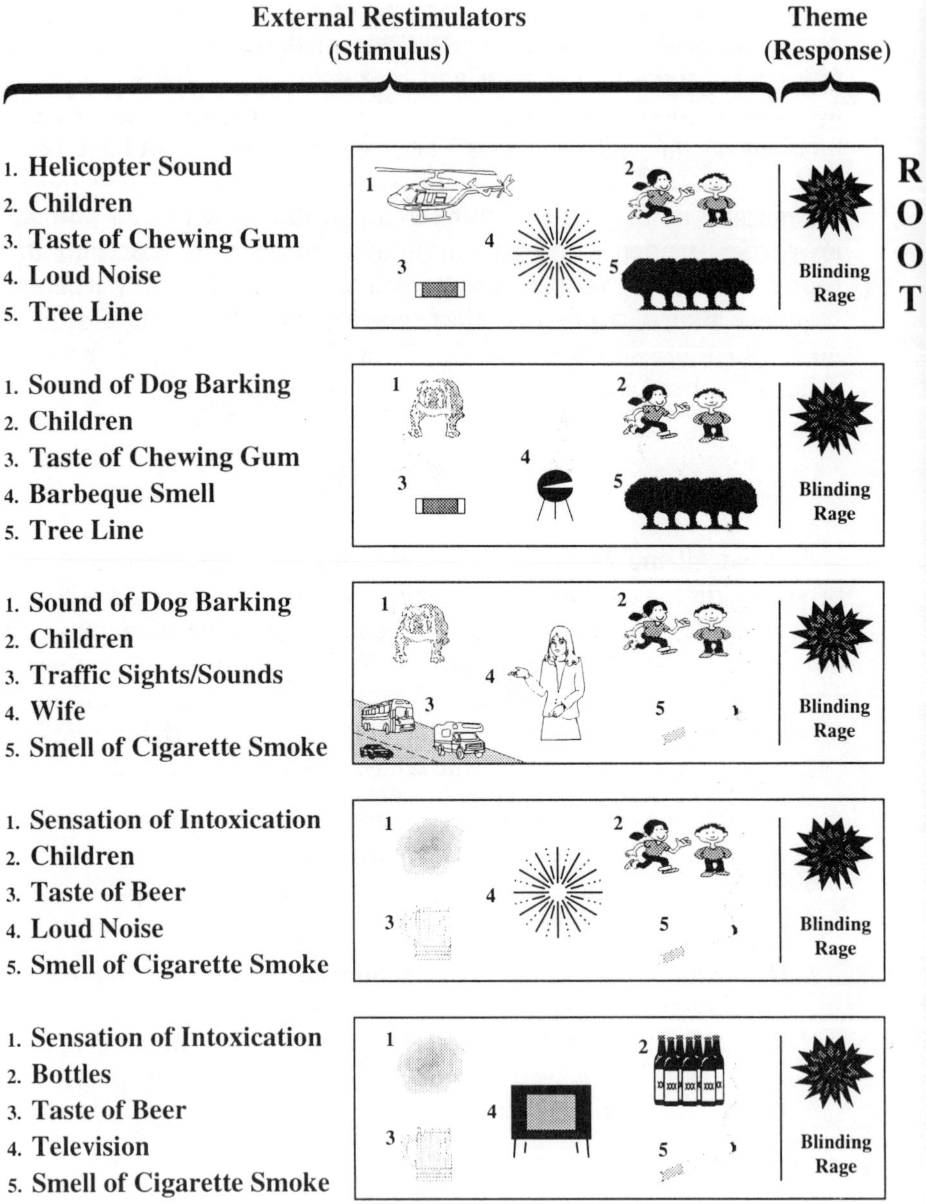
External Restimulators
(Stimulus)
Theme
(Response)
1. Helicopter Sound
2. Children
3. Taste of Chewing Gum
4. Loud Noise
5. Tree Line
Blinding Rage
ROOT
1. Sound of Dog Barking
2. Children
3. Taste of Chewing Gum
4. Barbeque Smell
5. Tree Line
Blinding Rage
1. Sound of Dog Barking
2. Children
3. Traffic Sights/Sounds
4. Wife
5. Smell of Cigarette Smoke
Blinding Rage
1. Sensation of Intoxication
2. Children
3. Taste of Beer
4. Loud Noise
5. Smell of Cigarette Smoke
Blinding Rage
1. Sensation of Intoxication
2. Bottles
3. Taste of Beer
4. Television
5. Smell of Cigarette Smoke
Blinding Rage

Figure 44. A sequence of traumatic incidents

Just because a theme is common to all the TI's on a sequence, however, does not mean that the theme is what holds the sequence together or what causes it to form in the first place. What links the TI's in a sequence is not the common theme but associated external restimulators that are similar from one TI to the next but probably *not* common to all the incidents in the sequence (See Figure 44). It is these restimulators that cause the restimulation that forms the sequence, not the presence of the theme.

If we look at restimulation as a Pavlovian stimulus-response process, the theme is the *response*, not the *stimulus*. In the formation of a sequence of TI's containing, say, the emotion "outrage", it is not outrage that triggers earlier TI's containing outrage. It is external *stimuli* (such as certain stresses or other environmental elements) that remind the person of earlier TI's, and the *response* is outrage.

That's how a sequence is formed in life. In session, using thematic TIR (see pp. 443-449), we use an "artificial" form of restimulation, not the type that normally occurs in life. We use the *response* — the theme — as a *restimulator* to find earlier TI's. By having the viewer locate a feeling that is contained in a sequence of TI's, we are able to restimulate (and therefore find) earlier and earlier incidents on that sequence, until eventually we locate the root. In so doing, however, we are not using the same type of restimulation as that by which the sequence was formed.

The concept of a theme and that of a sequence are inextricably intertwined. Every sequence has a common theme, and every theme that troubles the viewer has a sequence of TI's in which it is contained. There are no "narrative sequences" — only primaries that can be run out with narrative TIR.

On occasion, a traumatic incident can exist in isolation without being part of a sequence. Such a solitary incident must contain primary pain since it is not a restimulation. It is handled by being viewed by itself, rather than as part of a sequence. Recent traumatic incidents, such as operations, severe losses, illnesses, and injuries, can often be handled in this way. Usually, however, a traumatic experience is part of one or more sequences, each going back to a separate root. Often many sequences are involved. In order to *fully* discharge a traumatic experience, each of the sequences of which it is a part must be reduced back to its root. If only *some* of these sequences are reduced, the traumatic experience may, however, be *partially* discharged. In either case, the traumatic incident is said to be "reduced":

> **Definition:** Reduction is the complete or partial discharge of a traumatic incident or sequence.

The End Point of TIR

When a significant amount of charge has been reduced from a traumatic incident or sequence, a certain set of phenomena will appear, indicating that a proper end point for TIR has arrived. In order of importance, these are:

1. Very good indicators
2. Extroversion
3. Free needle (if done on a meter)
4. Realization

These phenomena usually do not appear until the root of a sequence has been reached and reduced. When such an end point occurs, it is time to stop working on that particular incident or sequence and start something else. That incident or sequence now ceases to be part of "present time", and the intention units or power that was tied up in maintaining it as part of present time is reclaimed. The viewer is no longer as liable to be affected by restimulators resembling the contents of that incident or sequence. She might still be somewhat capable of being restimulated in this area, however; some of the incidents she has addressed might be part of other, as yet undischarged, sequences. In this case, these other sequences can be addressed in order to reduce the remaining charge.

Themes

As I have said (pp. 437-439), the traumatic incidents in a sequence have in common a "theme":

> Definition: A <u>theme</u> is a negative feeling, emotion, sensation, attitude, or pain that is common to all the different traumas in a sequence. Since it is present in several incidents, it does not describe any specific incident.

Themes found in sequences of TI's are generally negative feelings:

> Definition: A <u>negative feeling</u> is an unwanted phenomenon, intention, or negative emotion, resulting from the restimulation of one or more traumatic incidents.

Negative feelings may include unwanted attitudes as well as negative emotions, sensations, and pains. The word "feeling" is being used in its broadest possible sense to include unwanted perceptions, sensations, pains, emotions, perceivable mental or bodily states, numbness, and *lack* of feeling. Although some unpleasant feelings (e.g., primary pains) have a "legitimate" basis in present-time circumstances, most result from restimulation. TIR greatly reduces the number and intensity of negative feelings caused by restimulation.

TIR Procedure

In order to give you a "feel" for what Traumatic Incident Reduction is like, I shall take the liberty of addressing you, the reader, in the second person, as though you were, or intended to become, a facilitator. Traumatic Incident Reduction may be addressed to a general area or subject, such as "school", "men", or "the Army", or it may be addressed to a specific item, such as "a feeling of being closed in". If you start from a general subject, you must first find a specific item, of which there are two types — narrative and thematic:

> Definition: A narrative item is an item that describes a particular traumatic incident.

> Definition: A thematic item is an item that describes a particular negative feeling or attitude, without any reference to a specific incident.

The narrative or thematic item serves as a starting place for a specific application of the TIR procedure.

The Assessment Step

It is important to determine which subject and, within a subject, which incident or negative feeling should be addressed first. For this purpose, you can use several different means of assessment. Each of these methods consults the viewer to a greater or lesser degree. Generally you have the viewer give you (verbally) a list of subjects that are troubling him, or a list of traumatic incidents or unwanted feelings. While the viewer is naming the different items, you observe carefully and note the viewer's reaction to each as it is presented. Such reactions may include flushing, twitches, grimaces, an emotional tone of voice or a response on an electrodermometer (if you are using one). You choose the item that seems to give the largest reaction as the one to handle first.

If the topic you select is a general subject like "school", the viewer must list any traumatic incidents that may be connected with it. If there are any such incidents, handle them first, using the procedure given below. If there are no such incidents, or if — despite all such narrative items having been addressed — the viewer is still disturbed by the area being addressed, have him list negative feelings or themes connected with the area. It is helpful to ask fairly specific questions. Thus you can ask for all unwanted feelings, then all unwanted emotions, then sensations, then attitudes, then pains connected with the general subject. You then choose the one among *these* that is the most live. If you are using a meter, this would probably be the one that engenders the greatest meter response; otherwise, it would be the one in which the viewer is most interested. Don't try to address items that are not accompanied by a meter response and an expression of interest, no matter how "obvious" or "suitable" they may seem. These items may become live in a later assessment, at which point they too can be addressed.

If a viewer presents a traumatic incident or negative feeling that he is obviously "in" — one that is absorbing his attention — there is no need to engage in any further assessment. That item is live and should be run forthwith. Otherwise, always check with the viewer to find out whether he is interested in running the item, unless he is already obviously interested or has so stated. This rule applies to all procedures. Don't attempt an action in which the viewer has no interest.[44]

The Viewing Step

Once you have found a narrative or thematic item (a negative feeling or an incident) to start with, you run that item, using the following procedure. When starting from an incident the viewer has already mentioned, omit Step 1:

---

44. It could be argued that checking for interest is too permissive and would allow the viewer to avoid or "get out of" doing an action that is "good for him" or that "he needs to confront". Such a concept may exist as a hold-over from the theory that psychotherapy operates by "breaking down the ego defenses". Facilitation does not operate in that way. It is extremely important that the facilitator remain aware of the close relationship between interest and attention. Interest is by far the best and most useful means of deciding which items can be fruitfully addressed.

INC   **Ask the viewer to find an incident that contains that theme.**

For instance, you could say: "Find an incident containing a fear of flying," or "Find a time when you were afraid of flying."

WHEN   **Ask her when it happened.**

If the procedure started from a specific incident, you can ask a more specific question, such as "When did your house burn down?"

Accept whatever "date" the viewer gives. It does not have to be precise. "When I was little", "A long time ago", or "When we lived in Seattle", are just as acceptable as "January 10th, 1943." She may "date" the incident by the *location* in which it happened, or by *subject*, for example: "When I was in high school."

LONG   **Ask for the length of the incident.**

Again, this can be approximate. If the viewer really has no idea, that's fine.

START   **Ask her to go to the starting point of the incident and tell you when she has done so.**

AWARE   **Ask her to close her eyes (if they are open) and tell you what she is aware of.**

What you want, here, is not a description of the *whole* incident but only of whatever scene she perceives at the very *start* of the incident. You might get something like, "There's a wooden door, a long hallway, and a man in a striped shirt." In some cases, especially if the incident is highly charged or the viewer is inexperienced, you may get an extremely tentative answer, like: "I can't really see anything; I just get a feeling of darkness and fear," or: "It's vague ... maybe a big room ... or cave, or something." Accept such answers without hesitation. Most viewers will experience heightened perception later on in the incident or on later runs through the incident. Most viewers will want to close their eyes on this step and while running through the procedure so they are not distracted by present-time perceptions; some will prefer to keep them open.

GO   **Ask the viewer to go through the incident to the end.**

It is usually best if the viewer does this step silently. She just runs the incident in her mind from start to end like a movie, getting as much detail as possible. Some viewers, however, seem to require the support of the facilitator while they are going through the incident, or they find that recounting the incident as they go along helps them to confront it. Most would probably find they can perceive the incident better while going through it silently.

TELL   **When she has gone through the incident to the end, ask her to tell you what happened.**

She should *then* tell you what happened in the incident, as well as her *reactions, thoughts, and feelings* at the time of the incident. You *must not* offer any comments or interpretations concerning what she has to say. It is absolutely crucial to avoid *any* evaluation or invalidation during TIR or any procedure. Confine yourself to simple acknowledgements, such as "Good," "Fine," or "OK". If this was her first time through the incident, have her run through it again, using **START**, **GO**, and **TELL**, above.

L/H   **Determine whether or not charge is coming off the incident being addressed.**

If you are running a narrative item, you will probably want to go through the incident several times before bothering with this step, since sometimes it takes awhile for an incident to "bite". On themes, you would check after the second run-through.

If the following indicators are present, then the incident is probably discharging:

a. The incident is changing in some way. *Change* is the most obvious signal that an incident is reducing.
b. The viewer is becoming more relieved.
c. He is manifesting an emotional discharge (such as crying or expressing anger).
d. He is recovering more memory of the incident; he is becoming aware of new aspects of it.
e. He is becoming able, or more able, to perceive the incident.
f. He is becoming more aware of the reactions and conclusions he had at the time of the incident and is re-evaluating these.
g. The needle is loosening or the baseline is moving downwards.

If it isn't *very* obvious from the above indicators, ask the viewer whether the incident seems to be getting lighter or heavier. Or you can ask whether he feels he should run through this incident again. If you do ask, or if he volunteers an opinion, you must always accept and act on his answer. If both or you are unsure, it is permissible to have the viewer run through the incident again. If the incident is discharging, have the viewer review it again, using START, GO, and TELL, above. If it isn't discharging, go on to the next step.

EI   **On a thematic item, if the incident is not discharging, ask for an earlier incident containing the same theme.**

On a narrative item, ask for an "earlier similar incident".

On a thematic item, if you don't get an earlier incident, check for an earlier starting point. Sometimes the viewer gets stuck in the part of the incident that is quiet — e.g., the unconsciousness that occurs after a severe trauma — but has not yet confronted the full trauma that exists earlier. Sometimes, too, an incident is much longer than the viewer originally thought it was. Asking for an earlier starting point can handle either of these cases:

ES   **Ask whether the incident you are working has an earlier starting point.**

On a narrative item, *first* check for an earlier starting point for the incident, *then*, only if you don't get one, ask for an "earlier similar incident" (**EI**).

As I shall discuss later (pp. 453-454), you should train the viewer not to reject or invalidate fleeting impressions he gets when you ask the question, nor to question the validity of any pictures he reports to you. Have him tell you whatever he gets, whether or not it seems "relevant". If it is really irrelevant you will find out soon enough, but in the vast majority of cases what may begin as a mere "irrelevant" impression will be found to "develop" into a valid incident after a few runs.

If the viewer cannot find an earlier incident, continue reviewing the same incident (from the earlier starting point, if there is one), using **START**, **GO**, and **TELL**, above.

Continue with **WHEN** to **TELL** on the new incident, until *that* incident ceases to reduce, then do **EI** or **ES** or both, as appropriate.

If the viewer spontaneously presents an earlier incident, accept it and take it up, using **WHEN** to **TELL**. In this case, do not bother to ask for an earlier incident, since the viewer has already given you one, and do not make the viewer continue with the incident he was on. Take up the earlier incident offered by the viewer and continue with Steps **WHEN** to **TELL** on the new incident.

Follow the above steps until you get very good indicators, extroversion, a free needle (if you are using an electrodermometer), and a realization. When these signs of an end point are present, STOP. End the session, or switch to another topic. Don't engage in any rehash or further analysis of what it all means.

If you began with a narrative item and it does not readily resolve, you can have the viewer list themes connected with that incident and handle each of them, in descending order of liveness, with the full TIR procedure for themes, as given in this section.

When an item is handled, check for interest in running other flows.[45] If the flow you just ran is an inflow, check for charge on the outflow — a time or times the viewer caused another to have the same negative feeling or the same type of incident. If you find something on one of the other flows and the viewer is interested in it, handle it with the above steps. Similarly, check for and — if the viewer is interested — run crossflows (another to another) and reflexions (times she caused herself to have that kind of incident or negative feeling). Some of the same incidents may crop up on the other flows. That is fine — she will benefit from running them from a different viewpoint. In each case, the earlier similar question should reflect the flow you are dealing with. So you would ask for "An earlier similar time you caused another to have _____ (whatever the item is)," and so forth.

Often the incident you *start* with is an inflow. But the viewer *may* begin by running a time she hurt someone else, a time she observed a friend being traumatized, or a time when she did something to damage herself. Other flows on an item can be just as upsetting and traumatic as the inflow. In such a case, after completing whichever flow you started with, check the inflow, along with the other unrun flows.

---

45. Assuming the viewer doesn't have her attention fixed on some other incident or item. See pp. 235-238 for a discussion of flows.

After fully handling the item as above, if you have started from a general subject, choose a new item relating to that subject and run it as above. Continue finding and handling items until the charge has been reduced from the entire area or subject that you started with and the viewer has experienced a major improvement in that area.

Note that when you are handling a specific subject, you should first run any traumatic incidents that come to mind, and then handle themes. It may take several sessions.

Then choose a new general subject or area to address. When you have run out of live subjects, TIR is completed.

The more charge the viewer can remove from a later incident, the easier it will be for him to contact an earlier one. That is why you continue to run through an incident until it is no longer discharging before asking for an earlier one. That is also why you *always take an earlier incident volunteered by the viewer*: the whole point of running through an incident repetitively is to make it easier to find an earlier one. If he has already found such an incident, there is no further purpose in continuing to run the later one. For this reason, too, if he offers more than one earlier incident, ask him to select the *earliest* of these, and continue from there.

Often, when you start off with a heavy individual traumatic incident, it may well be the only incident on the sequence — i.e., the root. Therefore it is a good idea, when starting with such an incident, to plan to stick with it for some time and make sure you really don't depart from it until it ceases to discharge. When running themes, however, it is usually necessary to find earlier similar incidents.

The Experienced Viewer

As might be expected, after a viewer has had some experience with TIR and has become familiar with the procedure — and when he has reduced a certain amount of charge — reducing traumatic incidents becomes faster and easier for him. He will:

a. Have greater certainty about what is happening during TIR.

b. Have greater awareness of whether an incident is reducing or whether to go to an earlier incident.

c. Find incidents more quickly and easily.

d. Need less guidance.

As the viewer reduces the charge in his Net, he has more and more personal power with which to address traumatic incidents, so he confronts and handles them more easily. The viewer may start doing several TIR steps at a time, or even discharging incidents simply by looking at them. Therefore, when the viewer starts moving fast and skipping steps, don't try to adhere robotically to the procedural steps given above since that would slow the viewer down and actually impede TIR. Recognize the viewer's ability to go faster and welcome it.

Summary of the Procedure

1. Select a live subject or area of life.

2. Choose a live traumatic incident or negative feeling connected with that subject.

3. Have the viewer "go through" (re-experience) the incident, and any earlier associated incidents, on a sequence from latest to earliest (root), to an end point and reduction. If you are starting with a heavy traumatic incident, you may not need to go earlier. If you are starting with a negative feeling, you probably will.

4. Handle any other flows on the same item by doing Step (3) on each flow, if the viewer has any available incidents on these flows.

5. Continue running different sequences and flows until that traumatic incident or feeling is handled.

6. Choose a new item to address, and handle as above.

7. Continue in this manner until the whole subject or area that you began with has been discharged.

8. Choose the next subject or area of life that needs to be addressed and handle it as above, until no more subjects remain to be addressed.

General and Remedial TIR

TIR can be used either as a remedy to handle incidents and sequences that are acutely in restimulation or as a more general action, intended to provide a thoroughgoing discharge of incidents in the Net, including parts of the Net that, though charged, are not currently in restimulation. The former is called "Remedial TIR", and the latter is called "General TIR":

Definition: Remedial TIR is TIR used to handle items that are currently in restimulation and areas of life that are currently bothering the viewer. Its intent is to relieve current stress and restimulation.

Definition: General TIR is TIR used to handle items that are not currently in restimulation and that are *not* currently bothering the viewer. Its intent is to reduce the likelihood of future restimulation and difficulties and to remove charge from the case, generally and thoroughly.

Although the degree to which traumatic incidents adversely affect a person is proportional to the degree to which these incidents are restimulated, all charged incidents have *some* chronic adverse effect. This effect tends to be cumulative throughout life. As people get older and accumulate more and more traumatic incidents and sequences without discharging them, their chronic emotional state tends to drop further and further down on the emotional scale. Discharging traumatic incidents reverses this tendency. When discharged, traumatic incidents cannot be restimulated and no longer have power over the person. Their contents *are* available to her as possibly useful experience. Hence, General TIR should be used at the appropriate time in the viewing plan, even though the viewer does not have any specific current difficulties or restimulations she wants to address.

Traumatic Incident Reduction is an exceptionally simple and powerful technique. By itself, it could resolve much of the world's misery.

Transcendent Experiences

Frequently (with most but not all viewers), certain events occur that give the viewer a clear impression of herself as a spiritual being, not co-extensive with her body. These experiences appear to transcend the limits of a purely physical model of the universe. They include:

1. Remembrances of past lives.

2. Contact with other beings, not inhabiting bodies, close to the viewer.

3. Out of body experiences (OBE's)

4. Extrasensory perception (ESP)

5. Religiously transcendent experiences.

A recent poll of Americans shows that 67% have personally had experiences they regarded as ESP.[46] According to Gallup Polls done since 1980, 43% said that they had had an unusual spiritual experience; 23% believe in reincarnation. Since facilitation requires a strictly person-centered and non-evaluative, non-invalidative *modus operandi*, when a viewer reports such a phenomenon, the facilitator must:

1. Accept it as valid data concerning the viewer's world.

2. Deal with it appropriately.

Past Lives

Whether the viewer expects to encounter them or not, what appear to be past-life experiences are commonly encountered in viewing. They often occur in the course of TIR or other deeply retrospective procedures.[47] When asked for an earlier similar incident, the viewer gets a flash picture of an incident that could not have occurred during the viewer's current lifetime. It has been found, empirically, that if such incidents are ignored or invalidated, the viewer is unlikely to reach an end point on the procedure being run, whereas *if they are taken up and handled like any other incidents*, a full end point is likely to occur. The viewer must also be instructed to give whatever comes up in response to a viewing question and not to invalidate her own first

---

46. A 1987 poll by the National Opinion Research Center of the University of Chicago.

47. Many therapists have employed a hypnotic technique of "past life regression". In fact, they have an organization: The Association for Past-Life Research and Therapies, Inc., in Riverside, California. We have found that past life experiences are also commonly experienced in the *absence* of hypnosis. Even some relatively "mainstream" psychiatrists like R.D. Laing and Carl Rogers have acknowledged the possibility of past lives as a source of influence on a person. In the face of the widespread belief in such notions, open-mindedness is essential in dealing with viewers.

impression. Self-invalidation can be at least as destructive to the viewing process as invalidation from an external source.

It is not a good idea to tell viewers that they are *supposed* to have transcendent experiences or that it is a likelihood. To do so would be evaluative, and the viewer might feel pressured to have such experiences or feel like a failure for not having them. Some people routinely fall into past lives in many different procedures; others do so rarely, if ever. The presence or absence of transcendent experiences is not relevant to the viewing process. What *is* relevant is to eliminate self-invalidation, and evaluation and invalidation from the facilitator.

Beings

It is not uncommon for viewers to experience the presence of what appear to be nearby disembodied "personalities" or "beings", not under their control:

> **Definition**: A being is a person or spiritual entity, considered to be separate from a body. A viewer may think of himself as a being. He may also experience the presence of disembodied beings external to himself, but, in some sense, close by — that seem to exert an influence on him.

Whether these beings are viewed as automatized sub-personalities, multiple personalities, or completely separate beings who are in some way "attached" to the viewer is not significant. A viewer who experiences such beings will form his own ideas about them. Some experience beings early in viewing. Most experience them — if at all — only after they have done a fair amount of viewing and have "quieted down" their internal mental "noise".[48]

---

48. Several current therapies deal explicitly with beings, such as those that do "microexorcism", "depossession", or "spirit releasement". Jung apparently

Whether beings are perceived as "autonomous" sub-personalities or as external beings, they are handled in the same way in viewing. Phenomenologically, it appears that beings are best handled by having the viewer himself adopt the role of a facilitator and treat them as ordinary viewers. In this act of "indirect viewing", the viewer talks to beings, acknowledges their responses and originations, handles their restimulations, and does other procedures with them, such as running them through traumatic incidents or doing selection procedures with them, as their individual needs seem to require. At some point during indirect viewing, a being may seem to disappear. This disappearance could be interpreted as the reintegration of a dissociated sub-personality or as the freeing of a trapped external being.[49]

In order to do indirect viewing, a viewer must either herself be a reasonably competent facilitator or be trained by one. She needs to be able to apply viewing procedures to herself and to any beings she may encounter. Generally, a relatively new viewer cannot handle these different functions at the same time. She cannot act as a facilitator for herself, let alone for beings. But when she has reduced her mental confusion and enhanced her ability to concentrate on the task at hand (i.e., when there are fewer distractions and restimulations), she can, given training, handle being a facilitator for herself *and* for beings.[50] As a solo

---

used techniques of talking to other beings. For that matter, other, more "mainstream" therapies deal with how a person "talks to himself": in cognitive therapies, such conversations are a form of corrective self-talk. Gestalt and transactional analysis also use talking to some aspect of the self. Sometimes they have the client "put" the dissociated aspect of himself facing him in an empty chair and get him to talk to it.

49. An interesting phenomenon can occur in the case of a viewer who experiences the presence of beings. She may misperceive some unwanted feeling or restimulation as being her own, when actually it is generated by an external being or group of beings. Or, she may misassign something to a being that is actually her own. When correct ownership is established, viewing — direct or indirect — goes more smoothly.

50. This occurs at what is called the "Turning Point". See pp. 468-470.

viewer — one who has been trained to act as her own facilitator — she can, in fact, make very rapid gains because she certainly can understand what *she* means when she says something, and none knows better than she when she has good or bad indicators. Solo viewing is an important and useful innovation that arises as a natural consequence of the person-centered viewpoint. Since outside interpretation and evaluation is neither necessary nor desirable in viewing, it stands to reason that a person should eventually be able to do it by herself.

Chapter Nine

Case Planning

Any skill or ability is acquired through a series of steps, each of which results in improvement. Taken together, they lead to the final attainment of the major skill or ability sought. A person has many subsidiary successes enroute to any truly significant accomplishment.

Spiritual and therapeutic methodologies have often followed a similar pattern. They generally include a series of steps a person goes through while approaching the ultimate goal of the activity — enlightenment, sanity, full functioning, rationality, or self-realization. A gradation of improvement is also implicit in many of the concepts of metapsychology. The different levels of the Emotional Scale are such a gradation; other-determinism, self-determinism, and multi-determinism are another; the six domains form yet another.

The Curriculum

In the context of metapsychology, the overall schema is called the "General Curriculum":

Definition: The <u>General Curriculum</u> is a case plan giving the usual or customary sequence of actions required, and abilities to be attained, in the course of viewing.

In constructing a case plan for an individual viewer, the technical director uses the General Curriculum as a guideline to form a specific curriculum for that viewer. This individually tailored curriculum is called an "Individual Curriculum":

Definition: An <u>Individual Curriculum</u> is a case plan intended to give the optimal sequence of viewing steps needed by a specific viewer. In planning an Individual Curriculum, a technical director starts with the General Curriculum as a guideline and tailors it to the specific needs of the individual viewer.

The General Curriculum contains a set of viewing procedures that form a proper progression toward the realization of potential. People work on and attain various specific abilities and freedoms while progressing through this Curriculum, such as the ability to communicate freely, the ability to solve problems, the ability to assert oneself, and freedom from unwanted effects of the traumatic incident network (Net).

Theory of the General Curriculum

Since for all people the Net is constructed in the same way and the mind operates by the same principles, it is possible to put together a General Curriculum that will work well for most viewers. The Net is layered in such a way that some parts of it are more accessible — easier to view — than others. These more accessible parts obscure the less accessible parts and therefore must be addressed first.

As we have seen, viewing and understanding any material has the effect of making it more "transparent".[1] This holds true whether the subject matter being viewed is one's case or, say, a foreign language. When I try to read a German book, my attention goes onto the written words that I see on the page and stops there. My relative lack of understanding of German makes the writing "opaque". As I improve my understanding of German, the words become more transparent. My attention penetrates the words, and the meanings begin to shine through. When I become a fluent reader of German, I am generally no longer conscious of the written words at all; I am not even aware that I am reading German. Rather, I just absorb the meaning "directly", as I do when I read English.

So it is with the Net. When I first address it, it seems that I can only penetrate its outside. My attention is fixed on the various upsets and other disturbances at its periphery. But as I examine and come to understand these disturbances, they begin to lose their opacity, and underlying incidents begin to make themselves evident. Eventually, as I attain greater and greater understanding of the Net, I can penetrate to its deeper regions (see Figure 45).

In reality, however, I am not located *outside* my Net but at its very *center*. The reason why disturbances are the first elements I can be aware of is that, being the most peripheral, they are the elements from which I am first capable of differentiating myself. While viewing disturbances, I am still failing to distinguish myself from the deeper elements of the Net. As I progress through the Curriculum, I become aware of and differentiate myself from deeper and deeper elements, so these begin to become apparent to me as well. Finally, I am able to differentiate myself from and view elements that are very close to the center. Not surprisingly, the closer we get to the core of the Net, the closer we get to the basic identities and characteristics of the person. At this level, we find "stacks", each stack being a series

---

1. See pp. 49-51.

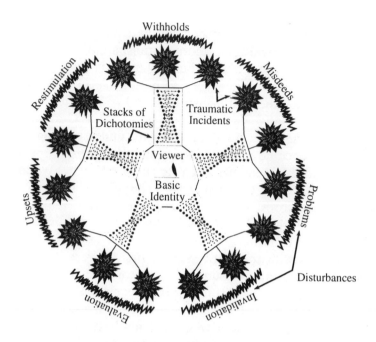

Figure 45. Layers of the Net

of pairs of opposing identities and purposes ("dichotomies") piled up on top of each other. It is on top of these basic structures that the entire edifice of the Net is built. By enabling the viewer to eliminate these stacks, we help him to eradicate the basis on which the Net rests and to become the stably happy, powerful, loving person he wants to be.

The curriculum can also be viewed as a way of addressing fixed or frozen "intention units", i.e., "charge". A person is in a less-than-optimal state largely because a large number of his intention units are trapped in various disturbances (such as upsets, worries, withholds, or misdeeds) or in past traumatic incidents. Personal power can be measured by the number of intention units one has available to spend. When intention units become trapped or frozen — as happens during traumatic incidents or when one is disturbed — one thereafter has fewer available intention units, hence less power.

Sections of the Curriculum

Since the Net is constructed in the same general way for all people, it can best be addressed by following an appropriate sequence of action, rather than by randomly trying to address elements of aberration or by only following the viewer's attention and interest. The General Curriculum used to address the Net is thus divided into sections. Each section is a preparation for later sections, so you must do them in proper order, completing each one to a point of major improvement before you move on to the next. What follows is a brief account of each section.[2]

The General Curriculum is divided into two major segments:

1. The Primary Curriculum
2. The Core Curriculum

The Primary Curriculum is called "Primary" because it is done first; the Core Curriculum is so called because it deals with matters that are very close to the core of a person's identity.

The Primary Curriculum

The Primary Curriculum starts with Stress Reduction and extends through the Rightness Section (see below, pp. 465-466). It is concerned with stripping away charge contained in the disturbances and traumatic incidents that form the outer part of the Net.

---

2. Detailed information on the curricular sections can be found in: F. Gerbode, *The General Facilitator Course*, IRM Press, Menlo Park, 1990.

Stress Reduction Section

The easiest thing for a person to confront is what she is *already* confronting. This is what lies at the periphery of the Net. Thus, in the first section of the Curriculum you do not attempt to direct the person's attention to issues she is not already concerned with. Instead, you take issues the viewer's attention is already on and reduce the charge so that she can release those issues (cease paying attention to them compulsively). Procedures used in Stress Reduction include Exploring, Unblocking, Remedial TIR, and Pre-Session Clearing procedures. But Stress Reduction may include any number of other procedures, including objective procedures, depending on the needs of the viewer and the knowledge and ingenuity of the technical director.

Help Section

Before the viewer is ready to embark on major actions that can provide permanent case change, it is crucial for her to handle any charge on the issues of help and control. Every viewing procedure involves both help and control. The viewer has to be able to both give and accept help and control before she can be properly engaged in viewing. The section contains a number of objective and subjective procedures which address these issues.

Recall Enhancement Section

The purpose of Recall Enhancement is to help the viewer recover the ability to contact her past easily. Objective and subjective procedures used in Stress Reduction and Help enabled her to contact the *present* with ease and to perform actions freely in the present. The next gradient is for her to learn to contact and handle the *past* with equal facility.

Communication Section

Recall Enhancement deals with non-traumatic incidents. The next four sections handle relatively light areas of charge — disturbances, not heavy traumas. They go one layer deeper into the Net. Once a viewer has established contact (in the Help Section) with her present, and (in Recall Enhancement) with her past, the next thing for her to do is to work on improving her contact with other people by addressing charge on the subject of communication. This, and the subsequent three sections of the Curriculum, are meant to give a very thoroughgoing handling of disturbances. As a result of doing these sections, the handling of disturbances obtained in Pre-Session Clearing and in Stress Reduction becomes more stable.

Enroute to a thorough handling of disturbances, we will find that communication is the key to resolving all difficulties, and the viewer's contacts with other people are usually what is most problematic for her. In dealing with disturbances, therefore, we start with a section that addresses communication and improves the viewer's ability to communicate. Communication comes first also because it is crucial that there be a clean and secure communication channel between the facilitator and the viewer.

Resolution Section

A person can begin to resolve problems when — and only when — he can communicate. Even if the viewer knows what the solution to a problem is, he generally cannot implement that solution without communicating with others. Most problems are best resolved by effective and thorough communication. Hence we address problems *after* addressing communication. It is important to deal with problems, because being fixed in a problem greatly inhibits future gain. That is why worries — problems in the here and now — are handled as a part of Pre-Session Clearing. And that is why a more thorough address to the whole area of problems is included as a major section of the Curriculum. As a result of doing this section, the viewer is much better able to resolve problems; he is no longer irresolute.

Reconciliation Section

When a person cannot forgive and achieve a reconciliation with himself or others after certain misdeeds have occurred, the result is guilt and hostility. Guilt and hostility mainly spring from a person's own misdeeds, which he has then withheld, or from charge connected with others' misdeeds. Here, we are dealing with two disturbances (withholds and misdeeds), which, if not handled definitively, will tend to recur at the start of each viewing session.

A person commits a misdeed when he has been unable to resolve a problem in a more constructive fashion. Unwanted situations, when encountered, must be handled in *some* way or other. Ideally, they are handled by confronting, understanding, and communicating, leading to a resolution of the problems contained therein that is optimal for all concerned. Being basically good, a person will naturally act in the best way he can for the good of all, but if he is weak in his ability to solve problems, he will feel "forced" to commit misdeeds. Therefore, handling misdeeds and the guilt connected with them is not optimal without first addressing problems. Completing this section should result in a major reconciliation, both with others and with oneself.

Resilience Section

People who are unable to communicate, to resolve problems, and thus to avoid committing misdeeds are more or less continually upset in life. Upsets are a third kind of disturbance that may need to be handled at the start of a session. People tend to get more upset at themselves than at anyone or anything else, and when they do, what upsets them the most is the fact of having committed misdeeds. Since people are basically good, when a person has committed misdeeds in a certain area it is difficult for him to remain in that area because he fears he will just continue to commit more misdeeds and continue to be upset with himself for hurting others. He therefore introduces a change of location or activity — he leaves the area.

Therefore the tendency to commit misdeeds must be handled before one's life can be stably free of upsets and before one can comfortably remain in one place for a period of time and thus avoid a major upsetting change. Handling of major upsets and change should therefore occur only *after* misdeeds, guilt, and hostility have been handled.

By the end of this section, the viewer has had a thoroughgoing disturbance handling and a release of lighter incidents. He should be stable and resilient — able to withstand change and upsets well and able to bounce back rapidly afterwards. Here, he comes to the end of that part of the Curriculum that concerns itself with the periphery of the Net, and he is ready to move closer to the core.

General TIR Section

The first step of moving closer to the core is to handle some of the root incidents on which the disturbances are based, i.e., to handle deep-seated traumatic incidents. We have seen that TIR can be used as a remedial action to handle charge contained in recent or already restimulated incidents. This is called Remedial TIR and forms part of Stress Reduction or of a case repair plan.[3] But after completing Remedial TIR, there still remain traumatic incidents and sequences that are *not* currently restimulated but that nevertheless use up intention units and *could* be restimulated at any time. When located and handled with General TIR, these are discharged and cannot be restimulated in the future.

Rightness Section

Up to this point, the viewer has been mainly dealing with "force" — uncomfortable feelings and disturbances that have been restimulated. Having handled a great deal of force at this point, she is better able to tackle significance without becoming embroiled in force. So she is ready to straighten out her belief system, i.e., her concepts and facts.

The viewer, like anyone else, is of the opinion that what she believes is right. Otherwise, she wouldn't believe it. But she can be *righter*. Wrongnesses can be caused by misconceptions, false information, or fixed ideas. This section addresses all three. Misconceptions are misinterpretations of written or spoken language. In the procedures called Word Clearing and Subject

---

3. See pp. 451-452, 462.

Clearing, we can trace down and correct misconceptions. By using Information Correction, it is possible to locate and correct false information.

Finally, because of pain, force, and confusion, a person has seized on certain ideas as aberrated cardinal points. These ideas are not changeable by reasoning alone because they are held in place by force — by an unwillingness or inability to confront certain things. All the work that has been done up to this point on the Primary Curriculum has eliminated enough force to permit the viewer to address fixed ideas directly. If fixed ideas are not explicitly addressed, they tend to remain in place just because she is used to them; they have become habitual and so remain, despite the fact that the factors that originally caused them to become fixed have been eliminated. In this section, the viewer becomes aware of what her fixed ideas *are* and acquires the ability to change her mind about them. The result of doing so is that the viewer is *actually* more right and doesn't need to *assert* her rightness so much.

The Core Curriculum

The Core Curriculum is the second part of the General Curriculum.[4] In a sense, the seven Sections that make up the Primary Curriculum are just a setup for the *real* work of handling issues at the core of the Net — core identities, and goals. Yet the viewer will realize major noticeable gains in life — almost as a "side-effect" of doing the Primary Curriculum.

---

4. The procedures used in the Core Curriculum are discussed in detail in Bill Nichols and Frank Gerbode, *The Unstacking Course*, IRM Press, Menlo Park, 1992. We will just give a brief sketch of them here.

Identity Section

At this point, the viewer has addressed various categories of disturbances, discharged a number of traumatic incidents, and handled some fixed ideas. Now she is ready to proceed to handle a deeper layer of the Net — the layer, quite close to herself, that has to do with identity and purposes. This section uses a procedure called "Unstacking" to deal with elements called "stacks" that lie at the very core of the Net.[5] These are sets of deep-seated but conflicting purposes and identities. The Identity Section identifies the basic identities and purposes in which a person is fixed and enables her to move out of them, as well as discharging the opposing identities and purposes. When all such fixed identities and purposes are discharged, a person is free to simply be herself and to pursue her true purposes.

Individuation Section

This section addresses beings or sub-personalities in and surrounding the viewer and her body with which the viewer may have confused herself. On completing this section, the viewer has succeeded in individuating herself from these other beings that are not herself.

Future Sections of the Curriculum

Future sections may include exercises that are closer to those found in the mystical traditions. These will be the subject of future research, although it is possible that reliable techniques already exist somewhere for enabling a suitably prepared viewer to achieve a state of enlightenment. Everything that has been done up to this point could be regarded as a preparation for this higher work.

---

5. This procedure was developed by Bill Nichols.

The Turning Point

In the course of his viewing, a person gradually eliminates more and more aberration and charge from her case. At the current state of our knowledge, it may be too much to ask to expect a viewer to be able to eliminate every scrap of charge and never again to have any form of aberration. Such an attainment, though theoretically possible, would be tantamount to the achievement of a high degree of sainthood, and no such saints have been created, at this writing.

It is commonly observed, however, that, at a certain point in a viewer's Curriculum, she will reach a Turning Point at which a marked change has occurred in her relationship to her case and in her view of her own identity. Prior to reaching this Turning Point, the viewer is susceptible to becoming immersed in her aberrations. At those times of immersion, while dramatizing or experiencing negative feelings she is unable to remain conscious of herself as a being separate from the aberration. Rather, she is *being* the aberration — *being* her case. After reaching the Turning Point, the viewer has attained the ability to be aware that her aberrated actions and negative feelings are coming from her case and are separate from her. This realization gives her a certain measure of control over her case, although not *total* control. Rather, the balance has shifted such that even when her case is restimulated she now has more control over her case than it has over her.

In summary, before the Turning Point, the viewer:

- Is liable to become completely immersed in her case.
- Is not generally aware that she is experiencing or manifesting aberration, when that, in fact, is what is occurring.
- Has no clear concept of herself as a being separate from her mind and her case.
- Is mostly the effect of her case when she is disturbed.

After the Turning Point, the viewer:

- Does not become completely immersed in her case.
- Is aware when she is manifesting or experiencing aberration.
- Has a clear concept of herself as a being separate from her mind and her case.
- Is mostly causative over her case, even when disturbed.

Although after the Turning Point the viewer is able to do all the types of viewing actions of which he was capable before, he is now able to do other viewing actions that were previously impossible for him. After the Turning Point, the viewer can maintain a separate viewpoint even when encountering charged material. He is therefore capable of solo viewing, in which he must alternately play the role of facilitator and viewer. Case influences are no longer likely to distract or sidetrack him from what he is doing in a session. Under certain circumstances it is still better to receive facilitation from another, but he *is* capable of solo viewing.

Having reached the Turning Point also enables a viewer to deal more easily with the issue of individuation, since he now has a clearer conception of who he is and who he isn't. He probably cannot do a fully adequate job in the Individuation Section until he has reached the Turning Point.

A viewer may reach the Turning Point at *any* point in his Curriculum,. You will have noticed, however, that the Curriculum is laid out in such a way that the issue of identity is addressed near the top. The likelihood is that if the viewer does not reach the Turning Point early on, he will have by the time he completes the Rightness Section. If not, he can always reach the Turning Point on another cycle through the Primary Curriculum.[6]

Undoubtedly, the General Curriculum will evolve as we gain more experience with it and make further advances in metapsychological knowledge. Nevertheless, as it stands, the General Curriculum provides an excellent preparation for the exploration

---

6. See below, pp. 474-475, for a discussion of cycling through the Curriculum.

of the more "spiritual" side of life, or of *any* aspect of life. If one
has a command of basic abilities like communication and
problem-solving, and if one is free from restimulation, then one
can pursue *any* future ability in an unhampered manner. One
cannot effectively pursue "spiritual awareness" without a clear,
quiet mind with which to do so. A more or less continuous state
of turbidity — anxiety, hostility, worry, or psychosomatic illness
— is incompatible with such a pursuit. Such mundane problems
cannot simply be bypassed or ignored, as some spiritual or therapeutic disciplines have tried to do. Contrary to the myth that
exists in the minds of some, suffering, pain and aberration do not
enhance knowledge or awareness — quite the reverse. They can
and should be thoroughly addressed and eradicated.

Clearing and Discovery

There are two basic kinds of viewing — clearing and discovery:

> **Definition**: Clearing consists of viewing actions taken to
> destimulate, deactivate or discharge material that is
> already inadvertently or accidently restimulated or
> activated in life or in session. The end point of clearing
> is a viewer who is clear (free of disturbances) and ready
> to move on to his next discovery action.

> **Definition**: Discovery consists of viewing actions that
> selectively address, explore, and reduce charge in
> currently unrestimulated or inactive areas of disability.

The major focus of clearing is to destimulate, deactivate or
discharge *existing* restimulation — restimulation that exists right
now. Discovery begins when a viewer is clear. Its major function
is to selectively restimulate and address specific areas of his
world, handling each area fully before going on to the next, in
order to enhance his ability and reduce the likelihood or magnitude of future disturbances in that area.

Corrective and Curricular Actions

Ideally, a person will simply move smoothly through the major actions of her Curriculum and become more and more able as she attains the end point of each. In practice, various events can derail her from a smooth progression through the sections. When such an event occurs, the situation needs to be addressed and handled so that she can return to her Curriculum.

The need to clear disturbances at the beginning of a session occasions one such "detour", usually a brief one. Other detours can be more lengthy. While a viewer is engaged, say, in the Communication Section, some major area of her life may suddenly emerge as a massive difficulty. Perhaps she gets sick or experiences a major trauma or loss, or perhaps some error occurs in viewing and needs to be corrected — a heavily-charged sequence that is incompletely handled or an important procedure that is carried on past its proper end point. When such things happen, one cannot simply forge ahead with normal curricular actions. In fact, a new case plan may need to be worked out to handle the obtruding situation, if it is a major one.

There is, therefore, another way of dividing up viewing actions — into *corrective* actions (or remedies) and *curricular* actions:

> **Definition**: A corrective action is an action taken to handle unforeseen errors or difficulties that make it necessary to take a detour from an individual Curriculum. The end point of a corrective action is a viewer who has handled the error or difficulty and is ready to move on to her next curricular action. Corrective actions are sometimes called "remedies".

> **Definition**: A curricular action is an action or procedure that is part of a general or individual Curriculum.

Most corrective actions are clearing actions, and most curricular actions are discovery actions, although there are exceptions on both sides. Stress reduction, for instance, is mainly a clearing action but it is also a curricular action. And a viewing program designed to handle a current difficulty might contain discovery actions, as well as clearing actions.

Following the Viewer's Attention

A cardinal rule of facilitation is that, if the viewer's attention is already fixed on some topic, he must handle that topic before addressing other matters. In other words, all necessary *corrective* actions must be done first, before *curricular* actions can proceed. If some error or difficulty has arisen, it will continue to distract the viewer until it is corrected. Also, all necessary *clearing* must be done before one engages in *discovery*. The purpose of clearing is to handle enough charge to unfix the viewer's attention from already restimulated material so that he can view the appropriate discovery material.

Suppose a viewer — midway through working on the section of his Curriculum that has to do with problems — is visited by a hostile relative and has a major asthmatic attack. If the facilitator tries to plough ahead with *curricular* procedures designed to handle confusions the viewer has concerning his career, the viewer will not be able to handle those confusions because his attention is fixed on his asthma and on his relationship with the hostile relative. So the viewing session will be fruitless. In this case, the technical director must first formulate a corrective plan to handle the asthma and the relationship with the relative before returning to the issue of problems connected to the viewer's career. This plan will undoubtedly include viewing, but there might be a need for the viewer to take certain other steps as well, such as obtaining medical treatment or getting into communication with the hostile relative and establishing some guidelines. When the situation is improved, the asthma gone, and the viewer's attention freed from the hostile relative and the asthma, he can go back to considering his confusions about his career.

Certain procedures, such as correction lists or simple retrospection[7], tend to be used as corrective actions; others, such as TIR, tend to be used as curricular actions. But there is no hard-and-fast rule about this. Sometimes TIR will greatly enhance a corrective plan; it can be a highly effective way of clearing a heavy disturbance. Correction lists or simple retrospective procedures can be used as part of a discovery plan to find new (not currently restimulated) material to handle. The same procedure can thus be used sometimes as a remedy and sometimes as a curricular action. In general:

Clearing actions destimulate, deactivate or discharge restimulated traumas and sequences, whereas

Discovery actions *activate* and then discharge currently unrestimulated traumas and sequences, as a way of eradicating aberration and preventing future disturbances, and

Corrective actions are intended to handle an immediate error or difficulty, whereas

Curricular actions are intended to provide long-term improvement.

Of course, if a clearing procedure results in discharge, it may also prevent future restimulation. A simple remedy can often have profound and permanent effects.

---

7. See later in this chapter (p. 489, 507-508) for a description of these procedures.

Cycling Through the Curriculum

In learning a skill, regardless of one's level of proficiency, one can always benefit from a review of basics. Even the greatest of musicians continue to practice basic exercises on a daily basis, and the same principle can apply to viewing. It is often advantageous for a viewer to "cycle through" various curricular sections, to revisit them at various times. Having achieved a certain ability to communicate, a viewer, say, goes on to do further discovery in the area of problems, hostility and guilt, upsets, and fixed ideas. Then, having eliminated a certain amount of charge and repression, she may become aware of charged areas having to do with communication of which she was previously unaware. With this new awareness, she can now redo some of the communication procedures and attain an even greater ability to communicate than before. Then, with an improved ability to communicate, she can take a deeper look at problems, and so forth.

Viewers sometimes become preoccupied with issues of status. This has been referred to as "spiritual materialism".[8] She may come to see higher ability as merely another possession, like a house or a car. The danger of spiritual materialism is greatest when the steps a person is supposed to take enroute to the final attainment are conceived of as absolute or permanent, i.e., when the progression is conceived as linearly "upward". Some viewers have become overly impressed with themselves or with others for having reached a "higher section" of the Curriculum. A concern for status generally indicates that a viewer is not getting adequate gains from what she is doing because if she *were* experiencing such gains, she would be mainly interested in using her new-found abilities, instead of being interested in the formality of having "attained a state".[9]

---

8. Trungpa, C. *Cutting Through Spiritual Materialism* (Shambhala, Boston, 1973).
9. A concern for status should probably be included as a "bad indicator". A person who has obtained a pilot's license but is a poor pilot will be reluctant

The cyclic approach to the Curriculum minimizes the issue of status because a person may start at any level of ability or reach any level of ability and still benefit from *all* the sections of her Curriculum. The fact of her being on a certain section of her Curriculum says nothing about her ability level. It only indicates what she is currently working on. It is true that if a person is doing relatively well, say, on the subject of communication and does not have a great interest in addressing the subject right now, it is permissible to skip that section and move on. But it is necessary to keep in mind the fact that the person will have an opportunity to cycle back through that section at a later date, so the fact of having skipped a section has no status implications. Simply stated, the end point of any section is a major improvement in ability or freedom with respect to the subject matter of the section.

Pre-Session Clearing

The action of pre-session clearing plays a part in a number of psychological techniques, and various methods have been advocated for handling the "day residue", "transference", and the like. In "Focusing",[10] the focuser is taught to examine each of the items that are currently bothering him, "being with them", not to dive into them, but to "clear a space" in which to work. Gendlin compares this action to that of making a "to-do list".

---

to fly. The only value the license will have for her is that of a status symbol. We have encountered this type of person in Chapter Six, as a "phony", pp. 321-323. Such a person may have a bumper-sticker that says, "I'd rather be flying," but, of course that's a lie. She'd rather drive around and show off the bumper sticker. A competent pilot simply goes out and enjoys flying.

10. See Gendlin, Eugene T. *Focusing* (Bantam Books, New York, 1982), for an account of this excellent technique.

This comparison is particularly apropos when we consider that restimulation creates a form of incomplete receptive cycle: one is given an opportunity to become aware of some repressed material and has a choice of either adding another repression on top of it or confronting the whole thing right now. But there is a third choice: to make a note of it so that one will neither have to keep it in mind nor lose track of it entirely. Although this action does not handle the charge in the repressed material, it prevents a further buildup of charge on the subject and tends to result in a feeling of relief, a feeling of being at least somewhat in control of the situation. And, of course, it allows hope that the subject *will* be fully handled in the future. It is a way of indicating that some charge has been left behind, instead of repressing the fact. Many other therapies employ a "progressive relaxation" technique to similarly "clear the air". In some cases, pre-session clearing can become the entire therapy, as in certain permissive techniques such as free association and other non-directive approaches, where the therapist just continues to follow the attention of the client wherever it leads. These techniques can be beneficial, but they do not penetrate as deeply nor as quickly into the core of a person's case as does clearing, when combined with subsequent discovery.

Procedures for Pre-Session Clearing

In this section, I shall again take the liberty of addressing you, the reader, as a potential or actual facilitator. Before starting the agenda for a session, you ensure that the viewer's attention is not fixed on present-time upsets, problems, withholds, misdeeds, or traumatic incidents. Often a simple, informal question, like "How are you doing?" or "How have things been going?" will elicit this information. An experienced facilitator can often tell whether the viewer is disturbed or clear by observing his physical appearance. And a meter can also be very helpful in this regard. If the viewer has good indicators and a free needle, he is probably clear, and there is no need to do any pre-session clearing: he is already ready to handle the session agenda. Anything short of free needle and very good indicators means that one or more disturbances are probably present and need to be cleared.[11]

As mentioned above (pp. 349-350, 400-403), disturbances fall into the following categories:

1. Upsets
2. Worries
3. Withholds
4. Misdeeds

Facilitators can and should be trained to spot various good and bad indicators and take the appropriate actions.

At the start of the session, if the viewer is not clear (with a free needle and very good indicators), but it is not obvious what the disturbance is and the viewer does not volunteer it, you must *find* what it is. In the presence of turbidity, *no further progress can be made until it is cleared.* Ignorance of this fact has caused many therapeutic hours to be wasted.[12] If the viewer is upset, worried, or in the grip of a stuck traumatic incident, trying to address anything else is a waste of time. You must handle the disturbances first,[13] and they need to be handled in a definite order. Obviously, if a person is locked into a traumatic incident, you handle that first. Next, you handle any upsets — especially if the viewer is upset with *you*.

---

11. Other reasons for not having a free needle and very good indicators at the beginning of session, such as tiredness, drugs, or hunger, should have been checked for and handled before starting the session.
12. Freud recognized the counter-productiveness of secrets and tried to handle it by making it a rule that one was to say everything that came into one's mind and not hold anything back.
13. This is true, incidentally, of *any* activity involving communication and interpersonal relationships. In the presence of problems, upsets, or withholds, it is very difficult to attend fully to some other activity, and the quality of one's performance and communication suffers as a result. Therefore, people whose disturbances have been cleared are at a great advantage in their personal relationships.

Handling Upsets and Worries

As we have seen (pp. 225-235), there is a close relationship between affection and communication. If a person is upset, her affection is down, and she will tend to be uncommunicative. Upset people are often silent. But the process of viewing is very dependent on the presence of an excellent communication channel between the facilitator and the viewer. Any upset tends to block this channel and therefore hinders the viewing process. In the presence of an upset, the only topic the viewer can talk about readily and with benefit is the upset itself. The communion between you and the viewer, if jeopardized, must be re-established immediately. So check for an upset first. If you are using a meter, keep an eye on it while asking whether there is an upset — and when getting a reply — in order to pick up any response.[14] If the viewer does have an upset, get him to tell you about it, to say what the upset was. Often, just a brief description, acknowledged without evaluation, will cause a deactivation, as evidenced by a free needle and good indicators. But if there is no free needle and good indicators, simply ask (as in TIR) for an earlier similar upset, and have the viewer describe that. This process of asking for earlier similar incidents (simple retrospection) continues until a free needle and good indicators are present:

Definition: Simple retrospection is the action of describing an incident or item, then tracing it back to earlier similar incidents or items, giving a simple description of each. Unlike TIR, it does not involve running through

14. If there is no response and the viewer says, "No" or is not sure, then it is safe to assume that there is no upset. If there *is* a response and the viewer is not sure, you can follow it up by asking whether the viewer had a thought when the question was asked. If the viewer cannot find an upset yet the meter responded, ask whether it was a false response or a protest (all the while keeping an eye on the meter) and get an answer to *that* question.

past incidents or contacting the same incident repetitively, nor does it involve a series of steps. It simply involves description, followed by finding an earlier similar incident or item, until an end point occurs (usually a free needle and good indicators and often a realization).

Occasionally, a viewer will volunteer two or more upsets. You note the relative magnitude of the meter response to each and the degree of interest in each and handle them by simple retrospection in decreasing order of liveness.[15]

When the upset or upsets are handled, if the viewer does not have very good indicators, "sobers up", starts to experience negative feelings, or cannot find an upset to handle, check for a current *worry*. A worry is handled by simple retrospection, in exactly the same way as an upset.

Handling Withholds

Next, if necessary, ask whether there is a withhold. Here, you are looking for a piece of knowledge that the viewer wishes to withhold from others because it seems dangerous in some way to reveal it. In handling such withholds make sure you get a full and complete description of what is being withheld without falling into the role of an interrogator. Check to make sure nothing is left out in the viewer's description. The presumption is that, if you have done a good job in establishing a safe space, the viewer will be willing to tell you everything she knows, so your attitude

---

15. Don't "pump" the viewer for more upsets after she has handled those that are immediately available. The purpose of pre-session clearing (or clearing of any kind) is to handle what the viewer *already* has her attention on, rather than to put her attention on something else. The latter course is followed in discovery, not in clearing.

should be that you are helping the viewer to become *aware* of the totality of the withheld information, not forcing her to tell something she does not want to tell.

Often a viewer is so concerned with hiding something from others that she hides it, at least partially, from herself as well. You are helping her reverse this repression by creating a safe space. If she does know something and is genuinely unwilling to tell you, then it can be assumed that you have failed to make it safe for her to do so. If you do not get a full description, some repressed material may be left behind, and an upset will almost certainly occur, sooner or later. When all the information is out in the open, inquire whether anyone might have found out about it or should have known about it.[16] Like upsets and worries, withholds are handled with simple retrospection.

A similar procedure is used in handling misdeeds, except that you ask the viewer (if it is not obvious) whether the misdeed is also withheld. Misdeeds are commonly, though not necessarily, withheld. If the misdeed is also withheld, you handle it as a withhold. Otherwise, you handle it with simple retrospection alone.

All pre-session clearing procedures are carried to a free needle and good indicators.[17]

Special Clearing Procedures

When you have handled all of the disturbances, the viewer should be clear, with a free needle and very good indicators, and ready to start the session agenda. But if you have diligently tried to handle the viewer's turbidity, and he remains unready to start the session, being preoccupied with some disturbance that pre-session clearing is not handling, you might need to do a special

---

16. This action will pick up times when the withhold was *restimulated*.

17. Besides the simple clearing procedures described here, there are also more advanced clearing procedures that require the use of an electrodermometer.

correction procedure. Or you might have to end the session and work out a new agenda. Don't try to work out a new agenda *during* the session — especially if things are not going well — because you may not be able to think clearly enough to come up with a good one under pressure. It is better to take a break and sort it out in your own space and time or get advice or supervision from the technical director (if you work with one). Then you can start a new session with an agenda designed to handle the specific difficulty that came up.

If a session agenda consists of a special remedy to handle a known recent difficulty in viewing or in life, then the facilitator need not launch into clearing at the start of the session. The session agenda itself is intended to handle the disturbance. So, on the assumption that the viewer is *bound* to have his attention on the difficulty in question, the facilitator does the specific remedy designed to handle it. When the remedy (such as a correction list) is completed, the viewer should be clear and ready for a major action. That is the proper end point of a remedy. If the viewer does not have a free needle and very good indicators or if he is not ready to carry on with a major action, then he needs additional clearing.

Types of Viewing Procedures

Many different viewing procedures have been found useful in helping another person improve the quality of her life. In order to talk about them intelligently, we need to be able to classify them. First, however, I would like to make a few general comments, by way of leading up to a suitable definition of "procedure". To start with, I will again resort to a computer analogy. Just as a person has a small number of very basic abilities that can be used in an infinite number of ways, so a computer has a very small number of fundamental actions that can be put together to construct programs. These "basic" actions of a computer are contained in a "basic instruction set" that contains the most primitive instructions that can be programmed into the computer, the simplest actions we can ask the computer to do. In an ordinary computer, these vary in number from a handful to several hundreds. The art of programming a computer consists in combining these basic actions in various patterns to produce a desired result.

One combines very basic actions to form basic procedures; then one combines these basic procedures in various ways to form "higher level" procedures, and so on. In order to understand what a computer can really do, one must know what the basic actions of a computer are. In understanding a person, one must know what *her* basic actions are.

What is a Procedure?

A procedure contains one or more actions. It consists of actually *doing* something.[18] The simple act of boiling water, for example, is a procedure consisting of several lower-level actions:

BOILING

1. Put water in a pot.
2. Put the pot on a burner.
3. Turn on the burner.
4. Wait until large bubbles start coming to the surface of the water.
5. STOP. (The boiling water is in the pot.)

I can now offer a definition of "procedure" that will help provide a useful classification:

---

18. It is possible, however, to conceive of a "null procedure" consisting of doing nothing, comparable to a "no-operation" computer instruction. Null procedures are used in various meditative practices. It is rather paradoxical to think of doing something that consists of doing nothing, but then some disciplines (particularly Eastern ones) do not seem to mind paradoxes.

Definition: A <u>procedure</u> is a pattern of purposeful actions, using objects of various types, involving a specific set of locations and directionalities, with one or more attainable end points.

We can classify procedures by type of:

1. Purpose
2. Pattern
3. Action
4. Object
5. Location
6. Directionality
7. End Point

Although a person is certainly not a machine, she can, like a computer, perform certain basic actions. It is through patterns and combinations of these basic actions that she does everything she does. Viewing procedures, like finger exercises on a piano or bowing exercises on a violin, tend to exercise *basic* actions, rather than complex "higher order" actions. An improvement in more *basic* abilities has a more generally beneficial effect on a person's world than an improvement in highly *specialized* abilities. A coach might improve a person's ability to play tennis, but that specialized ability is not easily generalizable to other areas of life. Improving a person's ability to *perceive*, however, has much more far-ranging effects on many aspects of her life — including her tennis game!

Basic Components of Viewing Procedures

The classification of viewing procedures follows the *basic* actions and characteristics of a person's world, since viewing is meant to have far-ranging, general effects on a person's life,

There is no limit, theoretically, to the number of viewing procedures that could be developed using different patterns and combinations of actions, objects, locations, directionalities, and end points.

Patterns currently used in viewing procedures are:

1. Simple action
2. Repetition
3. Loop
4. Retrospection
5. Checklist
6. Combinations of the above.

A simple action consists of only one step, such as "Think a thought." A repetition consists of repeating a pattern. The pattern repeated may be a single action — as in asking the viewer repeatedly to "Think a thought" — or any of the above patterns. When the pattern repeated is a checklist, then we have a loop, as in procedures that have a pattern like "A,B,C,D,A,B...". Retrospection is the act of repeatedly going backward in time, as in TIR and pre-session clearing procedures.

Actions demanded of the viewer in a session consist of some of the most basic actions of which he is capable:

1. Finding
2. Perceiving
3. Reviewing
4. Describing
5. Comparing
6. Listing
7. Selecting
8. Conceiving
9. Picturing
10. Postulating
11. Physical motion

Objects addressed in viewing include all the basic components of experience:

1. People and identities
2. Intentions and actions
3. Phenomena
4. Concepts

   5.   Facts

Locations used in viewing procedures include:

1.   Position (in various spatial locations)
2.   Tense
      a.   In the past
      b.   In the present
      c.   In the future
3.   Objectivity
      a.   In the mind (subjective)
      b.   In the physical universe (objective)

Directionalities include:

1.   Spatial (forward, backward, etc.)
2.   Temporal
      a.   Toward the past (includes retrospection)
      b.   Toward the here and now
      c.   Toward the future
3.   Polar
      a.   Creation (from person to world)
      b.   Reception (from world to person)

End points encountered include:

1.   No Change
2.   Release
3.   Discharge
4.   A disability or unwanted condition gone or diminished.
5.   An ability gained or improved.
6.   Procedure-specific end points.

These end points are manifested in various ways, such as by the presence of a free needle, very good indicators, realizations, a high level on the Emotional Scale, disappearance of unwanted feelings, and improved perception. Remedies and light procedures, like those used in clearing disturbances, tend to have fairly "mild" end points whereas major procedures are expected to have more major end points. Some procedures have very specific end points; most have only the more general ones given in (2) through (4), above.

A Classification of Viewing Procedures

Of all the possible ways of classifying the many viewing procedures, it seems best to make an initial division into **subjective** and **objective** procedures:

Definition: Objective procedures are viewing procedures that are directed toward physical objects and the physical universe.

Definition: Subjective procedures are viewing procedures that are directed toward mental objects and the mind.

These definitions divide procedures with respect to the **location** of their objects.

It is useful to make a second division of procedures into **creative** and **receptive** procedures. This division uses the criterion of **directionality** in the polar dimension (the dimension that extends between the person and his world):

Definition: Creative procedures are viewing procedures that require the viewer to perform *creative* actions, to create effects in his world.

Definition: Receptive procedures are viewing procedures that require the viewer to perform *receptive* actions, to perceive and understand his world.

Viewing procedures can therefore be classified as follows:

1. Subjective procedures
    a. Receptive subjective procedures
    b. Creative subjective procedures

2. Objective procedures
   a. Receptive objective procedures
   b. Creative objective procedures

Receptive Subjective Procedures

Receptive subjective procedures are designed to increase the viewer's degree of insight into, and understanding of, his past and his mind. Traumatic incident reduction is a typical example of such a procedure; procedures involving simple recall of past incidents are another. These procedures improve a person's ability to perceive, interpret, and understand parts of his subjective world. In making this improvement in his subjective vision, his view of the objective world will also improve. For instance, by viewing past incidents and getting rid of charge contained in them, a person attains a sharper perception of his present surroundings.

Creative Subjective Procedures

Creative subjective procedures exercise the viewer's ability to conceive and picture. Often, such procedures are useful in "taking over" automatisms — specifically, fixed ideas and phenomena stemming from the Net. If a person is compulsively recreating traumatic scenes from the past, *causative* creation of the same pictures can help her to regain control of her own world. This technique is used in some forms of cognitive therapy.[19] A fixed destructive pattern of thought can also be "taken over" by creative conceiving. The procedure "Invent something worse than

---

19. Beck, Aaron T., M.D. "Role of Fantasies in Psychotherapy and Psychopathology" *J. Nerv. Ment. Dis.* Vol. 150 #1 (1970), pp. 3-17.

_____ ", (filled in with something the viewer is fixated on as a bad thing) can have beneficial results when run repetitively at the appropriate point in the viewer's case plan.

Receptive Objective Procedures

Many objective procedures can be used outside a viewing session as exercises rather than as viewing actions. Receptive objective procedures used in viewing include those designed to bring the viewer's attention into the here and now and to increase her ability to be aware of the present-time world. These are called "locational procedures"; they mainly exercise the ability to find, to perceive, and to describe.

Creative Objective Procedures

Creative objective procedures mainly exercise the ability to control or move the body or other physical objects in various ways.[20] Like the subjective creative procedures, many of these involve breaking down or "taking over" automatisms — but *physical* rather than mental ones.

Some procedures fall in between subjective and objective and in between creative and receptive because they contain combinations of some or all of these elements. A procedure may involve both physical objects and mental objects or states. "Look around here and find something you could have affinity for", used repetitively, requires the viewer to be aware of her emotional level while at the same time locating a physical object. Or a procedure

---

20. Various martial arts procedures, sports, and physical exercises of other kinds (such as Hatha Yoga) are creative objective procedures. Though not part of viewing, they can be quite beneficial on their own or as adjuncts to viewing.

may involve perception combined with picturing or conceiving, as in the procedure that consists of a repetitive alternation of:

Notice that [room object].

with

What bad scene isn't that [room object] a part of?

Many different permutations and combinations can and do occur, but the above classification is useful.

Patterns of Viewing Procedures

Viewing procedures are put together in various patterns; they are never done randomly or arbitrarily. Apart from the content of the procedures or the objects with which they deal, the patterns themselves tend to have specific beneficial effects.

Retrospection

In my description of TIR (pp. 433-452), I have already given a good example of one type of pattern: retrospection. Retrospective procedures move backward in time along lines of similarity. A facilitator, using a retrospective procedure, asks the viewer to find earlier similar incidents or items. Because of the structure of the Net, systematic retrospection is an especially fruitful pattern to use.

Exploring and Inquiring

These are very informal techniques that can be used either to gather data about or reduce some charge from a topic that is of concern to the viewer. They have been discussed in detail in Chapter Eight, pp. 421-423. All other viewing techniques except Exploring and Inquiring are very tightly patterned.

Repetition

Apart from retrospection, the most common pattern used in viewing is repetition. Although deceptively simple, repetition is an extraordinarily powerful technique, when used with no duress and in a very safe environment. Repetition allows an action which if done only once would have a very superficial effect, to achieve a profound one. If a person wants to clean up a littered yard, just one iteration of the action: "Pick up a piece of paper and put it in the trash," will not create much of an improvement. But if this action is done repetitively, she will eventually have a clean yard. This characteristic is paralleled in repetitive handling of *mental* conditions.[21] A simple question like: "What could you say to me?", if asked once, has no great effect. But if it is asked many times — perhaps over a period of half an hour or an hour — it can have an astonishingly beneficial effect. The viewer feels increasingly safe about speaking as she perceives that no bad consequences arise when she says something.[22] Also, answering each question requires the viewer to take a fresh look at the subject, and her insight into that subject characteristically becomes increasingly more profound as she finds more and more insightful answers to the question.

To what does repetition owe its power? Repetition has different effects, depending on what is being repeated. Used in training, it helps a person acquire a skill. Repeating an action

---

21. The parallel is not totally exact, because in a repetitive subjective procedure, the viewer does not simply eliminate a certain number of individual items of psychological "garbage", but rather tends to penetrate more and more deeply into the core of her case. She moves "vertically" as well as "horizontally".

22. This assumes, of course, that the facilitator refrains from evaluating or invalidating anything the viewer says and limits herself only to acknowledging and repeating the question. It also assumes that the facilitator listens to, understands, and acknowledges any communication originated by the viewer.

many times seems to establish a habit pattern that can then be made automatic, or incorporated in an identity of a person. But although repetition *establishes* a non-aberrated habit pattern (skill), it can also *break* an already established aberrated habit pattern (automatism). If you can get a person to do self-determinedly and repeatedly something that was an automatism, the automatism eventually breaks down, temporarily or permanently. To illustrate this point, try the following:

Exercise 21. Taking Over a Habit

a. Pick out a nervous habit you have, especially one that you are currently engaged in, such as chewing your lip, wiggling your feet, or humming a tune — or wait to do this exercise until you notice you are doing something of the sort.
b. Notice exactly what you are doing.
c. Do it a few times deliberately.
d. Note what happens to the compulsion to do it.

Thus, conscious repetition *establishes* a skill and *destroys* an automatism. In either case, repetition is beneficial.

Of course, I must reiterate that if force, pain, or duress is involved in the repetition or if the repetition is not being done completely willingly then the opposite occurs. A repetition done under stress causes a sequence of similar traumatic incidents to be formed. The person becomes less skilled, less willing and able to act in the area, and he is *conditioned* into an automatism instead of *learning* a skill.

A safe space, a willing viewer, and complete absence of duress are essential prerequisites to successfully using repetitive procedures — or *any* viewing procedures. The viewer may experience various degrees of discomfort during the repetition — may experience boredom, frustration, and other negative feelings. That is to be expected, because most procedures cause a selective restimulation of parts of the Net before reducing the charge in those areas. But any degree of genuine unwillingness on the part of the viewer will change a procedure from beneficial to harmful.

Although an automatism is something that the viewer appears to be *doing*, he considers it to be something that is just *happening* without his awareness or control. When a person wiggles his leg nervously or compulsively interrupts others, he is generally not aware of doing so. To him, it seems to be happening "automatically".

One way in which automatisms may arise is as an attempt to resolve an incongruity between two intentions. A person may "resolve" such a conflict by taking responsibility for only one side of the conflict and repressing the other, regarding it as something alien or as something that is "happening" to him. A person who is in conflict about taking a drink may "resolve" that conflict by repressing the "side" of him that wants to take a drink, identifying with the side that wants to stop drinking, and saying that he is "compelled" to drink against his will. A person who is in conflict about a relationship and does not take responsibility for that part of the conflict that causes him to want to stay in that relationship may state that he feels "trapped" in the relationship.

I have mentioned incongruity as one form of "intrinsic" or "primary" pain or aversion.[23] Freud viewed intrapsychic conflict as *the* source of repression:

> "All these [repressed] experiences had involved the emergence of a wishful impulse which was in sharp contrast to the subject's other wishes and which proved incompatible with the ethical and aesthetic standards of the personality. There had been a short conflict, and the end of this internal struggle was that the idea which had appeared before consciousness as the vehicle of this irreconcilable wish fell a victim to repression, was pushed out of consciousness with all its attached memories and was forgotten. Thus the incompatibility of the wish in question with the patient's ego was the motive for the repression; the subject's ethical and other standards were the repressing forces."[24]

---

23. See pp. 295-298.

Many contemporary forms of therapy such as Gestalt and Hakomi use specific techniques to enable the client to become aware of and bring to expression the side of the conflict that is normally repressed, instead of, say, "sublimating" it into an altered, socially acceptable form, as Freud suggested. Perls[25] and Moreno[26] use alternate role-playing and other techniques to accomplish this purpose. Hakomi therapy uses an interesting variation of "taking over", in that the therapist takes over — often *physically* — the side of the conflict with which the client has identified himself.[27] If the client is trying to hold in his feelings by some physical motion (such as a tense posture), the therapist (sometimes with an assistant) "takes over" the tension that is holding back the feelings. She "helps" the client hold back the feeling by exerting the physical tension *for* him. By aiding the client's defenses, she makes it safe for the client to experience the other side of the conflict — the one normally defended against. Similar effects are created by the Interactionalists in their use of symptom-prescription.[28] In the latter practice, it is assumed that the symptom exists to hold back some opposing impulse. When the therapist tells the client to do the "automatic" action that is the symptom, the client gains control over it, because the ability to do something also entails the ability *not* to do it. By *doing* something, one acquires the ability to stop. Beck, for instance, has shown that by having a person causatively create pictures that have been "on automatic", the person can be helped to regain

24. Freud, Sigmund *Two Short Accounts of Psycho-Analysis* Translated by James Strachey (Penguin Books, Singapore, 1984) pp. 48-9.
25. Perls, F.C. *The Gestalt Approach* (Science and Behavior Books, Ben Lomond CA, 1973) p.93f.
26. Moreno, J.L. *Psychodrama* (Beacon House, 1970).
27. Kurtz, Ron *Hakomi Therapy* (Hakomi Institute, Boulder, CO 1985) Ch. 16, pp. 8-16.
28. See Weakland, J.H., Fisch, R., Watzlawick, P., and Bodin, A. "Brief Therapy: Focused Problem Resolution", in Watzlawick, P. and Weakland, Eds. *The Interactional View* (Norton, New York, 1977) p. 290f.

control over these pictures or fantasies.[29] "Desensitization" may work for similar reasons, although a different rationale has been given by behavior therapists for its workability.[30]

When one runs a repetitive viewing procedure like: "What could you say to me?", one is likely, at first, to get "automatic" or "social" responses, like "Hi!", or "It's a nice day." Then, because of the repetition, these socially conditioned responses and thought patterns break down and the person begins to *really* look at the possible things she could communicate. Eventually — if each of her answers is simply acknowledged and none is either evaluated or invalidated — she realizes that she is able and willing to say a wide variety of things. Some moment of "breakthrough" in her thinking will occur, and she will have a realization, very good indicators, and a reduction of charge.[31]

29. Beck, Aaron T., M.D. "Role of Fantasies in Psychotherapy and Psychopathology" *J. Nerv. Ment. Dis.* Vol. 150 #1 (1970), pp. 3-17.

30. Wolpe, Joseph *The Practice of Behavior Therapy* (Pergamon Press, New York, 1969).

31. Repetition is not the only way to break down cognitive and emotional automatisms. Another method, "Focusing", is beautifully described by Gendlin [Gendlin, Eugene T. *Focusing* (Bantam Books, New York, 1982).]. In Focusing, it is not repetition but continuous and patient contact with, and perception of, an area that leads to the breakthrough. In Hakomi therapy [Kurtz, Ron *Hakomi Therapy* (Hakomi Institute, Boulder CO, 1985).], Morita therapy [Reynolds, D.K. *Playing Ball on Running Water* (Quill, New York, 1984).], Gerdieffian "self-observation" [Tart, C. *Waking Up* (New Science Library, Boston, 1986).], and others, a similar use of "mindfulness" — patient and unhurried "pure" observation — occurs, with similar effects. In Gendlin's schema, one observes the area being worked on by trying to get the "felt sense" of the area. One then tries to find a verbal "handle" — a verbal expression that captures the essence of the felt sense — by "staying with" the felt sense until the proper descriptive word or phrase occurs. This "handle" is then verified by comparing it to (allowing it to "resonate" with) the felt sense. At a certain point, after all the automatic thoughts and responses have been allowed to die away, a breakthrough occurs and one gets a physical reaction, a "body shift", with a sense of relief, some sort of realization, and a generally good feeling. This description sounds quite close to what I have presented as the usual end point of a procedure: a realization and very good indicators. In viewing, the "body shift" is manifested by the presence of a free needle. At the end of his book, Gendlin states that a biofeedback device would be useful in detecting the

Often, it is not a single action that is repeated but two or more actions. Two actions may be repetitively alternated, as in:

"What could you confront?"
"What would you rather not confront?"

Such alternate-repetitive procedures allow the viewer to compare two different things or look at two or more sides of an issue repetitively, or sometimes to consider different "flows", as in the repetition of a multistep progression:

1. Tell me something another would enjoy about you.
2. Tell me something you would enjoy about another.
3. Tell me something others would enjoy about others.
4. Tell me something you would enjoy about yourself.

These are run in a loop: 1, 2, 3, 4, 1, 2, 3, 4, etc., to an end point.

The Checklist Pattern

In any endeavor, when a certain sequence of actions needs to be done in a certain order, a "checklist" pattern is used. A procedure for building a radio set or a model airplane, knitting instructions, and a countdown sequence for a rocket launch are examples. A checklist is a way of ensuring that everything gets done in the proper sequence.

TIR contains a checklist pattern, combined with repetition and retrospection. It is necessary to *find* an incident before going to the start of the incident. It is necessary to go to the start of an incident before running through (reviewing) the incident.[32] A

---

body shift [*op cit*, p. 168]. The electrodermometer may serve such a purpose, when supplemented by careful observation of the viewer and her reports. It is possible that a Focusing approach could be combined with repetition or with other patterns of viewing to reach even greater depth.

32. As noted earlier (p. 450), an experienced viewer can go through these steps

session agenda is a checklist, done in a certain order.[33] A viewer's Individual Curriculum is also a checklist, as is the General Curriculum, though these may also contain loops.

Using a checklist makes viewing much easier on the viewer and more precise in its actions than a more random approach. It gives the viewer a systematic schema for viewing, and it tends to keep her on the most fruitful topics, rather than letting her attention wander to unrelated topics.

All these patterns can be and are combined in various ways. After doing an exploration on a subject to locate charged items, one may run TIR on the items found, or some repetitive procedure. Repetition, retrospection, and a checklist pattern are all combined in TIR. Sometimes exploration contains retrospective steps. This ability to combine viewing actions into patterns gives viewing a great deal of richness and versatility.

Basic Viewing Actions

As implied in the term "viewing", most (but not all) viewing procedures are receptive — they are ways of perceiving, interpreting, and understanding experience. Having perceived, the viewer arrives at his *own* understanding, via his *own* interpretation of the experience viewed. Viewing procedures are non-evaluative in that they do not mandate how the viewer is supposed to interpret what he views, nor does viewing prescribe what the viewer is to perceive when he views. The viewing procedure merely

---

without having to have an explicit command for each, but the steps still need to be done, and in the proper order.

33. In a typical agenda, any disturbances are cleared first, then an assessment is done, then the items found in the assessment are run, in decreasing order of size of response (the largest response is run first).

prescribes a *means* of looking and a direction in which to look. What the viewer actually perceives is between himself and his world.

Some procedures direct the viewer's attention toward the world ("objective" procedures), others toward "mental" or non-physical objects ("subjective" procedures). More specifically, if something comes up as a charged item, like "father" or "sex", the facilitator may direct the viewer's attention toward the item in a variety of ways. But what the viewer is supposed to *perceive* is not prescribed. It is possible, in other words, for the facilitator to be directive without being evaluative.

Locating

One of the major actions the facilitator asks the viewer to do is locating — finding, spotting, or getting. In an objective procedure, the viewer may be asked to find an object in the room; in a subjective procedure she may be asked to find a particular kind of incident in her past or some other category of object, as in: "Locate a time when you were happy," or "Find something you wouldn't mind forgetting." Entities that cannot be found are absent or "lost". In a mental sphere, they are either never known, forgotten, or repressed — that is, the viewer does not currently *have* them. If a viewer can find something, that means she *has* it — it is there and is not too heavily repressed to be prehended. If a proper assessment was done and the item arrived at lies just below the awareness threshold, the viewer will start finding things that were repressed. That is, she will complete receptive cycles. So finding or spotting — especially when done repetitively or retrospectively — is beneficial in itself.[34]

---

34. It is also, of course, a necessary condition to doing anything else with an object. Obviously one cannot review an incident unless one has found it first!

Looking and Describing

Having located something, the viewer may be asked to look at it or review it. In certain objective procedures, he may be asked repetitively to look at walls or other objects, an action that tends to bring his attention into present time. In TIR, reviewing is the heart of the process. Either looking or reviewing brings into view aspects of an entity that were hitherto unknown. In fact, *viewing (or perceiving) is the very receptive cycle that was incomplete*, so looking or reviewing completes the cycle.

Looking and reviewing generally include giving a *description*. The facilitator often simply asks for a description of the object or event and, of course, the viewer must perceive it in order to describe it. Nevertheless, describing something to another person appears to confer a positive benefit that goes beyond what one would be able to accomplish simply by scanning something by oneself. The facilitator *facilitates* by helping the viewer to feel safe and supported, and by being *interested* in what the viewer is saying. It often feels, to the viewer, as though he gets rid of charge by communicating it to the facilitator in the form of a description. Fortunately, the facilitator does not, on her side, feel as though she is accumulating that charge.

Comparing

One special case of describing is that in which a viewer is asked to view two things and *compare* them, or to find something that is similar (or dissimilar) to something else. If a person has fixed attention on a problem that she does not seem to be able to let go of, one can ask for other problems of comparable or incomparable magnitude. The principal behind this action is the following: the main reason a person clings to a problem is that the problem she is attending to is relatively comfortable, compared to other problems she *might* be attending to. A person seems naturally to want to be involved in solving problems of one kind or another. If she cannot handle a higher-level problem, she selects a lower-level problem that is within her scope.

Part of what lies behind this phenomenon is that a degree of failure tends to introvert a person, causing the boundaries of her identity to shrink.[35] This "stepping back" gives her a chance to revise the way she is acting and to improve her skill so she can re-extend and be successful this time. If a person does not avail herself of this opportunity to relearn, if she puts her attention on a *lower*-level problem instead of working on her skills, then she remains at a lesser degree of extension. Having a viewer find or invent problems of comparable magnitude to the one on which her attention is fixed enables her to "take over" the automatism of fixing on a lower-level problem and allows her to regain her power of choice in doing so. Once she realizes she does not *have* to fixate automatically on a lower-level problem, she has an opportunity to confront the larger problem or failure she has been trying to escape from and to work on solving that. Of course, the viewing session must itself be safe and stress-free. Automatic and unproductive responses can occur when — as is often the case in life — one does not have a safe time and space in which to reflect on one's choices.

Selecting

An action related to comparing is selecting, which we have encountered as a form of assessment.[36] It is also a very powerful viewing action in itself. In selecting, one finds a charged subject that is unclear in some way and clarifies it by interpreting it in a certain way and understanding it. Selecting is done by asking a single question and then getting a series of answers to the

---

35. As discussed in Chapter One, p. 23.
36. See Chapter Eight, p. 424.

question. The question prompts the viewer to look at her experience and give the best answer to the question. There is generally one or more "right" answers to the question for that particular viewer at that particular time. The same question may generate other "right" answers at another time.

If, despite doing well in life, a person continually looks on herself as a failure, one might select with the question, "What would have to happen for you to know that you are successful?" This requires the viewer to look at the issue of success and failure and clarify her thoughts and feelings on the matter. The viewer might give a series of answers like the following:

"I'd have to stop feeling anxious."
"I'd have to receive praise from my boss."
"I'd have to become wealthy."

After giving a few such answers, the viewer will characteristically achieve an intuitive breakthrough and find what is, for her, the correct item, such as:

"I'd have to know what I want to achieve in life."

The viewer might have the realization that she has not been able to achieve success because she has never had a clear goal in terms of which success could be defined. Or the "correct" item for this viewer might be something entirely different, like:

"I'd have to stop comparing myself with others."

accompanied by the realization that, in comparing herself with others, she was setting up impossible standards that could never be realized.

When such a breakthrough occurs, whatever the content, the facilitator (if he is using a meter) will observe a major response — a baseline drop and a free needle — and the viewer will have a sense of certainty about her answer. It will *feel* right and, for that viewer at that time, it will *be* right. The facilitator must check with the viewer to make sure the item is correct. If the viewer manifests any doubt or bad indicators, it is *not* a right item — for her, which is all that matters — and the selection procedure must be continued, or a correction list must be used. A wrong item can cause a great deal of upset, so it is important to be sure.[37]

Selecting may also work as a means of finding a cardinal point. Although selection questions take many forms, they generally call for a single answer. Though there may be many answers to the selection question, one answer will generally stand out for the viewer as the most important, cardinal, or apropos. Often the cardinal point found is an *aberrated* cardinal point.[38] For instance, the viewer may be "making others wrong" in a number of ways, but the central or major way in which he does this is, say, by harping on his own deprived background, which has become an aberrated cardinal point for him — it "excuses" any deficiencies he may have. If you ask this viewer, "What idea do you use to make others wrong?", you might get such responses as:

"They are losers."
"They are snobs."
"They are no better than I am."
"They are luckier than I am."

Finally, the viewer will realize that these are all variations on a central theme:

---

37. Selecting has some similarities to parts 3, 4, and 5 of Gendlin's "Focusing" procedure [Gendlin, E.T. *Focusing* (Bantam Books, Toronto, 1978) pp. 55-60]. In Gendlin's procedure, the client puts her attention on a certain area, or rather on a "felt sense" relating to a given area, and asks what the reason is for the particular quality of this felt sense. The focuser gives a variety of answers until she experiences a "body shift" on coming up with the "correct" one. A meter, if present, would show a baseline drop and free needle at this point. The facilitator or therapist has her "verify" the item by checking it against the "felt sense". This is analogous to the facilitator checking the item with the viewer to make sure it "feels right", regardless of the nature of the item itself, and the bodily response (betokened by a free needle) confirms this feeling.

38. A point seized upon arbitrarily as a way of avoiding confusion or pain. See Chapter Six, pp. 301-303.

"Oh! I use the idea that *I come from a deprived back-ground!*"

At this point the facilitator (if she is using a meter) will see a baseline drop and free needle. The facilitator goes on to verify the answer, "I come from a deprived background" by checking it with the viewer. If the viewer agrees, with very good indicators and a widely free needle, the selection procedure is complete. Otherwise, the procedure has to be continued or corrected.

Selecting is quite effective because it tends to focus on central aberrated points, or aberrated cardinal points. The viewer discharges some of the charge by looking at some associated items, then quickly gravitates to the core of the situation.[39] When the central aberration is brought to light and discharged, the associated items will also be found to have discharged, since their charge lay in their connection to the central aberration. When aberrated cardinal points are thus spotted and eliminated, a considerable amount of beneficial restructuring of experience can occur.

This is also the case when the cardinal point found is *not* aberrated.[40] One can use selection to decide things — to decide what is important or what to do at a certain point. Selecting a doctor or a career is quite similar to the procedure given above. When a person has selected the correct item, it *feels* right to him. It is useful to consult one's feelings in making important choices.

---

39. Indeed, frequently the viewer will offer the correct item or answer immediately, without having to give a list of items.

40. For instance, as Gendlin points out, it is possible to use the Focusing technique outside a "therapeutic" context to gain insight into non-personal matters. One can consult a "felt sense" and focus on it to improve one's understanding of any subject and to make positive decisions of various kinds in life [*Op cit*, pp. 4, 165]. Gendlin mentions that he used this technique in writing his book. If so, the quality of the book speaks well for the effectiveness of the technique!

Creative Actions

Procedures using creative actions[41] are often used in viewing to "take over" automatic actions. If a person is automatically creating painful fantasies or having unwanted ideas, having him conceive or picture these things deliberately can bring the automatic action under control. As Fritz Perls points out,[42] we often deal with a state of inner conflict by taking ownership and control of one side of the conflict and alienating ourselves from the other side — repressing it without "unmaking" it. If the viewer were to become aware of both sides of the conflict at once, he would be confused and uncomfortable. But he would also have an opportunity to resolve the conflict, whereas if one side of the conflict or incongruity is repressed, the conflict cannot be resolved. Perls followed Moreno in using various techniques to bring out hidden conflicts, such as alternately role-playing the two sides.[43] All these techniques make it easier for the person to take over automatisms that he had previously felt to be "outside" of himself.

Creative actions play a central role in education, in training, and, of course, in life.

---

41. I.e., conceiving, picturing, and postulating.

42. Perls, F., Hefferline, R.F., and Goodman, P., *Gestalt Therapy*, (Dell Publishing Co., New York, 1951) Ch. IX, pp. 353-368.

43. Perls, F.C. *The Gestalt Approach* (Science and Behavior Books, Ben Lomond, CA, 1973) p.93f. The techniques of symptom prescription and of "taking over" in Hakomi therapy were described earlier in this chapter under the heading "Patterns of Viewing Procedures", pp. 493-494.

Stress Reduction

A person who is not overwhelmed by stress and is functioning adequately in life tends to be more responsive to personal enhancement methods of all kinds than is a person who is more severely disturbed. This fact is hardly surprising, since a person who is generally more able will also be more able at the process of self-discovery and self-improvement. Paradoxically, this means that the people who need help the most are the least likely to benefit from it. Unless a person is able to concentrate fairly well, he is unlikely to benefit from subjective procedures (such as certain viewing procedures and psychoanalysis).

The first step in helping a person, then, is to remedy his current state of distraction, worry, guilt and general turbidity so that he can attend to the major areas of his case that need to be addressed: those areas that are covered in his Individual Curriculum. The viewing step that accomplishes this purpose — Stress Reduction — is not really a curricular action; it is "pre-curricular", and its purpose is to do a thorough job of clearing current disturbances. What needs to be done in Stress Reduction varies greatly from person to person, depending on the particular disturbances to which he is subject at the time. People in different life-situations will have different forms and severities of turbidity. One may have just lost a spouse; another may have had a serious accident; another may be in a conflict with his employer or suffering from feelings of intense guilt because of some recent or past misdeed. The plan for Stress Reduction thus varies widely from person to person, whereas the rest of the Curriculum is more nearly uniform.

The Initial Interview

The first step for a new viewer is an interview, consisting of a fairly lengthy Inquiry. The facilitator collects data concerning the viewer's age, marital status, and occupation, as well as her:

1. State of health and medical history, including any chronic or psychosomatic conditions, severe illnesses, operations, or injuries.
2. Study and educational history (since most viewers have spent a significant part of their lives in school).
3. Sexual or marital relations.
4. Other familial relations (both her parental family and her own family, if she has one).
5. Friendships.
6. Work situations and other significant groups of which she is a member.
7. Religious background and views.
8. Significant losses or traumatic incidents.
9. Compulsions or inhibitions.
10. Drug history.

In short, all unwanted conditions and possibly problematic or upsetting areas in the viewer's life are asked about. Although the facilitator may work from a list of questions, and makes a point of being very thorough, this action is done quite informally.

With a new viewer, an electrodermometer is especially helpful in locating fruitful areas. The facilitator carefully notes all meter responses and any significant changes in the appearance or manner of the viewer. She traces down any areas that give heavy meter responses to discover more specifically where the charge lies. If possible, this interview is ended on a free needle and very good indicators, though often this may not be possible. Generally, however, the viewer gets a great deal of relief just from talking about these issues with a good listener.

Case Planning for Stress Reduction

Following this initial interview, the data obtained are then closely studied by the technical director, who writes a plan for a sequence of viewing actions that will handle the items found that most occupy the viewer's attention. Generally, only items that responded on the meter are handled. Others are assumed to be uncharged or too far below the awareness threshold.

Nevertheless, if the viewer is interested in a particular area and wants to handle it, it is necessary to address that area, regardless of a lack of meter response. A plan for Stress Reduction may start out with a series of objective procedures, which act in a general way to pull fixed attention off the past and to allow the viewer to attend to the present.[44]

Explorations are freely used in Stress Reduction. The informality and flexibility of the exploratory style of viewing is especially congenial to inexperienced viewers.

The techniques used in clearing can be applied to a variety of charged items. If a person has charge on his mother, one can ask for upsets, problems, withholds, or misdeeds connected to mother, handling each retrospectively to a free needle and very good indicators. One can also use various flows in clearing procedures, such as:

Inflow: "Did your mother upset you?"
Outflow: "Did you upset your mother?"
Crossflow: "Did your mother upset anyone else?"
Reflexion: "Did you upset yourself because of your mother?"

in each case handling the question with simple retrospection, as needed.

---

44. As discussed earlier (pp. 488-489), these objective procedures may be receptive (noticing or locating things in the environment) or creative (moving the body and other objects, touching things, etc.), or a combination of the two. They are generally repetitive.

Correction Lists

Another technique used in corrective viewing is calling lists and handling the items that show a meter response. Correction lists are directed toward handling errors and disturbances that occur in certain types of situations in life and in viewing.

> **Definition**: A correction list is a list of the most likely errors or unwanted conditions that can exist in a particular subject or procedure, designed to spot current items that are restimulated and to clear them. Some correction lists are specifically designed to handle difficulties that may arise in a particular subject, viewing procedure, or "in-life" situation. Others are more general. A facilitator may use a correction list when something goes wrong in life or in a viewing session.

Specific correction lists are designed to handle difficulties encountered in specific circumstances, such as TIR, selecting, and study difficulties. These lists contain the errors and disturbances that most often occur in those viewing or in-life situations. An experienced facilitator knows which list to select for which occasion. Some lists are best called all the way through and then handled in decreasing order of response or in some other order (a two-pass assessment). Others are best handled by taking up each responding item as it appears and completing its handling before going onto the next item (a one-pass assessment). Still others are best handled by asking the viewer individually about each item, and getting an answer on each, then further handling any that show a response on being asked or answered. A list can be called generally — without a prefix — or it can be called with a particular prefix. If a facilitator runs into trouble with a particular selection procedure, for instance, he can correct it with a list, prefixed by the phrase "Concerning this selection procedure...."[45]

---

45. The prefix is used to keep the viewer's attention on the specific charged area being addressed, so that she does not get dispersed into other aspects

The proper handling for each charged item found on a list varies with the nature of the item. Errors in selecting, or such items as wrong reasons or wrong identifications, are handled using the special techniques of selecting. Restimulated traumas, losses, and fixed incidents are handled by TIR. Other disturbances are handled by clearing procedures. Some lists are handled by simply running each item on the list in the form of a repetitive question, to the proper end point. For instance, one could have a list item "Suppressed", which (if live) could be handled by repetitively asking "Has anything been suppressed?", or "Concerning your mother [if that is the prefix of the list] has anything been suppressed?", until there is a free needle, realization, and very good indicators. Other lists require a simple retrospective handling of the items: one gets an answer to the question; then, if no end point is attained, one asks "Is there an earlier similar _____ ?", until an end point is reached.

It usually takes a greater degree of training for a facilitator to do corrective actions, or "remedies", than routine curricular actions, which are often simple repetitive procedures. To do remedies, the facilitator must be quite versatile: she must be able to shift styles and methods of facilitating as the need arises.

Handling Overruns

When a procedure is incomplete, the correct thing to do is simply to continue it until an end point is attained. When a procedure is overrun, it is necessary to "recover" the end point. This involves a recovery procedure:

---

of her case.

Definition: Recovery is a corrective action used to handle an overrun. In a recovery procedure, the viewer is returned to the favorable state he was in at the end point, before the point of overrun.

Different recovery procedures are used for different situations. They include:

1. Having the viewer recall the moment when the end point occurred.
2. Getting the approximate date or time of the end point.
3. Finding whether something relating to the end point was suppressed, invalidated, not acknowledged, or evaluated.
4. Finding what was deactivated at the time of the end point.
5. Finding what was reactivated when the end point ended.
6. Asking what occurred while running a procedure and looking for the specific end point of that procedure.

The first five procedures are those most widely used. The sixth is used where there is a very specific end point for a particular procedure.[46]

When to Use a Remedy

It is not difficult to determine when it is necessary to use a remedy, because it is easy to recognize when viewing is not going well.[47] Proper viewing leads to a free needle and very good indicators. When a viewer becomes unhappy during or after a session, when the facilitator cannot get a free needle or very good indicators, or when the viewer becomes frustrated and upset, then the facilitator knows something is not going well. Fortunately,

---

46. In-life activities can also be overrun, and sometimes it is necessary to recover the end points of these as well.

47. In Chapter Eight (p. 427), I list some of the bad indicators that may be encountered in viewing.

she has recourse. Often, she can just ask the viewer what is wrong and get the answer from him, then handle the situation. If the viewer does not know, the facilitator can discover what the actual charge is by doing a correction list or an Inquiry. Although neither the viewer nor the facilitator may know exactly what has gone wrong — if they did, they would not be at an impasse — the meter will respond on the appropriate item if the facilitator does an Inquiry or assesses a list that contains likely possibilities. Errors in selecting can cause some very dramatic upsets. Fortunately, there appear to be only a limited number of things that can go wrong in selecting, such as:

1. A wrong item was found.
2. The selection question was uncharged.
3. The viewer or facilitator rejected a correct item.
4. Earlier selection errors were restimulated by the current action.
5. The selection procedure was overrun.
6. The selection procedure was incomplete.
7. Other charge got in the way.

A list for handling difficulties that arise on selecting will contain these and a few other items. When called by the facilitator, the correct item(s) on the list — those that caused the difficulty — will respond and can then be handled.

In TIR, possible errors include:

1. There was no charge on an item in the first place (an unnecessary attempt to run an uncharged item).
2. The procedure was overrun.
3. The procedure was underrun or incomplete.
4. There was an undiscovered earlier similar incident or earlier starting point.
5. The facilitator asked for an earlier similar incident when there was none.

A TIR correction list can be constructed to cover these possibilities and any others that are likely to occur on TIR.

In addition, there are "all purpose" lists to handle general upsets in life or in viewing. Using such a list, it is relatively easy to find out what the correct charge is and handle it. The handling on a particular item might involve using a second, or even a third, list. For instance, if the responding item on an "all purpose" list is "Was there an error in selecting?", the facilitator might have to go to a more specific list concerning selection to handle this item.

Rarely, the situation proves too complex to handle with a routine correction list or elementary procedures like exploring or simple retrospection. In such a situation, the facilitator should end the session and get a new session agenda — one designed to handle the complexities. This allows enough time to study records of earlier sessions and to think calmly about what needs to be done.[48]

The concept of a correction list is largely unknown in the field of psychotherapy and personal enhancement. The reason may be that the idea of repairing an incorrectly done session is equally unknown. In viewing, the highly structured nature of the procedures, and the definiteness of the end points that are to be achieved make it quite apparent when the facilitator has been successful and when she has not. The concept of "correction" requires a concept of what is correct and what is not. I feel that correction lists are, in themselves, a major contribution to the field of personal enhancement.

Emergency Remedies

Some corrective procedures are useful for emergency situations such as illnesses, injuries, and severe emotional shocks. It is useful to have informal emergency remedies for these situations, including some that can be done in the absence of a meter and a formal session environment. These include physical contact procedures (such as body awareness procedures involving touching

---

48. A remedial plan so arrived at might include more correction lists or other elements such as objective procedures, TIR, or selecting.

and manual pressure) and physical "re-enactment" of a recent physically traumatic incident. Bodily awareness procedures restore awareness of the body that has been inhibited by pain and illness. These are done by the facilitator touching the viewer's body in different (non-sexually stimulating) places, each time telling the viewer to be aware of the touch. The viewer must let the facilitator know each time that he has felt the touch. Re-enactment is done by going back to the actual scene of an accident or injury and re-enacting it. The viewer assumes as closely as possible the exact physical position and location he was in when the injury occurred. He repetitively contacts what the body was touching at the time of the injury. Of course, dangerous items, such as corrosive or hot objects, where further injury could occur from contact, are avoided or rendered harmless before the re-enactment is started.[49] TIR and other subjective procedures can also be used.[50]

Handling Life

Certain situations commonly arise that require special handling in order to avoid the sort of continual or repeating upsets and distractions that inhibit viewing. Although a full handling of such a situation often includes viewing steps to reduce charge, additional steps, actually done in real life, are often helpful and sometimes essential in order to abate the upsetting situation and to prevent it from recurring.

---

49. Any reader who has a young child and wants to experience the remarkable efficacy of re-enactment should try the following: the next time the child has a minor injury that brings her to tears, get her to re-enact (slowly, and this time harmlessly) the exact motions that she went through in injuring herself. Have her do this several times, if necessary, until an improvement occurs.

50. These emergency remedies are given in greater detail in Appendix 1, pp. 541-549.

These situations include:

1. Illnesses
2. Continual misdeeds.
3. Failures

Handling Illness

Illness, of course, should first be handled with proper medical means. It can also be addressed with viewing remedies — emergency or otherwise. Even if an illness is psychosomatic, that is no reason why it should be considered curable solely by psychological means. Adequate medical care is usually an indispensable part of handling even clearly psychosomatic illness. Viewing, however, can help the healing process by eliminating the psychological factors that precipitated the illness and which would tend to prolong it if left unhandled.

Illness is often a response to environmental stress. Therefore, one can help a sick person recover by having her spot people and situations that are disturbing to her or traumas that may have either occurred or been restimulated. These actions are normally done in a session, although they may be done in a simple interview. Once the source of the restimulation has been identified (assuming that there is some present-time restimulator), the viewer can receive special help in handling the stressful person or situation after viewing is completed. Since the viewer has been *affected* by the situation, help consists in teaching her how to become *causative*. If the viewer has a sister who is antagonistic to her, she may benefit from communication exercises designed to teach people how to handle others without arousing antagonism. Often, the viewer learns what she has done to generate or perpetuate the ill-feeling. When she stops doing it, the antagonism vanishes or abates. It might be useful, in this sort of case, to arrange a brief exercise in which the viewer works with a partner who takes on the role of the sister and the viewer tries various approaches until she finds one that seems to work well.[51] Then the viewer can actually deal with the sister in such a way that she ceases being as antagonistic or ceases to be antagonistic altogether.

Although both parties to any dispute are responsible for any antagonism, it is best to assume that the person one is helping *can* take a causative role in handling situations. From this viewpoint, she will be able to see how changing her actions can cause an effect. In an interpersonal situation, the fact that one person takes responsibility for the situation does not mean that others cannot *also* take responsibility for it. Interpersonal events are multiply determined — they can be affected by all the participants. If a person is allowed to take an other-determined viewpoint, the viewpoint that she is a "victim of circumstances" or that others are responsible for what she does, she will not be able to handle a situation effectively.[52]

The technical director, if there is one, must decide whether viewing is what will help the person at a particular time or whether some other kind of help is desirable. Viewing should not be a *substitute* for medical care, nor for actual in-life handling of certain other situations (such as legal or financial troubles).

Continual Misdeeds

Sometimes, an in-life handling is needed because the viewer has been engaging in activities that he regards as ethically wrong. A person will generally not permit himself power or ability if he cannot trust himself. Continual misdeeds often result in conflict with the environment (with one's spouse or the police, for instance). So it is often necessary to find what the person is

---

51. Similar exercises are used in Gestalt therapy, assertiveness training, and elsewhere.

52. It is commonly thought that two people involved in a situation should share the responsibility 50—50. A better viewpoint is that each party should regard herself as 100 percent responsible for resolving it.

continually doing that is ethically wrong and get him to stop doing it, and possibly to repair the damage to or restore harmony with others he has injured.

The technical director or facilitator must make sure she is not being moralistic or imposing her own moral values on the viewer. There is a danger that the threat of being denied viewing could be used to coerce people into behaving in a way that suits the facilitator or technical director. Such a form of coercion would be a particularly nasty form of evaluation and would make establishing a safe space impossible. There is a delicate balance here because the facilitator or technical director also has the right and the duty to exercise judgment concerning what she thinks will be effective, and she must not be forced into practicing in a way that she thinks is ineffective or wrong. Some helpful guidelines for sorting out these issues are:

1. The facilitator or technical director must not try to handle a situation she — but not the viewer — thinks is ethically wrong. If the situation really is unethical, the viewer will become aware of that fact in the course of viewing and will mend his ways.[53]
2. The facilitator or technical director has a right and a duty to decide on the form of help she thinks is best for the viewer. She need not take orders from the viewer in this regard.[54] For instance, if a viewer is continuously committing what *he* considers to be misdeeds towards others, he will also tend to act in such a way as to reduce his own awareness and power. Such self-destructive actions can inhibit or prevent

---

53. Since the viewer is basically well-intentioned, removing charge and duress from his case will render him more and more capable of displaying those basic positive intentions. People who are doing well are easier and more pleasant to relate to than people who are in distress.

54. If the viewer knew what was wrong with him and how to right it, he would not need to do viewing in order to handle it. He would have already viewed — and resolved — the issue.

viewing, and it would not be correct to try to continue viewing until the pattern of destructive actions towards oneself
and others stops.

3. Although it is up to the facilitator or technical director to
    judge whether the next step for the viewer should be view-
    ing or some other action, she should not refuse to help
    someone altogether nor use the threat of such refusal to
    help as a form of coercion. There is almost always *some*
    way of helping.

4. It is up to the viewer to decide whether he wishes to accept
    the form of help offered. If the viewer disagrees with the
    case plan, he has, of course, the right to seek other opin-
    ions, and the technical director or facilitator should give him
    appropriate referrals.

Handling Failure

Failures usually cannot be dealt with by viewing alone. They
must be addressed in the physical world. If a person is upset
because her marriage is failing, she can temporarily feel better
after some viewing but unless the issues that are causing the marriage to fail are handled in real life she *may* come to feel the
sense of failure again every time she goes home — or even *thinks*
about her marriage. She has understandable reasons for feeling
upset because a real failure exists.

As I have mentioned before (pp. 137-144), success and
failure are tightly bound to emotions. Anyone who considers herself a failure in an activity will feel negative emotion with respect
to that activity. No amount of viewing will permanently eliminate
this negative emotion so long as this failure actually continues to
exist. This problem is encountered with chronically hospitalized
psychiatric patients. No amount of psychotherapy will help them
until they can achieve some kind of success. As psychiatric
patients, they are certainly unsuccessful in life, so they have very
"rational" reasons for feeling negative emotion, not the least of
which is that they are stigmatized and defined as social failures —
"mental patients" — a fact often stressed by R.D. Laing, Thomas

Szasz, and others.[55]

It is very desirable, then, to have a means by which people who have been failing can find a way to progress toward success. The proper handling of failure consists, simply, of learning the steps necessary to achieving success in *any* situation. These steps, as outlined below, may seem simplistic to the reader. When one is not involved in an adverse situation, it is fairly easy to be objective and to perceive what needs to be done. But when one is *in* such a situation — upset and overwhelmed — the needed steps are not usually apparent unless they are explicitly stated. The guidelines given below are, of necessity, stated in very general terms, in order to apply to the myriad activities in which one can have different degrees of success or failure. With appropriate rewording, they can be made to apply to *any* sort of activity, whether it involves other people or not.

Emotions and Conditions

For each level on the Emotional Scale, there is a corresponding success level, or "condition", as shown in Figure 46. The conditions are on the "world" side of the person-world polarity; the emotions are on the "person" side.

---

55. See Laing, R.D. *The Politics of Experience* (Ballantine Books, New York, 1967) and Szasz, T. *The Manufacture of Madness* (Dell Publishing, New York, 1970). That is one reason why I am avoiding the medical model of "mental illness". It actually has debilitating effects on people's well-being because of the stigma of being "mentally ill" or even "neurotic" — a pseudo-medical term.

EMOTION   CONDITION

                                           DISENGAGEMENT
ELATION · · · · · · · · · · · · · · · · · FINAL SUCCESS

ENTHUSIASM · · · · · · · · · · · · · · · · · · · SUCCESS

CHEERFULNESS ⎫
COMPLACENCY ⎬ · · · · · · · · · · · · NORMAL
CONTENTMENT ⎭

AMBIVALENCE ⎫
ANTAGONISM ⎪
ANGER   ⎬ · · · · · · · · DRUDGERY
RESENTMENT ⎪
HIDDEN HOSTILITY ⎭

ANXIETY · · · · · · · · · · · · · · · · · · EMERGENCY

FEAR · DANGER

GRIEF ⎫ · · · · · · · · · · · · · · · · · FAILURE
APATHY ⎭

                                           FINAL FAILURE
                                           DISENGAGEMENT

Figure 46. The emotions and their corresponding conditions.

Engagement

Beside the success-failure continuum, there is another continuum: a continuum of commitment to or engagement in a particular activity. The two continua are different but related. A person can engage in an activity in a half-hearted manner, or she can throw herself into it to a greater or lesser degree. On the person side of the person-world polarity, this can be regarded as the degree of *assumption* of an identity corresponding to the activity, while on the world side, it can be regarded as the degree of *engagement* in an activity:

Definition: Engagement is the degree to which a person assumes an identity, or the importance she places on a particular activity.

Engagement is "how much of herself she puts into" an activity or identity. A person can be quite versatile and still be able to be quite engaged in a particular activity. I can become fully absorbed in playing a guitar and, the next minute, do something entirely different (such as reading a book) with equal engagement. Assuming an identity engages a person with the world that corresponds to that identity. Becoming a guitar player engages me with the world of music, sounds, frets, strings, arpeggios, Fernando Sor, and appreciative (or unappreciative) listeners. Becoming a father engages me in the world of a wife, children, household rules, schools, tantrums, and familial affection.

Although engagement is not the same as success, the two are related. Successfully completing a moderately complex or difficult activity requires a certain minimal level of engagement. It is possible to fail at an activity such as landing a plane because one is not sufficiently engaged in it. On the other hand, a small degree of engagement is sufficient if an activity is relatively easy (like eating).

One way of improving the success level, with respect to a particular activity, is to increase the person's degree of engagement in that activity. To increase or re-establish one's engagement in an activity, one can apply the following "Engagement Procedure":

1. Verify and renew one's intentions and purposes related to the activity.
2. Establish contact with and control over the various entities involved in the activity by organizing them appropriately.
3. Establish communication with other persons involved in the activity.
4. Find out what needs to be done to achieve one's purpose and establish a plan of action.
5. Carry out the plan of action.
6. Continue Steps (1)-(5) at deeper levels of engagement.

If I have been disengaged from an activity, I will find myself, on getting engaged or re-engaged in it, at a certain level on the success scale. Since engagement is a form of cardinality or importance — the importance to me of an activity — it amplifies whatever emotion I may have with respect to that activity. Depending on the success level, I find myself feeling more strongly apathetic, frightened, angry, or enthusiastic as I become more strongly engaged in an activity. In fact, I often disengage from an identity or activity because the negative emotion associated with failure in that activity is too great. Disengagement — also known as "escape" — makes me feel better because it causes the intensity of my negative emotion to fade. Under these circumstances, a re-engagement is usually difficult and distressing because I must again confront uncomfortable emotions until I move up to a higher success level.

An "institutional case" (such as a chronically hospitalized mental patient) has typically disengaged from many activities, and on re-engaging will usually experience intense distress, a fact which tends to trap him in the institution. Addiction is a similar form of disengagement that can relieve uncomfortable emotions caused by failure in life. The institutional case could be regarded as being "addicted" to the institution. On coming off drugs (or TV, or gambling, or sex, or a cult, or whatever other means he has used to disengage), the addict re-engages with painful areas of life that are in bad condition, and the difficulty of confronting this pain and these conditions tends to keep him "hooked".

Emotions and their corresponding conditions contain their own "built-in" strategies.[56] At or below antagonism, these strategies tend to lead to failure. Therefore, it is necessary to bypass them and use more effective means for handling lower conditions.

Below Failure

Let us consider the emotions and conditions from the bottom up. There is a point *below* failure where a person has decided that a certain goal cannot be achieved and — since one cannot intend something that is thought to be impossible — has disengaged entirely from the activity. He has failed (past tense), but does not currently stand at the point of failure.

Failure

At failure, the person has not yet completely disengaged from the activity, but he has *almost* completely disengaged because of repeated traumas and losses that have caused him to feel overwhelmed. He sees himself as being unable to control or communicate with the area, entities, and persons connected to the activity. He lets others handle them because he feels incapable of doing so himself. The corresponding emotional level is from apathy to grief. The person has not totally given up, but he has not decided to do something about the condition either. The proper handling for failure is either to recognize that the activity is not something one wants to do anyway, and to stop all engagement in that activity, or to decide one really does want to do the activity and re-engage in it. Following the Engagement Procedure

---

56. See Chapter Three (pp. 141-144) for a fuller description of these strategies.

given above will resolve the issue. To help a person who has failed or is failing, it is therefore necessary to get him to:

1. Reassume the appropriate identity.
2. Re-engage in the activity.
3. Move up the success levels.

A facilitator, or a friend, can go over the re-engagement procedure with the person and help him to achieve a re-engagement. This would normally not be done in a viewing session.

Danger

When one re-engages in a certain activity after having failed in it, one often finds oneself immediately in danger. The corresponding emotional level is fear. Here, the person is faced with a threat or threats that seem overwhelming because he does not feel he can cope with them. He feels he is about to lose his status, his relationship, his job, or his rank or otherwise be ejected from the activity in which he is engaged, or else that he will probably have to leave in disgrace unless some desperate action is taken. His impulse is to flee, to disengage, but he has not yet done so. People are normally frightened when they go back to confront activities at which they have failed or are about to fail. The danger is real, and it is the danger of failing (or of failing again) and possibly being punished in various ways for doing so.

Although fear felt in response to an actual danger would tend to make one want to run away (thus again falling into failure), an *effective* strategy for moving up into a higher condition will usually be different:[57]

---

57. There are cases where running away *is* the adaptive thing to do, such as in avoiding an avalanche. These are mostly cases of immediate physical danger where one does not have an effective means of combating the danger.

1. Use the Engagement Procedure to establish greater engagement.
2. Confront and handle the danger in the situation, instead of running away from it.
3. Take effective steps to ensure future safety in the activity.

Unless this last step is explicitly executed, a person may be too preoccupied with running away, or with handling the danger, to look at the necessity of having a long-term strategy as well.

Emergency

When danger has thus been overcome, one progresses to a somewhat less stressful, though still subnormal, condition called "emergency". The emotional level corresponding to emergency is anxiety. A person at emergency is constantly coping with immediate threats; she is close to being overwhelmed. She builds up major backlogs (incomplete cycles) because she does not have time to handle *routine* cycles. She tries to be hyper-alert, to attend compulsively and indiscriminately to every detail in her environment that seems to be a threat, and to ignore or neglect other things that, though still needing attention, are less immediately threatening. She is not so severely under threat that she feels she has to run *away* from the threat. Rather, her attention is drawn compulsively *toward* the threat, and she loses sight of the importance of other things.

She becomes dispersed and has difficulty completing cycles because while she is in the middle of handling one threat, another will pop up and she will then abandon the first and go after the more immediate one. So she tends to be rather unproductive. Her backlogged cycles may, in turn, become threatening. The activity can thus become a continual juggling act. When too many items are being juggled at once, the whole activity can collapse and throw the person back into a danger condition, in which she now has an impulse to flee from the activity. The correct way to handle an emergency condition is to:

1. Make a list of all cycles that need to be completed, in order of urgency and importance. Make sure the list is really complete and that you have not neglected anything "routine".
2. Start from the top of the list and complete one cycle at a time as rapidly as possible, thus handling any backlogs. Allocate extra time, if needed, because part of an emergency is a real or apparent insufficiency of time.
3. Find out what other cycles you should be completing.
4. Make a list and complete these cycles, as in Steps (1) and (2).
5. Meanwhile, reorganize the way you do things and establish necessary skills, routine methods, and policies for handling the cycles you have to complete so that everything is not always coming up as an emergency or a special situation requiring a special individual decision.

Drudgery

When emergency is successfully handled, you can fall into a pattern where you are trying very hard to succeed, not making adequate progress, and not enjoying it. Here, the emotional level is between anger and ambivalence — "frustration" might describe the general frame of mind. The cycle is experienced as quite effortful and is regarded as drudgery, which is many people's concept of "work".[58]

The tendency of a person in this condition is to get into fights and to use force toward the various people and objects in her environment. She does what she needs to do, but does as little as possible and resists any additional responsibility. She feels under duress, feels that she has to work hard and that she is being

---

58. At a higher emotional level, it would be called "play". See Chapter Three, pp. 148-149.

exploited. No matter what she does, she cannot seem to get into a more comfortable position. She feels trapped in her situation, with little hope of improvement. Her strategy is to resist, to use force, and to fight back. She may or may not have the "guts" to do so. By antagonizing others, she often brings into being the hostile, uncooperative environment that she is resisting even if it was not there before, from the viewpoint of others. In this way, she is likely to *create* an emergency. In a job situation, if a person antagonizes a major client, she may create an emergency for the company. In a marriage, if a wife antagonizes her husband, the threat of divorce may emerge. Since her relationships and other aspects of the environment that pertain to the activity are somewhat compromised, she becomes less productive and tends to fall into emergency by developing a backlog of incomplete cycles.

The correct handling for drudgery is:

1. Do what you can to make the activity easier, such as putting the environment in order and, in certain cases, taking action to refine your skills.
2. Get into communication with each person with whom anger or antagonism has occurred and talk out and resolve any differences or bones of contention, or find more congenial people to relate to.
3. Take a long, hard, honest look at your role in the activity and see if you can expand that role without becoming overwhelmed.
4. Work harder than usual to put out more products and prevent backlogs.
5. Adopt a policy of being helpful, within the limits you have given yourself, and try to stretch those limits as much as possible.

Normal

If these steps are successfully carried out, you move up to the emotional level of contentment or complacency, where "doing what comes naturally" begins to be an acceptable strategy.[59] The natural impulse at this level is to keep doing what one is doing and not to change things. Everything tends to go smoothly. One feels satisfied, content, and conservative, though perhaps unexcited. Left to his own devices, a complacent person will remain in a normal condition indefinitely. In order to move up to a higher level of success, however, one must add other rules to the built-in strategy.

1. Keep doing what you are doing; do not change any successful actions.
2. If an improvement occurs, find out *what caused it* and reinforce that cause by incorporating it as part of the normal routine.
3. If a deterioration occurs, find the cause, remedy it, and alter the normal routine to prevent a reoccurrence.
4. Without interrupting your normal routines, test out some new ideas or procedures that you think might be improvements in a circumscribed area that will not affect your overall success if they do not pan out. Incorporate into your routine the ones that do prove workable.

---

59. In the 60's, it was fashionable to say, "If it feels good, do it." This makes sense when one is above ambivalence on the Emotional Scale, or above drudgery in one's condition. But if one is at ambivalence or below, this rule is no longer applicable. It may "feel great" to bash someone's head in when one is angry, yet such an action rarely leads to a favorable outcome.

Success

The emotional level corresponding to success is cheerfulness or enthusiasm. A successful person not only does well at routine activities but also actively seeks out a wider range of responsibility — new worlds to conquer. Such a person is continually improving his performance. He tries out new ways of doing things and incorporates successful actions into his routine. He seems to do everything that is needful and more while apparently being quite light-hearted and playful about it. The natural impulse when one is successful corresponds exactly with what one *should* do, which is similar to the strategy given above for handling complacency except that an enthusiastic person, being highly self-confident, tends to be more willing to take a chance. If he continues in this manner, he will tend to achieve a final success and move on to a new activity or to a higher phase of the same activity.

Final Success

The emotional level corresponding to final success is elation. At this level, a person has successfully won a game, completed an activity, or fulfilled an intention, and he will enjoy the condition for a short time, then formulate a new intention or activity and get ready to move up to a final success in the new activity. Final success tends to be quite short-lived.

What a person does when he has achieved a final success depends on the nature of the activity. If the activity is a limited one with a definite end point, such as winning a game or building a house, a successful person will complete the project and move up to exhilaration on the Emotional Scale, as he disengages from it by achieving final success. This, of course, is the ideal way to disengage from an activity. If the activity is an unlimited one, such as "painting pictures", then the enthusiastic person will set up a gradiently expanding series of sub-goals (e.g., "to have his own exhibition", "to have an exhibition in New York", "to get a picture into the National Gallery"), and engage in each of them, bringing each in turn up to final success and exhilaration. An enthusiastic person characteristically achieves final success in an activity and moves on to the next, higher goal, either in continued furtherance of an unlimited activity or — having completed a limited activity — by engagement in another activity.

Timing is important. A person should not deny himself the time to savor the rewards of success — a vacation, praise, self-validation — but this should be for a finite, limited time. Some people become the victim of their past successes by getting stuck in them (usually when these successes are scarce, being surrounded by failures).[60] There are few who are as unhappy as those who *used* to be successful and never went on to face a new challenge. The second-unhappiest are those who cannot permit themselves to enjoy a well-earned reward.

Sometimes a person can quite successfully apply these formulas by himself; at other times, particularly in the lower conditions such as failure or danger, it seems better to have another person to work with. The methods described in this chapter can be an important adjunct to the process of viewing when a person is confronted with an actual failure in life that cannot be handled by viewing alone. They can, of course, be used whether or not a person is engaged in viewing.

---

60. See Chapter Six, p. 320, for a more complete discussion of being stuck in a success. Ron Kurtz in *Hakomi Therapy* (Hakomi Institute, Boulder CO, 1985) Chapter One, pp. 4-8, calls final success "Completion" and (correctly) emphasizes the need to spend some time savoring it. A compulsive worker cannot allow himself this satisfaction. In viewing, this principle is implicitly recognized — as the practice of ceasing to run a procedure when an end point occurs.

CONCLUSIONS

I have attempted to present the outline of a new subject of study, the study of human nature and experience as viewed by the individual human, i.e., from the person-centered viewpoint. I have established some needed terminology that will, I hope, cut through some of the confusion of ordinary language without departing too strongly from it.

The book describes a theory of personal experience and action and a theory of personal disability. It presents, in outline, some examples of methods derived from these theories — methods that can be used to increase personal ability and the quality of life. Variants of most of the methods described have been used successfully over a period of years and have indeed resulted in a definite and rapid improvement in the quality of life for those who have used them. They include Stress Reduction — a way to provide immediate relief from psychological pain and difficulties — and other methods for a more thoroughgoing eradication of the root causes of personal unhappiness.

As a result of using these methods, many have reported positive results that can only be described as "spiritual". They have encountered out-of-body experiences, past lives, and other paranormal phenomena, all of which have confirmed for them their basic spiritual nature. But neither metapsychology nor its methods require anyone to accept any particular world-view, including the view that spirituality is a part of life.

Central to the person-centered viewpoint that pervades this book is a rejection of the medical model and of the idea that it should take many years of expensive training to learn how to help another person handle her confusion and unhappiness. The intention is to make it possible for *many* people to help others, not just an elite few, and for many others to receive help, not just those who are wealthy enough to afford therapy.

For all its impressive physical technology, present-day civilization has heretofore lacked an equally well-thought-out and agreed-upon technology for achieving personal happiness. Instead there have been a number of different technologies, some religious, some therapeutic, each adhering to its own ideology and methods. Yet truly effective and rapid helping techniques are desperately needed, as is a non-sectarian approach to helping.

This book contains the *beginning* of such an approach, not, as yet, a full-fledged metapsychological discipline. I hope that others will discover flaws in this formulation and create better formulations and so continue to build on these beginnings. With all the effective methods we have now, we have only begun to realize the potential that lies in the person-centered approach.

In the future, we must walk a careful line between dogmatism on the one hand and fuzzy thinking on the other. The struggle with terminology gives evidence of this dangerous dichotomy. I have consistently had to try to avoid ponderous Germanic or Latinate words and phrases, as well as tempting, snappy acronyms, which, if they were introduced into this subject, would act as a barrier between specialists in metapsychology, and non-specialists. On the other hand, careless use of ambiguous terms would result in such a lack of clarity as to make the subject unexplainable. Other writers on this subject will have to make the same judgments. I hope they make them wisely.

The struggle with terminology is only one aspect of the general struggle to strike a balance between finding a consensus that can be widely agreed-upon on one hand, and, on the other hand, avoiding dogmatism and preserving the spirit of free scientific inquiry. As with any other scientific endeavor, the make-break point lies in the question of whether the experiences of one person can be duplicated by another. In my presentation, I have tried to adhere to experiences that are completely duplicatable from person to person. Everyone can perceive, conceive, understand, and interpret. We all believe we exist and that we are surrounded by a world of some kind. We have all had traumatic incidents and the experience of having them restimulated — and of feeling lingering unwanted effects from these incidents.

Traumatic Incident Reduction, along with other very similar methods, has been used with hundreds of thousands of people and has proven astonishingly workable in the great majority of cases. This method, and all those mentioned in this book, will have to be verified in personal experience and by controlled studies. A great deal of research still needs to be done to show that these methods do, indeed, have duplicatable results.

I hope that my readers will be inspired to test these methods in their own experience and verify (or falsify) them for themselves. And I hope that some will, in time, be moved to subject these methods to empirical and statistical scrutiny in formal experimental studies. A great deal of work still needs to be done in discovering reliable objective indices of subjective experience. Some have asserted that subjective experience cannot be studied scientifically and that therefore we must confine our research to visible behavior. I think this is a defeatist viewpoint. We should not shrink from the methodological challenges of examining experience.

There is much to be learned, and we have a desperate need to learn it.

AFTERWORD

In attempting to describe experience consistently in a person-centered way, I have tried to confine myself to discussing entities to whose existence almost anyone could agree.

But I cannot refrain from seizing the opportunity to express a few of my personal opinions and to explore some of the larger implications of the ideas presented in this book.

It seems to me that as we learn more about the physical universe via the physical sciences, as the study of religion and spirituality moves away from dogmatism and becomes, for many, another field of free exploration, as philosophy escapes the bonds of logical positivism and begins to become more concerned with practical applications, and as therapies become more spiritual and more cognitive, the fields of religion, science, philosophy, and therapy tend to merge into a single concern: the search for truth and personal fulfillment.

In introducing the person-centered viewpoint as a practical tool for helping people improve the quality of their lives, I have not tried to make any assertions about what the "absolute truth" about the universe might be, nor even about whether there *is* such an absolute truth. Each person must reach his own conclusions about this issue, as about everything else in life. For *practical* purposes, it does not matter whether there really is a universe "out there" that stands completely apart from those who perceive, interpret, understand, and change it. Nor is there any point in *asserting* the "absolute" existence of anything unless one is trying to change the opinion of others.

In my view, assertions about "absolute reality" are simply a way of justifying fixed ideas, dogmatism, and ideological imperialism. Absolute truth means never having to change your mind. But the world is not like that. Even the physical sciences evolve: scientists change their considerations and their maps of the universe. Therapeutic practice continues to evolve; philosophy evolves. Even religions evolve and change.

When a person interprets the world in a certain way, that *is* the way the world becomes — for him. Any person — whether he be a philosopher, a theologian, or a farmer — has as a primary activity the job of arriving at a useful and valid view of the world. No amount of exhortation about absolute reality can excuse him from that obligation. It goes with the territory of being a conscious being.

In order to arrive at a valid world view, a person must *start* from his existing experience and build on that experience by interpreting it and using it to test various explanatory hypotheses. The conclusions he reaches — even conclusions reached about the physical universe, the brain, the nervous system, and mechanisms of perception — can never *invalidate* the existence of the data on which these conclusions are based: personal experience. If, from a set of data **A**, one reaches a set of conclusions **B**, one cannot use **B** to invalidate **A** because in so doing **B** would invalidate the basis of its own acceptability, thus disproving itself. So the contents of a person's direct experience will always be epistemologically prior to any model of the physical universe *derived from* that experience. Rather, assertions about the physical universe — or any other universe — must be firmly rooted in the commonalities of personal experience: i.e., in metapsychology.

In 1910, Edmund Husserl announced the creation of a new science — the science of subjective phenomena, or "phenomenology".[1] This science was to study the origin and nature of the

---

1. Husserl, E. *Philosophie als Strenge Wissenschaft*, (Vittorio Klostermann, Frankfurt, 1910).
   English translation by Lauer, Q. "Philosophy as an Exact Science" *Cross Currents* v.6 Summer-Fall (1966), Nos. 3,4; pp.227-246,325-344.

personal observations and experiences that underlie both the phy-sical sciences and all other aspects of life. Husserl's work suf-fered from his exceedingly complex way of thinking and from a lack of clarity in his writing. Whether his obscurity was a prob-lem of expression or one of thinking is itself not clear. Despite the efforts of others, such as Merleau-Ponty and Martin Heidegger, to clarify, correct, and expand upon Husserl's work, phenomenology, as a legitimate subject of study, has not been as widely accepted as it probably deserves to be.

The Human Potential Movement, however, led by Karl Jung, Fritz Perls, Abraham Maslow, Ken Wilbur, Charles Tart, and many others, gave wider currency to the notion that subjective — and even spiritual — states and perceptions can be a legitimate subject of study. In fact, the original meaning of "psychology" was "the study of the soul, or spirit".

Until relatively recently, enlightenment was the exclusive concern of religions, philosophies, and spiritual disciplines in their various forms. However, certain current forms of therapy[2] also have a form of enlightenment as their goal, and some progress has been made towards understanding what needs to be done in order to attain this state. Enlightenment, or high awareness, and the non-material nature of a person can also be the object of a formal discipline, science, or subject of study whose purpose is to under-stand life at its deepest level.

Up to this point, the study of these matters has generally been a "proprietary" matter, with a proper name or brand name attached. Thus Buddhism, Hinduism, Scientology, Freudianism, Jungianism, Existentialism, Vedanta, and other disciplines each follows its own path. Usually, each proprietary discipline asserts that its own product is the only really successful one. These dis-

---

2. Principally, the various "Humanistic" or "Transpersonal" therapies, including Existential and Jungian analysis.

ciplines fall short of being sciences, however, to the degree that each is committed to a certain proprietary doctrine.

Science, by its nature, adopts various hypotheses but remains committed to none, as a matter of principle. A person with a true scientific spirit, while willing to take a particular viewpoint for what can be learned from that viewpoint, remains open to the discovery of new, currently unknown viewpoints and stands ready to discard her hypotheses when she can explain things better and learn more by entertaining different hypotheses. The truths and observations so arrived at are made the object of public discussion, scrutiny, and ownership; they are not the property of any individual or group. Truths are refined by being subjected to intersubjective observation, use, testing, validation, and falsification.

Metapsychology ought to exist — and, I think, at this point *can* exist — as a *generic* field of study embracing the truths that have been discovered in all these disciplines. It does not need to be ossified and fixated into a proprietary religion, cult, therapy, or belief system that bears a proper name or trademark. Rather, it can be, and ought to be, regarded as a legitimate discipline in itself, like physics, chemistry, biology, and philosophy. As such, metapsychology can improve our understanding of the various non-generic mental and spiritual disciplines. It is no more incompatible with Buddhism or Freudianism than, for instance, the study of organic chemistry is incompatible with a study of Bayer's method of synthesizing aspirin or Exxon's method of refining oil. A study of metapsychology should lead to the discovery of basic truths about personal experience that underly the various sciences, psychologies, therapies, and religions, and should therefore be able to relate these disciplines to each other.

It is conceivable that by applying the principles of metapsychology we can discover truths that could revolutionize the fields of science, religion, philosophy, and therapy.

But most of all, an understanding of personal experience — its creation, its elements and its structure — is applicable to the improvement of the quality of experience, the attainment of personal happiness. If we can reliably bring personal happiness into being, we will surely have accomplished a great deal.

APPENDICES

Appendix 1

Emergency Remedies

A number of metapsychology-oriented techniques have been developed for the specific purpose of providing immediate help to someone who has had a physical or emotional shock. They can usually be done in a very informal manner. But before beginning any remedy, it is important to make sure the person is *willing* to do the remedy. *No* form of viewing will be successful if done under duress.

Despite their often remarkable efficiency, there is nothing either magical or difficult about any of these remedies. Should you wish to attempt them yourself, the descriptions that follow, though brief, contain sufficient data to allow you to do so.

Remedies for Injuries and Illnesses

Though emergency remedies for illness and injuries are usually helpful — and, on occasion, astonishingly so — they are not intended to replace medical handling of illness or injury but to supplement medical treatment by helping the patient deal with the psychosomatic aspects of the illness or injury. They are done only *after* any needed first aid or other immediately needed medical procedures are completed. If the person is not ill or severely injured, or if she has already begun medical treatment, these remedies can and should be done without delay.

The Touch Remedy

The Touch Remedy may be done for any kind of illness or injury. It consists of touching the ill or injured person on different parts of the body[1] to improve her state of communication with her body.

When a person suffers physical pain or discomfort, she tends to flinch, to repress her awareness of the affected body part. This act of repression uses a certain amount of energy and thus lowers the personal power of the individual somewhat. It also seems to inhibit the healing process. A systematic approach to helping a person become more aware of her body, particularly the affected parts, reduces the "flinch" and has been found, empirically, to be effective in speeding recovery, sometimes dramatically.

A fingertip or one or both hands may be used to make the contact. Finger contact seems to work best where there are specific, relatively well-circumscribed areas of pain or discomfort. Manual contact seems to work better with more generalized bodily distress. Finger contact can be used with the viewer seated in a chair, preferably one with an open back, so that it is easy to touch her back. Manual contact is best used with the person lying on a bed or other comfortable surface. Ideally (for you, as the facilitator) this surface should be raised approximately to waist height, as with a massage table. Otherwise you may have to kneel or squat next to the viewer.

You must first find out what the viewer considers to be an acceptable amount of pressure. The contact should be firm

---

1. Avoiding embarrassing or sexual body parts.

enough to be readily felt but not so strong that it is uncomfortable. You instruct the viewer to stay in good communication with you and to let you know if there are any changes in physical sensations, emotions, or thoughts. Touch remedies seem to work better when done with the viewer's eyes shut, but they do not have to be.

The basic procedure is as follows: you touch the viewer — with a finger or with your hands — and, after the touch, and while maintaining the contact, you tell the viewer to feel your finger (or your hands). The viewer indicates in some way that he has done so. Then you touch the viewer in another bodily location and ask him to feel your finger (or hands). After awhile, the viewer gets the idea and you do not have to keep giving the request. Just continue touching the viewer and waiting for an indication that he has felt the touch. Moving on to the next location can take the place of a verbal acknowledgment. The procedure continues in this way, repetitively, until one or more of the following signs of an end point occur:

1. There is no change for several minutes.
2. The viewer becomes very relaxed.
3. There is some improvement.
4. The viewer has a cognition and feels good.
5. The uncomfortable bodily symptoms are gone or alleviated.

These are listed in increasing order of desirability. On encountering one of these end points, you must use your judgment in determining whether to stop or try for a better end point.

While doing the procedure, you should keep your attention on the viewer and remain alert for any changes in skin color, facial expression, breathing pattern, or bodily attitude that might signify a change in the viewer's state, a cognition, or some other unexpressed thought, emotion, or feeling. When such a change occurs, you should gently ask whether anything is going on or whether the viewer wants to say anything. Avoid mentioning the physical change you observed because that tends to make the viewer self-conscious. And even if no visible changes are occurring, you should ask how the viewer is doing every few minutes. This is again a matter of judgment. Some viewers do not like to be interrupted when their attention is on trying to become more aware of the body. In any case, remain in physical contact with the viewer during this step; doing so seems to enhance the affinity.

A good pattern of touching, if the discomfort is fairly generalized, is to start on the head and alternate from side to side, moving down the body. Concentrate on sensitive areas like joints and more or less follow the pattern of the various nerve connections of the body. Avoid any embarrassing or sexual parts of the body. A typical pattern (alternating, always, left and right sides) would be:

> Top of head
> Forehead
> Cheeks
> Under or behind the ears
> Sides of the neck
> Top of the shoulders
> Shoulder tips
> Elbows (inside or outside)
> Wrists
> First joint of digits
> Second joint of digits
> Tips of fingers
> (Then return by the same route to the neck)
> Sides of the chest
> Flanks
> Stomach (You can use a circular [clockwise] pattern, here, to follow the direction of the intestines)
> Hips
> Thighs
> Knees (inside or outside)
> (Continue down to the feet and back, as with the arms, back to the hips)
> Sides of back (moving up)
> Shoulder blades
> Shoulder tips

Shoulder tops
Neck
Back of the head (just below the skull seems
to be a good spot)
Top of the head

and so forth. You can alternate going down the abdomen and up the spine with going down the spine and up the abdomen. When working with a viewer who is lying down, it is best to concentrate for several runs on either the front or the back half of the body, then get the viewer to turn over to do the other side. Often a minor end point is a good time to do such a switch. If a session is very short — say, less than 15 or 20 minutes — the whole session is probably best given on one side of the body; then a second session may be done later on the other side. The viewer may have a preference about whether to have his front or his back done first. Follow it.

When there is a specific area of discomfort, spend more time in and around that area. It is best not to start off too close to a painful spot. You start at a certain distance from it and then move further away, a practice that unfixes the viewer's attention from it. As the remedy continues, you may move closer to the affected area, though in some cases (such as with an open wound or if the pain is located in a sexual part) you do not actually touch it. You concentrate on any special areas of discomfort, but otherwise you follow the pattern more or less as given above, giving approximately equal time to all parts of the body.

The Touch Remedy can be used several times a day. If a person is very ill or very tired, it is best to do several short sessions, each to a minor end point instead of doing a few long sessions and trying to achieve a major end point on each.

The Re-Enactment Remedy

This remedy is used to help a person recover from recent injuries. It is done as a repetitive procedure. The viewer can do this one by herself, or it can be done with a facilitator. The viewer goes to the location where an injury or physically painful incident occurred and re-enacts the incident. Ideally, re-enactment is done as soon as possible after an injury (of course, *after* any needed medical care is rendered, and assuming the viewer is ambulatory).

The viewer carries any objects she was carrying at the time and goes through the same motions as she did when the injury occurred (except slowly and in a controlled manner), and she gently contacts the location where she was injured with the injured part of her body. Of course, if the object that did the injury is still dangerous (e.g., because it is hot, caustic, or electrically charged), it must first be rendered harmless before the re-enactment is done. The re-enactment is repeated several times. You will often observe that, at some point, a feeling of pain "turns on" intensely, and then, as repeated contact is made, it will "turn off". At that point, the procedure is usually complete. The procedure usually takes only a few seconds or minutes. If changes continue to occur, however, it may be beneficial to continue for much longer. If nothing is happening after a few minutes, it is probably a waste of time to continue.

Sometimes a person (especially a child) cannot confront recontacting the area where she was injured. In this case, you bring her as close as she can willingly tolerate and do the re-enactment at that distance. She will probably come to feel comfortable, in time, with a gradual approach to the point of injury.

Locational Remedy

This remedy is useful for helping someone who is overwhelmed, distracted, confused, intoxicated, nauseated, or disoriented and unable to concentrate well enough to run subjective viewing procedures. There are various ways of doing a locational. The right way is the way that the viewer prefers.

The general idea is to repetitively draw the viewer's attention to objects in the environment. Getting the viewer to touch or feel different (non-charged) objects usually works well. You say, for instance, "Touch that desk." (or "Feel that desk.") The viewer does so, and you acknowledge him by saying, "Thank you," "Good," or "Fine." Then you say, "Touch that door," and you continue on with other physical objects in the vicinity.

The Locational Remedy is done to a point where the viewer:

1. Experiences no further change,
2. Feels more awake or aware, more in control, or more in present time,
3. Has a cognition and very good indicators, or
4. Experiences some other improvement.

Variations on the procedure include asking the viewer, repetitively, to "Notice that book," "Notice that ashtray," and the like, or to "Look at that table," or asking him questions like, "Where is the door?", "Where is the window?" and getting him to point. Anything that gets the viewer in contact with his environment repetitively will work. He will tell you which kind of locational he likes best.

Remedies for Recent Traumatic Incidents

These remedies work well with children or adults who have had recent severe upsets, injuries, or illnesses.

Conversational Remedy

The simplest way to handle a recent shock is to let the person talk about it and to listen carefully. He may need some encouragement at first. You can encourage a person to say more in various ways. "Tell me what happened," "Did anything else happen?", "Is there anything (or anything *else*) you want to tell me about that?", and similar prompts can be used, until the person has finished telling you. *You must refrain from any hint of evaluation or invalidation.* Just acknowledge by letting him know that you hear him and comprehend what he has said. A person is usually only too eager to tell you about a traumatic incident if you are a safe person for him to talk to. You *become* safe by avoiding evaluation and invalidation and, generally, by following the rules laid out in Chapter Eight, pp. 387-394. Be prepared to receive a long account, and do not get impatient or try to cut it short. If the person has told you about the incident but still has attention on it, ask him to tell you about it again one or more times.[2]

It may very well be that no more than one or a few such recountings will prove necessary, after which the viewer may be quite happy, with no more attention trapped in the area. If that is not the case, ask him (if it seems appropriate) "What do you think you might be able to do about that?" or "How might you handle that?", or something with a similar meaning. What you are asking the person to do is to get the idea of being causative in the area, instead of being a victim (but you must not accuse him of being a victim). You can continue to ask variations on this question, until the person feels more in control.

---

2. This technique works quite well on children. For instance, when a child has had a nightmare, after one or more recountings of the incident, she will "come up" the Emotional Scale through grief or fear to a point above antagonism. She will then be able to relax and go back to sleep.

Past-Present Comparison

This is another way of handling a traumatic incident. Ask the viewer "Where was the incident?" (or you could ask, "Where did you get hurt?", or whatever the wording of the specific incident is). You get an answer, acknowledge it, then ask, "Where are you now?", get an answer, and acknowledge it. You alternate back and forth between these two questions until some improvement occurs for the viewer.

Traumatic Incident Reduction

One of the best remedies for a traumatic incident is, of course, Traumatic Incident Reduction (TIR). This is best done in a formal session, but in an emergency it can be done informally. The procedure is as outlined in Chapter Eight (pp. 441-451). Again, with a sick or exhausted person, it is best to give very short sessions. And with a very distracted or overwhelmed person, it is best to start with a Locational Remedy, so that the person can concentrate better. Even if a full end point is not reached in a short session, a person will usually feel somewhat better for having begun the process of reducing the charge. The procedure can always be picked up where it was left off — and should be as soon as possible — and continued until a fuller end point is reached.

To reiterate an important point: make sure the person is really willing to have the remedy done at this time. Ill or shocked people are sometimes extremely exhausted and are in greater need of sleep or rest than of anything else. At other times, the person *cannot* rest or sleep well until the shock has been alleviated by viewing. Therefore, some judgment needs to be exercised. The best guideline is the interest and willingness of the viewer.

Appendix 2

Goals

The purpose of handling goals is to help a person reduce the charge and confusion surrounding goals he has failed to achieve, to clarify his present goals, and then to help him see how they can be achieved. You can do these procedures "solo", but it is best to do them with another person you trust. Your partner acts as a facilitator and also ensures that you do not get bogged down. After you have completed an action, you and your partner can switch roles: he can do the action with you as the facilitator. If you get bogged down while doing these actions solo, find a suitable partner and do the steps with him. Don't just keep on struggling.

Clearing Past Goals

This is an exercise to handle charge connected with past goals and purposes, prior to setting or establishing new goals or purposes. The purpose of clearing past goals is to be able to have a goal or goals that you:

1. Can achieve
2. Want to achieve
3. Feel is worthwhile
4. Can enjoy working toward
5. Feel is helpful to yourself and others.

Select, as a partner, someone with whom you are comfortable. If you are doing this procedure solo, first take the role of the facilitator and ask *yourself* the questions, then take the role of the viewer and answer them. If another person acts as your facilitator, he asks the questions.

Do this exercise on a turn-about basis, going through it with Partner A being the facilitator while Partner B does the exercise. Then Partner B becomes the facilitator, while Partner A does the exercise. Remember: it is crucial to the success of *any* procedure for the facilitator to avoid offering any evaluations, interpretations, or invalidations in response to anything that is said. It is equally crucial to acknowledge anything that is said in such a way that the viewer knows it is understood but not to go beyond a simple acknowledgement.

1. Have the viewer find a past goal (preferably a major goal or purpose) and discuss it, using the following questions as a guide:

   a. What progress have you made on the goal?
   b. What hindrances have you run into? (Make sure you find out *what* was stopping the viewer, not just a *time* when she was not making good progress.)
   c. How have those hindrances affected you?

2. Do Steps (a), (b), (c), (a), (b), (c), etc., until the viewer runs out of answers. Then ask the following:

   a. Are there situations or people that have made less of the goal in some way?
   b. Have you invalidated your goal or your ability to reach the goal?
   c. What has working on the goal actually resulted in?
   d. Are there any other considerations, ideas, or decisions you have had about the goal?

  e. Has the goal been beneficial to you?
  f. Has the goal been beneficial to others?
  g. Has attaining the goal been within your abilities?
  h. Have you enjoyed doing the steps necessary to bring this goal about?
  i. Is it a goal you have really *wanted* to achieve or just a goal you have felt you *ought* to achieve?
3. Turn around (have Partner B do the same thing with Partner A).
4. Then see if there is another goal that the viewer has had in the past and repeat the procedure laid out in Step (1).

This exercise is complete when:

1. The viewer finds a major goal to work on, or
2. Realizes that she already has one and is working on it, or
3. Finds out what her goal already is, or
4. Finds she knew what it was all along,

and has no remaining charge or confusion on it.

---

2. This procedure for handling goals was designed, in part, by David Mayo, former Director of Research at the Institute for Research in Metapsychology.

Appendix 3

Metapsychology Practitioners

IRM has approved three categories of facilitators in the United States and abroad as being competent in facilitating some or all parts of the viewing methodology.

The first category is that of *Graduate TIR Facilitator* (GTF). A GTF has completed the TIR Workshop or equivalent and has practiced for a period of time under IRM supervision. While not fully trained in general metapsychology, a GTF has demonstrated competence in using unmetered Traumatic Incident Reduction (TIR) with trauma survivors.

The second is *Certified TIR Facilitator* (CTF). A CTF has completed the full TIR Course, is trained in biomonitoring, and is competent in applying objective procedures, handling disturbances, and performing all the actions that can prove necessary to prepare a viewer for TIR.

The third category is *Certified General Facilitator* (CGF). A CGF is fully capable of training and facilitating on all Sections of the Curriculum, including those which contain TIR.

Those with the title of *Certified Trauma Specialist* (CTS) have also been certified by the International Association of Trauma Counselors.

554   *Beyond Psychology*

Non United States

Australia

Alex D. Frater, MAHA, GTF, CTS
261 Queen Street, Suite #9
(P.O. Box 718)
Campbelltown 2560
AUSTRALIA
61-46-281-197
Fax: 61-46-252-925

Canada

Neill Neill, GTF, PhD
General Delivery
Alert Bay, BC
CANADA V0N 1A0
604-974-2494

Irene Schoenfeld, CGF, CTS
Toronto Centre for
Applied Metapsychology
880 Broadview Ave
Toronto, ON
CANADA M4K 2R1
416-778-7396
Fax: 416-778-8623
email: 75231.2071@compuserve.com

Europe

Monica Gabrielli, CGF, CTS
3 Chemin du Hameau
1255 Veyrier
SWITZERLAND
41-22-784-3301

Hildegard Jahn, Dipl. Soz., CGF, CTS
Motivationsberatung
Perlacher Strasse 15
D-8000 München 90
WEST GERMANY
49-89-691-5881

Madeleine Lejeune Vandergoten, CGF
Centre de Métapsychologie
Appliquée Bruxelles
6 Boulevard Jules Graindor 6 Bte 2
B-1070 Bruxelles
BELGIUM
32-2-520-8122

Chantal Piot, PhD, CTF
93 Route De Berne
1010 Lausanne
SWITZERLAND
41-21-653-6624

United Kingdom

Steve Bisbey, CGF, CTS
Lori Beth Bisbey, Ph.D., CGF, CTS
Bisbeys Partnership
Gainsborough House
9 Portland Rd.
East Grinstead
Sussex RH19 4EB
ENGLAND
email: LoriBeth@demon.co.uk
44-1-342-323107

Bill K. Casey, GTF
148 Cholmley Gardens
Mill Lane
London, NW6 1AB
ENGLAND
44-171-435-2696

United States

Arizona

Kate Sorensen, MA, CGF, CTS
Compassionate Technologies Ctr.
The Gateway Ranch
77 Leupp Rd.
Flagstaff, AZ 86004
602-527-2623
Fax: 602-774-3463

California

Janet Buell, CGF
27703 Ortega Highway #15
San Juan Capistrano, CA 92675
714-661-5779
email: jbuell@pipeline.com

Helen Burgess CGF
Marin Center for
Applied Metapsychology
111 Frustuck Ave.
Fairfax, CA 94930-1934
415-455-0933
Fax: 415-258-0306

Kim Carbone, CTF
P.O. Box 65
Mill Valley, CA 94942
415-388-6338

Gerald D. French, MA, CGF, CTS
IRM
431 Burgess Drive
Menlo Park, CA 94025
415-327-0920
email: BiaGer@aol.com

Frank A. Gerbode, MD, CGF, CTS
IRM
431 Burgess Drive
Menlo Park, CA 94025
415-327-0920
email: sarge@metapsy.starconn.com

Brian Grimes, CGF, CTS
1312 Addiewell Place
San Jose, CA 95120
408-927-8269
Fax: 415-325-0389
email: BKGrimes@aol.com

Kevin Haughey, CGF
4244 Via Marina #137
Marina del Rey, CA 90292
310-821-2532

Aldyn Jones, CTF
70 London Way
Sonoma, CA 95476
707-939-9885

William Nichols, CTF
6854 1/2 Tyrone Ave.
Van Nuys, CA 91405-4045
818-909-4834

Marjolaine Tourangeau, CGF
5954 Caminito Cardelina
La Jolla, CA 92037
619-456-9713

Margaret K. Turner, CGF
3652 McNulty Way
Redwood City, CA 94061-1129
415-568-3207

Florida

Teresa Descilo, CGF, CTS
email: XTPS83A@prodigy.com
Victor Lyons, CGF, CTS
email: 100340.556@compuserve.com
16313 SW 99th Place
Miami, FL 33157
305-255-1619
Fax: 305-254-7654

David Findlay, MA, GTF, CTS
6 North Aurora Ave.
Clearwater, FL 34625
813-449-8964

Robert Moore, PhD, GTF, CTS
2191 Burnice Dr.
Clearwater, FL 34624
813-443-2096
Fax: 813-443-1120

Judith Steiner, MA, CTF, CTS
Center for Personal Growth
of Southern Florida, Inc.
401 Johnson Lane Ste 103
Venice, FL 34292
813-485-8586

Maryland

Rhonda Dziuk, GTF, CTS
Re-Entry Associates, Inc.
225 Frederick Street
Cumberland, MD 21502
301-777-2813

Raggi Malnati, MSW, CGF, CTS
Ctr. for Applied Metapsychology
3909 Kincaid Terrace
Kensington, MD 20895
301-949-9365
Fax: 202-667-0139
email: 75511.1513@compuserve.com

Michigan

Marian Volkman, CGF, CTS
Ann Arbor Center for
Applied Metapsychology
5145 Pontiac Trail
Ann Arbor, MI 48105
313-662-6864
email: marian.volkman@hal9K.com

Missouri

Nancy Day, CGF
Ability Facilitating Center
13 NW Barry Road, Suite 214
Kansas City, MO 64155-2728
816-468-4945

Oregon

Aerial Long, CGF
Center for Applied Metapsychology
1270 NW 178th Avenue
Beaverton, OR 97006
503-531-7916

Wachington

Gerald Bongard, GTF
4163 Beach Dr. S.W
Seattle, WA 98116
206-562-0864
email: gerrygail@aol.com

Karyn Kuever, MSW, CGF, CTS
Seattle Center for
Applied Metapsychology
10819 N.E. 112th St.
Kirkland, WA 98033-4507
206-827-7893
email: kkuever@u.washington.edu

West Virginia

Margaret R. Melotti, GTF, CTS
Re-Entry Associates, Inc.
P.O. Box 842
Ridgeley, WV 26753
301-777-2813
Fax: 301-777-2827

GLOSSARY

Working out a proper and consistent vocabulary for metap-sychology has been a continual compromise between what sounds graceful in ordinary English and what conveys a precise meaning. Although I have tried to use ordinary English terms as much as possible and have assiduously counted syllables so as to have as few as possible, I have had to coin a few terms. Even some of the English terms I have used have a different and rather more precise definition in my usage than English gives them. In this I follow the lead of other sciences such as chemistry (with its use of such terms as "acid" and "reduce"), physics ("work", "energy", "mass"), and astronomy ("star", "galaxy"). In some cases, a three or four word English phrase could be substituted for one of my terms, but I have found it clumsy, sometimes, to have to use a whole phrase when a single (unusual or somewhat stretched) word would serve.[1]

---

1. Unlike Wittgenstein and some other modern philosophers, however, I feel that there *is* such a thing as a concept, apart from — and sometimes even in the absence of — words to express it. So words are not all-important, in my view, except as a convenient way to refer to concepts.

Aberrated Cardinal Point: An arbitrary stable point or entity selected as a reference point in a situation because a person is not willing or able to confront the situation. This unwillingness or inability causes the person to cling to that entity as a point of stability. An aberrated cardinal point serves to hide the repressed situation rather than to handle it. Compare **Arbitrary Cardinal Point**.

Aberration: Distortion of thought, perception, intention, identity, and behavior, caused by the traumatic incident network.

Ability: A combination of control and understanding. Control is what corresponds, on the person side of the person-world polarity, to order on the world side. Understanding corresponds to heuristics. "*An* ability" is the potential for performing a specific action or type of action, whereas "ability" (used without an article) means a more *general* capability or potentiality. Thus "*an* ability" could be regarded as the exercise of "ability" in a specific area.

Abhorrence: Aversion directed toward an *entity* (a thing, not a person). The impulse toward rejecting or continuing to not have an entity. A high degree of abhorrence might be described as "loathing". Compare **Desire, Disaffection**.

Acceptance: An absence of aversion for something or someone.

Access: The ability to receive something causatively. Also (as a verb) to exercise causation in a receptive mode. Compare **Influence**.

Acknowledgment: An indication given by the receiver of a communication to the originator of the communication that is intended to convey the datum that the communication was received and comprehended. It is also an indication, given by the issuer of a request to the person who complies, that the issuer is aware of the compliance.

Action: An instance of causation by a person. The exercise of an ability.

Active: An active sequence or traumatic incident is one that is easily restimulated.

Activation: See **Reactivation**.

Activity: The action or actions (creative or receptive) that a person takes in order to fulfill an intention.

Activity Cycle: See **Cycle**.

Aesthetics: The appreciation of beauty. It is a "positive" kind of pleasure, not a drive-reduction form of pleasure. Compare **Relief**.

Affection: Affinity directed toward a *person* (not a thing or entity). The wish to be close to another person, to share a common space, viewpoint, and identity. An impulse toward communion. A high degree of affection is referred to as "love". Compare **Desire, Disaffection**.

Affinity: A willingness to be close to, or to assume the viewpoint of, something or someone, to reach for it or him, or to share space with it or him. It is a willingness to *have* something, or to *be* something or someone. When directed toward a person, affinity is affection; when directed towards an entity, it is desire. See **Desire, Affection, Aversion**.

Agenda: A written list of the actions the facilitator plans to take in the next viewing session.

Alienation: A low degree of communication, comprehension, and affection which, together, form a descending triad: less communication leads to less comprehension and less affection, less comprehension leads to less affection and less communication, and less affection leads to less communication and less comprehension. The easiest way out of this descending triad is by communicating. The opposite of **communion**. See **Debilitation**.

Alignment: The tendency of different parts of a person's world to fit together properly or to work together harmoniously to further the intentions of the person. The opposite of **incongruity**.

Ambivalence: A level of the Emotional Scale between antagonism and complacency. When one is ambivalent, one is on the borderline between liking or disliking a certain identity, activity, or experience. This is the emotional level at which one has "mixed feelings". The likelihood of succeeding in the activity is viewed as about equal to the likelihood of failing. The condition in the world that corresponds to ambivalence is drudgery.

Anesthetic Idea: An idea introduced and adhered to in an attempt to avoid confronting something painful. Anesthetic ideas tend to be fixed ideas. See **Delusion, Fixed Idea**.

Appendage: Something unnecessary that is added to something that is better in its simple form.

Arbitrary Cardinal Point: A point of reference chosen arbitrarily as a cardinal point in order to begin to resolve a confusion. Generally, a person will prefer *any* point of reference to complete confusion. An arbitrary cardinal point need not be aberrated. Compare **Aberrated Cardinal Point**.

Ascending Triad: With respect to communion, power, and empowerment — an increase of one component leading to an increase of the next component, and so forth, the result being higher and higher levels of communion, power, and empowerment.

Assent: The action of agreeing, of saying "Yes!" to a concept. It is one possible outcome of considering, the other possibilities being dissent and assignment of a probability. Assent can take two forms: receptive assent is acceptance; creative assent is commitment.

Assertion: A statement or declaration that affirms the existence of a particular element of reality. Assertions include interpretations and evaluations. A facilitator must not make assertions about the viewer's world or his case, except by way of agreeing with something the viewer already knows consciously (an *indication*). He *may* make assertions about what the next viewing action should be. See **Interpretation, Evaluation, Indication**.

Assessing: The action of finding areas of the viewer's life to which one or more viewing procedures can fruitfully be applied, i.e., areas that lie just below the awareness threshold. See **Awareness Threshold**.

Assumption (of Identity): Particularization and extension of identity through the incorporation of previously external elements (such as skills, tools, and concepts) as part of the self. The opposite of **shedding**.

Assumption (*An* Assumption): A *fact* that refers to, indicates, or implies a concept or entity that might or might not exist. A fact that has *meaning*. A premise.

Attention: The intention to receive. Compare **Volition**.

Authority: A person or group that is a source of knowledge, pleasure (relief or aesthetics), or order and is therefore a cardinal point. Note that an authority is an authority *for a person*. For someone else, that person or group might not be an authority.

Automaticity: An action done by a person without her being focally aware, at the time, of doing it. She has only a *subsidiary* awareness of doing it. She may be aware that the action is *happening* but, if so, she does not see herself as the originator of that action. It seems to be "just happening".

Automatism: An aberrated, conditioned, automaticity. Compare **Skill**.

Aversion: A refusal or unwillingness to share a space, viewpoint, or identity with something or someone, an intention to withdraw from it or him. It is the lower or "negative" portion of the scale of affinity. It goes beyond a mere lack of inclination or willingness to a positive refusal.

Awareness: Receptive power. Awareness is what, on the person side of the person-world polarity, corresponds to validity on the world side. See **Validity**.

Awareness Threshold: The dividing line that separates those entities of which a person can be readily aware from entities that are repressed. A person can only become aware of the latter by using a special procedure (if at all).

Bad Indicator: A phenomenon that indicates that a person is not being successful in carrying out some activity. A bad grade in school, or shortness of breath in a heart patient, are bad indicators. Negative emotion is usually a bad indicator. Compare **Good Indicator**.

Baseline: See **Baseline Value**.

Baseline Action: Cumulative downward motion of the baseline value, indicative of reduced charge.

Baseline Counter: A display that counts baseline action.

Baseline Drop: A drop that is so large and of such duration that it requires an adjustment of the baseline control to keep the needle on the dial. See **Drop**.

Baseline Value: The number the baseline control is pointing to when the needle is centered on the dial. It gives the level of skin resistance around which fluctuations of the needle occur.

Basic Actions: A person's three most basic actions are prehending a phenomenon (perceptualizing), prehending a concept (conceptualizing), and prehending a fact (cognizing). These actions apply in both a receptive and a creative mode.

Basic Aversions: Basic types of circumstances a person has in her world that she does not like and would like to change. These include **Physical Aversions** and **Situational Aversions**.

Basic Creative Actions: Picturing, conceiving, and postulating — i.e., perceptualizing, conceptualizing, and cognizing in a creative mode.

Basic Identity: An identity that occupies the highest point in the hierarchy of identities that a person can assume, an identity from which a person cannot "step back", or that a person cannot shed. It is a matter of speculation what sort of identity this might be, if it exists.

Basic Receptive Actions: Perceiving, interpreting, and understanding — these are perceptualization, conceptualization, and cognition in a receptive mode. Intuiting might be another basic receptive action.

Beauty: That which generates positive pleasure or aesthetic appreciation in a person. It is the counterpart, on the world side of the person-world polarity, to aesthetic feeling on the person side.

Behavior: Motion of a person's body, caused by his postulates.

Being: A person or spiritual entity, considered to be separate from a body and a mind. A viewer may think of himself as a being. He may also experience the presence of disembodied beings — external to him, but, in some sense, close by — that seem to exert an influence on him.

Blankness: An experience encountered in study when there is a failure of comprehension. A feeling of emptiness or stupidity that results from the absence of a concept that should be there.

Body: The physical organism through which a person interacts with the physical world.

Body (of a session): That part of a session that comes after pre-session clearing. It contains the major actions of that session. See **Major Action**.

Boredom: A person's response to a non-heuristic situation, a situation where there there is little or nothing to learn or in which learning is otherwise difficult. It is the counterpart, on the person side of the person-world polarity, to monotony or tedium on the world side.

Built-in Aversion: Aversion to uncomfortable bodily sensations that under normal circumstances cannot be readily confronted without having a relatively strong intention to do so. These aversions appear to be genetically "built in" to our bodily identity, and most are clearly conducive to organismic survival.

Calling: A form of assessment in which the facilitator starts out with an item (sentence, phrase, or word) or a list of items and calls these off, noting the meter responses. The items that respond are either addressed as they come up or taken up after the whole list has been called, generally in descending order of size of response.

Candidate Fact: A concept or referent. It is something that offers itself as a possible fact but which may or may not yet be accepted as such. When a person gives assent to a candidate fact, she "elects" it to the status of being — for her — an *actual* fact.

Cardinal Point: An entity or person that, because of its (or her) tendency to promote pleasure, order and heuristics in a person's world or communion in her relationships, or because of its relationship to specific intentions of hers, has importance for her.

Cardinality: Importance; the quality of being a cardinal point. The cardinality of an experience or of an activity determines the "intensity" with which it is experienced, or the engagement with which it is done.

Case: The sum total of the charge a person has, together with the aberration that results therefrom.

Case Planning: The action of deciding which procedures should be used with a viewer and the order in which they should be done. Case planning is done before starting a session, not *during* a session.

Causation: Any action a person does is a form of causation. In a receptive action, he causes the *receipt* of a phenomenon, fact, or concept; in a creative action, he *creates* a phenomenon, fact, or concept. Both are causative.

Charge: Repressed, unfulfilled intention.

Checklist: A procedural pattern consisting of a linear sequence of actions, all of which must be done in the prescribed order.

Clear: Free of current restimulation and turbidity.

Clearing: Clearing is a corrective viewing action, an action taken to destimulate, deactivate or discharge material that is already inadvertently or accidently restimulated in life or in session. The end point of clearing is a viewer who is "clear" — free of turbidity and ready to move on to her next discovery action. See also **Discovery, Deactivation, Discharge, Disturbance, Pre-Session Clearing, Turbidity**.

Climbing Needle: A needle pattern consisting of a motion to the left, indicating a climb in skin resistance.

Co-Facilitation: A partnership between two or more persons, in which they alternate being facilitator and viewer for each other, so that both can get help and both can have the experience of helping. Sometimes it is best to have more than two and use a "round robin" schedule.

Cognition: A prehended fact, one of which a person is currently aware. Also, the act of prehending a fact. The term is also used to mean a *new* cognition — a realization, an acquisition of new knowledge. (verb: cognize)

Command Cycle: A cycle created when one person gives a command to one or more other people. It is complete when those to whom the command was given comply with the command or when the intention to get them to comply is ended.

Communication: The transfer of a token from one person to another, where the concept or phenomenon that the receiver interprets the token as representing is the same as the concept or phenomenon that the originator intended the token to represent.

Communication Cycle: A cycle that starts when one person attempts to communicate to another. It ends when the originator knows that his communication has been comprehended or when he gives up the attempt to communicate. Compare **Command Cycle**.

Communication Exercises: Exercises in which the various components of communication (confronting, delivering a communication, acknowledging, etc.) are practiced to a point of expertise. Abbr. **CE's**

Communication Section: A section of the Primary Curriculum that concerns itself with difficulties with and charge on communication.

Communion: A combination of communication, comprehension, and affection that characterizes a person's relationship with another person. These three factors tend to form an ascending triad: more communication leads to more comprehension and more affection, more comprehension leads to more affection and more communication, and more affection leads to more communication and more comprehension. The easiest entry point to this triad is through communication. Compare **Power**, **Alienation**.

Comparing: One of the basic actions that a viewer is asked to do in viewing. It is the act of describing the relationship between two entities or concepts.

Completing A Cycle: Since a cycle depends, for its existence, on the existence of an intention, the cycle is complete when the intention is either fulfilled or unmade. Failing to complete cycles clutters up a person's present time with too many ongoing activities.

Comprehension: The act of correctly identifying the concept or experience that an originator of a communication intends to convey. A co-experiencing or joint prehension of one or more concepts or phenomena between two persons. Comprehension is the result of communication. It need not involve agreement or concurrence. See **Prehension**.

Compulsion: An important or habitual creative automatism.

Conceiving: The act of creating a concept.

Concept: Something that may or may not exist, to which a symbol or statement may refer. A concept or thought, not a picture or phenomenon. It may be represented by a symbol, but it is not the symbol. A person converts a concept into a fact by assenting to it, into a fiction by dissenting from it, or into a certain probability by according it something in between full assent and full dissent. It is, in effect, a "candidate fact" or "potential fact". It is something that "offers itself" as a possible fact but which may or may not yet be accepted as such.

Conceptoid: A sort of intimation or the vague beginnings of a concept that has not yet attained enough clarity of meaning to have it make sense to agree or disagree with it. An unclear or incompletely-formed concept. See **Quasi-Entity**.

Conceptual Blankness: See **Blankness**.

Conceptual Skill: The ability to use concepts to understand or to create other concepts.

Conceptualizing: The action of prehending a concept (whether it is created or received).

Conclusion: A fact arrived at from data by the process of understanding (interpreting and assenting to an interpretation of) the data. Compare **Datum**.

Concurrence: An agreement between two or more persons that one or more entities exist, a shared assent to those entities. There are various degrees of concurrence, depending on how much is shared.

Conditioning: The creation of automatisms. Conditioning is based on "deficiency motivation", an attempt to avoid or relieve pain or discomfort. In a conditioning situation, a person has a "choice" of performing the conditioned action or experiencing pain or discomfort and, if the pain is not confrontable, the choice has to be to act. A series of such experiences creates an automatism. Compare **Learning**.

Condition: The degree of success a person is having in a given activity. A condition is the counterpart, on the world side of the person-world polarity, to an emotional level on the person side.

Confronting: Engaging in receptive actions with respect to an entity. Being aware of that entity. Compare **Handling**.

Congruity: The tendency of different parts of a person's world to align with each other, to work together harmoniously to further the intentions of the person. The absence of inconsistency or conflict, either with the person's intentions or with each other, between the parts of a person's world.

Consciousness: See **Power**.

Consideration: The act of considering. Also, the product of an act of considering, i.e., a judgment that a certain concept is true, false, or has a certain probability.

Considering: The action of coming to decide whether to convert a concept into a fact by giving assent to it, to convert it into an unreality by dissenting from it, or to convert it into a probability by giving it something between full assent and full dissent. In considering, one weighs the pros and cons of accepting a concept and then finally decides or determines that it is factual, probable, improbable, or non-factual.

Contacts: Cylindrical metal electrodes that are held in the hands and connected to an electrodermometer, used to measure palmar skin resistance.

Continuity: A type of simplicity consisting of an absence of fragmentation, compartmentation, or interruption.

Continual Misdeeds: Harmful acts that are done repeatedly or continually. A person has difficulty allowing herself to improve when she is continually committing misdeeds.

Control: The ability to perform creative actions on an entity or on the world. Control is on the person side of the person-world polarity. The counterpart on the world side is order.

Controllability: A type of stability that permits a person to create predictable effects in her world.

Core Curriculum: The part of the General Curriculum that follows the Primary Curriculum, so-called because it deals with issues that lie at the core of a person's identities and purposes. It includes the Identity and Individuation Sections — the sections beyond the Rightness Section. Compare **Primary Curriculum**.

Correction List: A list of the most likely errors or unwanted conditions that can exist in a particular subject or procedure, designed to spot current items that are restimulated and to clear them. Some correction lists are specifically designed to handle difficulties that may arise in a particular subject, viewing procedure, or in-life situation. Others are more general. A facilitator may use a correction list when something goes wrong in life or in a viewing session.

Corrective Action: An action taken to handle unforeseen errors or difficulties that make it necessary to take a detour from an Individual Curriculum. The end point of a corrective action is a viewer who has handled the error or difficulty and is ready to move on to his next curricular action. Corrective actions are sometimes called "remedies". Compare **Curricular Action**.

Counter-Intention: The intention that some entity *not* exist. The entity opposed may be an object, an event, a state of affairs, or another intention.

Creation: A creative action. The act of bringing into existence concepts, phenomena, or facts. It is a "pushing out", an outflow, of concepts, phenomena, or facts from a person to his world. Also, the product of such an action.

Creative: A directionality toward the world from the person. Giving, rather than receiving. Pushing out, rather than pulling in. Compare **Receptive**.

Creative Action: The action of creating a fact, phenomenon, or concept, of putting something out into the world or producing a change in the world. Basic creative actions include picturing, conceiving, and postulating. Compare **Receptive Action**.

Creative Procedure: A viewing procedure in which the viewer is asked to perform one or more creative actions.

Creativity: The ability to engage in creative actions; the ability to bring entities into existence. See **Creative Action**.

Crossflow: The causation of some kind of effect between two or more persons, or between one or more persons and one or more entities, as viewed by another person who is not directly involved. See **Flow**.

Curricular Action: An action or procedure that is part of an Individual Curriculum. Compare **Corrective Action**.

Curriculum: A plan giving the sequence of actions required and abilities attained in the course of self-improvement. This may be a *General* Curriculum that would apply to most people, or an *Individual* Curriculum that applies to a specific person. See **Individual Curriculum, General Curriculum, Primary Curriculum, Core Curriculum**.

Cycle: The entire history of an activity or of an entity, from beginning to end. A cycle has a point of creation (in the case of an object) or starting (in the case of an event or state of affairs); a period during which it is persisting, continuing, and changing; and a point of destruction (for an object) or stopping (for an event). For any given person, different times are defined by the cycles that exist for that person. Some cycles are brought into being by the intentions that rule the various *creative* actions, others by intentions associated with the various *receptive* actions.

Danger: A condition in which the person is faced with an overwhelming threat with which she feels she may not be able to cope. Her impulse is to flee, to disengage, but she has not yet done so. The corresponding emotion on the person side of the person-world polarity is fear.

Datum: Something that is "given" to a person, in other words *accepted* by her. A datum is either a phenomenon or a fact. Compare **Conclusion**.

Deactivation: A situation in which, because of passage of time, change of environment, or some other reason (such as the application of a viewing technique), an active sequence or traumatic incident becomes inactive. See **Active, Inactive**.

Debilitation: A relative absence of power (drive, control, and understanding) with respect to entities. It forms a descending triad, with less drive leading to less control and understanding, less control leading to less drive and understanding, and less understanding leading to less control and drive. The opposite of **power**.

Declaration: A statement of fact, delivered as a communication to another person, with the intention that the other person assent to it.

Declarative: A type of sentence that is used to make a declaration.

Deficiency Motivation: A term used by Maslow to refer to the pursuit of "negative pleasures". It is a motivation to escape from an uncomfortable situation, to obtain relief. See **Relief**.

Delayed Reaction: An electrodermometer reaction that occurs some time after the viewer has had an item presented to him. Compare **Response**.

Delusion: A falsehood introduced in the act of repression in order to help hide the repressed material. See **Fixed Idea**.

Denial: A refusal to accept an obvious interpretation of a datum as true. A failure to accept as a fact a concept that *would* be accepted if it were not for an inability or unwillingness to confront.

Describing: One of the basic actions a viewer is asked to do in viewing, consisting of viewing and communicating the characteristics of what is viewed.

Descending Triad: With respect to communion, power, and empowerment: a diminishing of one component leading to a diminishing of the other components, the result being lower and lower levels of communion, power, and empowerment.

Desire: Affinity directed toward entities. An impulse toward having or continuing to have an entity. A high level of desire is referred to as a "yearning". Compare **Affection**, **Abhorrence**.

Destimulation: The undoing of restimulation. Such factors as the passage of time, a change of environment, or a viewing procedure can result in a destimulation.

Detour: A necessary deviation from a procedure or program, designed to handle an emergent situation that the current procedure or program is not capable of handling. Although a detour is a deviation from the normal path, it is designed specifically to take one around an obstacle and to return one to the main route as soon as possible. Compare **Sidetrack**.

Dilemma: A conflict between two or more of a person's current intentions.

Dimension: A quality of a world that permits the separation of its component parts.

Directed Unawareness: See **Repression**.

Directionality: An orientation in a certain direction along a certain dimension, such as up, down, toward the past, toward the future, toward the world, or toward the mind.

Disaffection: Aversion directed toward a person. The characteristic of being unwilling to be close to another person, to share a space, viewpoint, or identity with him. It is an impulse toward alienation. A high degree of disaffection might be called "hatred". Compare **Abhorrence, Affection, Aversion**.

Disability: A personal characteristic or situation that lowers a person's level of power or communion.

Discharge: The bringing to awareness of the contents of a traumatic incident, including any intentions contained in it, usually with a consequent fulfillment or cancellation of the intentions and a movement of the traumatic incident out of present time into the past as a completed (and no longer traumatic) incident.

Discharge by Inspection: A discharge that occurs as soon as an entity is spotted.

Discovery: The act of selectively addressing, exploring, and reducing charge in currently *unrestimulated* areas of disability. Compare **Clearing**.

Disengaged (from viewing): The condition in which the viewer is either not interested in her case, not willing to talk to the facilitator about it, not willing to comply with viewing instructions, or some combination of the above. In other words, the viewer is disengaged from viewing when the query channel, the observation channel, or the report channel are not functioning properly.

Disengagement: The act of moving away from a particular identity or activity, of assigning it less importance or cardinality, of discontinuing it.

Dissent: The action of disagreeing, of saying "No!" to a concept. It is one possible outcome of considering, the other possibilities being assent and assignment of a probability. Dissent is really only a form of assent. To dissent with the concept "a red car in front of my house" is to assent to the obverse concept "no red car in front of my house". See **Obverse Concept**.

Dissonance: A lack of mental harmony. Dissonance is what corresponds, on the person side of the person-world polarity, to incongruity on the world side.

Disturb: To cause a person's traumatic incidents or sequences to be restimulated or to put a person's attention on an upset, problem, withhold, or misdeed. To create turbidity.

Disturbance: A subject, situation, or item that is currently in a state of restimulation. Such items include upsets, problems, withholds, misdeeds, and traumatic incidents. A disturbance is an area of charge on which the viewer has her attention fixed. This area may not be one of the major issues that were supposed to be addressed in the session. Nevertheless, it needs to be handled first by clearing (at the start of a session or as part of a corrective plan) so that the viewer can free her attention from the disturbance and thus be ready for the major action of the session.

Disturbed: Of a person: to be in a state of turbidity. To have disturbances. Compare **Clear**.

Domain: A sphere of responsibility. There are six domains: self, intimates, groups, mankind, life, and the Infinite. These domains are concentric; each successive domain contains the previous ones, with the self at the center. Each domain has a subjective or mental side and an objective or physical side, reflecting the polar relationship between a person and her world.

Downward Spiral: See **Descending Triad**.

Dramatization: Behavior that is caused by the restimulation of one or more traumatic incidents. It is an unconscious re-enactment of the behavior that occurred at the time of the traumatic incident or incidents as (usually rationalized) behavior directed toward present-time objects or people. The behavior may be appropriate to the past incident or incidents, but it is usually not appropriate to the present time situation. Therefore it often has destructive consequences.

Drive: The general capacity to desire. A person with a great deal of drive is capable of having many desires and strong ones; a person with little drive doesn't care much about things. Drive is an essential ingredient (along with ability) of power. Without drive, a person, however able, is not powerful. Compare **Power**, **Ability**.

Drop: An electrodermometer response (dropping needle) of moderate size (over 1/8").

Dropping needle: An electrodermometer needle pattern, consisting of a movement to the right, indicating a decrease in skin resistance.

Drudgery: A condition in which a person feels he is fighting his environment. He is trying very hard to succeed in an activity, not making adequate progress, and not enjoying it. The corresponding emotional level is between anger and ambivalence — "frustration" might describe the general frame of mind. The person feels trapped in his situation, with little hope of improvement. His strategy is to resist, to use force, and to fight back. He becomes less productive and tends to develop a backlog of incomplete cycles.

Electrodermometer: Galvanic skin response meter. An instrument that measures electrical skin resistance as a means of biomonitoring or biofeedback. It is useful in locating charged items and in determining when an end point has occurred. Abbr. **Meter**.

Emergency: A person in a condition of emergency is constantly coping with immediate threats. She is close to being overwhelmed, and she is building up major backlogs (incomplete cycles) because she does not have time to handle routine chores. She tries to be hyper-alert, to attend compulsively and indiscriminately to every detail in her environment that seems to be a threat, and to ignore or neglect other things that, while still needing attention, are less immediately threatening. She is not so severely under threat that she feels she has to run away. Rather, her attention is drawn compulsively *to* the threat, and she loses sight of the importance of other things. The emotional level corresponding to emergency is anxiety.

Emotional Scale: A series of different emotions felt by a person as he encounters varying degrees of success or failure in an activity or has varying degrees of affinity or aversion for something or someone A continuum of emotions, ranked in increasing order of adaptiveness and success, between final failure and final success.

Empowerment: The combination of pleasure, order, and heuristics that the person attempts to create in and receive from his world. A combination of value and validity. It is the counterpart, on the world side of the person-world polarity, to power. Compare **Validity**, **Value**, **Power**.

End Point: The point at which the cycle connected with an activity has been successfully completed. This is the point at which the activity should be ended. It is manifested by a set of phenomena that indicate the successful termination of the activity. These phenomena vary from activity to activity.

Engaged (in viewing): The state in which the viewer is interested in his case, willing to talk to the facilitator about it, and willing to follow viewing instructions. The opposite condition is one in which the viewer is **disengaged** — not interested in his case, not willing to talk to the facilitator about it, or not willing to follow instructions. When a person is engaged in viewing, the query, observation, and report channels are in full operation.

Engagement: The degree to which a person assumes an identity, or the importance he places on a particular activity. Engagement is "how much of himself he puts into" an activity or identity.

Entity: An object, event, or relationship (state of affairs) that is part of a person's world, i.e., that exists, for a person, at a certain moment. Compare **Quasi-Entity, Person**.

Environment: The person's entire world, including the physical world, her body, and her mind. The viewer's mind is part of her *environment*, not part of the viewer. Also, a part of the viewer's world that is close by, such as the facilitation room.

Ethics: Control of intention; intending to intend; the ability to choose amongst different intentions, identities, and activities.

Event: An entity that is described as something that is *happening*. A process, rather than an object or a state of affairs. Compare **Object, State of Affairs**.

Evil: That which is counter-intended.

Existence: From a person-centered viewpoint, the quality of being perceivable or of being accepted as factual. The quality of being an entity — a phenomenon, fact, or concept.

Explanation: An inferring of new entities from existing entities; an interpretation of given data.

Exploration: A relatively informal viewing procedure in which the facilitator asks questions to get the viewer to look at and talk about different items and records the answers given and (if an electrodermometer is used) the meter responses obtained. Exploration may be done as a separate interview or as part of a viewing session. Compare **Inquiry**.

Extroversion: Looking outward. Looking toward the world side of the person-world polarity.

Facilitator: A person who helps another to perform the actions of viewing. Her function is to help the viewer to view his world and thereby to alleviate the charge and aberration contained therein.

Fact: An imperceptible entity that exists for a person at a certain moment. A concept that is accepted as real; a concept to which a person gives assent.

Factoid: A belief, consideration, or opinion that a person holds to be probable but of which he does not have enough certainty to accept it as a fact. A concept that is accepted as more likely real than not. See **Quasi-Entity**.

Factuality: (Refers to a concept) The condition of being assented to or agreed with by a person. Truth.

Failure: A condition in which a person realizes that he is not being successful in carrying out an intention or engaging in an activity. At the point of failure, the person begins to disengage from the activity. Failure is the counterpart, on the world side of the person-world polarity, to grief and apathy on the person side.

Faith: A degree of certainty that is sufficient for action. Faith provides the demarcation point between quasi-entities and actual entities. Faith usually falls short of total certainty, but it is the point at which we feel we can cease considering something and begin acting. See also **Quasi-Entity**.

False Belief: A belief based on unawareness of entities with which it is incongruent.

Fifth Dimension: See **Polar Dimension**.

Final Failure: A degree of failure that mandates complete disengagement from an activity.

Final Success: The fulfillment of an intention, leading to a disengagement from the intended activity. It is the counterpart, on the world side of the person-world polarity, to elation on the person side.

Finding: A basic action in viewing, consisting of locating something, physically or mentally. Getting something. See **Get**.

First Consideration: The first decision a person makes on a particular topic. This consideration therefore cannot be a contradiction of another consideration on the same subject. It is possible, however, for the person to add a layer of delusion on top of the first consideration — a second consideration that is incongruent with the first, then to add a third that is incongruent with the second, and so forth.

Fixation: An important or habitual receptive automatism.

Fixed Idea: A concept that is adhered to because it serves to make it unnecessary for the viewer to confront something — such as a painful situation, a confusion, or a problem — or because it serves to hold a fixed identity in place and thus seems important for the "survival" of that identity. A fixed goal leads to a fixed identity, and a fixed identity has fixed ideas that hold it in place. To discharge and dislodge a fixed goal and identity, it is usually necessary to address and discharge the fixed ideas that go along with it.

Fixed Identity: An identity a person has assumed in an effort to avoid pain or unpleasantness, one which the person does not feel completely free to give up.

Fixed Incident: A receptive cycle or activity that is incomplete because of repression. The repression causes a period of past time to be carried along chronically as part of the person's present time.

Flow: A directionality of causation between persons or between persons and entities. See **Outflow, Inflow, Crossflow**, and **Reflexive Flow**.

Focal Awareness: Awareness of that to which a person is currently attending.

Force: Something that has coercive power because it involves things that are difficult to confront. In viewing, you are generally trying to have the viewer find and handle force, rather than significance. Compare **Significance**.

Free Baseline: A free needle that is swinging so widely that the facilitator must keep adjusting the baseline control to keep the needle on the dial.

Free Needle: A needle pattern, consisting of a smooth, backward and forward "floating" motion at smoothly varying and not overly rapid rates of speed, with no particular directionality to it. It generally indicates unfixed attention, as when a person is clear (free of turbidity) or when a person has successfully completed a cycle or procedure. It is one of the cardinal signs that a viewing procedure has been completed and, as such, is something with which any facilitator using a meter should become so familiar that she can recognize it without hesitation.

Fully-Realized Person: A major goal of applied metapsychology is the systematic clearing away of a person's traumatic incident network. A person with no network could be said to be fully conscious, fully unrepressed, fully able, fully self-actualizing (to use Maslow's term), fully-functioning (to use Carl Rogers' term), or fully rational (to use Albert Ellis' term). A fully-realized person is also able greatly to expand *or* contract his scope of identity at will, or to shift entirely to a different identity. This state is an absolute and, as such, is unlikely ever to be fully achieved, but it is useful as a direction.

Future: A directionality "forward" in time, opposite to that of the past. Also, that set of entities in a person's world which have a future tense.

Gain: To come to have, or to acquire the ability to get, an entity.

Game: An activity that is engaged in at an emotional level of cheerfulness or above.

General Curriculum: A case plan giving the usual or customary sequence of actions required and abilities attained in the course of viewing. The General Curriculum consists of two parts: the Primary Curriculum and the Core Curriculum. Compare **Individual Curriculum** and see **Primary Curriculum, Core Curriculum**.

General TIR: A section of the Primary Curriculum in which TIR is used to handle items that are not currently in restimulation or areas of life that are not currently bothering the viewer. Its intent is to prevent future restimulation and difficulties and to remove charge from the case generally and thoroughly.

Get: To come to prehend an entity. See **Having, Prehend**.

Good: That which is intended.

Good Deed: An action that aligns with the major intentions of the majority of people affected by the action.

Good Indicator: A phenomenon that indicates (implies, means, signifies, or suggests) that a person is being successful in carrying out some activity. Positive emotions, good skin color, and free needles are good indicators.

Great Man Syndrome: The condition of being fixed in an over-extended identity.

GSR Meter: See **Electrodermometer**.

Guiding: Watching for a meter response and then querying what the viewer is looking at. This should be used sparingly, since it tends to cause a viewer to become dependent on the meter.

Handling: Creative actions directed toward an entity. Compare **Confronting**.

Happiness: The knowledge that one is being successful at fulfilling one's intentions. The subjective state that corresponds to the progressive attainment of success. See **Success**.

Harm: Action that a person views as opposing her intentions. Compare **Help**.

Hatred: A high degree of disaffection. Compare **Loathing**.

Having: The ability to be causative (or to act) with respect to an entity. The ability to prehend, or to get. See **Get, Prehend**.

Help: Action that a person views as furthering his intentions. Compare **Harm**.

Help Section: That section of the Primary Curriculum that is concerned with handling the viewer's charge on the subjects of help and control.

Heuristic: Tending to promote learning or understanding. School should be an heuristic environment.

Heuristics: The quality of a world or part of a world by virtue of which it promotes learning or greater understanding. The opposite of "dullness", monotony, or tedium. Heuristics is the counterpart, on the world side of the person-world polarity, to understanding on the person side.

Identification With the Aggressor: A situation where one relives a past traumatic incident from the viewpoint of the person who was overwhelming one, rather than from one's own viewpoint. One tends to act like and feel the feelings of the aggressor in the incident.

Identity: A package of viewpoints, tools, subsidiary awarenesses, and conceptual, perceptual, and instrumental abilities that can be incorporated as part of the self in order to fulfill an intention. "Identity" can also include the way in which a person chooses to appear to others.

Identity Section: That part of the Core Curriculum that deals with fundamental identities the person has assumed in order to carry out fundamental intentions.

Immutability: Resistance to being changed by a person. For an object, immutability is solidity (resistance to transformation) or mass (resistance to translation); for an event or state of affairs, immutability is a tendency to persist, or momentum.

Imperative: A sentence that is an explicit request.

Imperception: A failure to perceive.

Importance: See **Cardinality**.

Inactive: An inactive sequence or traumatic incident is one that (because of the passage of time, a change of environment, or some other reason) is not easily restimulated. Compare **Active**.

Incident: A receptive activity. Compare **Task**.

Incomplete Cycle: An activity that is ongoing and occupies a person's present time because its ruling intention has neither been fulfilled nor unmade.

Incompossibility: A term used by Leibnitz to mean strong incongruity, the inability of certain entities to co-exist.

Incomprehension: A failure to understand or a weakness of the powers of understanding. This is the counterpart, on the person side of the person-world polarity, to unintelligibility on the world side.

Incongruity: An incompatibility, conflict, or misalignment between two elements of a person's world. It is what corresponds, on the world side of the person-world polarity, to **Dissonance** on the person side. The opposite of **Alignment**.

Indication: An deliberate assertion about something related to a person's case, personality, or situation. In the context of viewing, it must only be done as an *agreement* with something the viewer already knows consciously. Wrong indications may be a major source of difficulty, if given in or out of a viewing session.

Indicator: Something that shows how well or poorly an activity is going. See **Good Indicator**, **Bad Indicator**.

Individual Curriculum: A case plan intended to give the optimal sequence of viewing steps that may be needed by a specific person. In planning an Individual Curriculum, a Technical Director starts with the general curriculum as a guideline and tailors it to the specific needs of the individual viewer. See **General Curriculum**.

Inflow: The receipt of an effect by a person from an entity or another person.

Influence: The ability to be causative creatively with respect to something. Also, (as a verb) to exercise such causative creativity. Access and Influence are the two forms of having (receptive and creative, respectively). Compare **Access**.

Inquiry: An informal means of obtaining information from a viewer about a particular subject. As in an Exploration, you try to draw the viewer out on a particular subject and inquire more closely into topics that appear to be charged or to have the viewer's interest. In an Inquiry, however, you are not primarily trying to release charge on a subject, and you do not need to bring the procedure to an end point. You are merely gathering information in a systematic way. Compare **Exploration**.

Insensitivity: A failure to perceive or a weakness of the power of perception. This is the counterpart, on the person side of the person-world polarity, to opacity on the world side. (It is not used in the sense of not caring about other people or not paying attention to them.)

In-Session Clearing: Handling of disturbances that arise in the middle of a session.

Insight: A cognition of an underlying truth.

Instantaneous Free Needle: A response in which a needle that was not free becomes free when an item is presented to the viewer. A BDFN is a type of instantaneous free needle that begins with a baseline drop.

Instruction: See **Viewing Instruction**.

Instrumental Goodness: The quality of being useful as a means toward some end. Compare **Intrinsic Goodness**.

Instrumental Skill: Skill at performing creative actions directed toward the world.

Integrity: Congruity of intention and identity.

Intelligibility: The quality of a world or part of a world by virtue of which it can be understood by a person. It is the counterpart, on the world side of the person-world polarity, to understanding on the person side.

Intention: A combination of desire and ability. A goal or purpose. An impulse toward causation. The proximal part of an action, the part that lies closest to the person. A clear, strong intention with no admixture of counter-intention usually results in the successful completion of a cycle. A common cause of failure is the absence of a sufficiently strong intention or the presence of counter-intentions. See also **Attention, Volition**.

Intention Units: The degree of power, consciousness, or intention might be considered to be divided into "units", of which a person has a finite quantity at any given time. If some of these are "used up" in ongoing activities, he has fewer available to take on new activities or to succeed in existing activities.

Interest: Directed attention. Attention can be either other-directed or intentionally self-directed.

Interpreting: Finding a meaning, significance, or explanation a certain datum might refer to or imply, thereby arriving at a concept. An interpretation is not a fact until it has been considered, verified, and assented to.

Interrogative: A type of sentence that asks a question, i.e., that is used to request that information be provided.

Intimates: People who are close friends, lovers, or family members. This is the second domain. See **Domain**.

Intrinsic Goodness: The quality of being good as an end in itself, rather than as a means to some other end. Compare **Instrumental Goodness**.

Introspection: Looking toward the mind rather than toward the physical universe. A person or identity cannot, however, look "inside" herself.

Intuition: The receipt of concepts or facts by a person directly from her world, not via interpretation or explanation of data.

Invalidation: Attributing a negative value or invalidity to something. Also, saying or implying to another that she is a bad person or that her beliefs or perceptions are false.

Item: An entity or topic that is possibly or actually charged for the viewer. A word, phrase, or sentence that communicates such an entity or topic.

Justification: A mechanism for handling the dissonance a person experiences when she has committed a misdeed. Because a person does, basically, wish to improve conditions all around, when she finds out (after the fact, of course) that she has worsened them by some misdeed, a dissonance exists that can be painful for her. One means of handling this dissonance is by explaining, to herself or others, how her action was not really a misdeed. This explanation can then serve as a rationale for future similar misdeeds.

Learning: The acquisition of knowledge or skill by the learning cycle. Compare **Conditioning**.

Learning Cycle: The cycle by which a person moves from a datum or data to a new entity. The way in which a person acquires new knowledge. A great deal has been written about this subject under the heading of the laws of deduction and induction.

Listing: A type of assessment that consists of asking the viewer a question and having her give a list of items, while observing the reaction to each as she gives it. When listing, the facilitator expects to find multiple items, none of which is particularly "right" or "wrong". The facilitator records the items and their responses (or lack of response). These responses are then used to determine which items should be addressed, and in which order. Compare **Selecting, Calling**.

Live: Of an item: one that carries charge and lies just below the awareness threshold. Such an item will attract the viewer's interest and will tend to cause a response on an electrodermometer. See **Awareness Threshold**.

Loathing: A high degree of abhorrence. Compare **Hatred**.

Location: The area of operation of a procedure. A place used for some purpose in a procedure. In a viewing procedure, the location addressed might be the body, the room, the mind, the physical universe, and so forth.

Logical Consistency: One form of congruity, a form of conceptual compatibility.

Loop: A procedural pattern, used in some forms of viewing, consisting of the repetition of a checklist.

Lose: To cease to have an entity. See **Gain, Having**.

Love: A high degree of affection. Compare **Yearning**.

Major Action: A procedure, contained in the case plan and the session agenda, that is done as part of the body of a session. See **Body** (of a session).

Mass: The quality of an object that causes it to resist translation (change of location). Also, the presence of a phenomenon (as in study), as opposed to concepts or facts. Compare **Significance**.

Medical Model: The concept that people who are having trouble in life are therefore "sick" and must be treated by a doctor or para-medical person, and that the difficulties such a person encounters in life constitute, or are indicative of, a "disease" that has to be "cured" in a medical or quasi-medical way.

Metapsychology: The study of the individual person and her experience, as seen from *her* point of view.   Metapsychology is the study of the person and her abilities, the origin, structure, and function of the mind, and the relationship between person, mind, and physical universe.   It is the discipline that unifies mental and physical experience; it seeks to discover the rules that apply to both.   Central to metapsychology is a study of how the person, her mind, and her world are seen from a "person-centered" viewpoint in the absence of any external viewpoint or judgments. Metapsychology picks up where psychology, as the science of behavior, leaves off.   Hence the name "meta-psychology" has the correct connotation of being a study that goes "beyond" psychology — beyond the study of behavior to the study of that which behaves — the person himself, and the person's perceptual, conceptual, and creative activity, as distinguished from the actions of his body.   In this sense, "metapsychology" restores the original meaning of "psychology" as "the study of the psyche, or spirit", and the applications of metapsychology reflect the perennial common goal of therapies, religions, and traditional philosophies, whether one calls this goal the attainment of sanity, of enlightenment, of happiness, of wisdom, or of salvation.

Meter: See **Electrodermometer**.

Mind: The set of entities that exist for a person but that, under ordinary circumstances, other people cannot be aware of or act upon directly.   It is that person's set of "private" entities, that person's "private" world.   The mind, however, is part of a person's *environment*, not part of the *person*.   Mental actions — creative or receptive — are not experienced by the person as being mediated through the body.

Mind-Body Problem: The problem of how to explain mental causation of physical events and physical causation of mental events. The "mind-body problem" only arises when mind and body are considered as inhabiting different universes, with different characteristics, different rules, and different types of causation.

Misconception: A word, phrase, or sentence for which there appears to be no corresponding concept or for which the corresponding concept received is not that intended by the originator of the communication containing that word, phrase, or sentence.

Misdeed: An action that runs counter to the important intentions of the majority of people affected by the action.

Morals: Group policies that are based on an unknown rationale — i.e., whose relationship to the stated intentions of the group is unknown. A moral code, having an implicit or unexamined rationale, may "take on a life of its own". Perhaps the rationale was once stated explicitly, but, the rationale having been lost, the policy has remained. Thus the policy may appear to be *intrinsically* right, since no reason has been given for it, so it may become permanently inscribed as a moral imperative. There is, perhaps, a *feeling* of absolute rightness about it that is unexamined, yet it may, nonetheless, be firmly agreed upon by the members of a group. Adherence to morality ultimately rests on the notion (sometimes ill-thought-out or outmoded) that a breach of a group moral code is more or less automatically guaranteed to be against the interests of the group.

Multi-Determinism: The consideration that one shares responsibility for the intentions and actions of all persons involved in a certain situation. See also **Other-Determinism**, **Self-Determinism**.

Mutability: Capability of being changed.

Narrative Item: An item that describes a specific traumatic incident. Compare **Thematic Item**.

Natural Aversion: An aversion to a condition that is more or less universally disliked. Natural aversions include "built-in" bodily aversions as well as aversions determined by violations of the rules and principles people universally use to organize their worlds. See **Primary Pain**.

Needle: An indicator on an electrodermometer that shows small, moment-to-moment fluctuations from a baseline skin resistance. There is a sensitivity control that determines the breadth of the needle movement in response to fluctuations in resistance. At a high sensitivity, the needle will swing wide on a very small change of resistance; at a low sensitivity, it takes a much greater change in resistance to affect the needle in the same way. It is also possible to use non-mechanical displays (such as CRT's or LED's) in place of a physical needle movement. The term "needle" is meant to describe such electronic displays as well. The term "needle" can also mean a needle pattern. See **Needle Pattern**.

Needle Pattern: An ongoing type of electrodermometer needle behavior that reflects the mental status of the viewer. Abbr. **Needle**. Compare **Reaction, Response**.

Negative Emotion: Emotion connected with failure and aversion, i.e., emotional levels at or below ambivalence, such as anger, fear, and grief.

Negative Feeling: A phenomenon that is negative or unwanted, caused by the traumatic incident network (Net).

Negative Pleasure: See **Relief**.

Net: See **Traumatic Incident Network**.

No Change: One of the phenomena that indicate that an end point has been reached in a viewing procedure. This is when a procedure has been going on for a period of time without any particular changes occurring. It is one of the lighter or weaker indications that a procedure should be stopped.

Non-Complexity: A type of simplicity consisting of having few separate parts in a simple relationship to each other. It is one of the desirable characteristics of a world.

Non-Sensory Perception: Perception that does not occur through any physical senses. It is the means by which we can view mental pictures. Note that this is not exactly the same thing as what is called "extrasensory perception". In non-sensory perception, what is perceived need not be events thought to occur in the physical world or in someone else's mind.

No Response: A lack of needle response to a given item; it generally indicates that the item presented should not be addressed at this time, either because it is too heavily charged to be dealt with readily or because it is completely uncharged. The needle simply goes on doing what it was doing before without responding to the item at all.

Normal Operation: A condition in which a person feels basically content with, though unexcited about, an activity. The natural impulse at this level is to keep doing what one is doing and not to change things. In this condition, everything tends to go smoothly. The person gets along well with family members, fellow workers, or companions and acts in an adequate, conscientious, if uninspired, manner. Left to his own devices, a person in normal operation will remain in that condition indefinitely. The corresponding emotional level is contentment or complacency.

OBE: See **Out-of-Body Experience**.

Object: An entity that a procedure uses as a datum, manipulates, or changes. There are different types of objects, such as mental pictures, numbers, concepts, and tables.

Also, an entity described as a discrete thing, like a table or chair, as opposed to an event or a state of affairs. Compare **Event**, **State of Affairs**.

Objective Procedure: A procedure used in viewing that is directed toward physical objects. Receptive objective procedures include procedures designed to bring the viewer's attention into present time and to increase her ability to be aware of the present-time world. Creative objective procedures mainly exercise the ability to control or move the body or other physical objects in various ways.

Objectivity: The quality of an entity being on the world side of the person-world polarity.

Obverse concept: The concept that is the negation of a certain concept. "no unicorn in my garden" is the obverse of "a unicorn in my garden", and vice versa.

Occam's Razor: The principle that if two or more explanations of existing data are equally consistent with all these data, one should choose the simplest and most modest of the explanations.

Omitted Data: One of the problems encountered in study, particularly in a "linearly arranged" course. Later sections of such a course usually assume that the student knows and understands the material of earlier sections or earlier courses. If the student does not have these earlier data, she cannot continue to learn from the course materials.

Omitted Interpretation: A form of repression, consisting of a refusal to try to interpret a datum or to think about it. The person refuses to make the "obvious" interpretation, the interpretation she would make in the absence of aversion and repression.

Opacity: The quality of a phenomenon that causes it to resist perception, but that also (paradoxically) *permits* perception. This definition applies to all senses. Opacity is relative to the perceptual channel being used. It is also relative to the acuity of that perceptual channel, as well as to the strength of the signal coming through.

Other-Determinism: The consideration that someone else is responsible for one's own actions. See also **Multi-Determinism**, **Self-Determinism**.

Outflow: The creation of some kind of effect by a person on an entity or another person.

Out-of-Body Experience: A experience commonly encountered in viewing and in other situations, in which a person seems to be located outside her body. Different people report different degrees of ability to perceive when having out-of-body experiences. Abbr. **OBE**.

Overrun: The action of continuing an activity beyond its proper end point or the fact of having done so.

Pain: The presence of someone or something to which a person has aversion, or aversion to an entity or person that is present. It can vary from mild discomfort to intense agony. See **Physical Pain, Primary Pain, Secondary Pain, Situational Pain**.

Past: A directionality "backward" in time, opposite to that of the future. Also, that set of entities in a person's world which have a past tense.

Past Life Incident: An incident encountered in a viewing session that is known not to have occurred in the viewer's current lifetime. Whether such incidents are real or imaginary, ignoring or invalidating them will usually prevent a resolution of the charged material being addressed.

Pattern: The arrangement of the parts of a procedure. Patterns currently used in viewing are: simple action, checklist, repetition, loop, retrospection, and various combinations of the above.

Perceiving: The action of receiving a phenomenon.

Perceptual Skill: The ability to receive phenomena. Skill in the use of instruments or other means of perception.

Perceptualizing: A coined word, paralleling "conceptualizing", meaning the action of *prehending* a phenomenon. Perceptualizing of phenomena that a person *receives* from outside himself is called "perceiving"; perceptualizing of phenomena that the person *creates* is called "picturing".

Persistent Free Needle: A free needle that continues to swing idly, regardless of what the facilitator does — usually indicative of a major end point. It is generally considered a good point at which to end a session. A persistent free needle is always accompanied by very good indicators on the part of the viewer.

Person: A living entity or being, as distinct from his body, his mind, or any identity he may assume for various purposes. The center of consciousness and action. That which performs the basic creative and receptive actions. It is not something a person *has*, but what he *is*. Compare **Entity**.

Person-Centered Context: A context in which it is implicitly assumed that "I believe that ... " or "I feel that ..." is *automatically* prefixed to each statement made.

Person-Centered Viewpoint: A pragmatic and experiential approach to the study of persons and the worlds they inhabit. From this viewpoint, we cease talking about some hypothetical world outside of experience and limit ourselves to what each person experiences: his own world. When we talk about "reality" from the person-centered viewpoint, therefore, we must specify *whose* reality we are referring to.

Person-World Polarity: The relationship between a person and her world, which are both connected and separated by the person's receptive or creative actions. At the one pole there is the person and the identity she has assumed. At the other pole, there is that which the person perceives, that which she knows or understands, that upon which she acts, and that which she creates by means of that identity — the totality of what exists for that person at that moment — in other words, that person's world.

Phenomenoid: What a person experiences when she is not sure of what she is perceiving, but she has an idea of what she *might* be perceiving. See **Quasi-Entity**.

Phenomenon: An entity that is being directly perceived by a person, at a certain moment. If a person is looking at a chair, the chair is a phenomenon for her at that time. Compare **Concept**, **Fact**.

Phoniness: Incongruity of intention and identity. We think of a person as "phony" when she is pretending to be something she is not or claiming an ability or possessions that she does not really have, in order to influence, beguile, or impress people, or to otherwise do something that does not align with the real intentions of that pretended identity. Phoniness is the opposite of **Integrity**.

Physical Aversions: "Built-in" aversions to certain sensations, including the various sensations called "physical pain", most types of sensory overload (such as overly bright lights or loud noises), and certain other sensations, such as itching, the feeling of hunger, and nausea. They mostly have to do with preserving the body. They appear to be constant as long as a person firmly identifies himself with his body.

Physical Pain: A type of physical sensation to which most people have a "built-in aversion", including various aches, burning sensations, sharp sensations, and the like. The "painfulness" of physical pain, however, lies in the person's aversion to the sensation, not in the sensation itself.

Picturing: The direct creation of a phenomenon by a person.

Play: An activity that is done at an emotional level higher than complacency or in a condition higher than normal operation. The only difference between work and play is the emotional level at which it is done.

Polar Dimension: The dimension that extends between the person and his world. In this dimension, objects are separated according to their "objectivity". Entities that are less "objective" and more "subjective" appear closer, in this dimension, to the current identity of the person; more "objective" phenomena appear more distant. The person, in his current identity, is at the center in this dimension, and it appears that the person always looks "outward", i.e., toward the phenomena he perceives. The polar dimension is linear between the person and each entity in his world.

Polarity: A relationship between opposites of being dependent on each other for their existence or of being two aspects of the same thing. The person and his world, for instance, are opposite sides of the same person-world polarity, like the north and south poles of a magnet. The north pole does not exist without the south pole; both are part of the same magnet. See **Person-World Polarity**.

Positive Emotion: Emotion that lies above ambivalence, such as contentment, enthusiasm, and elation.

Postulate: A fact created by the combined actions of conceiving and assenting.

Postulate Section: That part of the Core Curriculum that is concerned with addressing and eliminating some of the basic fixed intentions or postulates that are causing the viewer to succumb or to act in a self-destructive manner. This section gives the viewer an enhanced ability to control his own postulates.

Postulating: The combined creative actions of conceiving and assenting, leading to the creation of a fact.

Power: A combination of drive, control, and understanding (or drive and ability) that characterizes a person's relationship with the entities that constitute the person's world. These form a triad, with more drive leading to more control and more understanding, more understanding leading to more drive and more control, and more control leading to more understanding and more drive. Power is the potential a person has for intending things, for making things happen. Power is the degree of "aliveness" or consciousness a person has. It underlies both awareness and creativity and relates to all the abilities of a person, both creative and receptive. Power can be expressed as the number of "intention units" a person has to "spend". Compare **Empowerment**.

Precedent: The principle that one should do things as one has done them in the past, or that events will follow a pattern they have followed in the past. Precedent is a sub-category of stability, which is itself a sub-category of order. In order to preserve stability, a person has a strong conservative tendency: it is much simpler to continue building on an old frame of reference than to go to the trouble of creating a whole new frame of reference and readjusting everything.

Predictability: A quality of the future by virtue of which it is knowable to a person. A sub-category of stability, which is itself a sub-category of order. If one can predict the future, the world seems more stable. Things can get very precarious and difficult if one has to prepare for a number of different outcomes at any given point. Ideally, one should have a future that is, to some degree, predictable and controllable.

Prediction: The act of knowing the future. See **Predictability**.

Prehend: To hold or grasp (an entity) as the direct object of a person's current action. See **Get, Having**.

Prehension: The condition in which an entity is the direct object of a person's current action. The act of prehending.

Premise: A fact that indicates or implies another fact. An assumption.

Presentation: The appearance of an item in the viewer's awareness. The viewer's getting of the item. See **Get**.

Pre-Session Clearing: The handling of disturbances and distractions, done at the beginning of a session or, as needed, during a session, to a point where the viewer's attention is relatively unfixed and can be directed toward the major actions in the session agenda. Compare **Major Action, Body**.

Primary Curriculum: That part of the General Curriculum that is done first, hence the name "Primary". It includes the sections of the Curriculum from Stress Reduction through Rightness. See **Core Curriculum**.

Primary Pain: Physical or situational pain, based on natural aversion. It is not derived from restimulation of a traumatic incident. See **Natural Aversion** and compare **Secondary Pain**.

Prior Reaction: A reaction that occurs before the viewer has had the item fully presented to her.

Problem: An incongruity that is of concern or importance to a person at a particular time. An entity that conflicts with or resists a person's intention.

Procedure: A pattern of actions, done for a certain purpose, using objects of various types, involving a specific set of locations and directionalities, with one or more attainable end points.

Quasi-Entity: Something that possibly or probably exists for a person, but of which the person does not have enough certainty to qualify it as something that definitely exists. Quasi-entities are of three types: factoids, conceptoids, and phenomenoids. Compare **Entity**, and see **Factoid, Conceptoid, Phenomenoid**.

Reaction: A *change* of needle pattern caused by a mental change in the viewer. Compare **Needle Pattern, Response**.

Reactivation: Restimulation of an inactive sequence or traumatic incident that makes it relatively easy for the person to be restimulated into it *again*. Compare **Deactivation**.

Reality: For an individual person, reality is that person's world, what the person believes to exist. Reality, for two or more people, is a "common world", a set of entities that are shared as a result of concurrence.

Recall Enhancement Section: The section of the Primary Curriculum that is concerned with helping the viewer recover the ability to contact her past easily. Objective and subjective procedures used in Stress Reduction and Help enabled her to contact the *present* with ease and to perform actions freely in the present. The next gradient is for her to learn to contact and handle the *past* with equal facility.

Recall Procedure: A receptive, subjective viewing procedure in which the viewer contacts past, non-traumatic incidents. In recalling, the viewer does not try to re-experience the past incident. He only makes contact with it. Recall procedures improve a person's memory for, and familiarity with, the past.

Receiving: The action of a person taking something in, getting something, inflowing something from her world. It does not create a change in her world.

Reception: See **Receptive Action**.

Receptive: A directionality toward the person from the world. Receiving, rather than giving. Pulling in, rather than pushing out.

Receptive Ability: See **Understanding**.

Receptive Action: An action of pulling in or receiving already-existing entities from the world or another person. See **Receiving**.

Receptive Procedure: A viewing procedure in which the viewer is asked to perform one or more receptive actions.

Recovery: A corrective action used to handle an overrun. In a recovery procedure, the viewer is returned to the favorable state he was in at the end point, before the point of overrun. Different recovery procedures are used for different situations.

Reduction: The partial or complete elimination of charge by a process of destimulation, deactivation, or discharge.

Referent: The concept to which a token refers.

Reflexive Flow: Causation from self to self. Also called **Reflexion**.

Release: To cease to prehend an entity. The opposite of **Get**.

Relief: Negative pleasure derived from a diminution of pain or discomfort. It is one of the major goals a person seeks in attempting to organize his world. See also **Aesthetics, Deficiency Motivation**.

Reliving: The unconscious re-experiencing or re-enactment of one or more traumatic incidents that have been restimulated but not discharged. It can cause aberrations, i.e., delusions, negative feelings, or dramatizations.

Remedial TIR: Traumatic Incident Reduction used to handle items that are currently in restimulation and areas of life that are currently bothering the viewer. Its intent is to relieve current stress and restimulation. Compare **General TIR**.

Remedy: See **Corrective Action**.

Repetitive Procedure: A procedure which consists of a repetition of a certain action. Repetition allows a procedure which if done once would have a very superficial effect, to penetrate deeply into the viewer's case. Repetition is used in exercises to help a person acquire a skill. Repeating something many times seems to establish a habit pattern that can then be made automatic, or incorporated into an identity of a person. But repetition *breaks* already established *aberrated* habit patterns (automatisms). If you can get a person to do self-determinedly and repeatedly something that was an automatism, the automatism eventually breaks down, temporarily or permanently.

Repression: The act of trying to become unaware of a specific entity, or the state of being the object of such an act. Unawareness based on aversion, or a flinch from pain. It is unconsciousness *of* a specific entity, and it is brought about by the presence of that entity or by the presence of a related (similar) entity. Whereas simple unawareness is caused by turning *toward* something else, directed unawareness, or repression, is caused by pointedly turning *away* from the entity of which one is trying to be unconscious.

Resentment: A level on the emotional scale that lies above hidden hostility and below anger. At this level, one feels angry but does not yet feel capable of doing very much about it. This is the level at which one "holds a grudge". The condition in the world that corresponds to resentment (and to all the emotions from hidden hostility through ambivalence) is drudgery.

Resilience Section: That part of the Primary Curriculum that addresses charge in the subject of change and upsets. On completion of this section, the viewer will be more resilient — less affected by and more easily recovering from upsets and changes.

Resistance: The quality of a world that stops a person from exercising his abilities fully but also gives him something to exercise his abilities *on*. It is the counterpart, on the world side of the person-world polarity, to deadness or inability on the person side.

Resolution Section: That part of the Primary Curriculum that addresses problems. On completing this section, the viewer will be more resolute and will have a better idea of where problems come from and how to resolve them.

Respect: Allowing another to be the identity that he is being.

Response: A reaction of the electrodermometer that occurs almost instantaneously after a charged item is presented to the viewer. Compare **Needle Pattern, Reaction**.

Responsibility: Causativeness.

Restimulate: To remind a person, knowingly or unknowingly, of a traumatic incident or sequence. To activate a traumatic incident or sequence, enabling the person to be reminded of it more easily. When this occurs, the person re-enacts or re-experiences parts of the traumatic incident or incidents of which she is reminded — she dramatizes them or experiences negative feelings or delusions.

Restimulated: Of a traumatic incident or sequence: the state of having been activated by restimulation.

Restimulation: An instance of being restimulated or the act of restimulating.

Restimulator: An entity that reminds a person, knowingly or unknowingly, of a traumatic incident or sequence.

Retrospective Procedure: A procedure that moves backward in time along lines of similarity; it goes "earlier similar". Because of the structure of the traumatic incident network, systematic retrospection is an especially fruitful pattern to use.

Revenge: A type of justification for a misdeed. It is the claim that, in acting against a person, you are merely paying her back for what she has done to you — "evening the score". This justification is characteristic of the emotional level of antagonism.

Review: To go through a past incident, reliving it in as much detail as possible. This is the heart of the Traumatic Incident Reduction procedure. Reviewing differs from simple remembering as a motion picture differs from a snapshot.

Rightness Section: The viewer, like anyone else, is of the opinion that what she believes is right. Otherwise, she wouldn't believe it. But she can be *righter*. Wrongnesses can be caused by misconceptions, false information, or fixed ideas. This section addresses all three. On completing this section, the viewer will actually *be* righter, and she will have less of a compulsion to *assert* her rightness when she isn't right.

Rough Needle: A needle pattern, consisting of a jerky, uneven motion, not occurring as a response to a presented item. It often indicates that the viewer is thinking about something but has not yet communicated about it. A rough needle can get in the way of reading a meter properly, and the undelivered communication gets in the way of viewing. A rough needle can be made smooth, generally, by asking for undelivered communications. When the viewer has told the facilitator what his attention is on, the needle action will become smooth. See **Needle Pattern**.

Root: The traumatic incident that is earliest in a sequence and on which the entire sequence relies for its existence. It contains natural aversion (primary pain). It does not merely contain aversion based on a reminder of an earlier incident (secondary pain). Compare **Sequent**.

Scope: The range of entities that is covered by a certain explanation. This is a sub-category of simplicity, which is itself a sub-category of order. Maximizing the scope of his explanations of his world is one of the major principles a person follows in attempting to organize it.

Secondary Gain: The "usefulness" of aberration, apart from its function in facilitating repression. For instance, a person may cultivate or exaggerate an upset or a psychosomatic condition in order to get help, attention, or money from others.

Secondary Pain: Pain derived from restimulation of an earlier traumatic incident or sequence. Compare **Primary Pain**.

Second Consideration: A consideration made that is incongruent with a first consideration that is already in place and not unmade. Making a second consideration is a means of repression. It consists of adding a layer of delusion on top of one's first consideration about something. There can also be a third consideration, a fourth consideration, etc. See **First Consideration**.

Selection: A form of assessment and also a powerful viewing procedure in its own right. In selecting, the viewer finds a charged subject that is unclear in some way and clarifies it by interpreting it in a certain way and understanding it. The facilitator asks a single question and gets a series of answers to the question. The question causes the viewer to look at his experience in order to find the best answer or answers. There is generally a "right" answer to the question for that particular viewer at that particular time. The same question may generate another "right" answer at another time. Compare **Calling**, **Listing**.

Self-Determinism: The consideration that one is responsible for one's own actions and interests but not for others'. See also **Other-Determinism**, **Multi-Determinism**.

Sensitivity Control: A control on the electrodermometer that determines the degree of deflection of the needle, given a certain change in skin resistance.

Sequence: A group of one or more related or associated traumatic incidents, connected by one or more types of restimulators, in which later traumatic incidents contain restimulators of earlier traumatic incidents.

Sequent: A traumatic incident that is not the root for a particular sequence but is based on restimulation of a root or another sequent. Besides a restimulator of an earlier traumatic incident in the sequence, it may also contain primary pain, as well as one or more other restimulators that fit a different sequence.

Session Agenda: A written list of the actions the facilitator plans to take in the next viewing session.

Shedding: The relinquishing of an identity in favor of a more general identity through the disincorporation of previously incorporated elements.

Shoplifter Justification: A justification of a misdeed that consists of devaluing the importance of, or denying, the intentions that are violated in harming another person.

Sidetrack: An unnecessary deviation from a procedure or program. A failure to follow through and complete an activity cycle. A sidetrack is intended to handle something that either requires no handling or would be handled adequately by merely continuing the current procedure. Compare **Detour**.

Significance: The conceptual and factual content of an experience, such as the ideas encountered in study, as opposed to the phenomenal content, such as pictures or objects. Compare **Mass, Terminal, Force**.

Simple Action: A viewing pattern consisting of only one step.

Simple Retrospection: The action of describing an incident or item, then tracing it back to earlier similar incidents or items, giving a simple description of each. Unlike Traumatic Incident Reduction, it does not involve running through past incidents or contacting the same incident repetitively, nor does it involve a series of steps. It simply involves description, followed by finding an earlier similar incident or item, until an end point occurs (usually a free needle and good indicators and often a realization).

Simple Unawareness: A normal and unaberrated unawareness; a consequence of the fact that a person does not have an unlimited ability to be aware of things. Examples include the unawareness we have of things we take for granted or that we do automatically, forgetfulness caused by the passage of time, unawareness of things that are irrelevant to a particular purpose or identity, and unawareness of things that were never known.

Situational Aversions: Situational aversions can be understood from an examination of the basic ways in which a person seems to organize her experience. These would exist whether a person had a body or not. A person seeks to maximize her *power* to handle her world and the degree of *communion* she has with other people. She has an aversion to circumstances or situations which would prevent her from doing so.

Situational Pain: Primary pain that is non-physical but derived from the presence of a situation (such as a misdeed, a withhold, a problem, disorder, lack of control, tedium, etc.) for which a person has a natural aversion because it decreases her power or communion.

Skill: An ability of which a person has a simple (not directed) unawareness, because the ability has been incorporated as part of an identity the person has assumed. A learned automaticity.

Smooth Needle: A needle pattern consisting of a lack of agitation or change in pattern (usually slowly climbing or slowly dropping).

Solidity: A form of immutability consisting of a resistance to transformation.

Solipsism: The notion that the whole world is one's own construct or does not exist and that no other persons really exist.

Space: A set of three dimensions that separate objects from each other by position.

Spiritual Materialism: Seeking after spiritual abilities or spiritual status in the same way that one might seek after physical possessions — as a form of self-aggrandizement or personal power.

Stability: A major sub-category of order. One of the main features that exists for a person in an optimal world. A very unstable world is a disorderly one that is hard to live in. Sub-categories of stability include precedent, predictability, and controllability.

Stack (of Dichotomies): A collection of mutually opposing proponents (identities the viewer has been) and opponents (identities the viewer has opposed), with opposing goals, that are thought to lie at the core of the Traumatic Incident Network. See **Unstacking**.

State of Affairs: An entity, described as a form or as a relation amongst other entities. One of three possible ways of describing an entity. Compare **Object, Event**.

Stepping Back: The action of shedding an identity and assuming a less extended, less specialized identity, from which it is possible (if one chooses to do so) to view the identity one formerly assumed. Also, looking at a datum as a conclusion from other data. The direction in which one steps when one "steps back" is toward the person side of the person-world polarity.

Still Needle: A needle pattern consisting of a virtual cessation of motion. It often accompanies a high baseline and indicates that the viewer has too much material in restimulation or has his attention solidly fixed on something.

Stopped Free Needle: A response in which a needle that was free ceases to be so. It indicates the presence of charge.

Stress: An entity that a person thinks might be capable of overwhelming him or that he considers he may be incapable of fully confronting or handling.

Stress Reduction Section: The first section of the Primary Curriculum, in which you address issues on which the viewer's attention is already fixed and reduce charge on these issues so that the amount of stress the viewer is suffering from is reduced. Although Stress Reduction often produces spectacular relief, it is really only a form of metapsychological "first aid" and not a complete case handling. It is best regarded as a preparation for a more thoroughgoing approach to the viewer's case.

Subjective Procedure: A viewing procedure whose object or objects are located in past or the mind. Receptive subjective procedures are designed to increase one's degree of insight into, and understanding of, one's past and one's mind. These procedures improve a person's ability to perceive, interpret, and understand parts of her subjective world. Creative subjective procedures exercise her ability to conceive ideas and make mental pictures. Often, such procedures (as with many creative procedures) are useful in gaining control of unwanted automatic actions or conditions, such as bad habits, fixed ideas and negative feelings.

Subjectivity: The quality of an object being on the person side of the person-world polarity (the mind). See **Objectivity**, **Polar Dimension**.

Subsidiary Awareness: Awareness of that to which a person is not currently attending, but knowledge of which contributes to an act of focal awareness. Compare **Focal Awareness**.

Success: The fulfillment of an intention or (equivalently) the completion of a cycle.

Taking Over: Taking control and responsibility for an automatism and thus causing it to cease to be automatic. By taking over an automatic action, a person regains causativeness over it. By taking responsibility for *doing* something, one acquires the ability to *stop* doing it.

Task: A creative activity. Compare **Incident**.

Technical Director: The person in charge of planning Individual Curricula, case plans, and session agendas. She is also responsible for ensuring that the facilitators are doing their jobs correctly, and she makes sure they get help promptly if they get into difficulties.

Tense: A directionality in time. There are two tenses: past and future.

Terminal: A person or thing that can be the object of action, communication, or perception. It is a thing or person you can relate to directly, not a mere concept or relationship. A mother, a rabbit, and a typewriter are all terminals. Motherhood, wildness, and typography are not. Compare **Significance**.

Thematic Item: An item that describes a particular theme — a negative feeling or intention that connects a sequence of traumatic incidents. Since it is present in several incidents, it does not describe any specific incident. Compare **Narrative Item**.

Theme: A common restimulator that links different traumatic incidents in a sequence. Themes are negative feelings, intentions, attitudes, or thoughts. The same theme need not be present in the entire sequence.

Time: A dimension that separates objects from each other according to *tense*. In time, as in space, the person finds herself in the present at the origin, and past and future are in opposite directions.

TIR: See **Traumatic Incident Reduction**.

Token: A phenomenon that indicates or refers to a concept or (candidate) fact. A phenomenon that has *meaning*. The word "red" (spoken or written) is a token that refers to the concept of a certain wavelength of light or a certain type of visual phenomenon; dark clouds can be a token of rain.

Trainer: A person who coaches, supervises, advises, tutors or otherwise helps another person with practical exercises or applications.

Transcendent Experience: An event that gives a person a clear impression of himself as a spiritual being, not co-extensive with his body, because the experience appears to transcend the limits of a purely physical model of the universe. These events include: the appearance of past lives, contact with other beings close to the viewer that are not inhabiting bodies, out-of-body experiences, ESP experiences, and religiously transcendent experiences.

Transformation: Internal motion, resulting in a change of shape or internal rearrangement of parts.

Translation: External motion, resulting in a change of position.

Transparency: An absence of resistance to perception; the opposite of opacity.

Trauma: See **Traumatic Incident**.

Traumatic Incident: An incident that is wholly or partially repressed and that contains a greater or lesser degree of pain — felt, created, or received. A receptive cycle that is undischarged because of repression.

Traumatic Incident Network: The traumatic incident network is the network composed of all of the person's traumatic incidents, with their various interconnections. Abbr. **Net**.

Traumatic Incident Reduction: A viewing procedure that is akin to certain early psychoanalytical procedures. It involves tracing back sequences of traumatic incidents to their roots while completing the incomplete receptive cycles that have accumulated in the sequences. Abbr. **TIR**.

Truth: The factuality of a concept, its condition of being assented to or believed with certainty by a person.

Turbidity: The state of having having one's attention fixed on one or more disturbances. A person in this state is said to be "disturbed". See also **Disturbance**.

Turning Point: The point in viewing at which one becomes aware that one is separate from one's case even when one is manifesting or feeling the effects of it. The state of being more causative over one's case than one is the effect of it, of not having to act on the dictates of one's case.

Two-Way Communication: An interchange of communication between two people.

Unawareness: Lack of awareness. There are two kinds of unawareness: simple unawareness and directed unawareness (repression).

Underlying Truth: A concept that is closer to a first consideration than the relative falsehood or falsehoods that it underlies. See **False Belief, First Consideration, Second Consideration**.

Understanding: The creation of a new fact from one or more data. An interpretation of a datum or data, being a concept, is a candidate fact. What makes it an *actual* fact is the act of assent (acceptance). The combination of interpreting and acceptance is called "understanding". When one understands one or more data, one arrives at a new fact, a *conclusion*.

Also, receptive ability, the ability to exercise receptive abilities on an entity or on the world. Understanding is that quality in the person that corresponds to heuristics or learning potential in the person's world. Compare **Control**.

Unintelligibility: That quality of a datum by virtue of which it resists understanding.

Unstacking: A procedure for locating and discharging sets of conflicting goals and identities ("dichotomies"). Unstacking is the procedure that is used in the Identity Section of the core curriculum. See **Core Curriculum**.

Upset: A sudden or unexpected lowering of communion, value, or validity.

Validity: The combination of — and balance between — pleasure, order, and heuristics that a particular concept or world-view offers to a person. A person accepts those concepts that create the best balance and rejects concepts that create an inferior balance. A person's view of the world is the most valid one the person can piece together, given the available data. Validity is the counterpart, on the world side of the person-world polarity, to awareness on the person side. Compare **Value, Empowerment**.

Value: The combination of — and balance between — pleasure, order, and heuristics that a person attempts, by his creative actions, to achieve in the world around him. A person strives, by his creative actions, to maximize the value of his world. Value, therefore, is what corresponds, on the world side of the person-world polarity, to creativity on the person side. Compare **Validity, Empowerment**.

Verification: The action of determining the correctness or acceptability of an interpretation or concept, following certain rules. These rules are the means by which the person moves, in the learning cycle, from having a mere concept or several different concepts as possible interpretations of his data, to an acceptance of one or more of these concepts as factual.

Versatility: The ability to assume or shed identities.

Viewer: The one in a viewing session whose role is to examine her world and arrive at insights concerning it. Viewing is done by the *viewer*, not by the facilitator. The viewer should not be concerned with the mechanics of the session or the session agenda. She should only be concerned with viewing.

Viewing: An activity in which a person systematically examines her world in such a way as to gain insight and ability by undoing repression.

Viewing Instruction: A part of a viewing procedure consisting of an instruction given to a viewer by a facilitator. The facilitator acknowledges the viewer's execution of the instruction.

Viewing Procedure: A procedure used in viewing.

Viewing Question: A part of a viewing procedure consisting of a question asked of a viewer by a facilitator. The facilitator acknowledges the viewer's answer.

Volition: The intention to create. Compare **Attention**.

Weakness: Inability to cause change. It is the counterpart, on the person side of the person-world polarity, to immutability on the world side.

Willingness: The absence of counter-intention.

Withhold: Something that a person knows but does not reveal to others when an occasion arises to do so.

Work: An activity engaged in at an emotional level of complacency or below. Compare **Play**.

World: That which the person perceives, that which he knows or understands, that upon which he acts, and that which he creates — by means of, and from the viewpoint of, an identity; the totality of what exists for a person at a certain moment, including his mind, other people, and what he perceives or knows of the physical universe.

Worry: A problem that is currently occupying the person's attention and will continue to do so until it is resolved.

Yearning: A high degree of desire. Compare **Love**.

Zero-Sum Game: A game in which the more there is for one player, the less there is for the others. If one wins a zero-sum game, the others lose.

INDEX

elimination of, 260
renunciation of, 27-28
ego defenses, breaking down of, 443
Einstein, Albert, 43, 118, 322
elan vitale, 115-116
elation, 144
as point of change of identity, 144
electrodermometer. *See* meter.
electroencephalogram, 411
Ellis, Albert, 359
people are basically ethically
neutral, 264 fn
emergencies in ethics, 265
Emergency, 523-524
as a condition, 523
how to handle, 524
emergency remedies, 511-512, 541-549
emotion(s). *See also* specific
emotions by name.
acute, 148
built-in strategies of, 521
chronic, 148
conditions and, 517-528
drugs and, 145
effect on success, 145-148
negative. *See* negative emotions.
physiology and, 145
positive. *See* positive emotion.
success and, 137-149
emotional level
criterion for selecting
companions, 147-148
lowered by duress in therapy, 147
Emotional Scale, 141-149, 457
affinity and, 183-187
ascending or descending triads
and, 200
closeness and, 183-187
defn of, 141
motion towards and motion away
on, 331-332
pain and, 325-326
strategies available on, 145-146
use of to handle life, 516-528
empirical possibility, 57 fn
empowerment
defn of, 166
value, validity and, 166-169

empty chair technique in Gestalt
therapy, 455
encounter groups, 147 fn
end point(s), 405-407, 428-433
body shift as EP in
Focusing, 494-495 fn
consequences of failure to
indicate, 431
defn of, 405, 428
indicators of, 407
individual styles of, 429
major vs. minor, 407
overruns and, 405-407
premature indication of, 430
pre-session clearing, EP of, 401
procedure-specific EP's, 48
recognition of, 406
religion, EPs in, 405
therapy, EPs in, 405
timing in indicating EPs, 430
TIR, EP of, 440
types of, 485
variable nature of, 407
ending a session, 403-404
enemy(ies)
external e., need for, 300 fn
withholds and, 294
energy as event, 49
enforced viewing, 392-393
engagement
continuum of, 519
defn of, 519
how to increase, 519-520
enhancement, personal. *See*
personal enhancement.
enlightenment, xvi, 359
as a concern of therapy, 535
enthusiasm, 144
entity(ies), 30-37
affinity for, 180-182
correspond to actions, 80, 84-85
defn of, 30, 61
incongruities amongst, 295-296
non-prehended, 66 fn
private vs. public, 100
quasi-entities and, 41
receptive and creative modes of
gaining, 81

weakness and, 44, 48
impatience, 70
imperative, question as an i., 216
imperative function of
statements, 218-220
imperialism, existential, 56
importance, 173-178. *See also*
cardinality.
affinity and, 182-183
in vivo handlings, 512-518
inability and barriers, 47-48
inactive, defn of, 356
incident
defn of, 110, 348
earlier i. *See* earlier incident.
traumatic i. *See* traumatic incident.
incompatibility. *See* problem,
dilemma, incongruity, conflict.
incomplete communication cycles,
effects of, 224
incomplete cycle(s), 117-119
restimulation creates an i.c., 476
traumatic incidents and, 344-347
incomplete viewing cycles, 384
incompossible intentions, 258-259
incomprehensible data, 310
incongruity(ies), 295-304. *See also*
problem, dilemma, conflict,
incompatibility.
aesthetic, 296
amongst entities, 295-296
automatisms and, 492-494
awareness of, 296-298
intentions, i.s between, 299
intentions, i.s with, 297-298
misdeeds and, 285
problems and, 295-299
relevance of, 298
resolution of, 299
incorporation as high degree of
closeness, 184
indecision, 335-336
independence, 175
indicators, 426-428
bad i.s in viewing, 427
end point, i.s of, 407
good i.s in viewing, 427-428
variations in, 428

indirect viewing, 455-456
Individual Curriculum, defn of, 458
Individuation Section, 467
induction, 153 fn
infant development of perceptual
skills, 19
inferiority, feelings of, 273
Infinite, the, as the sixth domain, 247
inflow, defn of, 236
influence, defn of, 181
initial interview, 504
injuries, remedies for, 541-546
"inner" experience, nonexistence
of, 101
Inquiring, 422-423, 489
Exploring, i. vs., 422-423
insight
defn of, 340, 380
opposite of delusion, 341
prevented by evaluation and
interpretation, 4
insomnia, 89
instantaneous free needle, 418
as a large response, 420 fn
defn of, 418
institutional case, 520
instrumental skills, 20
in children, 20
in learning, 22, 49, 312
integrity, 283
defn of, 258, 322
identity and, 258-261
techniques for improvement
of, 259 fn
intelligence, invalidation of, 282-283
intelligibility of phenomena, 45
intensity
cardinality and, 178
of affection depends on
cardinality, 231
intention(s)
action and, 91-92, 192
animals can't control i., 258
assent and, 67-68, 111-112
awareness required for unmaking, 139-14
built-in physical i.s, 140 fn, 145
cause of an activity cycle, 110
communication, i. behind, 216

secretarial function of the facilitator, 389
seekers, 164-165, 167
selecting, 424, 499-502
  cardinal point, in s., 501-502
  decisions, using s. to make d.s, 502
  errors in can cause major upsets, 510
  Focusing and, 501 fn
  handling errors in, 510
  mechanism of, 502
  right item in, 500
  viewing action, s. as 499
selecting companions by emotional
  level, 147-148
selective inattention, 330 fn
self, 14-15
  invisible man, s. as, 52
  first domain, s. as, 246
  invisible to the self, 184
  running away from, 357
  what it is not, 15
self-actualization, 359
self-confidence, intention and, 113
self-deception, 253-254
self-deprecation, 273, 318-319
  as a protection against attack, 25
  overlies feelings of contempt, 319
self-determinism, 241, 457
  defn of, 240
self-fulfilling prophecies, 89
  of regarding others as
    enemies, 294, 295
self-hate, 275
self-hypnosis as a reflexive action, 236
self-invalidation, discouragement
  of in viewing, 453-454
self-revelation, basic impulse
  towards, 283
selling, 253 fn
selling oneself on a decision, 253
senior identity, 26-27
sense data, 83 fn
sensitivity control, 414
sensory deprivation, 278, 307
sensory overload, 276
sentence as an abstraction, 203 fn
separation of self and entity by
  action, 19-20
sequence(s), 348-359

adding an incident to, 354
defn of, 350, 437
formation of, 353-355, 439
held together by external
  restimulators, 439
requires a theme, 439
roots and, 437-440
tree structure of, 351
sequence of reception, 85-86
sequent, defn of, 351
session, 399-404
  body of, 401
  division of labor in, 398
  ending of, 403-404
  fixed length of, 392 fn
  length of must be flexible, 406-407
  noticing rightness in, 426
  planning of, 408-409
  responsibility for lies with the
    facilitator, 389
  starting the s., 399
  structure of, 399-404
  taking attention off the s.
    when it is over, 403
  traumatic incident, s. as, 401
session agenda
  as a checklist, 495-496 fn
  defn of, 399
sex as the second domain, 246
sex goddess, 140
sex-related identities, 320-321
Shakespeare, William, 218
shamans, 273
sharing. *See also* comprehension.
  affection and s. of identity, 179
  significant others, complete s.
    with, 290
  viewpoints, s. of 229
shedding, defn of, 60
significant others, 232
  complete sharing with, 290
simple retrospection, 473
  defn of, 478-479
simple unawareness, 328-329
simplicity, 158-159
sin, 284 fn
situation comedies, fixed
  solutions in, 301